D0213348

Teaching American History

Essays Adapted from the *Journal of*
American History, 2001–2007

Teaching American History

Essays Adapted from the *Journal of American History*, 2001–2007

Edited by

Gary J. Kornblith and Carol Lasser

Oberlin College

BEDFORD/ST. MARTIN'S   BOSTON ♦ NEW YORK

In memory of Roy Rosenzweig, our cherished friend

For Bedford/St. Martin's

Publisher for History: Mary V. Dougherty
Executive Editor for History: William J. Lombardo
Director of Development for History: Jane Knetzger
Developmental Editor: Kathryn Abbott
Editorial Assistant: Alix Roy
Production Supervisor: Sarah Ulicny
Executive Marketing Manager: Jenna Bookin Barry
Project Management: Books By Design, Inc.
Text Design: Julie Phinney
Cover Design: Sara Gates
Composition: Books By Design, Inc.
Printing and Binding: RR Donnelley & Sons Company

President: Joan E. Feinberg
Editorial Director: Denise B. Wydra
Director of Marketing: Karen R. Soeltz
Director of Editing, Design, and Production: Marcia Cohen
Assistant Director of Editing, Design, and Production: Elise S. Kaiser
Manager, Publishing Services: Emily Berleth

Library of Congress Control Number: 2008907227

Copyright © 2009 by Bedford/St. Martin's

All rights reserved. No part of this book may be reproduced, stored in a retrieval system, or transmitted in any form or by any means, electronic, mechanical, photocopying, recording, or otherwise, except as may be expressly permitted by the applicable copyright statutes or in writing by the Publisher.

Manufactured in the United States of America
3 2 1 0 9 8
f e d c b a

For information, write Bedford/St. Martin's, 75 Arlington Street, Boston, MA 02116
(617) 399-4000

ISBN-10: 0-312-48416-X
ISBN-13: 978-0-312-48416-3

PREFACE

This book represents more than the culmination of our seven years as editors of the "Textbooks and Teaching" (T&T) section of the *Journal of American History* (JAH). It also represents the quarter century that both of us have been offering courses in American history at Oberlin College. Our interest in effective and engaging teaching dates back to our time in graduate school, but for us (as for most teachers) it was the challenge and excitement of teaching students that prompted us to reflect on our pedagogical approaches and to rethink the way we pursued our educational objectives as teacher-scholars. Our students over the years have been delightfully creative, passionate, and intellectually intense. They are never dull and only rarely deferential. We developed strategies to engage them as much as possible in the joy of *doing* history, rather than require them to memorize and regurgitate established narratives based on our disciplinary expertise.

It was through this experience of trying to engage student interest in historical inquiry that we clarified our focus for our years as editors of T&T. We wanted to share with others—and have others share with us—the excitement of historical study that binds teachers and students together and to each other. In this volume, you will read the ideas of instructors at all levels. Some are (or were) relatively new to the profession when they contributed to T&T; others had many years of classroom experience. All contributed their enthusiasm to these studies of teaching and learning. Part One (from the 2001 JAH) is a roundtable of instructors, both veteran and novice, about teaching the survey. In particular, participants discuss the tension between coverage (or uncoverage) and teaching historical processes. Part Two examines the writing, editing, and production of college history textbooks, a topic that provokes a wide range of opinions among teachers, students, and even state legislators in the debate over textbook pricing and revision. This section includes the contributions of two long-time textbook authors, Mary Beth Norton and Alan Brinkley; a view from the inside from textbook editor Steve Forman; and an assessment of the place of the textbook in the U.S. survey classroom.

Part Three looks beyond the classroom and explores ideas for teaching and learning "outside the box." Taking the show on the road—literally—contributors to this section conducted classes and research online, in theaters, in museums, and in local communities to create wide-ranging, experiential environments for their students. Part Four considers the scholarship of teaching, learning, and testing and includes a multi-author article on the different ways that visual evidence helps students engage with and understand history. Finally, Part Five, taken from our last issue as T&T's editors, explores alternative foci for the U.S. survey class—sexuality and ethnicity in particular.

We are very excited to be able to present this synthesis of our years as the editors of T&T. We hope that this volume will inspire our fellow teachers to reflect on their own educational practices and to adapt them in inventive ways to their particular student audiences both in traditional classrooms and in non-traditional teaching spaces.

We are deeply grateful to our late friend Roy Rosenzweig for the generous help and wonderful guidance that he provided us during our term as editors of the "Textbooks and Teaching" section of the *Journal of American History*. Roy was a founding editor of the section in 1992, and he was instrumental in our appointment as the section's co-editors eight years later. Although we had the pleasure of sharing with him our enthusiasm about the essays in this volume, we are heartbroken that he is not with us to see the final product.

It is a pleasure to acknowledge the support, skill, and wisdom of the staff at the *Journal of American History* who so expertly supported us and the contributors to this section over the years. Special thanks to editors Joanne Meyerowitz and Ed Linenthal, to associate editor Susan Armeny, to information technology manager Melissa Beaver, and to production manager Nancy Croker.

We have enjoyed working with all the committed teacher-scholars who have written for the "Textbooks and Teaching" section. Unfortunately, for reasons of space and timeliness, we have had to omit from this volume some of the essays originally published in the *Journal of American History*. We wish to thank for their fine contributions John J. Grabowski, Michael J. Guasco, Timothy A. Hacsi, Kriste Lindenmeyer, Richard Rothstein, and Mark Tebeau. We also thank our many colleagues at Oberlin who have shared with us their love of teaching and their commitment to pedagogical excellence.

We offer sincere thanks to Mary Dougherty, Bill Lombardo, and Kathryn Abbott at Bedford/St. Martin's for their vision and talent in bringing this volume together. And of course we thank our students for teaching us so much.

NOTES ON CONTRIBUTORS

AMY BASS is associate professor of history and director of the Honors Program at The College of New Rochelle and has worked as research supervisor for NBC for five Olympic Games. She is the author of *Not the Triumph but the Struggle: The 1968 Olympic Games and the Making of the Black Athlete* and editor of the collection *In the Game: Race, Identity and Sports in the 20th Century*.

NED BLACKHAWK is an associate professor of history and American Indian studies at the University of Wisconsin, Madison, where he teaches American Indian, U.S. Borderlands, and early American history. His publications include *Violence over the Land: Indians and Empires in the Early American West*, which won five professional book awards in 2007, including the 2007 Frederick Jackson Turner Prize from the Organization of American Historians.

CHARLES BRIGHT is professor of history and director of the Residential College, a small liberal arts unit dedicated to undergraduate teaching, at the University of Michigan.

ALAN BRINKLEY is the Allan Nevins Professor of History and provost at Columbia University.

LENDOL CALDER, author of *Financing the American Dream: A Cultural History of Consumer Credit*, is associate professor of history at Augustana College, Illinois. Since his selection as a Carnegie Scholar in 1999, he has been working with others in the emergent field of the scholarship of teaching and learning to invent and share new models for teaching and learning at the post-secondary level.

DANIEL J. COHEN is an associate professor of history and the director of the Center for History and New Media at George Mason University. He is the author of

Equations from God: Pure Mathematics and Victorian Faith, and the coauthor, with Roy Rosenzweig, of *Digital History: A Guide to Gathering, Preserving, and Presenting the Past on the Web*.

MICHAEL COVENTRY teaches in the Communication, Culture & Technology Program at Georgetown University. His research interests comprise gender, media, and soldiers' culture in the twentieth-century United States.

A. GLENN CROTHERS is assistant professor of history at the University of Louisville, director of research at The Filson Historical Society in Louisville, Kentucky, and co-editor of *Ohio Valley History*. He is the author of numerous articles about southern Quakers and economic development in the early national and antebellum South and is completing a book, *The Quakers of Northern Virginia, 1730–1865: Negotiating Communities and Cultures*.

ALLISON DORSEY is an associate professor of history at Swarthmore College and the author of *To Build Our Lives Together: Community Formation in Black Atlanta, 1875–1906*. She recently completed an NEH summer seminar on the black freedom struggle at Harvard University and is currently working on a project involving the history of black freedmen on the Georgia Sea Islands.

CHARLES W. EAGLES has taught at the University of Mississippi since 1983. His latest book is *The Price of Defiance: Ole Miss, Race, and James Meredith*.

DOUGLAS R. EGERTON is professor of history at Le Moyne College in Syracuse, where he teaches and writes about race in early America. His publications include *Death or Liberty: African Americans and Revolutionary America* and *He Shall Go Out Free: The Lives of Denmark Vesey*.

PETER FELTEN teaches history and directs the Center for the Advancement of Teaching and Learning at Elon University.

STEVE FORMAN is senior editor and vice president at W. W. Norton. He focuses on college and trade books in history.

JOSEPH J. GONZALEZ is a member of the Department of History at Appalachian State University, where he teaches in interdisciplinary programs devoted to general education. He is working on a book on the U.S. occupation of Cuba from 1898 to 1902, in addition to contributing to the scholarship of teaching and learning.

LESLIE GENE HUNTER retired, after thirty-eight years, from Texas A&M University-Kingsville (TAMUK), where he was a Regents Professor of History and a Minnie Stevens Piper Professor.

CECILIA AROS HUNTER was a public school history teacher and administrator before becoming the University Archivist at TAMUK. The Hunters often collaborated on historical projects as they worked to make the archives a laboratory for students of history.

KARL JACOBY is an associate professor of history at Brown University and the author of *Crimes against Nature: Squatters, Poachers, Thieves, and the Hidden History of American Conservation*. His new book is *Shadows at Dawn: A Border Massacre and the Violence of History*.

DAVID JAFFEE teaches American Material Culture and is the director of New Media Research at the Bard Graduate Center for Studies in the Decorative Arts, Design, and Culture. He is the author of *People of the Wachusett: Greater New England in History and Memory, 1630–1860*; the visual editor of *Who Built America? Working People and the Nation's Economy, Politics, Culture, and Society*, and the author of numerous articles on artists and artisans in early America.

SCOTT KURASHIGE is an associate professor of history, American culture, and Asian/Pacific Islander American studies at the University of Michigan. He is the author of *The Shifting Grounds of Race: Black and Japanese Americans in the Making of Multiethnic Los Angeles*.

PAULINE MAIER is the William Rand Kenan Jr. Professor of American History at Massachusetts Institute of Technology. She writes primarily on the American Revolution and its impact.

PABLO MITCHELL is an associate professor of history at Oberlin College. He is the author of *Coyote Nation: Sexuality, Race, and Conquest in Modernizing New Mexico, 1880–1920*, which was awarded the 2007 Ray Allen Billington Prize by the Organization of American Historians, and is currently completing *West of Sex: Making Latino America, 1900–1930*.

MARY BETH NORTON is the Mary Donlon Alger Professor of American History at Cornell University, where she has taught since 1971.

CECILIA O'LEARY is a professor of history at California State University, Monterey Bay. She is the author of *To Die for the Paradox of American Patriotism*, is on the editorial board of *Social Justice*, and has spoken broadly on radio and television on the meanings of patriotism.

CATHERINE BADURA OGLESBY has taught U.S. history, U.S. women's history, New South, historiography, and other U.S. history courses at Valdosta State University in Georgia for the past ten years. Her book *Corra Harris and the Divided Mind of the New South* appeared in 2008.

ELISABETH ISRAELS PERRY teaches women's history and women's studies at St. Louis University. Her latest publication is *The Gilded Age and Progressive Era: A Student Companion.*

LEWIS PERRY became emeritus at St. Louis University in June 2008, where he had been John Francis Bannon Professor of History, a position he co-held with Elisabeth Israels Perry.

ALYSSA PICARD is a staff representative at AFT-Michigan, an affiliate of the American Federation of Teachers. She also teaches history and economics in the labor school program at Wayne State University in Michigan.

JOSHUA PIKER teaches early American and Native American history at the University of Oklahoma. He is the author of *Okfuskee: A Creek Indian Town in Colonial America.*

DAVID A. REICHARD is an associate professor of history and legal studies in the Division of Humanities and Communication at California State University Monterey Bay. His teaching and research interests include nineteenth- and twentieth-century U.S. social and political history, law in society, and the scholarship of teaching and learning.

DOUGLAS C. SACKMAN is associate professor of history at the University of Puget Sound. He is the author of *Orange Empire: California and the Fruits of Eden* and the forthcoming *Wild Men: Ishi and Kroeber in the Wilderness of Modern America,* which will appear in Oxford University Press's New Narratives in American History series.

VIRGINIA SCHARFF is professor of history at the University of New Mexico and the author of *Taking the Wheel: Women and the Coming of the Motor Age* and *Twenty Thousand Roads: Women, Movement, and the West;* editor of *Seeing Nature through Gender;* and coauthor of *Present Tense: The United States since 1945,* as well as *Coming of Age: America in the Twentieth Century.* As Virginia Smith, she has written mystery suspense novels, including *Brown-Eyed Girl, Bad Company, Bye, Bye, Love,* and *Hello, Stranger.*

WILLIAM B. SCOTT is professor of history at Kenyon College. He is the author of *Pursuit of Happiness: American Ideas of Property* and coauthor with Peter Rutkoff of *New School: A History, New York Modern: The Arts and the City,* and *Flyaway: Four Paths of the Great Migration.* He is currently completing *The War Against Slavery: The Siege of Charleston, 1861–1865.*

KATHRYN KISH SKLAR is distinguished professor of history at the State University of New York, Binghamton, where she co-directs the Center for the Historical Study of Women and Gender. She is the author of many books and articles in U.S.

women's history and with Thomas Dublin is co-director of *Women and Social Movements in the United States, 1600–2000*, an online journal and database.

NANCY C. UNGER is associate professor of history and women's and gender studies at Santa Clara University. She is the author of *Fighting Bob La Follette: The Righteous Reformer* and her current book project is *Beyond Nature's Housekeepers: American Women in Environmental History*.

MARIS VINOVSKIS is the Bentley Professor of History and a faculty member at the Institute for Social History and the Ford School of Public Policy at the University of Michigan. He has published nine books and over 100 articles and has a forthcoming essay, "No Child Left Behind and Highly Qualified U.S. History Teachers: Some Historical and Policy Perspectives."

TRACEY WEIS is an associate professor in the Department of History at Millersville University. She also coordinates the university's Women's Studies Program.

JOHN WERTHEIMER is a professor of history at Davidson College in North Carolina. He specializes in modern U.S. history and American legal history and dabbles in the history of Latin America.

JAMES P. WHITTENBURG is professor of history at the College of William & Mary, where he teaches courses on colonial and revolutionary America. Whittenburg was the founding director of the National Institute of Early American History and Democracy, a joint project of the College of William & Mary and The Colonial Williamsburg Foundation that sponsors educational programs in American History, Material Culture, and Museum Studies.

SAM WINEBURG is professor of education and history (by courtesy) at Stanford University and the co-director of the National Center for History Education, a collaboration between Stanford University, George Mason University, and the American Historical Association.

MICHAEL ZUCKERMAN has been teaching American history at the University of Pennsylvania since 1965. He is indebted beyond repayment to Lee Benson, who persuaded him twenty years ago to add elements of community service to his courses.

ABOUT THE EDITORS

GARY J. KORNBLITH is professor of history at Oberlin College, where he has taught since 1981. He has published numerous articles and edited *The Industrial Revolution in America* (1998). He is currently working on *Slavery and Sectional Strife in the Early Republic* and, with Carol Lasser, *Elusive Utopia: A Historical of Race in*

Oberlin, Ohio. He was co-editor of the "Textbooks and Teaching" section of the *Journal of American History* from 2001 to 2007.

CAROL LASSER is professor of history at Oberlin College, where she has taught since 1980. She was the co-editor, with Marlene Merrill, of *Friends and Sisters: Letters between Lucy Stone and Antoinette Brown Blackwell, 1846–1893* (1987) and editor of *Educating Men and Women Together: Coeducation in a Changing World* (1987). She is currently working on *Antebellum American Women: Private, Public, Political* (with Stacey Robertson) and *Elusive Utopia: A History of Race in Oberlin, Ohio* (with Gary Kornblith). She was co-editor of the "Textbooks and Teaching" section of the *Journal of American History* from 2001 to 2007.

CONTENTS

Preface   v

Notes on Contributors   vii

Introduction: Reflections on Textbooks and Teaching   1

PART ONE

TEACHING THE AMERICAN HISTORY SURVEY IN THE
TWENTY-FIRST CENTURY: A ROUNDTABLE DISCUSSION   5

PART TWO

WRITING, PRODUCING, AND USING AMERICAN
HISTORY TEXTBOOKS   39

Mary Beth Norton, Reflections of a Longtime Textbook Author;
or, History Revised, Revised — and Revised Again   42

An Interview with Alan Brinkley, The Challenges and Rewards
of Textbook Writing   50

Steve Forman, Textbook Publishing: An Ecological View   58

Daniel J. Cohen, By the Book: Assessing the Place of Textbooks
in U.S. Survey Courses   65

PART THREE

TEACHING OUTSIDE THE BOX   77

Amy Bass, Exploring the Wide World of Sports: Taking a Class
to the (Virtual) Olympics   79

Charles Bright, "It Was As If We Were Never There": Recovering
  Detroit's Past for History and Theater — 85

A. Glenn Crothers, "Bringing History to Life": Oral History,
  Community Research, and Multiple Levels of Learning — 91

Cecilia Aros Hunter and Leslie Gene Hunter, La Castaña Project:
  A History Field Laboratory Experience — 97

Catherine Badura Oglesby, Re-Visioning Women's History through
  Service Learning — 103

Alyssa Picard and Joseph J. Gonzalez, On the Road and out
  of the Box: Teaching the Civil Rights Movement from a
  Chrysler Minivan — 108

David A. Reichard, "Forgotten Voices and Different Memories":
  How Students at California State University, Monterey Bay,
  Became Their Own Historians — 114

Kathryn Kish Sklar, Teaching Students to Become Producers of New
  Historical Knowledge on the Web — 119

John Wertheimer, The Collaborative Research Seminar — 125

James P. Whittenburg, Using Historical Landscape to Stimulate
  Historical Imagination: A Memoir of Climbing outside the Box — 131

Michael Zuckerman, A Modest Proposal: Less (Authority)
  Is More (Learning) — 138

PART FOUR
THE SCHOLARSHIP OF TEACHING AND LEARNING . . .
AND TESTING — **145**

Lendol Calder, Uncoverage: Toward a Signature Pedagogy
  for the History Survey — 148

**Michael Coventry, Peter Felten, David Jaffee, Cecilia O'Leary,
  and Tracey Weis, with Susannah McGowan,** Ways of Seeing:
  Evidence and Learning in the History Classroom — 163

Sam Wineburg, Crazy for History — 200

PART FIVE
TEACHING RE-CENTERED SURVEYS IN THE
TWENTY-FIRST CENTURY — **215**

Ned Blackhawk, Recasting the Narrative of America: The Rewards
  and Challenges of Teaching American Indian History — 217

Allison Dorsey, Black History Is American History: Teaching African

American History in the Twenty-first Century 224

Scott Kurashige, Exposing the Price of Ignorance: Teaching Asian
American History in Michigan 232

Pablo Mitchell, Playing the Pivot: Teaching Latina/o History in Good
Times and Bad 241

Nancy C. Unger, Teaching "Straight" Gay and Lesbian History 247

INTRODUCTION: REFLECTIONS ON TEXTBOOKS AND TEACHING

Teaching American History: Essays Adapted from the Journal of American History, *2001–2007* brings together articles written about the way college professors teach the American past and published during our seven years as co-editors of the "Textbooks and Teaching" (T&T) section of the *Journal of American History* (JAH). If history is the study of change over time, then the history of "Textbooks and Teaching" is no exception. When this feature first appeared in the JAH in 1992, its founding editors Roy Rosenzweig and Sara Evans explained that they sought to "offer a critical analysis of the state of historical knowledge as communicated through textbooks." They pointed out that textbooks are "the single most important written source through which college students learn about the past."[1] Between 1992 and 1995, the section published reviews evaluating how different textbooks dealt with a wide range of topics, including the trans-Mississippi West, popular culture, family history, Reconstruction, and the origins of the Cold War. In 1996, Peter Filene and Peter Wood assumed editorial responsibility for T&T and widened its scope, declaring, "We want to provide a site where teachers exchange exciting ideas about how they convey history to their audiences."[2] Over the next four years, they published a potpourri of case studies highlighting innovative pedagogical practices.

When we became the editors of T&T in 2000, we decided to reshape the section to emphasize a series of annual themes. This volume presents a selection of the essays published under our aegis between 2001 and 2007. As we traced our own evolution as editors, we found that we increasingly focused on the ways in which teaching connected both to scholarly developments within the discipline and also to new research on student learning. We discovered that many historians wanted to talk about their classroom practices and to think about how students process what we teach them. We also found that "practicing" historians—people with research agendas who are trying to keep up with the accelerating rate of new scholarship—wanted their teaching to do justice to the broader issues, ideas, and themes of history in an age of increasing specialization and of an evermore diverse student body. Models of "active learning" interested these historians, who nearly all hailed from institutions that had poured money into educational technology designed to promote new pedagogical options. Yet conversations on teaching and learning methods had barely spread beyond a few experts.

Too often, our students arrive on college campuses telling us that high school history, even in advanced classes, bored them. To them, history seems to be "just one damn fact after another." As educators, we want our students to engage with history and to understand the excitement and possibilities we find within our discipline. Further, we want our students to develop foundational habits of mind so that the facts of history are meaningful. Still, when we look for information about teaching, we want something more than the "plug-and-play" lesson packages marketed for middle school social studies teachers, in which lesson plans include directions on how to arrange classroom desks, quantities of paper to supply, and the color of markers to use in delivering scripted content. We strive for something that brings history to life but does not sacrifice its complexities and paradoxes, its nuances, its analytic challenges, or its unanswered questions.

In addition, we balk at the notion that, to become good teachers, we need the wholesale immersion in the complex theoretical apparatus and empirical literature of cognitive psychology that would qualify us as authorities in "the new scholarship of teaching and learning." David Pace has suggested that without such expertise we are doomed to be "amateurs in the operating room," failing not only our students but also a broader public by remaining in "total ignorance of what is known about the field" of teaching. We take his point seriously. Much can be learned from the research on teaching; however, we believe few historians today are completely uninformed.[3]

For many years, some scholars have recognized their responsibility for taking classroom teaching earnestly, and some colleges and universities have directed attention toward enhancing the pedagogical effectiveness of their faculty. Harvard, for instance, established the Center for Teaching and Learning in 1975, and members of its history department were among the first to express a concern for undergraduate education. Indeed, in offering advice to a group of eager young graduate students in underpaid teaching assistantships (circa 1978), the venerable Oscar Handlin opined: "If a student thinks that Jackson came before Jefferson, it is our duty to help the student discover why that could not possibly be true." Though hardly a champion of radical innovation, Professor Handlin, perhaps unwittingly, articulated a fundamental commitment to what we today call "student-centered learning." He knew that our job was not to *tell* the student the answer, but rather to help the student develop the answer through analytic reasoning.[4]

In editing T&T, we sought to encourage historians to be conscious about how they teach (and about how students learn) without expecting them to master educational psychology. In our classroom work, we strive to introduce students to a rich and compelling discipline, where research in primary sources allows us to construct narratives, to create interpretations, to locate meaning, and to trace change over time. How can we help our students develop the skills that will permit them to engage with the past as we do? What are the key habits of mind that allow students to become budding historians?

During our term as editors, we developed a "compass" for charting the direction of our teaching in the hope of guiding our students toward meaningful appreciation of and reflective participation in "history-making."

Our basic design for understanding and teaching history consists of three intersecting axes. Axis "A" runs between seemingly opposite reasons for why we study history: to recover the *pastness* of the past and to recognize the *presentness*

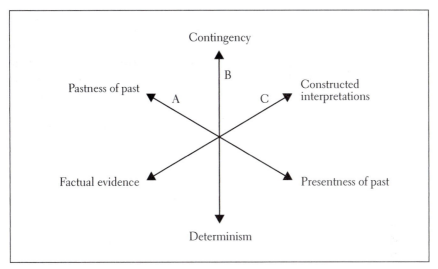

The History Compass

of the past. Axis "B" connects the contrasting poles of historical causation: contingency, with its emphasis on free will and individual agency, and determinism, with its emphasis on the role played by forces beyond individuals' control. Finally, axis "C" stretches between divergent methodological positions: the need for research in primary sources to locate evidence and establish historical facts and the need to construct historical interpretations in dialogue with other scholars because the facts do *not* "speak for themselves."

In connecting the pastness of the past and the presentness of the past, axis A represents what Sam Wineburg has called the "unnatural" character of historical thinking. We want our students to learn to balance along the taut line between a view of the past as a world incommensurately different from the one in which they live and a consciousness of the world that they inhabit as a product of past events and developments. We want students neither to assume that they possess an intuitive understanding of historical actors—projecting their own values and assumptions onto peoples from different times and in different places—nor to assume that they are themselves outside of history and thus less shaped by the context in which they have grown up than were their ancestors. Mediating between the pastness of the past and the presentness of the past promotes a kind of reflective self-awareness, a humbling departure from the self-referential egoism that pervades contemporary American culture.[5]

Axis B speaks to our struggle to understand the enduring theoretical debate between contingency and determinism. Most historians believe that no single explanation is adequate to explain what was done—or undone—by people in a given historical context. History is an exploration of how the pieces fit together in flawed, twisted, rusted, sometimes imaginary, and sometimes disrupted chains of events. To practice—and to study—history means grappling with the balance of choice, chance, and inevitability in any causal sequence. It means reveling in the myriad of possibilities for explanation. If we, as professional historians, struggle with this second axis, our students—so used to understanding history as a straight line of facts to be memorized for the test—often find it all the more incomprehensible.

Finally, in axis C, we seek to help our students understand that historians develop interpretations based on factual evidence but also through a process of analytical construction that involves debate and contestation, a dialogue that takes place not only in the present, but also with reference to prior interpretations. To rephrase Marx, historians write histories based on facts of their own choosing but not of their own invention and not in an intellectual vacuum. We look for patterns in the evidence we collect, and our search for patterns is informed by social theory and the arguments of other scholars, past and present. Our work—and that of our students—involves far more than mastering names, dates, and data. It entails asking why particular facts mattered within particular contexts and why human actions often produced momentous consequences unanticipated by those who undertook them. In the end, we hope our students can locate themselves in relation to the historians whose works they read, aware of how and why scholars have shaped their inquiries in specific ways and conscious of the changing course of the dialogue—the change over time that defines our field.

These three axes emerged from discussions of teaching and learning in T&T between 2001 and 2007, and they now guide us in our classrooms. In the articles collected here, we bring together much of the material that we found so dynamic and so vital. While the chapters that follow are largely arranged according to the themes we chose for different annual T&Ts, we have reorganized some material to enhance the intellectual coherence of this book.

Notes

1. Sara Evans and Roy Rosenzweig, "Introduction," *Journal of American History* 78 (1992): 1377.

2. Peter Filene and Peter Wood, "An Introduction," *Journal of American History* 83, no. 3 (1996): 943.

3. David Pace, "The Amateur in the Operating Room: History and the Scholarship of Teaching and Learning," *American Historical Review* 109 (2004): 1172–91.

4. Carol Lasser attended this event.

5. Sam Wineburg, *Historical Thinking and Other Unnatural Acts: Charting the Future of Teaching the Past* (Philadelphia, 2001).

PART ONE

TEACHING THE AMERICAN HISTORY SURVEY IN THE TWENTY-FIRST CENTURY
A Roundtable Discussion

We began our tenure as editors of the "Textbooks and Teaching" section with a discussion of the "traditional" American history survey, conceived of as a course on "mainstream" American experience from the first settlement of Europeans in North America forward. Although not all colleges offer, much less require, such a course, the survey still serves as the entry point for historical study for more undergraduates than any other American history course. What follows is the edited version of an electronic discussion we conducted during the summer of 2000 and published in the JAH in 2001. The participants were eleven scholars — at the time, some were relatively junior and others more senior. They discussed courses taught at a wide range of American colleges and universities. Participants included Charles W. Eagles (University of Mississippi), Douglas R. Egerton (Le Moyne College), Karl Jacoby (Brown University), Pauline Maier (Massachusetts Institute of Technology), Elisabeth Israels Perry (St. Louis University), Lewis Perry (St. Louis University), Joshua A. Piker (University of Oklahoma), Douglas C. Sackman (University of Puget Sound), Virginia Scharff (University of New Mexico), William B. Scott (Kenyon College), and Maris A. Vinovskis (University of Michigan). These practicing historians commented on prioritizing broad themes, specific content, and interpretive approaches and on formal and informal constraints on pedagogy in different classroom settings. From this dialogue emerged general agreement that, in our teaching, "less is more." Efforts to achieve comprehensive "coverage" backfire because they tend to overwhelm rather than to inspire students. Yet we want to make sure our surveys do not convey the false impression that the study of history is a settled matter and that it is a student's (boring) job to master facts and truths already well established by others. By engaging students in an understanding of history as multi-vocal, contested narratives, we invite them to participate in a more exciting, generative activity than mere memorization and regurgitation.

The first part of the roundtable explores the discussants' main goals in teaching the American history survey to today's undergraduates. While the participants acknowledge that comprehensive coverage is impossible, their comments reveal important differences in priorities, which range from teaching reading and writing skills and conveying essential content to introducing students to the problems of historical interpretation and instilling a passion for the discipline.

The second part of the discussion focuses on the structure and organization of the survey. The discussants debate the centrality of politics as an organizing theme. Several advocate widening the definition of politics to encompass the struggles of groups long excluded from citizenship and governmental power. Although many express reluctance to advertise their approach as multicultural for fear of alienating their audience, all of the participants embrace an inclusive notion of who constituted the American people over time.*

In the third and final part of the roundtable, the participants discuss pedagogical strategies. Many identify informal constraints on how they teach the survey, including student resistance to heavy reading assignments and competing pressures on students' time. Not surprisingly, class size proves to be a major factor in determining the mode of instruction, especially the degree to which various participants rely on stand-up lectures and student discussions. The utility of educational technology emerges as a point of controversy. Yet despite important differences everyone agrees that teaching the survey remains a critical mission for professional historians dedicated to educating the rising generation of college students.

---

*In reflecting on the roundtable in anticipation of its republication in this volume, Karl Jacoby was nonetheless "struck by how little [the] discussion touched upon Native American history." "Even though the human presence in North America dates to at least 12,000 years ago (and likely far earlier)," he observed, "our comments in the roundtable focused on the last few hundred years of this experience. As a result, we inadvertently left the vast majority of North America's human history virtually untouched. Figuring out the connections and disjunctures between this early history and the rest of the American past remains, it seems to me, one of the fundamental challenges for all those who aspire to teach the survey."

Roundtable Discussion

GOALS OF THE SURVEY

KORNBLITH AND LASSER: When you begin constructing the survey, what are your foremost objectives? Do you think about goals primarily in terms of coverage and chronology or of themes and interpretations? Are you trying to teach specific content or "how to think historically"? Are you concerned with introducing students to different historical methodologies? How does your conception of the audience for the course influence your goals?

SACKMAN: While content is important to me, I prioritize other things in the survey, and this has to do with how I think about what content is, and what kind of container American history is.

I have a sense that my stance reflects my generation's experience with the discipline. Certainly, every generation of American historians has grappled with the epistemological problems of the enterprise—with objectivity as an unrealizable, if noble, ideal. But in the early 1990s, when I entered graduate school at the University of California at Irvine, the so-called postmodern challenge was at high tide, threatening to sweep away, many thought, the pilings on which social science had been built. The discourse did more than raise questions about how we know what we know, for it forced us to grapple with how any particular body of knowledge gets institutionalized.

I doubt that there is a foundational stratum of knowledge that all students should learn before they can go on to more specialized study. My sense is that in many places the American history curriculum was set up with this notion in mind. I see problems both with the idea of coming up with a unified knowledge that is American history and with the logic of building a curriculum in history on the notion that students must first learn the known and fixed before they are ready to explore the unknown and contested.

The practical side of my experience in the Ph.D. program compounded the predicament that the theorists put us in. Of course, I was expected to master a body of knowledge in order to pass my exams (or so I thought). The naïve graduate student assumes that the body of knowledge is more or less fixed and assumes quite reasonably that there is a standard set of books and articles that form the reading list. I soon found out that reading lists and much of the character of exams had to be worked out with committee members. It may be then that I came to believe that history is always a product of negotiation. Students came up with their own lists—negotiating in advance the history that they would come to know and thus shaping themselves as scholars rather than submitting themselves

Journal of American History 87 (2001): 1409–41. All articles published with the permission of *Journal of American History*.

to an externally produced and authorized body of knowledge that would do the molding. After going through that process, it would take a fanciful leap for me to go into the lecture hall and position myself as an expert who commands a body of knowledge that is American history.

All of this said, I can still be shocked that the recently publicized poll of college seniors revealed that fewer than 30 percent could correctly identify Reconstruction on a multiple-choice test, and I begin thinking that some way of drilling content, content, content into students' minds must be pursued. Certainly, I don't want to leave students with the idea that any interpretation is as good as another or that there aren't important events and developments that they should know about. I do like to make it possible for them to realize that American history is not a fixed set of facts, figures, and events, that it is not a done deal. History was contested all along and continues to be contested. Conveying this is for me a big part of trying to make history come alive for many students who consider it inert, dead, and distant from themselves and their world.

JACOBY: The issue that preoccupies me is what causes students to enroll in a survey course in American history, especially at a time when interest in the liberal arts seems to be eroding. Like many other institutions, Brown University, where I teach, does not require students to take the American survey to graduate. And considering what one can earn with a computer science degree nowadays and that business is now the most popular major at four-year colleges, it is clear that few students see any practical reasons for studying history. Under those circumstances, I have come to see teaching the survey as taking on the peculiar responsibility of being an advocate for the discipline and convincing undergraduates that the study of the past is a crucial component of what it means to be an educated person.

This concern for drawing students to the study of history influences much of what I do in the survey. At the most basic, I stress to my students that the study of history teaches important skills that can prove useful outside the academy: the ability to read analytically, to write clearly, to discuss matters with one's peers in a constructive way, and so on. For many of those same reasons, I make historical methodology a central component of the survey. Weekly readings are weighted toward primary sources in the hope that through an exposure to the building blocks of historical scholarship, students will begin to understand how historians formulate analyses of particular events. I follow that approach, not because I think that a knowledge of basic historical facts is unimportant—indeed, it seems to me that content is inextricable from methodology—but because I feel certain that in ten or fifteen years, students' recollections of the exact details of the Northwest Ordinance will fade, but they can still retain an understanding of how to construct a persuasive argument based on a close reading of the available evidence. Moreover, it is in the interpretative realm that the truly creative aspects of history tend to be located, and if a key part of my job is getting students excited about the study of history, it is essential to expose them to one of the discipline's most alluring facets.

It may seem that I have reduced the survey to an advanced form of vocational training. Yet my secret hope for the survey is that, even if it attracts students for other reasons, ultimately it will persuade undergraduates of the sheer pleasure of thinking historically—that is, that it will inspire students to see themselves as creations of history and to believe that by studying events in the past, they can reach a deeper understanding of the human condition. While I doubt such a realization has much immediate value in the marketplace, I would like to think that it makes for a more self-aware, and therefore more fulfilling, life.

SCHARFF: Thanks to Doug Sackman and Karl Jacoby for their thought-provoking messages. I've taken a somewhat different approach and answered the questions in a less formal way.

I want students to care about, and be curious about, United States history. I want students to understand that the people they're studying weren't always dead—that they had to make choices based on constraints and options—some similar to those the students themselves face, others different.

I don't think choosing between coverage and themes is an either/or matter. I don't even know how to conceptualize what counts as good coverage or rational chronology without thinking about themes. Some opening questions: What is the United States? Where is the United States? Who counts as an American, and on what terms?

Regarding interpretations, I don't think University of New Mexico (UNM) freshmen can handle historiography as such. I might say, in the course of a lecture, "Historians have argued about the causes of the Civil War," but in the end, I have found that presenting too many arguments as plausible confuses the heck out of students. I guess that means they get *my* interpretation of history, and I'm comfortable with that. I've seen enough cases where "thinking historically" gets confused with the idea that there are no facts, only interpretations. To understand mercantilism, for example, it's incredibly useful to show students how the Navigation Acts changed over time and how and why people in the colonies reacted to the acts in the way they did. It's even fun to do that—let's recall, we're talking about such fascinating human activities as consuming drugs and smuggling.

I believe it's possible for anyone to think a complex thought, but I realize that my students have lives that get in the way of extended concentration on intellectual pursuits. Here at UNM, the average student age is twenty-eight. Many of our students have families, jobs, very heavy responsibilities, continuous interruptions. Thus I tend to assume the best way to teach is not to require sustained attention to discrete questions, but to pick a few themes and come back to them again and again in the course of the semester.

SCOTT: Doug Sackman's and Karl Jacoby's thoughts were provocative, but for me teaching the survey rarely comes down to philosophical concerns, although they are critical in understanding what American history is and can be. The survey for me is a defined task that is self-evidently valuable. Consequently I address most teaching issues pragmatically: What is likely to work best for my students?

I want students to understand why the United States is the way it is and how it became that way. I also want them to understand their own connections to the past and to appreciate that historical figures were not importantly different from contemporary people.

I try to teach a comprehensive course, one that moves chronologically from the late sixteenth century to the present. I don't think it is possible to think historically without historical content. People, places, events, motivation, and circumstance are the content for rigorous historical thinking. A provocative argument without such content would not be good historical thinking. Like Virginia Scharff, I see content and historical thinking as complementary to one another. At times in the course, I introduce students to competing interpretations to help them understand that history is an ongoing and, often, contentious discussion over past events. But I view the survey as a survey and do not devote much time to historiographical concerns.

My survey at Kenyon College enrolls mainly first- and second-year students, eighteen to nineteen years old. They are not otherwise employed, but they have little knowledge of life. My students come largely from upper-middle-class backgrounds. They have had little contact with the working class, small towns, or racial minorities. One goal of the course is to make them aware of the breadth and diversity of the United States and how Americans' histories have varied. Many of the readings I assign are designed to open new windows for them. I assume that they have no prior knowledge. Most take the course out of interest in the subject since it is required neither for the major nor for graduation. That means they are well motivated.

VINOVSKIS: Most of the students who take our introductory history surveys at the University of Michigan are not history majors, but individuals who may be interested in the subject matter or need to fulfill a broad distribution requirement. Moreover, they are quite diverse in terms of their year in school (most are first- or second-year students, but a large number are juniors and seniors). As a result, they have diverse backgrounds and needs, and I see my course as a broad introduction that provides the average college-educated person with the framework, chronology, thematic foci, and methodological tools needed for understanding United States history. I have also been greatly influenced by my reading of the results of various surveys of what seniors in high school and adults know (or don't know) about history, as well as my experiences with students over time.

When I first taught the first half of the survey course almost twenty-five years ago, I did not use a textbook. Instead, I lectured about various themes in American history placed within a rough chronological sequence and used monographs and primary documents as the readings for the discussion sections. Over time, I came to realize that many of the students, but not all, had a very weak background in American history. As a result, I now use a textbook and continue to gear my lectures to broader themes and issues—again within a rough, chronological approach. But rather than using the textbook as a point of reference or general reading, I have found that I have had to reinforce some of the general ideas and issues in the textbook so that the students will take the text seriously and pay attention to its content. With considerable effort, I now have made the textbook an integral piece of the survey, supplemented with some monographs and primary sources (although, as a result, I have had to reduce the additional reading in favor of the textbook).

Previously I taught the first half of the survey with a little attention to the Native American population in place before Christopher Columbus and then some comparison between Spanish and English settlement. But basically, the story became one of English westward settlement after the first few lectures. Now, I devote more attention to the longer and more complex history of the initial settlement of the Americas even before twelve thousand years ago and the diverse Native American peoples and empires. Being in Michigan, I devote some attention to French settlement and try to remind students of the importance of seeing history from the sixteenth century through the nineteenth not only from the vantage point of English settlers. Indeed, I argue that one could write a very different history of America from the Spanish/Mexican perspective—but I only touch on these in passing due to time constraints. Thus, issues of who occupied or settled North America have become much broader for me over time—partly due to a better appreciation of the diversity of American life, but also as a result of the richer and more sophisticated literature on America.

PIKER: Perhaps because I have taught two very different sorts of survey classes, I find that my approach to the "coverage versus methodology" debate varies according to the institutional constraints I face. In the honors version of the class— where enrollment is kept low (nine students last spring) and expectations for reading are high—we spend time juxtaposing primary documents and secondary literature. I insist that students think of themselves as historians, as people who have the ability and knowledge to engage with primary sources, professional historians, and their peers. We talk about the different readings that are possible, the assumptions we bring to the texts, the ways certain questions or problems have been embraced or elided.

By contrast, in the class with 220 students and no discussion sections, I stress coverage. I may use a brief overview of a historiographical debate to introduce a subject, and I do assign primary documents (in addition to a textbook and three monographs), which I refer to frequently in my lectures. For the most part, though, this version of the survey presents, as Virginia Scharff put it, "my version" of American history. The "conflicts" that I teach are those between historical actors, between people who were debating the central issues of their day. In other words, the contingent nature of American history (the choices people made) is foregrounded in this course, while the contingent nature of historical interpretation (the choices we all make as we evaluate the past) is not.

I've adopted this approach in the larger class for two reasons. The first has to do with simple logistics: in a class this large, supervised discussions are impractical, and requiring my teaching assistants (TAs) to respond to frequent writing assignments is cruel. I decided that asking students whose names I do not know and whose written work will be read very quickly to take part in the debates that surround historical interpretation was impractical and artificial. Analysis and interpretation divorced from debate and discussion is not "doing history." The second reason I've decided on this sort of strategy has to do with the background of my students at the University of Oklahoma (OU). They tend to be from small, relatively homogeneous towns. That has some advantages (religious topics—for example, the Puritans—go over really well), but it also presents me with some obvious challenges. I am committed to teaching a multicultural version of American history; my own research focuses on ways to incorporate Native Americans into our narratives of the American past. In the honors survey, because of the intimate nature of the class, I can guide our analyses away from certain flawed and (to my mind) pernicious interpretations of the American experience. In the regular survey, however, I worry that, because I can't directly engage with individuals, the students will leave the class without having truly questioned some of their beliefs about the American past.

ELISABETH PERRY: In constructing any survey, I think both of coverage and chronology *and* of themes. I agree with others who've said they can't be separated. In selecting material, I ask myself: What do students "need" to know about the past in order to function as informed citizens in today's world? On the assumption that boredom will turn them off from history, I try to find material that will fascinate them but also help them establish guiding principles for how they will live. A tight thematic focus helps the selection process, which is never easy.

I begin *every* course I teach by attempting to raise student consciousness about issues of diversity, inclusion and exclusion, etc., in how the past gets "constructed." Some students come to their college experiences already sensitized by sophisticated high school teachers, but most do not. They expect a survey that's geared toward some standardized test. As a result, if you're not talking about presidents and wars, you're not talking about "real" history. So, I lead off by asking, "Is history an art or a science?" and see where that takes us. Usually, pretty far! We end up discussing selection and exclusion, what constitutes evidence, the role of interpretation, how mainstream narratives get constructed, and so forth. And as we proceed along the course, at relevant moments I remind them of that opening discussion so that it becomes concrete for them. If I don't go through that exercise at the start (or have TAs do it), I get comments such as, "I signed up for a United States history course, not a women's history (or black history) course!"

EAGLES: The basic objective of my classes is to help students learn to read and write more effectively. It is essentially a skills development approach that almost incidentally uses American history. I work with students on how to take notes, how to read essays and books (always scholarly works), and how to write papers; I distribute a handout on each of the three general tasks, and some initially find them insulting but soon profit from them. I have found that many (most?) students have never been taught basic skills but instead have had to develop them on their own if they have them at all. All this may sound too elementary for many professors, but I see too many of our colleagues' manuscripts and eventual publications that suffer from sloppy thinking and writing, not to mention intellectual laziness, so I am confident that our undergraduates need such instruction.

My approach to the coverage question has been called a "posthole" as distinct from a "ball of string" one. Each lecture is a self-contained unit on a particular topic or theme, and the lectures are arranged chronologically with some overlap and omissions. My lectures do not string together to form a narrative but examine discrete topics in considerable detail and depth, with some connections suggested but others left to a textbook.

Content as such is not as important as organization and significance of material. The larger significance often leads to a discussion of interpretations and historiography. My own interests are largely historiographical, and I find students often find the debates intriguing and sometimes exciting—and definitely a new way of studying history. My first class in the second half of the United States survey, for example, deals with race relations from emancipation to 1900 and ends with a brief discussion of the views of C. Vann Woodward, Joel Williamson, and Howard Rabinowitz. If this is what "thinking historically" means, then I do it.

Nearly twenty years ago, I learned not to assume that students know much about history. They often know far more than I do about many things, but not history or even contemporary public life. I cannot assume they know where anything is or who anybody was. So I try to begin at the beginning but am constantly surprised that I did not really start at their beginning point. Students in 2000 seem even less oriented toward books and history than they were in the late 1970s when I started teaching. My commitment to reading and writing assignments has only deepened as students seem to have moved away from traditional academic work.

EGERTON: I suppose my first priority is content, although I wish it didn't have to be. The liberal arts college I teach at (Le Moyne College) is fairly exclusive, yet I often find that I have to provide the basics for my students, most of whom are sophomore history and political science majors. A good number have had supposedly college-level Advanced Placement (AP) courses in high school, but virtually none of them had to read anything for those classes besides a basic text. Like Douglas Sackman, I not only worry about polls that demonstrate that a solid majority of students cannot correctly identify Reconstruction; after fifteen years of teaching I have solid data to support that concern. (A student once identified the Reconstruction Act as a law passed to reconstruct damaged bridges after the Civil War!) Most of our history majors wish to teach high school, and given their lack of preparation, I can't help but feel that my main responsibility is to provide them with some basic information.

I also agree with Virginia Scharff that content and chronology, on the one hand, and themes, on the other, are not mutually exclusive. My two-semester survey course does include a theme of sorts: the question of what constitutes an American and how a good many non-elite groups struggled to broaden what was initially a very exclusive definition. But I don't try to hammer every lecture or topic into that hole—although most of my readings are organized around that broad topic.

I also try to get my students to think historically, by which I mean I want them to understand that there are more interpretations or views than those being presented by their instructor. Because my survey classes are rather small—about twenty-five students—I integrate a good deal of discussion into my lectures. I want my students to feel free to disagree with my interpretations, and so I remind—inform?—them on the first day of class that there is no such thing as capital T historical Truth. That does not mean that all positions are historically sound, but rather that we all carry a good deal of cultural baggage about. Historians can come to different conclusions based upon their reading of the relevant data—and they can even disagree about what are the relevant data! Many of my students are conservative, and I am not, so I encourage them to dissent from my interpretation of specific people or events. That is not the way they have learned in high school, and it takes them some time to adjust to the strange new notion that there is no single correct way to view the past. Many appear confused when I disagree with something written in one of the assigned monographs, as they have never been told that they can disagree with the written or spoken word.

Most of my students come from the Northeast; most are middle- or working-class; a majority are Catholic; a majority are women; most are bright but have to be pushed to do first-rate work. Beyond that, my students are a rather homogeneous lot, which is both good and bad. I rarely have either especially gifted students or especially ill-prepared students, and perhaps only one or two out of twenty-five will be above the age of twenty-one. That allows me to teach to the middle. On the other hand, there is a depressing sameness in their views as they have such similar backgrounds.

Over the past fifteen years, even as our SAT scores have gone up, it seems as if the students not only know less but are less eager to do the necessary work. I've had to resort to unhappy gimmicks such as book quizzes to force my students to read carefully, indeed, sometimes to read at all. But I refuse to lower my standards—or the number of assigned monographs—from what I began with in 1985. One concern I do have is that many of my students work long hours off campus. When I stop to get gas, there they are at the desk. I know their schedules are tight and their dollars are short—even as the price of books rises yearly—but I feel that I do them (or their future high school students) no favor if I reduce the reading load and cut back on my expectations of them.

LEWIS PERRY: There has to be a theme, but it has to be a capacious one, and I do not believe there is any single "right" theme for the survey. Years ago I had several chances under a National Endowment for the Humanities (NEH) grant to teach a survey focusing on the development of theater in the United States. I loved it, and I know many of the students got a lot out of it (especially those who "don't like history"). But when I moved to another university, it just didn't fit in the curriculum. I used to imagine teaching United States history in a school for the performing arts, but no such opportunity ever arose.

It is certainly necessary to keep in mind the needs, interests, preparation, and institutional context of the "audience." I don't talk about "methods" as I do in seminars for majors. But I do emphasize close reading and historical reasoning, both in discussions and essays. For that reason, I would be reluctant today to take on the huge enrollments I enjoyed a few times in the past (though large lectures can work well with well-planned and coordinated discussion sections).

Thirty years ago, I took for granted much more "basic" knowledge of United States history than I do today. More of the students seemed to be planning to teach history, and more of them were thinking of majoring in the field. And that was before students tested out of United States history based on AP scores. Today, I am less likely to focus on a series of topics without providing a clear sense of change and development over time. I no longer believe one can assume even the most rudimentary acquaintance with the "colonial" period, the "Revolution," Jacksonian "democracy," "Reconstruction," or the "industrial revolution," for example.

I certainly adjust topics and readings on the basis of the students in the course. I am well aware that the texture of examples discussed in my courses has changed as I moved from the Northeast to the Midwest to the South. That doesn't trouble me. I believe that if we taught history as often to senior citizens as to young adults, many new topics would be standard in the surveys (and in our research). But I think a constant in my approach, as in that of others of my generation, has been the amplifying and testing of core American beliefs about the progress of liberty in the light of advancing knowledge about the diverse experiences of American people. As we all know, some of our colleagues charge that the survey has lost all coherence. Some of the problems they point to are undeniable. But graduate students have been answering "race, class, and gender" questions for some time now. And thousands of teachers have been working out coherent approaches in their classrooms. We will never have a single true United States history, but I believe a very creative period of synthesis has already begun.

MAIER: I have taught the survey since finishing graduate school in 1968, but now I teach only the first half—which for me ends with the Civil War and perhaps a brief discussion of what it accomplished. I like teaching the survey; it gives me an excuse to keep up with a broader part of the field than I might otherwise do and to keep synthesizing, or trying to synthesize, new scholarship into some general understanding of the past that I convey to students. Perhaps I should say "try to convey"; what we actually accomplish is not so clear.

I did not, thank God, go to graduate school at a time when we agonized over the possibilities of objectivity or the extent to which and the process by which bodies of knowledge became institutionalized. I don't think we had or have illusions about discovering "truth" (although we recognized some versions of the past were less erroneous than others), nor did we remain oblivious to the way certain versions of the past became established at definable points in time.

In the 1960s there remained, perhaps curiously, a sense that there were certain parts of the past that every student should know about, and chunks of specialized information passed from the antiquarian to the historical by being related to some unfolding story that was history. Even as narrowly focused studies began to multiply, a certain faith remained—for a time—that, in the end, those specialized studies would lead to a redefined story or history. More recently, I sensed that that faith had corroded and in its place a hostility set in (how general I can't say), not just toward the idea that there is somehow one "master narrative" out there, but toward all efforts to define an organizing narrative. That form of postmodernism seems incompatible with the day-to-day work of being a historian, and certainly of a historian who teaches the survey or, as in my case, now and then writes parts of a textbook.

Random pieces of specialized knowledge hold in the head no more than pieces of dry sand cohere; the human mind, I and others believe, makes sense of experience by constructing narratives. History is a story. The problem is deciding what story or stories we tell and what we choose to incorporate in our story and what to leave out. I'm prepared to say that will change with the teller—although, postmodernism notwithstanding, I have the distinct impression that many of us are telling stories that aren't all that different. How could they be? We live in the same world, were trained in a common field, and read the same books and journals. And we're all part of a special cohort of historians who teach the survey.

If you assign a variety of sources—family trees, autobiographies, tracts, books, etc.—the questions of how you use them and what you can learn from them arise automatically. And the skills conveyed are "life skills," relevant no matter what students do in life. So is the substantive history they learn. If students realize that people didn't always think as they do, that assumptions have shifted over time, they've learned something of enduring human value. The moral purpose of the humanities, I was once told, is to make people realize what it is to be someone else—and that someone else can be from a different time period. In understanding the distinctions of people in other times we are simultaneously defining what's distinctive about ourselves and our time. Getting the "self" out of history is no easy thing, and maybe a silly objective, a courting of irrelevance, though a history that's overly self-referential strikes me as both morally and intellectually problematic.

STRUCTURE OF THE SURVEY

KORNBLITH AND LASSER: How do you structure the survey chronologically and thematically? What periodization do you employ and what themes do you emphasize? Do you focus on certain "turning points" in American history or do you highlight long-term trends and historical processes? Do you address (either explicitly or implicitly) recent debates over multiculturalism in the teaching of American history?

SCOTT: For me, whatever else an American survey includes, it should address the central political events and structures of the United States. It should give students a basic literacy in American political history. Beyond that, I place political history in its economic, social, racial, gender, ideological, cultural, and natural contexts. Even though I am not a political historian, I think the "political narrative" is a critical and necessary foundation for the American survey.

The subject of the course is the nation, its origin, its transformations, its constitutional and legal system, the character of its people, and the formative events—all issues under discussion and debate, often quite heated. Those contested issues make up the nation's historical discourse. It is not, however, a static discourse of fixed events, fixed interpretations, fixed meanings, nor fixed content, even though the most important events that punctuate the discourse have remained fairly fixed. The years 1492, 1607, 1620, 1630, 1688, 1763, 1776, 1789, 1812, 1819, 1848, 1861, etc., have precise historical meaning for most American historians. Had our graduate committees known that we did not "know the historical significance" of those dates, we would never have received our doctorates. Individuals' abilities to participate in the discourse of American history and to be taken seriously depend on the extent and depth of their knowledge of the discourse and their own scholarly contribution to it. One task of an American survey is to provide students a literacy of the American past or, if you prefer, the discourse of American history.

No two-semester survey can address all possible questions relating to American life since 1492. Each of us has to make choices appropriate for our students and their interests. In that sense we are storytellers more than social scientists. Our use and manipulation of data may be logical and even empirical, but our choices are determined by our sense of drama and our moral preferences.

Unum, however, is as important as *E Pluribus* or it would not be an American survey. The American survey, regardless of where or by whom or to whom it is taught, is largely understood to mean the "history of the United States." The category itself has privileged political concerns. The story goes far beyond narrow political history, but without attention to the formation and changes of the nation, the category "American survey" is meaningless and, probably just as important, not interesting for most students.

EGERTON: As I mentioned before, my survey course does have an explicit theme: the old question of what constitutes an American and how most non-elite groups had to struggle to force that definition to include them. As a result, my two-semester class does implicitly address diversity and multiculturalism, and I say implicitly because I consciously avoid using those terms in class. If I simply present the diversity of cultures, peoples, and religions in this country as a historical reality, my students accept this reality as a given. Curiously, I've discovered that if I employ politically loaded terms such as "multiculturalism," at least some of my students resist confronting this reality. Certainly, my selection of monographs— from Graham Hodges's *Root and Branch* to Catherine Clinton's *Divided Houses*, and from Anthony Wallace's *Death and Rebirth of the Seneca* to David Szatmary's *Shays' Rebellion*—implicitly recognizes themes of diversity and struggle in the American past.[1]

Having said that, I do agree, in part, with Will Scott's emphasis on political history. Although I do not agree that we must embrace a "political narrative" in our survey courses, it certainly is true that the one commonality upon which most early Americans could agree was their desire to be included as citizens. One might wish to note obvious exceptions to this drive for political inclusion—Denmark Vesey and Handsome Lake come to mind—but certainly a discussion of diversity in the antebellum era should include Frederick Douglass and Elizabeth Cady Stanton. If a "political narrative" means merely a chronology of presidential elections, as important as many of those were, we can probably expect our students' eyes to glaze over. But if properly understood to be the way that society, including those not yet included as political citizens, organizes its priorities and cultural values, then political history may be employed as a bridge between commonality and diversity.

Finally, I do emphasize "turning points" in history. I suspect that most of my students believe that it was somehow inevitable that the present would turn out pretty much as it has. I wish to emphasize in class that the actors we are discussing were real people with real options and that there were moments when there were roads not taken that might have considerably altered the rest of the American saga. I often inform my students that they are now advisers to King George III or Lyndon B. Johnson and must make policy decisions regarding the colonies or Vietnam. I'm less interested in having my students judge these people—although often they end up doing so—than I am in making them understand that, say, the Founding Fathers had a range of options when it came to slavery and freedom and that they made certain conscious choices that made America what it is today.

VINOVSKIS: I use a combination of chronological and thematic approaches. I follow Will Scott's plea for political history and developments to a large degree but leave myself ample opportunity to do thematic lectures on social, demographic, and economic topics.

There is no one overall theme—but several themes. Some, like the institution of slavery, I follow in considerable detail across the time periods using different perspectives (political, social, intellectual, etc.). Similarly, concerns about the threats to liberty and the responses of Americans to such fears in different periods are pursued. Other topics are more single issues, such as changing attitudes toward the elderly or changing views of abortion. With those more individual topics, I try to illustrate the variety of histories available and the richness of our past; here I sometimes shift the specific topics to reflect my own interests and readings as well as interesting work in the area.

Perhaps more than some, I try to present broad, overall trends and changes in areas such as social and economic history—and whenever possible to add some comparative information from other parts of the Americas or the world. I also try to make periodic references to developments in American life that students taking courses in other disciplines such as political science may find useful. I often focus on events such as the Revolution and the Civil War that have a particular impact on subsequent developments—examining the continuities and discontinuities as a result. Sometimes, I use obscure events, like Dorr's Rebellion, to illustrate how changes have taken place in American life that otherwise might not have been noted at the time.

Given my interest in history and policy making today, I frequently refer to the present to provide some interest in the past for students—but usually not with the intention of providing lessons or insights for developments today. Thus, when discussing changing attitudes and behaviors on abortion in colonial and nineteenth-century America, I start out by acknowledging the controversies today and the ahistorical views many Americans have about those issues—but the focus is on the past. On the other hand, when I discuss the rituals of death and dying in the past and the idea of the "good death," I remind the students that we have our own myths about dying today (such as Elisabeth Kubler-Ross's so-called stages of dying). Similarly, when talking about children and education, I point to the similarities between early-nineteenth-century infant schools and Head Start today—and leave students with questions about why Americans are so quick to put their faith in early childhood education rather than other types of more fundamental social and economic reforms.

PIKER: I'd like to begin by responding to Will Scott's well-stated brief for a politically based survey. I do, in fact, spend a great deal of time on politics in my pre-1865 survey class, but that material is backloaded. That is, slightly more than the first third of the course focuses on the period prior to 1763, and that section deals primarily with issues that my students would identify as "nonpolitical"—race, ethnicity, gender, ecology, religion, economic life, all the stuff that goes into the messy but fascinating processes involved in intercultural encounters and the setting up of colonial societies. Each of those issues has its own political dimension, but I'm not convinced that "politics" is at the center of what I'm discussing during those weeks. That is especially true because I try to go beyond the temporal and spatial bonds of what's often considered American history. So, for example, pre-Columbian Indian societies get a fair bit of coverage, as does fourteenth- and fifteenth-century Europe. Moreover, Spanish and French colonial efforts surface frequently in my lectures.

I use this material for a variety of purposes, but one of them is to set up the political debates that will play a large role in the class as we consider the period from 1763 to 1865. As we move from the Revolution and the Constitution through the early republic and antebellum periods, I try to give my students as broad a take as possible on what politics involved. They should leave my class with a general understanding of the various ways "American" has been defined, of the interests served by particular definitions, of what it means to be "in" and "out," of how "we" deal with "them." I hope my students will see the United States as both a nation and a process, and I hope they will see the way politics shapes and is shaped by the broader sociocultural milieu.

As the above suggests, my version of the survey is broadly multicultural. Like Doug Egerton, however, I have elected not to mention the M word. Why borrow trouble? I've found, instead, that I can get my students to engage with diversity (and with "bottom-up" history more generally) by insisting that they take seriously the idea that we live in a democracy. I ask them to consider what material they'd want to include in a history of the past year and suggest that a history that focused only on Bill Clinton and George W. Bush, on the marriage penalty and Social Security, would be unsatisfactory. What if we added Mark McGwire and Britney Spears? Better, perhaps, but they quickly recognize that this list doesn't begin to touch on the things that really matter in their lives. I tell them that it is those things—family and friends, work and play, faith and fear—that will be at the heart of this class.

JACOBY: Teaching the first half of the survey can be a curious experience, for the periodization employed is simultaneously very fixed and very fluid. One temporal boundary—the end point—is rigidly set. Is there any survey sequence that does not break at 1860–1865 or 1877? But the beginning and other turning points are left completely open to interpretation. In my own class, I try to use this vagueness, especially in relation to the starting date, to get the students thinking about how the concept of "American history" has shifted over time. Since the American history survey at Brown dates to the 1920s (the course number for the class I teach, History 51, has not changed in over seventy years), I am in the convenient position of simply historicizing my own course. In the 1920s, the survey at Brown had a fixed starting date (1783), presumably because American history began only when the United States came into existence. I show my students how subsequent scholarly trends have pushed this starting point backward in time. That exercise helps underscore the different assumptions about who Americans are and what America is contained within each starting point and, in turn, within the larger exercise of history as a whole.

Not every date receives such methodological massaging. I do emphasize many of the standard dates—1492, 1675, 1763, and, yes, 1877—in large part because I think it is vital that students be able to construct their own chronologies of the past. One of the hardest aspects about teaching the survey, I have learned, is conveying a sense of simultaneity—that events treated in separate lectures and in separate sections of the textbook (such as, say, King Philip's War, Bacon's Rebellion, and the Pueblo Revolt) were going on almost simultaneously. Having the ability to draw comparisons across regions and notice larger trends is only possible if students have a clear chronological framework on which to build.

Much like Douglas Egerton and Joshua Piker, I do not explicitly pitch my course as an exercise in multiculturalism, not because I think it is a particularly loaded term at my school, but because I am not exactly sure what constitutes a multicultural analysis, other than a general impulse toward inclusion. I do make consideration of race, class, and gender systems a fundamental part of my course, but I also try to historicize those very concepts. I approach race, for example, through the prism of race formation—the processes by which different ethnic groups from Europe began to think of themselves as white, different native tribes began to think of themselves as "Indians," Africans from different ethnic groups conceptualized themselves as black, and so on. Likewise, my discussion of class is bound to the development of labor systems, both slave and free, in the New World. My goal is not just to be inclusive on some surface level but to showcase the new identities that emerged out of the crucible of American history.

LEWIS PERRY: My remarks apply to the first "half" of the survey. First of all, I believe more and more firmly in the need to start with the best current information on pre-Columbian America. I expect to take my class next spring to the Cahokia mounds in western Illinois. Some of my historian friends get nervous about how much of that information, in general and specifically at Cahokia, is speculative and uncertain. But I think it is misleading to simply begin with the European terms of the story.

I probably will give less time than many others (and less than I used to) to the colonial period. Among the themes I will stress are "national identity"— English and "American." I like to ask when "American" history begins and present it as a problem with a range of answers. I don't think there's anything unusual about my treatment of the Revolution, except that I focus more each time on national identity and citizenship issues, with some comparisons to France. I will definitely spend some time on the Confederation and the Articles of Confederation (which I have found upperclassmen often know nothing about) and try to make the Constitution a historical event (as opposed to a sacred event).

Maybe because I also teach the early republic or early national period, I work hard on it in the survey. If I don't, it's very hard to make the democratic partisanship beginning in the 1820s comprehensible to my students as something new and dramatic. I suppose much of my emphasis is political, though I don't think of the course as primarily political. There will be at least a week on economic change, on the West, on the South, on reform, then all the time I have left will be devoted to slavery, the 1850s, the Civil War. Last time my emphasis in the Civil War was on the freedmen and citizenship. Even restricting my time in the colonial period as I do, it is hard to get past the Civil War.

I present this as more than a series of topics. I was interested in Maris Vinovskis's comments on how he used to focus on topics, without assigning a textbook, but has changed his approach. So have I. I feel some responsibility to give students a sense of development and change even as we discuss particular texts and issues.

I suppose you could say that I "implicitly" raise issues from current debates on "multiculturalism." But I don't think of what I am doing in that way. I prefer to keep the focus on historical development and change and ask students to suspend their current opinions and prejudices. But this gets into a *big* set of issues, I know.

EAGLES: For the last eighteen years I have taught only the second half of the United States survey, so I will restrict my comments accordingly. The course usually breaks roughly into thirds: 1865–1877 to 1900, 1900 to 1941–1945, and post–World War II. The selections result, not from some grand intellectual consideration, but rather from my mundane decision to give two exams during the course, in addition to the final exam, which means having three parts to the course. Within each third, lectures combine broader analyses of change and more discrete discussions of particular events or even individuals; sometimes one class can accommodate both in an inductive or deductive fashion. Within each third, the material follows a rough chronology, but otherwise the order is determined by what seems most sensible (for instance, an explanation of the changes in the nature of work in the late nineteenth century comes after an examination of the developing industrial organizations). Classes present long-term trends and within them highlight significant events, maybe even turning points such as the Spanish-American War.

The trends in the second half of the survey cannot surprise anyone: from small-scale production to dominance by large corporate interests; from an almost insignificant government to a large and powerful federal bureaucracy; the emergence of mass, popular, consumer culture(s); the increasing liberation of minorities, etc. National politics is not the focus of the course, but it takes on a larger importance as the course proceeds (the New Deal still strikes me as more important than the Chester A. Arthur administration). The themes tend to recur throughout the course, with or without my highlighting them for students. As I have said before, I use the "posthole" approach, largely because I realized long ago that everything could not be covered, that selectivity was unavoidable, and I opted for a more complicated presentation of fewer topics instead of a more rushed attempt to cover nearly everything. An additional benefit to a deliberately topical method is that the course can easily be changed from one semester to the next by switching individual topics. Each class is told, more than once, that class lectures and discussions do not offer comprehensive coverage (that's what the textbook is for). Adding and deleting topics helps keep the course fresh for me and thereby, I hope, for the students.

The topic of multiculturalism does not, for several reasons, arise. First, it would disgust some of the more alert conservative students at the University of Mississippi. Second, any unfamiliar polysyllabic word loses a certain percentage of students. Third, like so many things, doing it is better than talking about it; I prefer to present variety rather than preach about it. The same thing goes for historiography. I never use the word (can you see undergraduate minds close at the mere use of the word?) but rather demonstrate it. I became self-conscious of this years ago when a friend told me he had trouble explaining "fundamentalism" to his students. After we talked about it, I suggested he try explaining the concept to them and then maybe use the big word to tell them what it was but that he definitely not start by writing the word on the blackboard (does anyone else still use a blackboard?).

ELISABETH PERRY: There appears to be quite a bit of agreement in the responses: Everyone seems to follow a general politically based outline; no one makes a big deal out of "multiculturalism," but everyone tries to "be" multicultural by example rather than preachment; most everyone breaks the survey around the Civil War and Reconstruction, etc. Instead of saying those things over again, let me challenge some of the assumptions that I see as lying underneath.

First, the issue of coverage. If we continue to break the first half of the survey at the Civil War or 1877, aren't our chances of making it through the twentieth century in the second half declining? There's just too much to cover. Our students need a foundation in early American history, but isn't it increasingly important that we give them *first* a strong sense of their parents' and grandparents' generations? I wonder if we ought to think in terms of a different kind of chronological breaking point or figure out (somehow!) if there's a way to teach the survey backward from contemporary times.

Second, the issue of periodization. As a teacher of women's history, I often find myself at odds with standard periodization. Take the Progressive Era, my own period of specialization. To confine that era to the first two decades of the twentieth century diminishes the importance of how women set reform agendas in the late nineteenth. It also leaves out enfranchised women's continuing (and partially successful) efforts during the 1920s and 1930s to legislate progressive agendas. How does one handle such issues in the survey? One way that I do it is to make explicit that periodization is not some historical "fact" but reflects interpretive decisions that historians make and is contingent upon historians' own sense of what is important.

Third, the issue of "political" history. I agree with some of the other participants that any survey has to have a general political structure. But, as one person said, we cannot march our students from election to election. What to do? We need to establish at the start a broad definition of what we mean by politics. We don't mean just elections and voters, but the whole set of issues, ideas, and controversies over which Americans have argued, negotiated, and fought. Starting with such a concept more easily allows us to integrate the disfranchised, the unelected, and the citizen-activist into United States history and make that history a more compelling experience for the undergraduate student.

SCHARFF: Like Liz Perry, I won't go over familiar ground, and I also share some of her concerns about "traditional" periodization and a too narrowly defined political history. I'd be very surprised if there's anyone out there still doing history from one president to another. (Why waste time with Millard Fillmore when you need so badly to get to Abraham Lincoln? Shall we tarry with Calvin Coolidge when Franklin D. Roosevelt awaits?) So maybe the question is less one of what counts as politics but who counts as a political actor.

There's politics and politics, of course. Oddly, no one so far has used the word "conquest" to talk about the process of nation building in the United States. A couple of people have mentioned the importance of "liberty" as an American political concept. I like to draw lots of maps on the blackboard, showing the way in which the United States invents itself geographically as well as politically as an "empire for liberty." Under that kind of umbrella, I can bring in everyone from Sacagawea to Dred Scott to Abraham Lincoln, Susan B. Anthony stumping the Northwest for suffrage, all kinds of Roosevelts, Bill Haywood, Earl Warren, Rosa Parks.

The question of where to break the survey is baffling, but I find myself not unhappy with 1877. At that moment, the United States as a territorial entity was only very provisionally continental. I remind my students that any number of

Americans in eleven states had very recently died for the idea that those states weren't part of the United States and that in much of the West, the locals were, at best, grudgingly acquiescing to American authority. The end of Reconstruction is a good place to look back and say, OK, the United States map looked then pretty much the way it does now, aside from Alaska and Hawaii—the empire now stretched across the continent, from the Rio Grande to the forty-ninth parallel. The United States really was moving into a new phase with plenty of unresolved issues still on the plate. The question of *where* it was, was solved. *What* and *who* remained open.

SACKMAN: My basic themes are how the promises of liberty and equality have played out and what it has meant to be an American. For the most part, I do, as Elisabeth Perry puts it, try to "be" multicultural rather than preach multiculturalism. But at the end of the second half of the survey, I address multiculturalism as an explicit topic. We look at the "new immigration" since the 1960s and look back at earlier immigration debates; we look at affirmative action debates and the legacy of the Great Society—and, more broadly, the continuing significance of race and how race is more than a black and white issue; and we look at the politics of history and memory as it has been involved in the culture wars. Here, I talk a little about the two controversial exhibits at the Smithsonian Institution— "The West as America" and the *Enola Gay* exhibit ("The Last Act: The Atomic Bomb and the End of World War II")—using them as examples of how pervasive history continues to be in American life and as a way of looking back at material we covered on the conquest of the West and on World War II.

Like Elisabeth Perry, I embrace an expanded definition of politics. On the syllabus I set out provisional definitions of politics, as well as economics, society, and culture. My initial definition of politics there is "the character and operations of power in a nation, including but not limited to the roles of political parties and elected officials, and involving such issues as life, liberty, and the pursuit of happiness." "Culture," "society," "economics," and "politics" are all intensely debated and elusive terms (and they blur into one another), but by introducing the set of terms, I hope to help students see the complicated ways that the nation was put together and give them some initial tools for social analysis.

MAIER: How do I organize the survey? I say something about explorations and pre-Columbian America, including the impact of contact, then settle down with colonial Virginia and New England, looking at them separately and drawing comparisons. I use the "free time" in the first class after explaining the syllabus and requirements by having students look at a family tree—one that's attached to "John Dane's Narrative," a brief autobiography of a seventeenth-century Puritan (published in the *New England Historical and Genealogical Magazine* for 1854) that is one of my favorite teaching documents. It's amazing how much demographic data can be culled from one family tree. ("Hey," one student said, "this guy lived to be eighty-two! And look how many kids he had!") We read the narrative itself a week or two later. Deciphering seventeenth-century language (in modest quantity) can be like solving a puzzle—and to go from there to grasping a very different mind-set feels almost natural.[2]

Given time constraints, I have to move quickly to the Revolution. But first I assign something on the origins of slavery. I spend time on the independence movement and the creation of republican governments on the state and federal levels and take a close look at the federal Bill of Rights against Antifederalist demands. We discuss politics in the early republic, economic development, reform and abolitionism, expansion, the political crisis of the 1850s, secession, and the Civil War. That seems pretty standard: there are things we want kids to know about. Politics is included (though I do not, as Virginia Scharff put it, trace the story from one president to another) because, however we feel about politics today, it was central to American culture in earlier times, and the politics of time past helps explain the world we have inherited.

Is my treatment of survey material chronological or topical? It's both. It cannot be comprehensive; I need to make choices, as we all do. So some themes are privileged in the chronological narrative. The beginnings of slavery, early emancipation, the participation of free blacks in pushing for the end of slavery and genuine equality, the growth of abolitionism and its place in exacerbating sectional tensions, etc.: How could anyone teach the first half of the survey without addressing those issues? Can we understand the constitutional questions of 1861, much less our current government, without examining the institutional heritage of the Revolution? In theory I suppose an instructor could cover different topics, and no doubt we give different treatment to—or treat at different lengths—Indians, the western movement, immigration, the Supreme Court, popular culture, domestic life, religion, science, and technology. Surely I give much more attention to Indians, women, and race and less to theology and certain political topics than when I first began teaching. But certain things remain, I think, central to the story, though sometimes their place in that story is new or different from what it was in 1968. There's a reason Doug Sackman was shocked that students didn't know what Reconstruction was. Like it or not, there's a core of information we're still involved in conveying, and not because that information was institutionalized at some point in time, but because it's part of the unfolding story of this country. And the American history survey traces a national history.

PEDAGOGY OF THE SURVEY

KORNBLITH AND LASSER: Given the formal and informal constraints you confront in teaching the survey, what mix of lectures, discussions, and other modes of instruction do you employ? When you develop your schedule of reading assignments, to what extent are you concerned about page limits, cost, and "entertainment value"? If you assign a textbook, what is its function in the course? If you assign primary sources, how do you use them? How important are maps, photographs, films, and other visual media in your pedagogy? Do you use Web sites or other interactive technology?

PIKER: I'm going to focus my comments on my experiences teaching the large version of the University of Oklahoma's survey, rather than the honors course.

Formal constraints are almost entirely lacking at OU: no one looks over my shoulder as I design the syllabus, pick the texts, write lectures, etc. As a result, the sections of the survey that my department offers vary a great deal from professor to professor, which seems to me to be a plus. Informal constraints do, however, surface repeatedly, as I suspect they do at most institutions. I've mentioned some of those: very large classes, no discussion sections, a relatively homogeneous and conservative student body.

The class consists almost entirely of my lectures. I open the class up for questions periodically, but I do not attempt to use the students' questions as the basis for discussion. I try to assign several movies during the course of the semester, and I'm working on integrating small clips of films into my lectures as a way of illustrating a larger point and of "hooking" the students.

I find the lecture-only method of teaching disconcerting, to put it mildly. It often feels like I'm walking the line between pedagogy and performance art. In the best of all possible worlds, I would give one lecture a week (as a framing mechanism for the week's discussion), and then students would meet twice more in small TA- or professor-led discussion sections. OU is actually moving toward offering more discussion sections, but the sticking point is money to hire discussion leaders.

I assign a textbook (Mary Beth Norton et al., *A People and a Nation*), three monographs (one for each third of the class), and a document reader. Last semester, the monographs were William Cronon's *Changes in the Land*, Alan Taylor's *William Cooper's Town*, and Noel Ignatiev's *How the Irish Became White*.[3] I use the monographs as a chance for the students to investigate in detail a particular issue, place, or theme that might get slighted in the lectures. I need to work on referring back to the monographs in my lectures. I'm still learning not to assume that the students will see how Indian land-use strategies relate to King Philip's War or how William Cooper's experience fits into the debates surrounding Federalism.

The textbook is a supplement to the lectures, a chance for the students to preview (or, more likely, review) some of the material I cover in class. When I've taught other classes (say, colonial America) without assigning a textbook, my students get nervous; they're unsure of their ability to get "the point" of a lecture, and they're used to having the textbook as a fallback position.

As for the primary documents, I try to find material that they'll think is either "fun" (a Puritan writing about wigs, for example, or a captivity narrative) or "important" (the Declaration of Independence seems to qualify). The documents should be compelling enough to draw the students in, and their relation to the week's themes should be easily grasped. It's here, however, where I most feel the need for discussion sections. Engaging with the documents without engaging with others' interpretations of those same pieces can be a very sterile exercise.

Beyond making sure that all the books are in paperback, I haven't focused on cost. Pages-per-week, however, is a big issue. Anything more than 100 is a problem. The goal is to find the line between "We finished it but that last assignment was tooooo long" and "We've got so much reading that we're not even going to try to do it."

SCHARFF: I was amazed at how much my course patterns, approaches, and perplexities resemble Josh Piker's.

The only constraint at the University of New Mexico is scheduling—we teach either three fifty-minute classes per week (Monday, Wednesday, Friday) or two seventy-five-minute classes (Tuesday and Thursday). We usually run several large sections per semester, and my classes run anywhere from 90 to 150 students. The largest ever was 250, which was, unfortunately, scheduled in an auditorium with 800 seats. I couldn't see the top third of the room but once did become aware of people at the back—a couple, in carnal embrace. They were noisier than they realized.

With classes this large, like Josh Piker, I find myself mostly lecturing. I try to conduct big, crazy discussions now and then, and it depends entirely on the chemistry of the classroom whether they work or not. All it takes is a couple of bright, engaged, brave students to ask provocative and thoughtful questions, and the whole class can come alive. On the other hand, there are those semesters where the students seem mostly disengaged. One memorable morning I realized that a woman in the twentieth row of a crowded classroom must have overslept and was spending the entire class finishing her grooming: hair, makeup, and, the last straw, putting lotion over her entire body. By the end of the period, I had joined the students in watching her. Does this happen to other people?

I use the same text as Josh Piker, along with two supplementary readings. This semester, the first is a novel, Hugh Nissenson's *Tree of Life*—a harrowing, breathtaking novel of the frontier. The second, a book I've used pretty much every semester for ten years, is Frederick Douglass's *Narrative*. I'll be interested to see how the Nissenson works—the Douglass has never failed me.[4]

Ever since a student told me that he had to do his readings in the post office locker room when he was on breaks, I've seen the constraints in the amount I can assign. The limit is about 100 pages per week. Cost is also a factor. I wouldn't dream of asking students to pay more than $100 each term for books for the introductory survey. I try to take care of entertainment value in the lectures and hope they'll be hooked enough that they'll think history is per se entertaining. For example, I try to pick interesting individuals and return to them, over the course of several lectures, as witnesses and historymakers. Examples: Thomas Jefferson, John and Jessie Frémont, Frederick Douglass. I like to do the same thing with places—see New York as Dutch village, as growing commercial center, as site of immigration, as setting for the draft riots. I also tell stories about various people who avoided or resisted or simply survived the spread of American domination— the maroon communities in Florida, the Pueblos of the Southwest.

I use a couple of movies each term and this year will be integrating some of the video lectures (twenty-four minutes each) from *Biography of America*, a telecourse of American history produced by WGBH in Boston. As for maps, I've experimented—bringing paper maps, bringing transparencies—but in the end,

I've come to rely on the act of drawing very schematic maps on the blackboard. I treat the map drawing as an inside joke between me and the whole class—a statement that says, "Look, if I can get you to imagine the shape of the nation, the rivers and lakes, the battles or events, with a picture this childlike, you'll get a kick out of it and maybe look for a better map when you've got more time."

JACOBY: For the past three years I have taught the first half of the survey, which typically enrolls 100–150 students. The course currently features two lectures a week; then, on Thursdays and Fridays, the class is broken up into groups of twenty or so for discussion sections, led by me and two or three TAs. In theory, this format allows students both to get a basic overview and to debate the readings and lectures in an intimate setting. It is a constant struggle to keep section size down to an appropriate number. And once the lecture classes balloon to more than fifty people, it can become difficult to sustain the question-and-answer interplay that I like to employ during lectures.

For me, the paramount issue involved in selecting the weekly reading is how well the book or article can stimulate a lively and thought-provoking discussion section. Even though the sections take place only once a week, I consider them the heart of the class, since it is here that students learn to form their own interpretations of past events and to test them against those advanced by other students. Most weeks, this means that I assign primary sources. Like others, I use Frederick Douglass's *Narrative*; I also assign Mary Rowlandson's *The Sovereignty and Goodness of God*, Harriet Beecher Stowe's *Uncle Tom's Cabin*, Thomas Jefferson's *Notes on the State of Virginia*, and excerpts from the WPA slave narratives, the *Lowell Offering*, and the *Cherokee Phoenix*.[5] If I do a good job contextualizing those materials during my weekly lectures, we can have stimulating discussion sections. In contrast, when I assign secondary sources, the students often lack the historical knowledge to step outside the author's narrative, and so we are confined to narrower discussions about the author's thesis, use of evidence, and so on. Those are important discussions to have, but I find that having such discussions week after week can lead to diminishing returns.

Cost and readability enter into my calculus. Since many sources from the pre-1877 era are in the public domain, they tend to be available in cheap paperback editions. By keeping the cost of the books low, I hope to make it possible for more students to buy the books and thus to read them at their leisure and with greater care. Moreover, since many of the books I assign are foundational works of American history and literature, I would like to think that I am helping my students build useful personal libraries that they can turn to after leaving college.

I do assign a textbook, but we rarely discuss it in section. Instead, it functions as a fallback for students who want to check a name or date that they missed in lecture. I also rely on it to give the details of certain topics that I do not have the time to cover in depth in lecture, and I am very explicit about directing the students to it for this purpose during lectures. Between the textbook and the primary sources, I probably ask students to read in the vicinity of 200 pages a week (I have the luxury of teaching at a school where most students do not have full-time jobs in addition to full course loads).

Today's college students are intensely visual, and as a result I have made the reluctant decision to use slides every class. This has made preparing for lectures much more involved, but student feedback has been overwhelmingly positive. Although I worry about turning the survey into little more than highbrow entertainment and students into passive consumers, having slides has in fact created new opportunities for student exchange. Often I will show a slide and ask students to describe what they see as significant about the image. Students who seem tentative when discussing written documents frequently have far more to say when talking about a painting or an early political cartoon.

I have not done much with the Web other than including a few significant Web sites in my syllabus. I have yet to be persuaded that the research materials available on the Web are that much better than the primary sources already available in book or article form. There is also the question of whether I can reasonably expect students to have regular access to a Web-connected computer on which to do their class work.

MAIER: I choose a text that seems to offer reasonable, intelligent coverage. This year I'm using the concise version of James West Davidson et al., *Nation of Nations*, though I have to say I'm not sure concise histories do what I need. I always assign something on the origins of slavery—I used to use Peter Wood's *Black Majority*, which also introduced students to a Restoration colony, but I am substituting parts of Ira Berlin's *Many Thousands Gone* this year. Of course, I assign the Declaration of Independence (with Congress's editings—which opens everything up), the Constitution, and some ratification debates; I assign some William Lloyd Garrison, George Fitzhugh, *Uncle Tom's Cabin* (it's long but they love it), and a selection of Abraham Lincoln's letters and speeches. I explore some themes that aren't standard, assigning Pat Malone's *Skulking Way of War*, a short book that examines firearms technology and Indian-white relationships during the seventeenth century in a very memorable and useful way. I also assign Oscar Handlin's *Boston's Immigrants*, now sixty years in print and out of sync with modern interpretations, but it gives me a chance to explore the different ways concrete information can be "read."[6]

Many books are overlong for the survey. I could not assign all of the Ira Berlin book, for example; I assign parts of it for two weeks. And price *does* make a difference. I am delighted with the Dover Thrift editions of primary sources, which sell for a dollar or two (though they lack introductions, so I need to supply necessary background information).

EAGLES: No restrictions on teaching exist at the University of Mississippi, but the pressures of the students do have an impact. Long ago I realized that if I taught the course the way I thought it should be taught, the result would be very small classes. To maintain credible enrollments, I adjusted my expectations and demands, but that was a bargain I could easily accept. Survey class size is further constrained by an 8:00 A.M. starting time, which does not bother me. As a result, my survey classes are never more than thirty-five to forty, and often only in the twenties (therefore usually no graduate assistant, but I never use one for grading or teaching anyway). Though my reading and writing assignments cause many to drop after the first class, most students know about the course before they enroll. Student tolerance for academic work here has improved significantly in the last decade, but the overall climate still is not as supportive of the academic process as it is at more selective institutions.

For every class session, I am prepared to lecture for the entire period; my hope, however, is that discussions will emerge from the material presented and from the readings. I try to promote interaction by asking questions, some rhetorical and some directed at individual students, and the results vary from class to class. Seldom do I talk for the entire time, so I wind up cutting and compressing the material (which is far easier with the posthole method than with the ball-of-string narrative approach). I would like to be able to assign more readings, to depend on students to read them, and maybe even to think a little about them before class. When key participants are unprepared, discussions are tough.

Several factors influence my selection of reading assignments: length, cost, topic, approach, etc. My paramount concern is that students read history books, that is, books written by historians, and there are plenty of good ones. How can we expect to reach a reading public if we do not introduce them to real scholarly work in our classes? I try to combine different types of history and disparate subjects. For example, a biography of a labor leader might be combined with a book on an urban race riot and another on the Vietnam War, but not three biographies or three on labor or three on foreign policy. Instead of three monographs, which is about the top limit here for freshman classes, the last couple of times I have assigned two collections of essays, James West Davidson and Mark Hamilton Lytle's *After the Fact* and William Graebner's *True Stories from the American Past*. The textbook is *America: A Narrative History* by George Brown Tindall and David E. Shi.[7] And, yes, cost is a major factor because many of the students cannot spend zillions each semester on books. The problem grows worse every semester, with some textbooks costing more than $50 in paperback.

I may be the only person who does not use documents and primary sources. My goal is not to teach freshmen to be historians or necessarily to appreciate how historians do their work (I would not expect them to write poetry in a literature class). I want them to learn to enjoy reading history and grappling with arguments. Frankly, I find analyzing a couple of documents not a real example of how historians actually work, at least not twentieth-century historians who confront mounds of material. As for slides, maps, etc., even the most basic textbook has plenty of illustrations and maps, and the more elaborate ones have a surfeit. The latest in technology appeals to me very little. I am dedicated to the written word in a form that can be easily read anywhere: under a tree, in bed, in a hall waiting for class, over lunch. Students attracted to the latest technology may not find my courses enticing, but so far a sufficient number do, and I see no need to offer more of what they are already getting plenty of everywhere else in our culture.

SCOTT: My survey is a two-semester course. I limit the course to seventy students and do not have any graduate or teaching assistants. It meets three times a week and I usually lecture two of those days and engage in "discussion" the third day. In a class of seventy students, discussion cannot include everyone and is somewhat contrived since I assign the material and ask the questions. It is more like an orchestrated, participatory lecture.

During the semester, I require about 1,600 pages (eight books) of supplementary reading that includes primary works and historical monographs. I use Paul S. Boyer et al.'s *Enduring Vision* as the text.[8] I expect students to read 150 to 200 pages a week. Text and supplemental readings come to about $125 a semester. I use many of the same books each year and rarely change the text. On the used book market the required books can be obtained for about $50 a semester. I choose material, not just for its content, but also for its interest. If students are fascinated by a book, I use it again. If they found it boring, I don't use it again. This is true of primary sources as well as historical monographs. Once students realize that reading is a treat and not a punishment, they are willing to do it.

Students are not just more visual than ever, visual media are rich and valuable historical materials. When appropriate, I use music, art slides, architecture, news photographs, film clips, films, and maps. These are especially valuable to stimulate discussion since students do not have to read their assignments to participate in an informed way. It also makes them aware of the enormous variety of cultural stimuli that have formed our historical memories. The Web offers rich and rapidly growing resources for this, especially the American Memory Web site sponsored by the Library of Congress.[9] Unfortunately, I do not take full advantage of this, probably because of my age. It's not comfortable for me to use in class.

I do, however, use e-mail a great deal. E-mail has immensely improved my communication with students. They ask questions about lectures or readings, set appointments, and explain why they missed class (a serious infraction). I find that with e-mail, I can effectively reach my entire class, nudging them, encouraging them, or inquiring about problems. I can also make course announcements through my class lists. Still, on the whole, my course is low-tech: lectures, discussion, maps, slides, CDs, and videos with a few out-of-class films such as *Black Robe, The Last of the Mohicans, Amistad, Glory, The Birth of a Nation, On the Waterfront, Eyes on the Prize, Rebel without a Cause,* and *Medium Cool.*[10]

EGERTON: There are no formal constraints on how I teach the survey. I suspect that many of us wandered into this profession in part because we couldn't imagine being part of a culture where we had to take and give too many orders. But informal constraints include the refusal on the part of my survey students—most of whom are sophomores—to read monographs longer than 300 pages.

It appears, however, that among the participants in the roundtable I have the smallest survey courses—about thirty students per section (I teach two fifty-minute sections, back to back). As a result, my course is about 80 percent lecture and 20 percent discussion on any given day. I devote entire class periods to discussions of the four monographs I assign. I use a text—John M. Murrin et al.'s *Liberty, Equality, Power*—not only as background to my lectures, but as a source of data that I expect my students to know and be ready to discuss when they walk in the door.[11]

Cost is a factor, and I never assign a monograph that runs more than $20 new. The combined, hardcover textbook is $83 new, but my students use it for both semesters, and it costs less than two paperback splits. A majority of my students plan to teach high school, so I encourage them to keep the text rather than to sell it back for a few dollars in May.

I never give a lecture without an overhead map behind me. My students' geography is shaky enough, and it would be impossible to explain Robert E. Lee's second invasion of the North or the Missouri Compromise without a proper map.

Luddite that I am, I do not use Web sites or other online sources, in part because I'm not up on them, but also because I'm old-fashioned enough to believe that there is no substitute for a thick book and an overstuffed chair. Many of my sophomores cannot distinguish between a legitimate Web site that has legitimate primary documents or reprinted (refereed) articles and pop history sites or chat rooms where the wildest conspiracies are transformed into reality.

I do use videos in the classroom. As Karl Jacoby noted, our students are intensely visual, and so I use brief clips from videos to illustrate points I'm trying to make in my lectures. I rarely show more than a five-minute clip, but it helps my students to personalize abstract debates. Examples include a wonderfully concise debate between Alexander Hamilton and James Madison on funding and assumption from the otherwise ahistorical Washington miniseries (*George Washington: The Forging of a Nation*), Denmark Vesey speaking in Charleston's African Methodist Episcopal (AME) Church, or bits of *The Birth of a Nation* when I talk about Woodrow Wilson and civil rights.[12]

VINOVSKIS: Basically, the survey at the University of Michigan is divided into two parts—I teach the first half, which has about 175 students; the second half has about 350 students (this is each semester—both halves of the survey are given in both the fall and winter semesters). The first half of the survey could be larger, but we cap it at 175 to reflect the number of TAs we have for the sections. Our lectures are given twice a week (fifty minutes), and the sections meet twice a week (one hour for each section discussion—about twenty-five students per section). I always teach the honors section, which has about ten to fifteen students.

We have a lot of autonomy in how we teach the survey, but over time a basic format has been used by all of us. What we teach and how we handle it can be altered to suit the interests of the faculty member teaching it. (We try to rotate the teaching of the survey, but some individuals are more willing to volunteer to teach it than others.)

Having taught the survey for many years, I discovered that it is useful to revise the course just after I have finished teaching it—while it is still fresh in my mind. I always ask the students to evaluate the individual readings at the end of the course. Students are asked: Given the orientation of the course, would you recommend that the particular book being evaluated should be retained or dropped (using a five-point scale)? They are also asked for their favorite and their least favorite book in the course as well as any other comments or suggestions about the books or other aspects of the course. In addition, I ask some personal data (gender, grade in school, etc.) and cross-tab the results to see how the readings worked with different subgroups of the students.

Based upon those replies, the feedback from the TAs, and my own observations, I tentatively revise the course. Thus, I continue to use the Norton et al. textbook as it is the second most popular book, as well the Frederick Douglass volume (the most popular work). But I find a substitute for a book that I liked but that proved to be too hard and/or unpopular—unless there are compelling pedagogical reasons for keeping it. After completing the revision, I show it to my TAs and sometimes discuss it with a few colleagues; then during the early summer I review the revised list to make any final changes. In general, the textbook has remained the same, but the supplementary monographs and primary readings are frequently shifted.

While I use maps as overheads, most of the lectures are not illustrated, nor do I use PowerPoint or other devices. I think these might be very effective, but I simply have not had the time to go in that direction yet.

LEWIS PERRY: As it happens, I have never taught in a department where I was told what to teach. I have taught fairly huge sections (about 400 students), with graders but no discussion sections, at two state universities. I have also taught more comfortable sections of fifty to ninety students at one of those universities. Of course, I lectured more than anything else, but like Virginia Scharff, I found some ways of leading discussions (without requiring everybody's participation).

I am now planning a class limited to nineteen freshmen at St. Louis University on the first half of the survey. I did something similar at Vanderbilt a couple of years ago. I will not give any lectures, though I will present information and viewpoints, planned and unplanned. I will take the class to Cahokia Mounds at the start of the term and look for another field trip later. I like to play music (even though there are no recordings from the period, and there are issues of interpretation to discuss). I have used "Peg and Awl" from the Harry Smith Folkways Collection, for example, and recordings of the Sea Island Singers and of songs by the Hutchinson Family.[13] I will most likely use films and slides, too, but I will avoid having students sit too long without exercise. There will be considerable discussion of documents, considerable writing, and an emphasis on active inquiry on the student's part.

There are a number of very good textbooks, but it is hard to find a collection of primary sources fitting the themes I want to develop. I was very unhappy with the one I chose last time (and I chose it out of unhappiness with others). I am sorry that *Sources of the American Republic*, edited by Marvin Meyers, Alexander Kern, and John G. Cawelti, is out of print. I began with it when I was a graduate teaching assistant and still like its well-chosen documents, which are more than just snippets and do not simply lead to one conclusion. I have David Brion Davis and Steven Mintz's new *Boisterous Sea of Liberty* on my desk as something to think about. I may also build my own document collection from the Houghton Mifflin "BiblioBase." But I like the intelligent introductions of the two collections I've mentioned. I would also like to assign at least one work in its entirety—last time, at Vanderbilt, it was David Walker's *Appeal*.[14]

ELISABETH PERRY: When teaching classes of thirty to forty, I alternate between lecture and discussion. For the latter, I often put students into groups of five or six to work on specific issues or use something I call the "double circle." I ask them to count off "1, 2" and ask all with one number to form a circle in the center; those who got the other number encircle the inner group. The students "inside" do not have to raise their hands to speak; those on the outside do. I sit in the inner circle and moderate. After about twenty minutes, the groups switch. Between that and small groups I get a very high percentage of participation. We don't always get "through" all the topics I want to talk about, but everyone has a good time and, since I never know how a particular discussion is going to come out, I don't worry about going stale.

The Internet can be a wonderful resource, but I find that students do not use it wisely. They accept a great deal of what they see uncritically (the "As seen on TV" approach). And when they can't find something on the Web, they often decide that it doesn't exist and give up. Moreover, if they aren't wired in from their rooms, they tend not to use Web-based resources. I use e-mail to communicate back and forth with students, but, again, since some are not wired in, I can't rely on such forms of communication without leaving students out.

SACKMAN: Much of what Charles Eagles says on using history books I find persuasive, but I think it can also be valuable to have students grapple with primary materials. Consequently, I have come up with a grab bag collection of texts: a textbook, primary sources, and a set of monographs that are meant to complement one another as well as meet needs for coverage. For this fall, my first time teaching the first half of the survey, the monographs I ended up with are Colin G. Calloway, *New Worlds for All*; Elizabeth Reis, *Damned Women*; Jon Butler, *Becoming America*; and Stephen Aron, *How the West Was Lost*.[15]

After I developed the week-by-week organization of the course, I found that John Mack Faragher's *Out of Many* melded closely with what I wanted to do, so I went with it. I decided to use the brief edition mainly because of price.[16] Last year, I used the document set that has been prepared for *Out of Many*, which includes ten short documents for each chapter. Some weeks, discussion sections were done only on the documents for a particular chapter. This was a way of varying the amount and type of reading (I share Karl Jacoby's views on the limits of discussing monographs *every* time). My course (excluding the textbook) averaged about 100 pages a week, but some weeks had twenty to thirty pages of reading while others had about 200.

The silver lining to cutting out longer works on important topics is the discovery that there is more than one way to skin a fact. Two years ago, I had planned to use *The Grapes of Wrath* but finally decided it was just too long.[17] I was left with a gaping hole on the Great Depression. To address this, I had students do a "document-gathering assignment" for that week. I gave them two options: collect a magazine article or advertisement from the 1930s out of a mass-circulation magazine (I was fortunate that we had many of these available in the stacks) or collect a document specifically concerning the Dust Bowl and Dust Bowl migration from one of several Web sites that I identified. We started the discussion with a round of show-and-tell and then built from that. Initially skeptical of the assignment, students tended to appreciate the license they were given to explore the material culture of the past in such an open way.

Visuals and film are integral to the course. Especially for the twentieth century, I don't view them as gimmickry used to entertain students, since the development of a visual culture is itself an important component of the last hundred years. I've been lucky to be able to teach the survey in "smart classrooms"— rooms equipped with a digital projector to which I can easily connect my laptop computer. Every lecture I use fifteen to thirty images. Some are more illustration than anything else, but some are used as primary sources. I used to make slides, but now I can simply scan images in and incorporate them into a PowerPoint presentation. This has many advantages over the use of slides: it's less time-consuming (though it's not a snap), cheaper, possible to do at the last minute, and has slightly fewer technical glitches than the slide projector. A good slide, though, is far superior to the projected images in terms of resolution. I also like to show a few documentary films during the term. They can do things that I could never do in a lecture—unless, perhaps, I could spend a month "producing" each lecture.

But I don't think my approach to the survey is better than someone else's because I use visual media. I can only say that it is better than the course *I* would teach if I could use no visuals. We have raised some issues concerning the use of information technology, but I'd like to explore them further, and I'll do so in an alarmist fashion. With the creative use of Web sites, I think that each of the various publishers is trying to become the sole source for our classes. They can offer much that is enticing, helpful, and impressive, especially as it is our talented colleagues who provide much of the content for these sites. As these textbook plus Web site packages become more sophisticated and comprehensive, might they become, to put it baldly, master rather than tool, eroding that autonomy most everyone in the discussion feels we enjoy in putting together their courses? I ask myself if it would be wise to move more toward the position of Charles Eagles, who sees "no need to offer more of what [students] are already getting plenty of everywhere else in our culture." My answer so far has been to wheel in that Trojan Horse, uncover where it came from, and then analyze its promise as well as its danger. But, undoubtedly, the belief that we can simply incorporate it as a tool and keep our critical distance is in part illusory, and it will, for better and worse, change the very environment in which we work and in which we become who we are as teachers.

AFTERWORD

At the close of the roundtable, participants were invited to offer advice to new faculty teaching the survey for the first time. Several veterans cautioned against trying to cover too much in a single class. "Think of what you want the students to have in their heads when they leave the classroom, and structure the class accordingly," recommended Pauline Maier. "When I began teaching I was, like so many new Ph.D.'s, terrified I'd run out of material, and prepared the most information-packed lectures imaginable. By the second year I realized that what I had tried to teach in one class was enough for a full week." Charles Eagles recalled the advice he had received from a colleague many years before: "You can only tell a class two or three things in fifty minutes." Likewise Will Scott counseled "patience," while Elisabeth Perry encouraged novices to "take chances." Karl Jacoby advised, "Identify for your students what it was that first attracted you to the subject of history and try to pass this enthusiasm on to them. Students need to see firsthand the intellectual excitement that the study of the past can bring." Added Lewis Perry, "I think young faculty members and graduate students sometimes need to be assured or reminded that teaching is one of the most worthwhile things a person can do." In the end, the advice most often proffered was simple: "Have fun"—coupled with the reminder that, in Virginia Scharff's words, "You're not in this for the money."

Notes

1. Graham Russell Hodges, *Root and Branch: African Americans in New York and East Jersey, 1613–1863* (Chapel Hill, N.C., 1999); Catherine Clinton and Nina Silber, eds., *Divided Houses: Gender and the Civil War* (New York, 1992); Anthony F. C. Wallace, *The Death and Rebirth of the Seneca* (New York, 1969); David P. Szatmary, *Shays' Rebellion: The Making of an Agrarian Insurrection* (Amherst, Mass., 1980).

2. John Dane, "John Dane's Narrative, 1682," *The New England Historical and Genealogical Register* 8 (Boston, 1854): 147–56.

3. Mary Beth Norton et al., *A People and a Nation: A History of the United States*, 5th ed. (Boston, 1998); William Cronon, *Changes in the Land: Indians, Colonists, and the Ecology of New England* (New York, 1983); Alan Taylor, *William Cooper's Town: Power and Persuasion on the Frontier of the Early American Republic* (New York, 1995); Noel Ignatiev, *How the Irish Became White* (New York, 1995).

4. Hugh Nissenson, *The Tree of Life* (New York, 2000); Frederick Douglass, *Narrative of the Life of Frederick Douglass: An American Slave* (Boston, 1845).

5. Mary White Rowlandson, *The Sovereignty and Goodness of God, Together with the Faithfulness of His Promises Displayed: Being a Narrative of the Captivity and Restoration of Mrs. Mary Rowlandson and Related Documents*, ed. Neal Salisbury (Boston, 1997); Harriet Beecher Stowe, *Uncle Tom's Cabin* (Boston, 1851); Thomas Jefferson, *Notes on the State of Virginia* (London, 1787); James Mellon, ed., *Bullwhip Days: The Slaves Remember* (New York, 1988).

6. James West Davidson et al., *Nation of Nations: A Concise Narrative of the American Republic*, vol. I: *To 1877* (New York, 1996); Peter H. Wood, *Black Majority: Negroes in Colonial South Carolina from 1670 through the Stono Rebellion* (New York, 1974); Ira

Berlin, *Many Thousands Gone: The First Two Centuries of Slavery in North America* (Cambridge, Mass., 1998); Stowe, *Uncle Tom's Cabin*; Patrick Malone, *The Skulking Way of War: Technology and Tactics among the New England Indians* (Lanham, Md., 1991); Oscar Handlin, *Boston's Immigrants, 1790–1865: A Study in Acculturation* (Cambridge, Mass., 1941).

7. James West Davidson and Mark Hamilton Lytle, *After the Fact: The Art of Historical Detection* (New York, 1982); William Graebner, ed., *True Stories from the American Past*, vol. II: *Since 1865*, 2nd ed. (New York, 1997); George Brown Tindall and David E. Shi, *America: A Narrative History*, 5th ed. (New York, 1999).

8. Paul S. Boyer et al., *The Enduring Vision: A History of the American People*, 4th ed. (Boston, 1999).

9. American Memory Web site <http://memory.loc.gov>.

10. *Black Robe*, dir. Bruce Beresford (Vidmark Entertainment, 1991); *Last of the Mohicans*, dir. Michael Mann (Twentieth Century Fox, 1992); *Amistad*, dir. Stephen Spielberg (DreamWorks, 1997); *Glory*, dir. Edward Zwick (Tri-Star Pictures, 1989); *Birth of a Nation*, dir. D. W. Griffith (Republic Pictures, 1915); *On the Waterfront*, dir. Elia Kazan (Columbia Pictures, 1954); *Eyes on the Prize: America's Civil Rights Years*, prod. Henry Hampton (Blackside, Inc., 1986); *Rebel without a Cause*, dir. Nicholas Ray (Warner Bros. Pictures, 1955); *Medium Cool*, dir. Haskell Wexler (Paramount Pictures, 1969).

11. John M. Murrin et al., *Liberty, Equality, Power: A History of the American People*, 2nd ed. (Fort Worth, 1999).

12. *George Washington: The Forging of a Nation*, dir. William A. Graham (MGM, 1986).

13. Harry Smith, ed., *Peg and Awl*, performed by various artists (compact disk; Smithsonian Folkways, 1997).

14. Marvin Meyers, Alexander Kern, and John G. Cawelti, *Sources of the American Republic: A Documentary History of Politics, Society, and Thought* (Chicago, 1960); David Brion Davis and Steven Mintz, eds., *The Boisterous Sea of Liberty: A Documentary History of America from Discovery through the Civil War* (New York, 1998); BiblioBase is an online ordering system that permits the user to create a customized text. For more information, see www.bibliobase.com. David Walker, *Walker's Appeal in Four Articles* (Boston, 1829).

15. Colin G. Calloway, *New Worlds for All: Indians, Europeans, and the Remaking of Early America* (Baltimore, 1997); Elizabeth Reis, *Damned Women: Sinners and Witches in Puritan New England* (Ithaca, N.Y., 1997); Jon Butler, *Becoming America: The Revolution before 1776* (Cambridge, Mass., 2000); Stephen Aron, *How the West Was Lost: The Transformation of Kentucky from Daniel Boone to Henry Clay* (Baltimore, 1996).

16. John Mack Faragher et al., *Out of Many: A History of the American People*, 3rd ed. (Upper Saddle River, N.J., 2000).

17. John Steinbeck, *The Grapes of Wrath* (New York, 1939).

PART TWO

WRITING, PRODUCING, AND USING AMERICAN HISTORY TEXTBOOKS

In introducing the inaugural "Textbooks and Teaching" section of the *Journal of American History* in 1992, Sara Evans and Roy Rosenzweig wrote, "Textbooks are the single most important written source through which college students learn about the past."[1] That remains the case today. Yet complaints about American history textbooks abound. Chester E. Finn Jr., president of the Thomas B. Fordham Institute, has characterized them as "fat, dull, boring books that mention everything but explain practically nothing."[2] His criticism pertained to secondary-school textbooks, but college-level textbooks have also come under fire, especially for their high cost. A coalition of Student Public Interest Research Groups has launched the Campaign to Reduce Textbook Costs (MakeTextbooksAffordable .com), and elected officials across the country have debated—and in some states passed—legislation designed to restrain textbook prices. Still, most teachers of American history survey courses assign a textbook as core reading, and many assign only a textbook. For better or worse, American history textbooks shape how American college students encounter their nation's history and their society's cultural heritage.

Given the role played by American history textbooks, we decided to focus the 2005 T&T section on how they are written, produced, and used. We invited Mary Beth Norton and Alan Brinkley, two long-time and highly successful textbook writers, to discuss how they first got involved in textbook writing and how they viewed the process in light of their many years of experience—the choices and constraints they faced, their sense of audience and market dynamics, the trade-offs between writing textbooks and doing other kinds of scholarly work. A coauthor of *A People and a Nation*, now in its eighth edition, Norton discussed how that pathbreaking book—the first major textbook to incorporate the "new" social history—came to be and how it has evolved over time. She reflected on the challenges of working collaboratively with other authors and on the importance of regularly revising a textbook to incorporate new scholarship and to address readers' criticisms based on actual classroom use. She made clear that she and her coauthors, not editors or market specialists, decided what to retain and what to drop from edition to edition, though she also highlighted how page limits are inevitably restrictive.

Alan Brinkley's comments are excerpted from an interview we conducted with him on July 9, 2004. Brinkley explained how he "inherited" authorial responsibilities for *American History: A Survey* in the early 1980s and why, in his opinion, that textbook, now in its twelfth edition, has attracted a large readership for more than forty years. He also reflected on his sense of audience, the general parameters of the textbook genre, and the special difficulties of writing about the whole of American history as a sole author who must sometimes reach far beyond his area of specialization. Like Norton, he addressed the question of authorial independence, the recurrent process of preparing new editions, and the pros and cons of devoting large blocs of time to textbook writing.

To compose the text of a textbook is one thing; to convert that text into a printed volume and to place the final product (including ancillary materials) into the hands of teachers and students is a related but distinct process. For a view of textbook production and distribution from the perspective of an editor and publisher, we turned to Steve Forman, a veteran member of W. W. Norton & Company. We asked him in particular to address the explosive issue of textbook pricing and to explain why American history textbooks today cost so much. In response, Forman offered an ecological analysis of the textbook industry and its relationship to academic consumers. The cause of recent price hikes, he explained, is not pure-and-simple profit mongering by publishers but a growing disequilibrium within a complex system of producers, sellers, buyers, and resellers, in which behavior that appears rational to each participant in the short term may undermine the long-term interests of all concerned. Highlighting shifts in the operation and culture of higher education, Forman suggested a few systemic "adjustments," but he left open the central question of whether equilibrium can be restored.

Finally, we wanted to learn more about how instructors actually use textbooks in their courses. Daniel J. Cohen, developer of the Syllabus Finder, agreed to analyze data on the nearly eight hundred American survey courses included in this database of online syllabi. According to his analysis, many instructors rely almost exclusively on textbooks to supply curricular content in the survey—a tendency he deemed quite worrisome. He inferred that many instructors adopt textbooks as packaged courses, relieving themselves of the hard work of teaching creatively. He also found that, although no single title dominates the field, a handful of publishers produce the vast majority of textbooks commonly assigned in college courses. The combination of instructor dependence on textbooks and corporate concentration in the publishing industry raised serious questions about the health of history education. Even if top-flight textbook authors retain their independent voices, the range of perspectives to which students are exposed in college classrooms appears likely to diminish.

Notes

1. Sara Evans and Roy Rosenzweig, "Introduction," *Journal of American History* 78 (1992): 1377.

2. Chester E. Finn Jr., "Foreword," in *A Consumer's Guide to High School History Textbooks*, by Diane Ravitch (Washington, D.C., 2004), 5.

Mary Beth Norton

Reflections of a Longtime Textbook Author; or, History Revised, Revised—and Revised Again

About three decades ago, I agreed to join a textbook team being organized for Houghton Mifflin by my friend and former University of Connecticut colleague Tom Paterson. When I signed the contract for what became A *People and a Nation* (APAN), it never crossed my mind that I would still be writing and rewriting the same book well into the twenty-first century, nor that our book would reshape the entire field of American history survey textbooks.

We—Tom, myself, Howard Chudacoff, Bill Tuttle, and, at the initial planning stage, John Blassingame—knew we wanted to write a textbook different from any then on the market. Already friends before we became a writing team, we had all attended graduate school in the 1960s. There we had been influenced by the growing emphasis on social history and by a critical stance toward American development generally and American foreign policy in particular. As young associate professors, we were all regularly teaching the survey course, and we liked none of the available texts, which uniformly stressed political, economic, and traditional diplomatic history. Therefore, from the outset we planned a different type of textbook.

In the mid-1970s the few social history texts on the market were all quirky in one way or another. Adopting any one of them would require an instructor largely to remake a survey course. We wanted to write a book that would be traditional in organization but untraditional in content—one that employed a standard chronological structure and included politics yet focused on the experiences of ordinary people and paid significant attention to race and gender. We planned a narrative that covered such subjects continuously, not episodically. Each of us brought a different scholarly emphasis to the project, and we thought it important to integrate our own pioneering research and analytical perspectives into the book. For instance, my growing interest in women's history led me to the belief, welcomed by my coauthors, that we needed to incorporate extensive discussions of women and the family throughout the book.

We made a number of decisions at the very beginning that have continued to affect the text ever since. We concurred that APAN belonged to all of us and that we would not be proprietary about our individual chapters. Every edition would

Journal of American History 91 (2005): 1383–90.

be planned collectively. To the extent possible, we would read and comment on others' drafts, and we would not pull our punches if we saw a reason to criticize. We would share our areas of topical expertise by directing the others to relevant scholarship. We all detested the boxed sidebars that repeatedly interrupted the narratives of so many other texts, in part because those sidebars were often the sole vehicles for the incorporation of nontraditional material. We vowed to create as seamless a narrative as possible and to avoid such distracting features.

We planned to begin each chapter with an opening vignette focusing on a person or a group of people, using their story to introduce subsequent themes. We insisted that illustrations be contemporary and appropriate to the time period, a decision especially important for me because textbooks at the time often used misleading nineteenth-century pictorial reconstructions to illustrate colonial or revolutionary scenes. We would help select the illustrations, and we would write the captions ourselves rather than having them drafted by in-house editors; thus the pictures and captions too would become part of our comprehensive narrative.

We all had other projects underway when we signed the contract, so we did not begin to write the textbook immediately. John Blassingame, in fact, decided that one of his other projects took priority, and he chose to leave the team. Because our deadline was looming ever closer at the time he did so, we could not find one author to replace him; so we recruited two, David Katzman and Paul Escott, each of whom agreed to write four chapters. Howard Chudacoff and I each initially wrote seven, and Tom Paterson (the coordinating author) and Bill Tuttle each wrote six.

In textbook writing, developmental editors are crucial. Houghton Mifflin assigned one of the best in-house editors to that first edition. She helped us to pull the book together thematically, stylistically, and conceptually, for no amount of pre-edition planning could foresee all the problems we encountered while trying to write a book that varied so significantly from the norm at the time. In recent years, we have worked with freelance developmental editors hired by Houghton Mifflin, but the process and the role of the editor remain as critical as ever, for each edition brings revisions that must be incorporated unobtrusively into the existing text. The editors assist in ensuring that our writing styles and interpretations mesh throughout the various sections.

The first edition, published in 1982, was so successful it surprised everyone, including the authors, Houghton Mifflin, and other publishers.[1] We were relieved that we had correctly reassured a few nervous Houghton Mifflin editors who had worried about how far we were straying from the standard textbook content of the day: there *was* a huge demand for a text based on social history that nevertheless included all the usual political events, though not at such great length as in competing books. Other publishers soon recognized that their textbooks too needed to take such recent social history scholarship into account, and within the next decade many other new texts appeared on the market. We frankly never anticipated the alterations in U.S. survey textbook publishing that have followed *APAN*'s success. We thought only of writing *our* book, not expecting it to cause a sea change in U.S. survey textbooks generally. With each revision, we try to maintain our leadership position.

Even with the great success of the first edition, Houghton Mifflin editors emphasized to us that the second edition, scheduled to appear four years later, would be crucial to the long-term future of the book. Despite our careful planning and our own experience with survey courses, problems had cropped up when people taught with our book. The publisher commissioned a number of reviews from instructors who had assigned *APAN* to help us with this critical first revision. In preparing the second edition, we had to fix the problems they identified in addition to updating material. In my own section, it turned out that the major difficulty was caused by the organization of chapter 2, which began in the middle of the seventeenth century. Convinced of the significance of the large-scale introduction of slavery in the following decades, I had decided to highlight that fact by starting with the slave trade. But students in many universities found the rest of the chapter confusingly organized. So, somewhat reluctantly, for the second edition I adopted a different scheme that began with the founding of the Restoration colonies in the 1660s and 1670s. That section still begins the chapter in the current seventh edition, but this time around I significantly reorganized the rest of the chapter once more.

Now, too, the chapter in question is the third, not the second. My section expanded from seven to eight chapters in the fourth edition, in the wake of the Columbus quincentenary in 1992, for I convinced our editor that I simply could not incorporate into seven chapters the flood of exciting scholarship on early European exploration and discovery and on Native Americans prior to Europeans' arrival and in the initial contact decades. Nearly simultaneously, users of the third edition told us that the late nineteenth and early twentieth centuries received more attention in *APAN* than they usually devoted to the subject, so Howard Chudacoff condensed his seven chapters into six. In the sixth edition—for which we were joined by our first new author, David Blight, after Paul Escott left the team—we significantly reorganized the antebellum chapters but did not change their number. For the seventh edition, in which Beth Bailey and Fredrik Logevall replaced Bill Tuttle and Tom Paterson, respectively, we substantially rearranged the post-1960 chapters.[2] The last chapter in every edition is always completely redone the next time around, for obvious reasons. Since 1984, we have also produced a brief edition that appears two years after the long version; we have hired another historian to cut our prose, knowing we cannot do it ourselves. That historian updates the final chapter appropriately and receives coauthor credit on those volumes.[3]

Excerpts by Mary Beth Norton in *A People and a Nation*

4TH EDITION

There were two reasons for the rapid end to the crisis. First, the accusers grew too bold. When they began to accuse some of the colony's most distinguished and respected residents of being in league with the Devil, members of the ruling elite began to doubt their veracity. Second, the new royal charter was fully implemented in late 1692, ending the worst period of political uncertainty and eliminating a major source of psychological stress. King William's War continued and, although the Puritans were not entirely pleased with the charter, at least order had formally been restored.

6TH EDITION

In October, the crisis ended rapidly, for three main reasons. First, the colony's ministers, led by the Reverend Increase Mather, formally expressed serious reservations about the validity of the evidence used to convict many of the accused. Second, the full implementation of the new royal charter ended the worst period of political uncertainty, eliminating one of the sources of stress and regularizing legal procedures. Third, opponents of the trials gained the ear of the new governor, publicly disparaging the "hysterical girls" who had begun the crisis and casting doubt on their credibility.

7TH EDITION

In October, the worst phase of the crisis ended when the governor dissolved the special court established to try the suspects. He and several prominent clergymen began to regard the girls' descriptions of spectral tortures as "the Devil's testimony"—and everyone knew the Devil could not be trusted to tell the truth. Most critics of the trials did not think the girls were faking, nor did they conclude that witches did not exist or that confessions were false. Rather, they questioned whether the guilt of the accused could be *legally* established by the evidence presented in court. Accordingly, during the final trials (ending in May 1693) in regular courts, almost all the defendants were acquitted, and the governor quickly reprieved the few found guilty.

Changes in my account of how and why the Salem witchcraft crisis came to an end illustrate in a nutshell how my own scholarship has affected the contents of *A People and a Nation*. The fourth edition (written in 1992, published in 1994) adopted the standard interpretation. By the time I wrote the sixth edition language in 1999, I had begun researching the subject; I dropped a part I knew to be wrong and added two new explanations. The version published in 2005 differs from each of the other two, reflecting my conclusions in *In the Devil's Snare* (2002). Revisions drawn from other authors can be as dramatic but commonly only require one edition for full incorporation. *Mary Beth Norton et al.,* A People and a Nation: A History of the United States, *fourth edition, copyright 1994; sixth edition, copyright 2001; seventh edition, copyright 2005. Courtesy Houghton Mifflin Company.*

Each of APAN's seven editions has contained many small and large changes, ranging from condensations of sentences to the creation of new sections. For each edition Houghton Mifflin commissions a large number of reviews of the previous one. Some reviewers have used the book; others are potential adopters; still others are subject specialists in areas at the cutting edge of scholarship we wish to incorporate into a new edition. The reviewers are asked what they would change, add, and subtract. Unfortunately, reviewers commonly request additions and rarely tell us what we should cut. They can, however, see things that we do not; a reviewer of the sixth edition, for example, pointed out that current Atlantic world scholarship would suggest the second major reorganization of chapter 3, which I indeed undertook for the seventh edition.

The key to planning all the revisions is the two-day author team meeting that Houghton Mifflin convenes at its corporate headquarters in Boston two years before a new edition is to appear. After studying the reviews, each author prepares for presentation at the meeting a plan for revision of his or her chapters, identifying emerging themes and topics, possible reorganizations, and vignettes or features that need replacing. Collectively we go over all the plans with our editor, discussing their ramifications and seeing how they accord with one another. In particular, we deal with reorganizations that involve more than one author—for example, when material is moved from one chapter to another or when chapters are reordered. One such re-arrangement occurred after I assigned *APAN* in the first half of the survey course, which I teach every few years in rotation with my Americanist colleagues. I realized from teaching with the then-current edition that some material was presented in a confusing sequence that needed correcting.

The meetings are intense and exhausting, sometimes producing significant differences of opinion that must be resolved before we leave. The remaining original authors were so accustomed to the highly charged give-and-take of these sessions that we were surprised by the stunned reactions to them of our newer recruits. Through it all, however, team members—old and now new—have maintained a firm friendship that continues to characterize our interactions. Historians usually work alone, or at most with one other person whose expertise is similar; our joint enterprise has created an unusual partnership we all continue to appreciate and enjoy.

Following the planning meeting, we prepare initial drafts of our chapters, a task that usually requires months of concentrated effort. The next stage is less demanding, being devoted to refining edited prose, working on illustrations and other graphics, proofreading, and the like. Still, from start to finish each edition takes a full two years to produce.

For a textbook author confronting a requisite steady-state universe, in which each chapter must have essentially the same word count as its predecessor in the previous edition, every word can be precious. (Thus the condensation of sentences; one or two words saved from each of a hundred sentences gives an author a new paragraph.) Simply updating an interpretation is easy as long as one can use the same number of words. (When Harry Stout's biography revealed that George Whitefield was not, after all, a Methodist, I just had to replace *Methodist* with *Anglican*.) But if an author must suddenly find room for a major scholarly advance, something has to go. That happened to me in the sixth edition when I had to incorporate a detailed discussion of colonial slavery based on important works by Ira Berlin and Philip Morgan.[4] What went? A lengthy treatment of the Halfway Covenant and its gendered implications. Yet passages can also reappear, and the Halfway Covenant might eventually be reincarnated. A reviewer of the fifth edition called for an expansion of my treatment of the Enlightenment's impact in America; I concurred, and so I reinserted a revised version of a passage I had excised a couple of editions earlier.

I am often asked about how much of our revising is market-driven. The answer is: some. No reviewer, for example, told me that I should revamp chapter 3 to make room for the findings of Berlin and Morgan. I alone made that decision. On the other hand, we authors do respond when a reviewer writes, "I would use this book if it discussed x," and if we then conclude collectively that that reviewer has indeed identified an important gap in our narrative. We also pay attention when the Houghton Mifflin College Division marketing manager reports that sales representatives making calls on professors at a variety of universities are learning that people want more coverage of y, or that we could lose sales because competing volume Z is evidently handling a certain topic better than we are. Do I then rush to read and imitate that competitor? No, but I think about ways to improve my treatment of that subject in my chapters. In addition, the publisher learns about the market by occasionally surveying professors to ask how they teach the course, what texts they use, and what they like and dislike about those texts or others available to them. The marketing manager then shares the results with us. Houghton Mifflin always leaves it up to us to decide how to respond to any of these findings.

In short, the market for a basic college textbook consists of the instructors teaching the survey course, and we try to be responsive to what those instructors tell us they want. That does not mean that we abandon our own vision of APAN and what it should accomplish. We will not, for example, include boxed excerpts of primary sources in the text, despite some professors' requests for them, because of our general resistance to such features and because we do not think they advance students' learning, especially when so many primary documents are now readily available in their entirety on the Web. Yet we have added features over the years. For the sixth edition we developed the "Legacy" feature that ends each chapter and brings one story up to the present day. In our most recent revision, we decided to drop a feature introduced in the fourth edition, "How Do Historians Know," illustrations of sources with extended captions that discussed how scholars used them. In its stead we added to each chapter "Links to the World," a brief essay with a relevant global theme, because we wanted to broaden the subject matter of the book. These decisions grew out of a consensus among the authors and the publisher, driven in part by instructors' comments ("the market") and in part by our own understanding of recent scholarly trends.

One aspect of APAN, though, has been entirely market-driven, and that is the timing of publication. In the 1980s, new editions appeared in October; the assumption was that adopters would use the second volume for spring term classes and the first volume the following fall. Eventually, driven by the demands of adopters and college bookstores, we published APAN during the summer so that the new editions could be used throughout the academic year, but that meant professors had to assign the book without actually examining it. With the seventh edition, we have moved publication to late January, because potential adopters now want to see the new edition when they make decisions in March or April of the spring semester on book orders for the fall term. These timing changes have important implications for the authors, because they alter the due dates for final copy. Our deadlines have moved around the calendar, mirroring those changes during the year before the final publication date.

I have learned to think of *APAN* as a work in progress. What is not done in this edition might be done in the next. The accumulation of new scholarship over a period of years sometimes requires a major reworking of a chapter that can be predicted more than one edition in advance. As soon as one edition goes to press, I start to collect references for the next. By forcing me to revise my thinking every four years, *APAN* allows—even requires—me to change my mind in print, something that historians rarely do. I have to keep up with trends in scholarly literature covering the entire period before 1800, regardless of whether I am teaching a particular lecture course that semester. Although the process is occasionally tedious and always time-consuming, the imperative constantly to rethink the parameters of my field is what keeps textbook writing intellectually challenging for me. At the moment, the chief issue for me is how far to go in the "Atlantic world" direction; the seventh version of *APAN* contains more extended discussions of the Caribbean, Brazil, and Africa than have previous editions. Do I go even further in the eighth edition? The scholarship that appears in the next couple of years will answer that question.

Working on the textbook has unquestionably made me both a better teacher and a better writer—being constantly concerned about clarity has never hurt a lecturer or an author of any type of prose. And the monetary rewards have been considerable. But there are trade-offs. Any textbook, no matter how innovative, commonly brings little acclaim from one's fellow scholars or one's own department. Consequently, writing a textbook is not a task an untenured professor should undertake. In many ways the textbook's four-year revision cycle (two years on, two years off) determines the rest of my scholarly life, especially now that with the seventh edition I have acquired the additional duties of *APAN*'s coordinating author. My third monograph, *Founding Mothers & Fathers*, which took fifteen years from conceptualization to publication, would probably have been produced in a decade had I not had to set it aside three times during that period to revise the textbook.[5]

Yet simultaneously it is immensely gratifying to realize that hundreds of thousands of American college students (and high school students in honors or Advanced Placement courses) have read *my* version of early American history. Sometimes they write to tell me how much they learned from the book or to ask about an interpretation novel to them. I was thrilled when a young African American woman history Ph.D. came up to me at a professional meeting to tell me that our textbook, assigned in her sophomore U.S. history survey course, had inspired her to become a historian. Through *APAN* my ideas are having an impact far beyond my monographs and my classroom teaching. What more could any historian ask?

Notes

1. Mary Beth Norton, David Katzman, Paul Escott, Howard Chudacoff, Thomas G. Paterson, and William Tuttle, *A People and a Nation: A History of the United States*, 1st ed. (Boston, 1982).

2. Mary Beth Norton, David Katzman, David Blight, Howard Chudacoff, Fredrik Logevall, Beth Bailey, Thomas G. Paterson, and William Tuttle, *A People and a Nation: A History of the United States*, 7th ed. (Boston, 2005). Authors who leave the team continue to be listed on the title page for one further edition.

3. Mary Beth Norton, David Katzman, Paul Escott, Howard Chudacoff, Thomas G. Paterson, William Tuttle, and William J. Brophy, *A People and a Nation: A History of the United States, Brief Edition*, 1st ed. (Boston, 1984).

4. Harry S. Stout, *The Divine Dramatist: George Whitefield and the Rise of Modern Evangelicalism* (Grand Rapids, Mich., 1991). Ira Berlin, *Many Thousands Gone: The First Two Centuries of Slavery in North America* (Cambridge, Mass., 1998); Philip D. Morgan, *Slave Counterpoint: Black Culture in the Eighteenth-Century Chesapeake and Lowcountry* (Chapel Hill, N.C., 1998).

5. Mary Beth Norton, *Founding Mothers & Fathers: Gendered Power and the Forming of American Society* (New York, 1996).

An Interview with Alan Brinkley

The Challenges and Rewards of Textbook Writing

On Becoming a Textbook Author and Taking over
American History: A Survey

When I was a graduate student at Harvard University in the 1970s, my adviser was Frank Freidel, one of the three original authors of *American History: A Survey*, a very successful book in the 1960s and 1970s. Shortly after I received my Ph.D. in 1979, Frank approached me about the possibility of assuming responsibility for the book. To test out my suitability, he asked me first to revise his other textbook, *America in the Twentieth Century*, and it was a good experience. It was my own field, I was just starting out in the profession, and it was a great way to think through how I wanted to approach the twentieth century. I revised the book quite substantially. Everybody seemed to be reasonably pleased with it. Knopf published the book, and I went on to the big book.[1]

By then, T. Harry Williams had died; Frank was no longer participating actively; and Richard Current, who was maintaining the book, no longer wanted to do so. The question was whether the book would just expire or whether we would try to keep it going. The book had a distinguished history and an established market. First published in 1959, it had been called *A History of the United States* and was twice as long as it is now—a huge book in the mold of the 1940s and 1950s when the massive two-volume Morison and Commager was the standard.[2] At that time there were fewer universities; they were more elite and more traditional in their curriculum. It was realistic to expect students to read a huge two-volume textbook. But by the time *A History of the United States* was published, it was already almost obsolete. Two years later, the authors condensed it into what became *American History: A Survey*—with a title that was supposed to differentiate it from the longer book, which ceased to be published very soon after.

It may seem strange to think that a textbook that made its appearance in the late 1950s could survive through the extraordinary changes in scholarship we have seen since then. I think this book survived in part because it was written by people who were outside the northeastern, consensus school type of scholarship that dominated the 1950s. The three authors had all been graduate students together at the University of Wisconsin, and had, one way or another, all worked

Journal of American History 91 (2005): 1391–97.

with William Best Hesseltine, to whom they dedicated the book. They were part of the old Wisconsin school Progressive tradition. The book was built around conflict, around battles over power. It wasn't polemical—it wasn't like reading Charles Beard—but it was different from the other textbooks of its time. And this made the book more compatible with the world of the 1960s and 1970s.

I took the book over in the early 1980s. Although there were lots of things missing, the basic framework actually held up reasonably well in the areas it did cover. It was not a book that needed to be jettisoned; it needed to be augmented and revised. It was, as most books of the time were, overwhelmingly a political and diplomatic history with a little intellectual history, and just a smidgeon of social and cultural history. It had to become more balanced. A *People and a Nation* had just come out, aimed at people who wanted the new social history. There was great pent-up demand for such a book, and there was an immediate and very strong response. But my book had an established constituency that I didn't want to alienate; it was a book for people who wanted to do the old history. It did very well in the Midwest, in the South, in Texas, in areas in which this old Progressive history was still alive. I knew then that one of the characteristics of the book would always be that it would take political history very seriously. But it couldn't be just political history; it had to incorporate very significant amounts of African American history, labor history, social history, and all of the other new areas of scholarship that had recently become important.[3]

So I set a schedule for myself, pegged to the four-year revision cycle. I planned something for each new edition. On two occasions, I have made women's history the principal focus of a major revision. One revision attempted to incorporate some of the new western history; another revision focused on Hispanic/Latino history and environmental history. In every edition I pick something that I want to emphasize: cultural history, history of technology and science; sometimes more than one thing; and that's how the book evolves over time.

Revising the book also means going through the existing material to see what needs to be updated. The scholarship doesn't change so rapidly that everything needs to be revised every four years, but there are always some things that need reconsideration. In these revisions, the political history, which was the core of the original book, kept getting condensed and condensed and condensed—because that was the only thing there was to condense. Political history still has a larger role in my book than it does in many books, but it is no longer even the majority of the book, so only relative to other books is it a political history book.

For each edition, four more years of history at the end must be incorporated, and I revise the last two or three chapters each time. There are now twenty-five years of very substantial history at the end of this book that did not exist when I took it over, and the book is not much longer than when I started. You naturally write at much greater length about recent events than you would write about something, say, forty years ago, because you write in part from memory. So for each edition I shrink and update these last chapters to make them more compatible with the rest of the book and more responsive to what scholarship there is on the very recent past.

In some ways, these may seem to be the least important chapters of the book, because most survey courses never get to them. But both teachers and students always look at these final chapters. They want to know what you have said about things they remember. This was particularly difficult for the most recent edition, 2003. I was finishing revisions on that edition in September 2001 in New York. I spent the first weekends after September 11 working at ground zero, serving food to rescue workers. This was traumatic for everyone in the United States, but particularly for those of us living in New York, and then to have to come home and write about it was really hard. I don't know how many students ever get to September 11 in class, but I've received more correspondence in response to what I said about it than I've ever gotten about anything else.

So this book is never stable; it is never fixed. If a textbook doesn't change, then it will die, or should die. If you look at the book I inherited and the book as it is now, I doubt you would find very much at all that is really the same.

NARRATIVE, VOICE, AND AUDIENCE: THE DISTINCTIVE CHALLENGES OF TEXTBOOK WRITING

Narrative is a major issue in the historical profession. There seem to be three views:

First, there's the view that we should give up on narrative because any kind of narrative privileges one kind of history over another. Some historians have argued that we should give up the narrative line, at least for now, because new areas of historical scholarship are fragile, and the inevitable political narrative would crush those areas we are working to legitimize and expand.

The second view argues for an integrative narrative that brings all the various historical fields together. Liz Cohen's book, *Making a New Deal*, succeeded in bringing together labor history, cultural history, and to some degree political history, exemplifying an integrated history, albeit for a very contained period and framework.[4] But no one has come up with a master narrative of American history that effectively integrates all of the areas of history across the vast expanse of time.

Many of my colleagues in political history take a third view: that political history is the only basis for narrative, and we should fit other things in as we can. I don't agree with that either. Yet, to the degree that my book has a coherent narrative line, it is more the political narrative than anything else. As I see it, this is a necessary device, but it is always an artificial and limiting device. Textbooks have to be readable. You have to have some kind of narrative line, providing a sense of connection between various things. But it's a very frail line.

It is common to criticize today's textbooks for the absence of a strong narrative and to claim that this is why they are not as easy to read as older books, which did have a clear, coherent narrative structure. And this criticism is often used by those who also believe that textbooks now lack a literary merit that many used to have. In my occasional reading of older textbooks, I find that some were indeed beautifully written, but on the whole I don't see any significant decline in the literary quality of the books over the past forty years. I think the narrative structure of recent books has perhaps become less cohesive. But that's the necessary price we pay for the different and much larger view of history that we have embraced over the last generation.

I balk at the notion that my "voice" is the core of the book. But you can't be completely neutral. I think I am more sensitive to alternative views of events in my textbook than I would be in my own scholarship. I am also inclined to reflect the scholarship I most admire. For example, the book was already pretty good on Reconstruction when I inherited it. Richard Current was an early revisionist scholar in this area. But the text was still heavy with Thaddeus Stevens, Charles Sumner, congressional Reconstruction, and presidential Reconstruction, with little sense of African American agency. My own view of Reconstruction was very much influenced by Eric Foner, whose book came out not long after I began my work with *American History*.[5] And that has helped shape the view of Reconstruction I present. Similarly, on a wide range of twentieth-century topics, I do clearly have a point of view—the New Deal, dissent, the Cold War, liberalism, civil rights, the Vietnam War. I try not to present them polemically, but I wouldn't say I'm neutral.

At the same time, though, I try at least to suggest options and to create a certain degree of openness in how readers might evaluate things. I avoid language that seems too directive or opinionated. I at least gesture towards the existence of alternative views, sometimes in the text and especially in the feature "Where Historians Disagree." I inherited this feature, but in my time on the book, I've substantially rewritten the existing ones and added many new ones, in part in recognition that any book—and certainly this book—has a point of view but that there are other points of view. I want to help students understand that what they are reading in my book is one view of the past—but a view, like all views, that can be contested.

You have to be aware of who your audience is. These are not books that are going to be sold in Barnes and Noble, and they are not books that many scholars are going to buy and read. These are books that are going to be force-fed to tens of thousands—or even hundreds of thousands—of undergraduates who didn't choose the book themselves. Their faculty chose it for them—and the teachers are in marketing terms the most important audience. But presumably there is a relationship between how teachers choose the book and how students respond. Teachers won't continue to use a book that students don't like. As I write, I try to think about the students who will ultimately read the book, and I try, imperfectly to be sure, to be aware of what they need to the degree that I can imagine it. I don't feel that I am a free agent. You have to keep your readers in mind.

The market for these books is eighteen- to twenty-two-year-olds, and perhaps sixteen- to twenty-two-year-olds, and their teachers, in a huge swath of the United States and in some other parts of the world as well. The adoptions range from Ivy League universities to community colleges to high schools. So the book can't be so simplistic as to alienate the top or so sophisticated as to alienate the bottom.

I don't want to exaggerate the degree to which I give deep thought to the philosophy of the textbook. When I write, I'm not usually thinking consciously about how this will work in a high school classroom in Texas, or in a community college in California, or at Oberlin College or Columbia University. But part of me is always aware of the ultimate audience. Nobody chooses to read a textbook. They read a text because they are told to; and I do think there is something about the purposes the textbook serves that works against an entirely good reading experience. As best I can, I try to fight that, try to make it as engaging a reading experience as I can given the many competing purposes that the textbook has to serve. I try to make it a book that presents diverse peoples within every area of history to help diverse readers see and understand their own experiences and their own assumptions. But I also try to make it something that people will feel comfortable reading. I get e-mail comments from students who say they really like reading the book. Many students who never write to me may hate reading the book. But I hope on balance the people who like it outnumber those who don't.

QUESTIONS OF CONTROL: BEING A SINGLE AUTHOR AND RELATIONS WITH EDITORS AND PUBLISHERS

There are a lot of disadvantages to being a single author; I don't have equal expertise in all the areas I am required to write about, and there's a credibility problem with a twentieth-century historian writing about, for example, pre-Columbian history or a political historian writing about women's history. That's why in new textbooks the group of authors is determined not just by the periods they cover but by other specializations; these teams are designed to represent a whole range of scholarly points of view and expertise. I've never worked with other authors, so I can only guess what it's like; in some ways I'm sure it's easier—I can imagine how relieved I'd be if there were some other people doing parts of the books that are more difficult for me to do.[6] But how do you bring together the work of four or five active authors? When I hear about the very significant roles that the editorial staffs of some publishing houses play in these books, I assume that they are necessary roles, because someone has to make the work of several different authors compatible.

   I myself have never experienced any editorial interference from my publishers. I have never had the experience of editors saying to me "You should do this," or "You shouldn't do that," or "You can't say this," or "We don't like this passage and you should rewrite it." My editors do surveys of readers, and out of those surveys come suggestions, but it has always been up to me to decide which suggestions to take. I suspect that being a single author reduces the role of editors. I have really been left alone to do what I want, and I'm very fortunate never to have had any interference either from Random House–Knopf, the original publishers of the books, or from McGraw-Hill, their successors.

   Before each revision, I work with publishers to commission reviewers whose views I would especially like to solicit. I seek out reviews from people who don't use the book but have an expertise in some field I'm interested in—for example, early American history. In addition I use reviews from faculty who assign the book. In the introduction to my books, I invite students to respond, and I give them my e-mail address. They don't usually offer a general critique of the book, but they do point out errors or ask such questions as "I have to write a paper on — — —; what should I do?" I receive a lot of e-mail from high school students, more than from college students, even though more than three-quarters of the adoptions for this book are from colleges and universities.

PACKAGING AND REPACKAGING: THE SHORT VERSION, ANCILLARIES, AND FEATURES

The Unfinished Nation was proposed by an editor at Knopf in the late 1980s, seven or eight years after I had taken over the big book. I was very resistant to the idea of a shortened version of the big book, in part because I didn't see the market for it. The only book on the market then that was significantly different in size and format was the Tindall book; it was lower in cost and smaller in size, and it lacked colored pictures and the multitude of features then common in larger books.[7] I then had two textbooks in print, *American History* and the twentieth-century book, and I really didn't want to spend more time on textbooks. But I had gotten married, moved to New York City, and was having a child. Having extra income sounded appealing, and it didn't sound like that much more work, and so I finally agreed.

The goal was to reduce the size of the book by 40 to 50 percent, to use a new format, and to reach a new audience. I took the text of the big book and tried to rewrite it pretty thoroughly. I tried to give it a more coherent narrative, although without any illusions about how far I could go in that direction. I also worked on the writing. I thought that the process of condensation would be a way for me to bring my writing style more centrally into the book. I actually found it a rewarding process. I did feel that, for the first time, I was really making the book mine. I was reasonably pleased with how it came out. So doing *The Unfinished Nation* was part of the process for me of feeling that I was taking ownership of these textbooks. And when I went back to *American History*, I felt more confident that I had a grasp of the whole of the book and where it should go. Now, in the cycle of revisions, I generally revise the big book and, two years later, incorporate a version of those revisions into *The Unfinished Nation*.

I have no relationship to the ancillaries marketed with the textbooks. I play no role in their creation; many of them I have never seen. That part is entirely in the hands of the publishers. The exception is the Web site, in which I don't play a large role, but for which I make suggestions. Over time some parts of the text have moved out of the book and onto the Web site; for example, the extensive bibliographies that used to be part of the book.

There are also features inside the book. At first, I fought against them, but gradually I found I actually liked them. One of the first I introduced was a feature called "Patterns of Popular Culture." I really enjoyed doing this. It was an area with which I didn't have any scholarly connection, but there was a lot of interesting material. I had some wonderful graduate assistants at Columbia University who helped me gather material and think about how to present it.

In the last edition (2003), I added a feature called "America in the World," which took events in American history and tried to place them in the context of the events of the world. For example, the American Civil War roughly coincided with wars of national consolidation such as the Italian and Latin American revolutions and German unification. I think these are useful additions given the character of our time.

CLOSING REFLECTIONS

I do sometimes feel that I'd be able to do more serious scholarship if I didn't do these books, and I worry about being drawn away from my scholarship. My own scholarship does play a role in the textbooks, but only in a very small part of them. On the other hand, I feel that writing these books makes me a much broader historian than I would otherwise be. I feel that I have an awareness of a much larger range of scholarly activity than I would otherwise be involved in, that I have a larger context for my own scholarship. I can't keep up with all the monographic literature, but I do read reviews of new books. And when important new syntheses come out, I read them. I ask my graduate students for their views. So writing textbooks certainly does interfere with my own scholarship, but it also benefits it. In addition, I don't think that there's anything that I do that reaches more people, that has more of an impact on the way history is understood, that has a greater influence on the lives of students. If part of being a scholar is to reach people and affect their understanding of the field, one could argue that this is the most important thing I do. Although I didn't realize it at the time, agreeing to move into textbook writing was a profound decision that shaped my life in very significant ways. But I don't regret having made that decision.

Notes

1. Richard N. Current, T. Harry Williams, and Frank Freidel, *American History: A Survey*, 1st ed. (New York, 1961). Frank Burt Freidel, *America in the Twentieth Century*, 1st ed. (New York, 1960); Frank Burt Freidel and Alan Brinkley, *America in the Twentieth Century*, 5th ed. (New York, 1982).

2. T. Harry Williams, Richard Nelson Current, and Frank Burt Freidel, *A History of the United States*, 1st ed. (New York, 1959). Samuel Eliot Morison and Henry Steele Commager, *The Growth of the American Republic*, 1st ed. (New York, 1930); the fifth edition appeared in 1962.

3. Mary Beth Norton et al., *A People and a Nation: A History of the United States*, 1st ed. (Boston, 1982). Richard N. Current, T. Harry Williams, Frank Freidel, and Alan Brinkley, *American History: A Survey*, 6th ed. (New York, 1983).

4. Lizabeth Cohen, *Making a New Deal: Industrial Workers in Chicago, 1919–1939* (Cambridge, Eng., 1990).

5. Eric Foner, *Reconstruction: America's Unfinished Revolution, 1863–1877* (New York, 1988).

6. *Editors' note*: Brinkley is listed as a coauthor of two textbooks for students at the secondary level, but by his account his role in their development has been largely advisory.

7. Alan Brinkley, *The Unfinished Nation: A Concise History of the American People*, 1st ed. (New York, 1993). George Brown Tindall, *America: A Narrative History*, 1st ed. (New York, 1984).

Steve Forman

Textbook Publishing: An Ecological View

Imagine an ecosystem in which the major organisms are faculty, students, text-book publishers, and bookstores. As producers, consumers, and decomposers, they circulate the nutrients of higher education up and down the food chain. The system has sustained a long-term equilibrium, with change coming in grad-ual, evolutionary form. But in recent years, some of the system's core conditions have changed, disturbing that equilibrium. Some observers see a crisis at hand, a version of global warming in which textbook prices are rising to dangerous levels.

As a longtime inhabitant, I can confirm that the system is troubled. To judge from the current controversy, though, one problem is a lack of understanding of a producer organism in the system—the publisher. To restore the system's in-tegrity, a measure of mutual understanding is necessary. Toward that end I would like to explore the physiology of that ungainly organism, the textbook publisher.

I must admit that my own perspective may not be representative. The orga-nization that has been my publishing home for more than twenty-five years is an exceedingly odd, even unique, creature. In a publishing landscape dominated by corporate conglomerates, W. W. Norton and Company is one of the few inde-pendent publishers left, and the only one that is both independent and employee owned. What difference does that make? It means we enjoy an unusual stability, with continuity in decision making that aligns the books we publish into a profile of the house. It also means we subsist only on the money generated by the books we publish and distribute. The decision making at Norton is primarily editorial, but in order to survive and grow we must pay close attention to the ledger of costs and revenues.

Norton is a two-armed creature that relies on flexibility, quickness, and expe-rience to compete with the megacorporations of publishing. Trade and college are our two main divisions, and there are strong connections between them. Authors often migrate within the firm, first publishing a trade book and then a textbook, or the other way around. Often a single title can succeed in both markets, such as Jared M. Diamond's *Guns, Germs, and Steel*, or Jonathan D. Spence's *The Search for Modern China*, a textbook first published in the trade division and also a *New York Times* best seller.[1] The differences between trade and college from an editorial point of view are instructive. Despite the allure of

Journal of American History 91 (2005): 1398–1404.

trade publishing, I have found in college books a more challenging set of problems and a richer array of opportunities for editorial enterprise. The college market also operates in a reassuringly rational way. Much like the long baseball season that allows the good teams to prove themselves over a 162-game schedule, the large, fairly discriminating college market enables textbooks that are well crafted to succeed over time. The trade market does not display such rationality: it is a short three-out-of-five series in which anything can happen—and usually does. Good books are too often sent home early. But even then the discerning college market can come to the rescue: some failed trade books enjoy long and successful lives as paperbacks assigned in colleges.

This rationality encourages college publishers to shoulder the staggering investments in time and money required to launch an introductory textbook—years of work, millions of dollars spent before a single copy is sold. The trick is developing and publishing a book that hits its target or creates a new target worth hitting. How do we do this?

Publishers for elementary through high school (K–12) classrooms target huge state adoptions that are governed by clear and specific guidelines for coverage. Their approach is to produce heavily managed texts in which committees of authors write to specifications with little individuality. In Texas in 2003 an adoption of social studies texts for all grades represented a $233.7 million purchase. The books in consideration had to navigate an elaborate selection process that included a public hearing with speakers from seventy different special interest groups.[2]

College publishers enjoy more flexibility because of the structure of the college market. Most adoptions in the U.S. survey course, for instance, are made by individual instructors employing their own criteria in the choice of a text. In some departments a committee decides on the use of a single text in the survey, and those are the big prizes publishers lust after, but they are too few to skew publishing strategies in a meaningful way. This Jeffersonian cast to the college market also means that we do not face the ideological pressures that K–12 publishers do. College textbooks can show more individuality and still succeed commercially.

So why do we so often hear the charge that all textbooks are the same? In part it reflects a certain homogenizing effect in the way textbooks are developed and marketed, an effect that becomes more pronounced in a book's later editions. The market we enter may be large and diverse, but it does impose some limits on what we can do. The U.S. history survey course has undergone significant change in the last twenty-five years, with the field of social history maturing in a generation, but the Declaration of Independence still has to turn up on time, and Warren G. Harding has to put in a (brief) appearance. The basic chronology of American history is a given in a U.S. survey text, with the result that the tables of contents of most books look the same. Moreover, in the development of a text, the publisher and the author always draw on reviews of content by period and subject specialists—twenty to thirty in all—a process that makes for a more accurate and representative book but may also efface some identifying features. When this process is repeated over many editions, the homogenizing effect grows stronger.

In part, though, the charge that all textbooks are the same suggests that the viewer is not looking closely enough. Recall Ronald Reagan's observation in opposing the expansion of Redwood National Park in 1966: "A tree is a tree. How many more do you need to look at?"[3] As a city boy I am tempted to concede Reagan's point—so let us look at another analogy. A jazz standard such as "Skylark" has been performed by many different artists. Although the basic song structure remains the same, the Sonny Rollins version is different from Miles Davis's, each personal and unique. Part of the appeal of publishing new texts in American history is the challenge of taking the standard core of the course and molding it into something new. It takes an author with command of the field—one who combines a solid grounding with a distinctive vision—to do this.

Of course, there is no guarantee that an author's vision will align with the demands of the market. The fun for editors is in working toward a reasonable overlap between those things. That may call for modifications in the author's approach, but the market can be malleable too, sometimes in ways that are hard to predict. Build it and they will come: the right text, with effective marketing and sales support, can crystallize and mobilize what had previously been a nebulous market demand. The wrong text, however, can be a very costly failure. So some publishers opt to place their bets squarely on the market and have found commercial success with what are essentially paint-by-the-numbers textbooks. It is an approach that characterizes any number of consumer-goods industries. But it is a bit like betting heavily on the favorite to show: the upside is limited, and with a stumble the downside is still significant. And there is not much joy in it.

Publishers are moved to hedge their bets because the risks in launching a new introductory text are so high. Before the first copy is printed, the publisher has spent more than a million dollars on author advances, grants, and plant costs (cartography; photo research, permissions, and processing; other artwork if needed; copyediting; book and cover design; typesetting; proofreading and indexing; paper, acetate, and electronic ancillary costs). Manufacturing costs (paper, printing, and binding) add another couple of hundred thousand dollars to the entry fee. Advertising costs can equal that, with the main item being the free copies of the text that we send as samples to instructors. For a new survey text published in one-volume cloth and two-volume paperback formats, we give away upwards of six thousand to eight thousand copies. We also give away instructor's manuals, computerized test banks, transparencies, Web site entries, and CD-ROMs—all significant components of the total cost of publishing a survey text.

Those are the direct costs of books sold, forming the big hump a book must overcome during its edition life if it is not to be DOA, a total loss, a nightmare in write-offs. To be a success it has to soar over that hump by a comfortable margin because it must also contribute to the indirect costs of running an effective publishing operation. Those include warehousing and distribution, selling and travel expenses, editorial expenses, salaries, and other administrative costs, including ever-escalating health insurance premiums. After a due contribution to indirect costs and taxes, a successful text will yield a net income that we can invest in new projects.

How does the price of a book relate to those costs? Consider a new survey text priced at $89.05 on the shelf at the campus store. That retail price, which the student pays, represents an average 30 percent markup by the bookstore from the net price set by the publisher—in this case, $68.50. The bookstore gets $20.55, or 23.1 percent of the retail price, which the stores hold to be their margin. (There is very little risk for the store in this commerce: bookstores can return every unsold new college book to the publisher for a full refund.) The direct costs of publishing this survey text come out of the net price as follows: A royalty set at 15 percent of the publisher's net price would yield the author $10.28, about 11.5 percent of the retail price the student paid. Plant and manufacturing costs (including ancillary costs) account for $15.95, or 17.9 percent of the book's retail price. Advertising, including free copies, accounts for $6.53, or 7.3 percent. Indirect costs, such as those I mentioned above, account for $30.48, or 34.2 percent, and taxes another $1.84, or 2.1 percent. Of the $89.05 retail price this leaves $3.42, or 3.8 percent, as net income for the publisher.[4]

A used copy of the same book on the shelf will cost students $66.79, a 25 percent discount on the new-book retail price. The bookstore will have paid anywhere from 10 percent to 50 percent of the new-book price to obtain the used copy. At the highest buy-back price, the bookstore pays the student $44.53 and earns 33.3 percent on the resale of the book (compared to 23.1 percent on a new-book sale). The author and publisher, having created the commodity itself and the content that is the basis of its value, realize $0.00 in this transaction. There are no payments from bookstore to publisher or author on the sale of used books.[5]

The vision of on-campus student buyback fills me with nostalgia. These days a massive and efficient national market fills new adoptions on one campus with used books from another. Google "textbook buyback" and you will get more than one hundred thousand entries, ranging from Web sites for Amazon and Barnes and Noble to sites for BooksIntoCash.Com and the Bowdoin College bookstore. The University of California, Irvine, bookstore page offers as book-buyback categories "The Good Ones," "The Not Bad Ones," and "The Dreaded Additions to Your Personal Library." BooksIntoCash.Com helpfully describes history as "a broad subject including historical ideas, . . . historical events, . . . civilian thoughts and theories, . . . and the history of a great deal of things. History can truly be an exciting subject." Not exciting enough, however, to warrant holding on to your books: the site buys new copies of textbooks at 30 percent of the average retail price. Like many other buyers of used textbooks, BooksIntoCash.Com offers to buy instructor's copies as well, including those clearly marked "instructor's edition" or "free copy."[6] A dismayingly large number of those copies we give away to instructors are in turn sold into the used-book market.

The effect of all this is to choke down new-book sales in the second semester of a book's life. With the average college book resold three to four times, the used-book market stifles new-book sales by the second and third year of an edition. Although it has gathered force in recent years, this decomposing process has been part of the ecosystem for a long time, and the inhabitants make their adjustments. For oxygen-needy publishers, revised editions clear the market for a brief time at prices that reflect costs and market conditions. We at Norton offer instructors discounted packages consisting of textbooks and monographs on our list, or ancillary materials such as readers or study guides. Those measures have helped maintain an equilibrium of sorts. But other types of change in the system have shifted the publisher's niche in relation to the instructor's, increasing the costs publishers must shoulder and feeding the current controversy over textbook prices. Notable change has come in three broad areas: technology, teaching conditions and practice, and student culture.

The arrival of digital technology has enriched the teaching and study of history. The Web makes it possible to convey the sights and sounds of the past and to offer a vast array of traditional documentary sources with speed and convenience. Students can go to the Web site for a textbook, listen to the thrilling cadences of Martin Luther King Jr.'s "I have a dream" speech, and find a rich sampling of writings, speeches, music, and images of the freedom movement. Those riches come at the cost of steep permission fees and additional authoring fees for the necessary pedagogical elements.

The first edition of Eric Foner's *Give Me Liberty! An American History* features a dedicated student Web site replete with hundreds of primary-source documents, images, audio selections, and video material gathered specifically to supplement the text, including an extensive taped interview with the author on the book's major theme.[7] Much of that material is also provided to adopters free on a CD-ROM for use in illustrating lectures, preparing handouts, and generating other course materials. (We pay another round of permissions for that use.) Another CD-ROM gives instructors the materials they need for course management with the text in use. In short, the publisher now offers not only the basic text for a course but an extensive array of multimedia materials to enhance the text and enrich the course.

The demand for those materials arises in part from a second basic change in the ecology of higher education: the massive shift in the academic work force away from a full-time or tenure-track faculty. According to a 2001 U.S. Department of Education report, 70 percent of the 1.3 million members of the instructional work force in higher education were either part-time adjunct faculty, full-time contract faculty, or graduate student employees. Adjuncts alone accounted for 35 percent of the total.[8] This development has many important implications for everyone involved in higher education. Time-strapped instructors and budget-conscious departments increasingly rely on the course-support materials publishers can provide. Textbook prices reflect the attendant costs.

The third, and perhaps the most disturbing, recent campus phenomenon is that students are increasingly willing to opt out of the purchase of books entirely, whether new or used. More students are arriving on campus unconvinced of the utility or inherent value of books, a stance the cynical rhetoric of the used-book industry reinforces. This may be related to a broader cultural trend revealed in *Reading at Risk*, the summer 2004 report of the National Endowment for the Arts. The report documents a steady decline in literary reading by Americans over the last two decades, a trend especially strong among eighteen- to twenty-four-year-olds.[9] We all should do what we can to stem this tide. Publishers have launched efforts to show students how best to use their books and ancillary materials. Faculty can help by making active use of the textbooks they assign. The often unspoken condition for student resentment of textbook prices is the under-use of those books in the classroom.

The murky complexity of our ecosystem belies the reductive picture conveyed in the public controversy over textbook prices. The title of the recent California Student Public Interest Research Group report, *Ripoff 101*, purports to say it all; it does not. That and many of the news reports on the issue ignore or misconstrue the conditions and the ways in which publishers operate. Instead of coming to grips with the operational details, they blame publishers for discretionary and unreasonable increases in textbook prices.[10] The charge of publisher profiteering is not only wide of the mark; it is an obstacle in the path to a solution. If we remove that unwarranted assumption from the current debate, then we can see the degree of convergence in the interests of publishers, professors, and students.

And that is a starting point for a constructive set of responses to the current situation. A number of publishers are beginning to offer lower-cost and lower-price versions of their textbooks. Norton has been taking this approach for twenty years with George Brown Tindall and David E. Shi's *America: A Narrative History*, and it has been a considerable success.[11] Almost all survey texts are available in lower-priced brief editions, and a growing number are coming out in "value" editions. Those are one- or two-color books with fewer illustrations and maps, no pedagogy, and no supplements. We and other publishers are also experimenting with low-price online versions of our introductory textbooks. We will see in coming years whether the market shifts decisively in this no-frills direction. There may develop a sequencing of formats akin to the hardcover-to-paperback sequencing of trade books, in which an initial publication of a text in full uniform is followed by a stripped-down, low-price version.

Some colleges are bringing back textbook rental systems that formalize the workings of the current system: students essentially rent books now, effectively paying not the retail price but the difference between it and the buyback price. Rental systems lower textbook costs to students by creating a chain of payments for access to a book. If we can assume that the initial purchase by the campus store is for new books, rental systems might also benefit publishers. They do, however, limit the flexibility of faculty in choosing books.

According to one informed estimate, the used-book industry will soon pull in $1 of every $2 spent on college textbooks.[12] With a massive secondary market occluding the atmosphere and a host of rising costs sending temperatures up, the ecosystem of college publishing is no doubt under stress. There are practical adjustments to be made, as we have seen. Publishers will respond to actual book-ordering and book-buying decisions by faculty and students, and we might even arrive at a new equilibrium. But with the system configured as it currently is, will it be sustainable?

Notes

1. Jared M. Diamond, *Guns, Germs, and Steel: The Fates of Human Societies* (New York, 1997); Jonathan D. Spence, *The Search for Modern China* (New York, 1990).

2. "Pearson Education Storms the Alamo. . . ." *Educational Marketer*, Aug. 4, 2003.

3. Politics, *President Reagan* <http://wais.stanford.edu/Politics/politics_president reagan.htm> (Nov. 15, 2004).

4. The cost structure and figures above reflect industry-average amounts for an introductory survey text.

5. These figures also reflect an average according to the standard textbook buyback Web sites. The rationale for the absence of royalty payments on the resale of goods, as opposed to that of rights, warrants further scrutiny. Why, for instance, can a single copy of *The Great Gatsby* be resold umpteen times without payment to the rights holder on any of those sales, whereas each use of a passage from the novel requires permission and a payment to the rights holder? The argument from practicality—that it would unreasonably clog commerce to require book purchasers to negotiate a price with rights holders as well as booksellers—is easy to remedy. And the economic argument that the publisher and author capture the full value of the good on its first sale is clearly inaccurate.

6. Amazon, *Sell Your Stuff* <www.amazon.com/exec/obidos/subst/misc/sell-your-stuff .html> (Oct. 26, 2004); *Barnes and Noble* <http://barnesandnoble.com> (Oct. 26, 2004); BooksIntoCash.Com, *Sell Textbooks* <www.booksintocash.com> (Oct. 26, 2004); Bowdoin Bookstore, *Textbook Buyback* <www.bowdoin.edu/bookstore/annex/buyback.shtml> (Oct. 26, 2004); The UCI Bookstore, *Buyback* <www.book.uci.edu/coursebooks/faqs/ buyback> (Oct. 26, 2004).

7. Eric Foner, *Give Me Liberty! An American History* (2 vols., New York, 2004–2005).

8. American Federation of Teachers, *Academic Staffing Crisis* <www.aft.org/topics/ academic-staffing> (Nov. 15, 2004).

9. National Endowment for the Arts, *Reading at Risk: A Survey of Literary Reading in America* (Washington, D.C., 2004) <www.nea.gov/pub/ReadingAtRisk.pdf> (Oct. 26, 2004).

10. Merriah Fairchild, *Ripoff 101: How the Current Practices of the Textbook Industry Drive Up the Cost of College Textbooks* (Jan. 2004) <http://calpirg.org/reports/textbook ripoff.pdf> (Oct. 25, 2004).

11. George Brown Tindall and David E. Shi, *America: A Narrative History* (New York, 2004).

12. Kevin Nance and Mike Thomas, "The End of Books?" *Chicago Sun-Times*, July 22, 2004 <www.suntimes.com/output/lifestyles/cst-nws-insight22_book.html> (Oct. 26, 2004).

Daniel J. Cohen

By the Book: Assessing the Place of Textbooks in U.S. Survey Courses

In a roundtable published in the *Journal of American History* [in 2001], professors from ten different colleges and universities spoke of the thoughtful, creative ways they approached the design of their American history survey courses. Most suggested that the textbook was of secondary importance, mainly used to supply background information to students, and they highlighted the pedagogical role of additional readings. Yet a study of nearly eight hundred syllabi posted on the World Wide Web reveals that the roundtable discussion may not be representative of how the survey is taught at most colleges and universities in the United States. Many U.S. history instructors appear to take a more pedestrian, by-the-book approach. They depend heavily on a textbook, on a textbook-based course's favorite type of graded work—the examination—and on the conventional ways of teaching American history that a textbook enshrines. Those findings lend a dark tone to the proclamation that Sara Evans and Roy Rosenzweig made in introducing the "Textbooks and Teaching" section of this journal in 1992: "Textbooks are the single most important written source through which college students learn about the past."[1]

The proliferation of syllabi on the Web presents for the first time the possibility of gaining a comprehensive picture of how history survey courses are taught and how textbooks are used in them. Since all documents on the Web, including posted syllabi, use text that is machine readable—and thus swiftly locatable and searchable—we can now assemble and analyze a substantial collection of course materials through electronic means. To exploit that possibility, in 2002 I wrote some experimental software, now called the Syllabus Finder, to locate, scan, and store syllabi from the Web. Thus far the software has found and tagged over three hundred thousand syllabi—probably the largest set of syllabi ever cataloged. Freely available on the Center for History and New Media Web site, the Syllabus Finder allows one to look up courses on specific topics, narrow or broad, to examine how history is taught at thousands of educational institutions, and to see which courses assign a certain primary or secondary source.[2]

To examine the role of textbooks in teaching the U.S. history survey, in early July 2004 I fed into the Syllabus Finder a list of forty-one titles that account for

Journal of American History 91 (2005): 1405–15.

virtually all college-level American history textbook sales. The program located 792 different survey courses, taught at 462 different educational institutions, that used those textbooks. (A secondary, broader search estimated that only 5 percent to 10 percent of American history survey courses do not assign a textbook.) Multiple sections of the same course at a single university were cataloged as distinct courses when the section leaders designed their own syllabi using individually chosen textbooks. Multiple sections with identical syllabi and textbooks were pared down to a single record so as not to skew the data. Similarly, I cataloged only the most recent version of a syllabus when a course taught by the same professor appeared for multiple years. The syllabi range in time from a single 1995 course to 258 syllabi from the first half of 2004. (Although instructors have probably removed some older syllabi from the Web, the volume of course materials online has clearly exploded. My research shows that it has almost doubled each year since 1997.)

I transferred the 792 syllabi to a specially constructed database and indexed them for key words and other distinguishing properties. Since computerized methods can go only so far, each syllabus was manually double-checked and parsed to highlight additional elements, such as primary-source readers. Obviously, this study leaves out the numerous syllabi that are still paper only, as well as syllabi that reside behind the electronic gates erected by popular course-management software such as Blackboard and WebCT. If the age distribution of the instructors who have posted the syllabi (information that this study could not determine) mirrors the age distribution of creators of Web sites in general—a sensible assumption, though possibly countered by the growing number of universities that require professors to post their syllabi on the Web—then the dataset may tilt toward courses taught by younger faculty members. If so, this study provides a sense not only of the current state of the American history survey but also of where it is headed.

Regardless of the composition of the faculty who have posted the syllabi, the sheer number of them, along with the wide range of institutions with one or more courses identified, most likely means that the dataset is a decent, though certainly not complete, representation of how American history is taught at the introductory college level. Yet it is important to distinguish among different kinds of colleges and universities. Of the syllabi this study examined, four-year colleges accounted for less than 9 percent of the total, community and junior colleges for 31 percent, and universities for 60 percent.[3]

Across all types of institutions, the periodization of U.S. survey courses is exceedingly rigid, matching the design of two-volume U.S. history textbooks. Virtually all courses fall into one of four main categories: American history to 1865 (21 percent of the total); since 1865 (23 percent); to 1877 (24 percent); since 1877 (23 percent). Only 3 percent of courses cover the entire history of the United States in a single semester, while slightly fewer (2.5 percent) use a different dividing year (ranging from 1776 to 1918) than the most popular choices of 1865 and 1877. Since World War II, two-semester American history surveys have used the Civil War as a natural breaking point. It remains to be seen how many more decades can go by before more professors shift to a later year to split the survey more equally in two.

Unless many instructors are failing to list additional reading on their syllabi, the data show that fully one-third of U.S. history surveys in which a textbook is assigned use no other books, although a small minority of those courses also employ the primary-source reader that can be purchased with their textbooks. The kind of educational institution in which a course is taught largely determines the likelihood that a course relies exclusively on a textbook: 47 percent of U.S. history surveys taught at community and junior colleges in spring 2004 depended entirely on the textbook for readings, while another 8 percent added a primary-source reader. Thirty percent of four-year college courses depended solely on a textbook, while another 3 percent added a primary-source reader. Twenty-six percent of university courses depended completely on the textbook, while another 6 percent added a primary-source reader.

Though as a whole far less popular than unabridged editions, concise editions of textbooks appear to be more popular in survey courses taught at universities than in survey courses at other types of schools, and their use seems to correlate with somewhat greater use of nontextbook works. Of the fifty courses the Syllabus Finder clearly identified as including brief versions of textbooks, almost three-quarters were at universities and almost all of the rest were at community or junior colleges. Only 23 percent of the courses using concise editions failed to assign either a primary-source reader or other books, while another 4 percent included just a primary-source reader. In other words, if one focuses just on supplementary books, 73 percent of U.S. survey instructors who select concise-edition textbooks assign additional books of their own choosing, compared to only 59 percent of instructors who use unabridged textbooks.

Among the 60 percent of courses that include books beyond the textbook and primary-source reader, there is considerable diversity in the additional volumes instructors assign. Thus, there are only fourteen titles that appear on 1 percent or more of all the syllabi cataloged by the Syllabus Finder. Only four of the fourteen are secondary works (one of which is over forty years old). (See table 1.)

Except in two classic works of early American history (by Edmund Morgan and John Demos) and in some primary sources that have been part of American history courses for decades (by Upton Sinclair, Thomas Paine, and Benjamin Franklin), the most obvious theme of the assigned books is the African American experience, especially under slavery. (See the books by Frederick Douglass, Anne Moody, Harriet A. Jacobs, Harriet Beecher Stowe, Henry Louis Gates Jr., and Malcolm X.) Many instructors apparently use one or more of those works to make up for a perceived deficit in textbook narratives. The historian Peter Kolchin has observed that few American history textbook writers are experts in the history of slavery, and only one of eight major textbooks he examined in the late 1990s addressed "the shift in historians' focus from slave treatment to the lives of slaves and 'the slave community,' a shift based on 'taking seriously first-hand accounts previously discounted as unreliable.'"[4] Scores of history teachers evidently agree with Kolchin's criticism and look to primary sources to fill in that

TABLE 1

Most used supplementary books in U.S. survey courses, ranked by course adoptions, 1995–2004

Author	Title	Number of courses	Percentage of courses
Frederick Douglass	*Narrative of the Life of Frederick Douglass*	41	5.2
Anne Moody	*Coming of Age in Mississippi*	31	3.9
James Davidson and Mark Lytle	*After the Fact: The Art of Historical Detection*	18	2.3
Upton Sinclair	*The Jungle*	16	2
Thomas Paine	*Common Sense*	15	1.9
Harriet A. Jacobs	*Incidents in the Life of a Slave Girl*	12	1.5
John Demos	*The Unredeemed Captive*	11	1.4
John Hollitz	*Thinking through the Past: A Critical Approach to U.S. History*	11	1.4
Harriet Beecher Stowe	*Uncle Tom's Cabin*	11	1.4
Benjamin Franklin	*The Autobiography of Benjamin Franklin*	10	1.3
Edmund Morgan	*The Puritan Dilemma*	10	1.3
Thomas Bell	*Out of This Furnace*	8	1
Henry Louis Gates Jr., ed.	*The Classic Slave Narratives*	8	1
Malcolm X	*The Autobiography of Malcolm X*	8	1

NOTE: N = 792 courses.

NOTE: For bibliographical information, see "Appendix A: Most Used Supplementary Books."

textbook gap—and perhaps also to make up for their own perceived lack of authenticity when discussing African American culture.

Professors of American history survey courses use electronic resources sparingly, which most likely reflects a continuing skepticism about the quality and value of online historical materials.[5] In an age of rapid expansion in the number of historical Web sites and Web syllabi, the use of the Internet to teach topics in U.S. history is growing at a far slower pace. Of the U.S. survey courses taught in

spring 2004, 9 percent used the official Web site of a textbook publisher for additional materials, while only 6 percent ventured out onto the broader Web for supplementary primary and secondary sources—not much better than the running
average of 5 percent for all syllabi from 1995 to 2004. Survey instructors eschew
film as well: merely 3.5 percent of all survey courses in the study include one or
more films, a rate that has held steady over the past decade.

If most U.S. survey instructors rely heavily on a textbook, they disagree about
which textbook to assign. Syllabi for 258 courses taught in the spring 2004 semester show twenty-seven different textbooks in use, with only one title assigned by
over 10 percent of instructors. (See table 2.)

Since courses do not have equal numbers of students, the figures in table 2
do not accurately represent the distribution of textbook sales—data that textbook
publishers are loath to release. Yet by any measure of market share—whether it
be the proportion of all volumes sold or the proportion of courses that have
adopted a particular title—it appears that no single textbook dominates the
American history classroom. The 102 community college and junior college
courses included in this analysis used 24 different textbooks; the 18 courses at
four-year colleges used 11 different textbooks; the 132 university courses used
27 different textbooks. The kind of institution did influence textbook selection,

TABLE 2

Most used textbooks in U.S. survey courses, ranked by course adoptions, spring 2004

Author	Title	Publisher	Number of courses	Percentage of courses
Roark et al.	The American Promise	Bedford, Freeman and Worth	31	12
Nash et al.	The American People	Pearson	23	8.9
Davidson et al.	Nation of Nations	McGraw-Hill	21	8.1
Faragher et al.	Out of Many	Pearson	21	8.1
Brinkley	American History: A Survey	McGraw-Hill	14	5.4
Divine et al.	America, Past and Present	Pearson	14	5.4
Tindall and Shi	America: A Narrative History	Norton	12	4.7
Goldfield et al.	The American Journey	Pearson	10	3.9

(continued)

TABLE 2 *(continued)*
Most used textbooks in U.S. survey courses, ranked by course adoptions, spring 2004

Author	Title	Publisher	Number of courses	Percentage of courses
Henretta et al.	*America: A Concise History*	Bedford, Freeman and Worth	10	3.9
Boyer et al.	*The Enduring Vision*	Houghton Mifflin	9	3.5
Carnes and Garraty	*The American Nation*	Pearson	9	3.5
Norton et al.	*A People and a Nation*	Houghton Mifflin	9	3.5
Brinkley	*The Unfinished Nation*	McGraw-Hill	8	3.1
Murrin et al.	*Liberty, Equality, Power*	Thomson Learning	8	3.1
Ayers et al.	*American Passages*	Thomson Learning	7	2.7
Divine et al.	*The American Story*	Pearson	7	2.7
Maier et al.	*Inventing America*	Norton	7	2.7
Jones et al.	*Created Equal*	Pearson	6	2.3
Boydston et al.	*Making a Nation*	Pearson	5	1.9
Lichtenstein et al.	*Who Built America?*	Bedford, Freeman and Worth	4	1.6
Berkin et al.	*Making America*	Houghton Mifflin	4	1.6
Henretta et al.	*America's History*	Bedford, Freeman and Worth	4	1.6
Carnes and Garraty	*American Destiny*	Pearson	3	1.2
Kennedy et al.	*The American Pageant*	Houghton Mifflin	3	1.2
Zinn	*A People's History of the United States*	HarperCollins	3	1.2
Carnes and Garraty	*A Short History of the American Nation*	Pearson	1	0.4
Carroll	*We the People*	Thomson Learning	1	0.4

NOTE: *N* = 258 courses.

NOTE: For bibliographical information, see "Appendix B: Most Used Textbooks."

however. Instructors at community and junior colleges preferred 2 titles in spring 2004, while no single textbook was used in more than 10 percent of the university courses. (See tables 3 and 4.)

The diversity of the assigned textbooks masks growing concentration within the publishing industry. The publishing giant Pearson Longman supplied textbooks to 99 of the 258 spring 2004 courses in the database (38.4 percent of the total), followed by the Bedford, Freeman and Worth Publishing Group (49 courses, 19 percent), McGraw-Hill (43 courses, 16.7 percent), Houghton Mifflin (25 courses, 9.7 percent), W. W. Norton and Company (19 courses, 7.4 percent), Thomson Learning (16 courses, 6.2 percent), and HarperCollins (3 courses, 1.2 percent). Interestingly, the study reveals a significant divergence in the character of courses that use different publishers' textbooks. Instructors who assign works beyond the textbook are far more likely to use textbooks by Bedford than by other publishers. Only 25 percent of spring 2004 courses that used one of the four Bedford textbooks failed to assign additional books, while 53 percent of courses that used Pearson and McGraw-Hill textbooks did so. But hold the applause for

TABLE 3

Most used textbooks at community and junior colleges, ranked by course adoptions, spring 2004

Author	Title	Number of courses	Percentage of courses
Nash et al.	*The American People*	18	17.6
Roark et al.	*The American Promise*	17	16.7
Faragher et al.	*Out of Many*	8	7.8
Davidson et al.	*Nation of Nations*	8	7.8

NOTE: *N* = 102 courses.

TABLE 4

Most used textbooks at universities, ranked by course adoptions, spring 2004

Author	Title	Number of courses	Percentage of courses
Davidson et al.	*Nation of Nations*	12	9.1
Roark et al.	*The American Promise*	12	9.1
Faragher et al.	*Out of Many*	11	8.3
Brinkley	*American History: A Survey*	8	6.1
Tindall and Shi	*America: A Narrative History*	7	5.3

NOTE: *N* = 132 courses.

professors using Bedford volumes for their willingness to move beyond the text-book. Courses using *The American Promise*, the most popular textbook from Bed-ford—indeed, the most frequently assigned textbook in this study—also had on average some of the most exam-intensive grading schemes and assigned the least amount of writing and the fewest class projects. Almost three-quarters of the final grade in an *American Promise* class in spring 2004 typically came from tests, 15 percent from papers, and roughly 5 percent each from class participation and other assignments.

Those data match another finding of this study: courses using more popular textbooks tend to rely more heavily on examinations. In spring 2004, exams counted, on average, for 72.4 percent of the final grade in a class using one of the textbooks adopted by ten or more courses nationwide. Courses using less popular textbooks tend to count papers and class discussion as a higher percentage of the final grade. On average, exams accounted for 64.5 percent of the grade in classes based on textbooks adopted by fewer than ten courses nationwide. Both of those percentages are quite high, of course—probably much higher than for a nonsur-vey history course. Indeed, the U.S. history survey courses that the Syllabus Finder located overwhelmingly rely on tests and quizzes over assignments that allow students greater latitude, such as essays or class projects. Examinations con-stitute 67 percent of the final grade in an average U.S. history survey that uses a textbook. Papers account for 20 percent, class participation a mere 7 percent, and other assignments constitute 6 percent of the grade. Notably, however, those grade weightings vary significantly by the type of educational institution. Four-year college courses emphasize written work and class participation more than community college or university courses do. (See table 5.)

Table 5, along with statistics that demonstrate the centrality of textbooks to the courses that use them, reveals how textbooks give professors a relatively sim-ple way to construct and teach a U.S. history survey course. Choose a popular textbook from one of the large publishers, throw in a few quizzes, a midterm, and a final, and instructors quickly have a ready-made course. While professional his-torians may complain about standardized testing in secondary schools and what it does to history education—the peril of "teaching to the test"—they should worry just as much about the "textbook and testing" character of so many Ameri-can history survey courses at the college and university level—courses being taught in the classroom next door.

TABLE 5
Percentage of course grade based on each type of assignment, U.S. history survey courses, 1995–2004

Type of school	Examinations	Papers	Participation	Other
Community/junior college	71.0	16.8	4.5	7.7
Four-year college	50.9	33.2	10.0	5.9
University	67.0	19.5	8.1	5.1

On a more hopeful note, this study suggests that we can improve our understanding of the teaching of history using digital resources such as the often overlooked and underappreciated course syllabus. Not surprisingly, the most creative history teachers seem to write much of the literature on teaching history, which may create a false impression of current instruction. Given the wealth of data on the Web and advanced ways of analyzing them, discussions of curricular and pedagogical practices should become less anecdotal and less dependent on the close analysis of a small sample of courses. For instance, although there is much talk about the centrality of race, gender, and class in contemporary academia, and a corresponding complaint about the absence of religious history within survey courses, the words "religion" or "religious" appear on nearly 30 percent of the 2003 syllabi in the Syllabus Finder dataset, only slightly lower than the 32 percent garnered by "race."[6] Educational specialists and historians will surely find more grist for the research mill as a higher percentage of course syllabi appear on the Web and as tools such as the Syllabus Finder become more refined and more widely available.

Appendix A: Most Used Supplementary Books (as Ranked in Table 1)

Frederick Douglass, *Narrative of the Life of Frederick Douglass, an American Slave* (1845; Cambridge, Mass., 1960).

Anne Moody, *Coming of Age in Mississippi* (New York, 1968).

James West Davidson and Mark H. Lytle, *After the Fact: The Art of Historical Detection* (New York, 1982).

Upton Sinclair, *The Jungle* (1906; Cambridge, Mass., 1971).

Thomas Paine, *Common Sense* (1776; New York, 1986).

Harriet A. Jacobs, *Incidents in the Life of a Slave Girl* (1861; Cambridge, Mass., 1987).

John Demos, *The Unredeemed Captive: A Family Story from Early America* (New York, 1994).

John Erwin Hollitz, *Thinking through the Past: A Critical Thinking Approach to U.S. History* (Boston, 1997).

Harriet Beecher Stowe, *Uncle Tom's Cabin* (1852; New York, 1952).

Benjamin Franklin, *The Autobiography of Benjamin Franklin* (New York, 1941).

Edmund Sears Morgan, *The Puritan Dilemma: The Story of John Winthrop* (New York, 1958).

Thomas Bell, *Out of This Furnace* (1941; Pittsburgh, 1976).

Henry Louis Gates Jr., ed., *The Classic Slave Narratives* (1987; New York, 2002).

Malcolm X, *The Autobiography of Malcolm X* (New York, 1965).

Appendix B: Most Used Textbooks (as Ranked in Table 2)

The American Promise: A History of the United States. Second edition. By James L. Roark et al. (Boston: Bedford, 2002. xxxv, 1,183 pp.).

The American People: Creating a Nation and a Society. Sixth edition. By Gary B. Nash et al. (New York: Pearson, 2004. xxxii, 1,106 pp.).

Nation of Nations: A Concise Narrative of the American Republic. Third edition. By James West Davidson et al. (Boston: McGraw-Hill, 2002. xlviii, 992 pp.).

Out of Many: A History of the American People. Revised third edition. By John Mack Faragher et al. (Upper Saddle River, N.J.: Pearson, 2003. xlvii, 991 pp.).

American History: A Survey. Eleventh edition. By Alan Brinkley. (Boston: McGraw-Hill, 2003. xlvii, 951 pp.).

America, Past and Present. Revised sixth edition. By Robert A. Divine et al. (New York: Longman, 2003. xxxi, 1,014 pp.).

America: A Narrative History. Sixth edition. By George Brown Tindall and David E. Shi. (New York: Norton, 2004. xxii, 1,512 pp.).

The American Journey: A History of the United States. Combined volume, third edition. By David R. Goldfield et al. (Upper Saddle River, N.J.: Pearson, 2004. xlvii, 1,023 pp.).

America: A Concise History. Second edition. By James A. Henretta et al. (Boston: Bedford, 2002. xxxii, 958 pp.).

The Enduring Vision: A History of the American People. Fifth edition. By Paul S. Boyer et al. (Boston: Houghton Mifflin, 2004. xliv, 1,023 pp.).

The American Nation: A History of the United States. Eleventh edition. By Mark C. Carnes and John Arthur Garraty. (New York: Longman, 2003. xxiv, 528 pp.).

A People and a Nation: A History of the United States. Sixth edition. By Mary Beth Norton et al. (Boston: Houghton Mifflin, 2001. xxiv, 977 pp.).

The Unfinished Nation: A Concise History of the American People. Fourth edition. By Alan Brinkley. (Boston: McGraw-Hill, 2004. xxxix, 948 pp.).

Liberty, Equality, Power: A History of the American People. Third edition. By John M. Murrin et al. (Belmont, Calif.: Thomson Learning, 2002. xlv, 1,115 pp.).

American Passages: A History of the United States. Second edition. By Edward L. Ayers et al. (Belmont, Calif.: Thomson Learning, 2004. xxxii, 904 pp.).

The American Story. First edition. By Robert A. Divine et al. (New York: Longman, 2002).

Inventing America: A History of the United States. First edition. By Pauline Maier et al. (New York: Norton, 2003. xxvii, 1,086 pp.).

Created Equal: A Social and Political History of the United States. First edition. By Jacqueline Jones et al. (New York: Longman, 2003. xlvi, 1,033 pp.).

Making a Nation: The United States and Its People. Prentice Hall portfolio edition. By Jeanne Boydston et al. (Upper Saddle River, N.J.: Pearson, 2003–2004. xvi, 768 pp.).

Who Built America? Working People and the Nation's Economy, Politics, Culture, and Society. Second edition. By Nelson Lichtenstein et al. (Boston: Bedford, 2000. 786 pp.).

Making America: A History of the United States. Third edition. By Carol Berkin et al. (Boston: Houghton Mifflin, 2003. xxxii, 1,014 pp.).

America's History. Fifth edition. By James A. Henretta et al. (Boston: Bedford, 2004. li, 950 pp.).

American Destiny: Narrative of a Nation. By Mark C. Carnes and John Arthur Garraty. (New York: Longman, 2003).

The American Pageant: A History of the Republic. Twelfth edition. By David M. Kennedy et al. (Boston: Houghton Mifflin, 2002. xxiv, 1,034 pp.).

A People's History of the United States: 1492–Present. Third edition. By Howard Zinn. (New York: HarperCollins, 2003. 729 pp.).

A Short History of the American Nation. Eighth edition. By John Arthur Garraty and Mark C. Carnes. (New York: Longman, 2001. xxxii, 820 pp.).

We, the People: A Brief American History. By Peter N. Carroll. (Belmont, Calif.: Thomson Learning, 2003. xxviii, 799 pp.).

Notes

1. Gary Kornblith and Carol Lasser, eds., "Teaching the American History Survey at the Opening of the Twenty-First Century: A Roundtable Discussion," *Journal of American History* 87 (March 2001): 1409–41; Sara Evans and Roy Rosenzweig, "Introduction," *Journal of American History* 78 (March 1992): 1377.

2. To create the Syllabus Finder, I downloaded several hundred syllabi from the Web, broke them apart into single words, and ranked those words by frequency, thus producing a statistical word profile of the average syllabus. The Syllabus Finder scans the database of Google with that profile and plumbs other databases of educational institutions and course materials at the Center for History and New Media at George Mason University; thus the software accurately locates syllabi. The Syllabus Finder takes advantage of a direct connection to Google's massive index of Web pages, available to researchers and software developers under a special program and license. (For more information about this program, called the Google Web APIs service, visit <www.google.com/apis> [Nov. 8, 2004].) The supplementary algorithms and databases make the Syllabus Finder much more adept than Google alone is at locating courses across the Web. The software generally can identify the college or university where each course is taught and can pull out book titles and other features of individual syllabi. It can also find syllabi that are posted as Microsoft Word documents or in portable document format (pdf) in addition to regular Web pages. Simon Kornblith greatly improved the complex regular expressions, or text pattern-matching algorithms, for book titles. Center for History and New Media, *Syllabus Finder* <http://chnm.gmu.edu/tools/syllabi> (Nov. 8, 2004).

3. The gap between community college and university instruction narrows if we look just at the numbers for spring 2004 (the most recent semester in the dataset): 7 percent of the courses were at four-year colleges, 41 percent at community or junior colleges, and 52 percent at universities.

4. Peter Kolchin, "Slavery in United States Survey Textbooks," *Journal of American History* 84 (March 1998): 1435.

5. For more on skepticism about Web resources, see Kornblith and Lasser, eds., "Teaching the American History Survey at the Opening of the Twenty-First Century"; and David Jaffee, "'Scholars will soon be instructed through the eye': E-Supplements and the Teaching of U.S. History," *Journal of American History* 89 (March 2003): 1463–82.

6. Paul Boyer, "In Search of the Fourth 'R': The Treatment of Religion in American History Textbooks and Survey Courses," *History Teacher* 29 (Feb. 1996): 195–216.

PART THREE

TEACHING OUTSIDE THE BOX

If the traditional American history survey and conventional textbook represent the standard way of presenting American history—that is, teaching "inside the box"—then what are the creative alternatives? Part Three reports on efforts to expand the teaching of college-level history courses beyond normal classroom formats and boundaries.

K–12 social studies teachers know that physically moving their students outside the traditional enclosure of their schools to new spaces—local museums and historical sites—can help history "come alive" even for the most disinclined. Until recently, college professors have been less adventurous. But upon posting a call for papers on teaching American history "outside the box" in 2001, we quickly discovered the abundance of energy and experimentation among historians teaching in institutions of higher education. Some faculty had broken out of the traditional lecture/discussion format to create new collaborations and learning communities; others had relocated the sites for their teaching beyond the four walls of their institutions; still others had found ways to empower their students to create new "texts"—from oral histories to material culture. Some efforts were unabashedly activist, making explicit connections between community service, social change, and the study of history; others stressed engaging students in writing history for, and sometimes with, new audiences. Reports came from beginning instructors and distinguished senior professors, from community colleges and flagship research institutions, from large schools and small, and from both urban and rural environments. What all shared was an evident commitment to participatory education and to the cultivation of a passion for "doing"— not just reading—history.

In this volume, we have chosen to present eleven reports from the field, demonstrating the astonishing vitality and range of innovative teaching. The reports describe service learning, community-oriented public history projects, collaborative research seminars, and traveling classrooms that educate both head and heart. Topics covered in these reports include the use of material culture and electronic resources in history courses and the destabilization of classroom authority that historians confront when they move away from traditional formats. In these case studies, first-year students find their way into new historiographical frameworks while advanced undergraduates thrive as researchers and publishers. Clearly, no one size fits all in these new approaches to teaching. Most impressive is the ability of inspired faculty to collaborate with students in the creation of new engagements with the past. Here is evidence of the success of historians who, with imagination and perhaps audacity, connect their students to both real and "imagined" communities. As John Dewey wrote in 1916, the purpose of the study of history is "to enrich and liberate the more direct and personal contacts of life by furnishing their context, their background and outlook."[1] Our reports suggest that teaching outside the box can accomplish that end.

Note

1. John Dewey, *Democracy and Education: An Introduction to the Philosophy of Education* (1916; New York, 1966), 211.

Amy Bass

Exploring the Wide World of Sports: Taking a Class to the (Virtual) Olympics

I teach cultural history at Plattsburgh State University, a regional public university located on Lake Champlain. The sixty-one hundred enrolled students are, without question, the faculty's top priority, so faculty constantly struggle to balance scholarship and teaching. When I was offered the opportunity to work as a research consultant for NBC Sports at the Olympics in Sydney, Australia, in fall 2000, I faced a formidable challenge: How could I, in only my second year at Plattsburgh, possibly obtain the time to travel "down under" for seven weeks at the beginning of the academic calendar? The answer I worked out, with help from my chair, my dean, and the Honors Program director, embraced the Olympic opportunity as a classroom experience that would benefit Plattsburgh students. The end result, a history honors seminar entitled "The Black Athlete," was a pedagogic innovation that combined distance and classroom learning by using contemporary and historical materials to enrich each other. Rather than a logistical nightmare, the course was an overwhelmingly positive academic experience for those involved and resulted in an impressive outpouring of original student research and writing on a variety of historical subjects. While all my courses deal with historical concepts of time and space, this unique learning experience required students to move constantly between figures and events of the past and those in the "real-time" present.

With the Sydney Olympics as our focal point, we concentrated on historically grounded topics from my own scholarship: nationalism and internationalism, postwar mass media, alternative methods of civil rights struggles, and the varied and changing constructions of race and racism in American culture.

From a Distance: Designing a Course without a Professor

Since the students were going to be professor-less for the first weeks of the semester, I developed a plan to keep the course on track. At a meeting the semester before, I talked to students about what I wanted to accomplish. I recast my absence as an opportunity and emphasized how I hoped to bring them to Sydney virtually.

Journal of American History 88 (2002): 1435–40.

I stressed their responsibility for making the seminar a success. Lastly, I conveyed the message that this was an experiment, and that it might not work at all.

That fall, a detailed reading schedule of scholarly historical articles greeted students. Their central task during the Games was what I designated the "Olympic Viewing Assignment." For the duration, students were to create personal, mixed-media journals based on multiple sources: NBC sports coverage, domestic and foreign news publications, the Internet, and (because of our close proximity to Montreal) Canadian print and television coverage. In addition, each student was to produce a written chronicle of the Olympics based on a set of common questions regarding media, celebrity, globalization, amateurism, commerce, spectacle, and, especially, identity. Specific questions included:

How are different sports represented?

How are identities—nation, race, class, gender, age, ethnicity—performed in Olympic rituals?

What is the role of the media in creating an athlete's identity?

Which nations seem to dominate the media coverage?

How is the culture of the host country represented?

ELECTRONIC CONVERSATIONS: USING THE INTERNET AS A CLASSROOM

In my absence students interacted with each other via the course Web page and its online discussion forum; they also corresponded with me via e-mail. As they shaped the dynamics of the online classroom, they used it to confer about readings, to set up times to watch Olympic events together, and to inform each other about relevant features in media organs. The students, who had yet to spend quality "face" time together, became a cohesive group, sharing ideas and insights. Drawing on the news sources available to them, they became skilled at identifying incidents and topics that corresponded to the central themes of the course. They discussed, for example, the Australian jumper Jai Taurima's boast that because of Sydney's cool temperatures, "You can pretty much knock out all the dark athletes." They pondered Canadian and American broadcasters' different styles of commentary and wondered how major league baseball broadcasts might affect the U.S. TV ratings for Olympic coverage. They debated amateurism, athlete drug use, and what one student termed "the business of the Olympics." They marveled at the Parade of Nations and at how North and South Korea, at least symbolically, marched as one. They heralded stars such as Marion Jones, Cathy Freeman, and Ian Thorpe; relished sports rarely seen on American television (table tennis!); and embraced underdogs such as Eric Moussambani of Equatorial Guinea, who swam slowly but to a standing ovation.

Because of the time difference between Sydney and Plattsburgh, students who watched NBC's coverage carefully noted how the Olympics were packaged for a prime-time audience, often twenty or so hours after an event took place. Those who watched Canadian television (CBC), which aired live footage into the wee hours of the morning, gave "spoiler alerts" ("DON'T READ THIS IF YOU DON'T WANT TO KNOW ABOUT. . . .") to classmates who wanted to watch it for themselves. One student preferred CBC coverage because, as a Canadian citizen, he was "incredibly offended and annoyed by the NBC coverage," especially when commentators used the word "Canucks" to describe Canadian athletes. "I apologize if I'm being over-sensitive," the student posted online, "but the term 'Canuck' isn't exactly something Canadians relish being called."

I kept my own contributions to the forum to a minimum. Students became accountable for the quality of the discussion, understanding that it could be only as good as they made it. They appreciated that, in one student's words, the forum helped them "keep up with class reading and work." It became for another an "interesting, unusual, and fun way to conduct class." As one student recapped the experience, it "helped us all stay in contact with one another."

An added benefit of the electronic dialogue was the contact with celebrity guests who joined us. Throughout my work in Sydney, I urged colleagues and contacts to enlist in the forum. The lively discussions ran the gamut of topics. When several gymnasts fell, for example, because the vault was set at the wrong height, a group of students expressed concern that it might negatively affect one young American's overall performance. Michelle Dusserre-Farrell, who won a silver medal in gymnastics in 1984, responded: "You're absolutely right. No matter how good of a competitor you are, a fall like Elise Ray's can mentally make the difference between success and failure." When another student asked about the impact of the Olympics on Australia's racial relations, NBC's Bob Costas replied:

> I believe the Olympics will have a positive effect on aboriginal relations here. We've already seen a display of important symbolism at the Opening Ceremony. Cathy Freeman lighting the torch is similar in ways to some of the important civil rights moments we have had. At the same time, the problems are complex, and goodwill alone won't solve them. It will require much more resolve than that—much more than just good feelings.[1]

The negative reactions of the international media to the newest installment of America's basketball "Dream Team" probably generated the most heated conversation. Evan Silverman, the director of Internet Services for the National Basketball Association (NBA), sparked an animated discussion when he wrote:

> Working for the league, I have helped deal with an anti-NBA backlash for several years, but the disdain for this year's Olympic team really struck me as out of the ordinary. . . . Putting aside whether you thought their play was inspired or not, did they really deserve the derision they received? A few things to think about . . . : 1) Is a team comprised of twelve African American NBA players too easily stereotyped by a largely non-African American media? 2) Does the world resent the Dream Team because they are some of the richest athletes at the Games? 3) Is the world's anti-U.S. sentiment simply re-directed to these well-known lightning rods? 4) Do people feel that the Dream Team does not genuinely care about winning a gold medal and is simply a product of the NBA marketing machine?[2]

Going Home: Merging Distance and Classroom Experiences

When I returned from Sydney, I found a group of students who were radically disappointed that the Olympics were over. However, we dived into the classroom portion of the course, beginning with individual meetings to discuss their Olympic journals, the size and quality of which were astounding. We began to study a series of common topics: the history of scientific racism, the Berlin Olympics in 1936, the Mexico City Olympics in 1968, the legacy of Jackie Robinson, Wilma Rudolph and the collision of race and gender, the racial politics of high school football, and Michael Jordan's global corporatism. As we worked through the readings, students recognized how our subject, the black athlete, implicated much broader societal issues. As one student remarked, "The concepts behind the content have many applications." Another concurred, surprised that she could "combine my major of biology with the course content of the black athlete."

For some, the academic journey became personal. Students continually challenged themselves to use the historical content of the course to rethink deeply embedded beliefs; one student displayed tears when admitting that she—like all of us—had fallen victim to accepting some racial stereotypes. "We dealt with issues that everyone has strong feelings about," another student remarked in his/her course evaluation. "We were headed in new directions where nobody knew what the answers were, so we all went along." Another student observed, "Social questions that transcended race were often brought up and showed me things by challenging my own feelings and conceptions of race, equality, racism, sports and general perceptions of life." Still another agreed: "The seminar assignments were key in getting me to ask myself questions of my own ideas and ingrained attitudes that I probably wouldn't have dealt with otherwise."

Those discoveries translated well into their research endeavors, which produced highly original and thoughtful papers of substantial quality. Students, such as one math major, seemed exceptionally excited about their work: "I feel as though this is the most important paper I've ever had to write." Many used their Olympic journals as the basis for more extensive inquiry, attaching the historical themes they had found in course readings to their observations about the Sydney Games. Some maintained the contacts they had established during the Olympics. One student, after watching the documentary about Muhammad Ali that NBC aired during the Games, interviewed two NBC writers who had worked on Ali, Joe Gesue, and Brian Brown. The end result was a wonderful paper on documentary images of the boxing legend entitled "Making Muhammad: The Cinematic Legacy of the Boxer Who Shook Up the World."

Others, interested in the racial politics of Australia's "stolen generation," struck up an online relationship with the aboriginal rights activist Geoff Moore. Because aboriginal culture had played such a large role in the Opening Ceremony, many opted to write about the aboriginal runner Cathy Freeman, inarguably the star of the Sydney Games. One student deconstructed the aboriginal content of the Opening Ceremony, during which Freeman lit the Olympic flame, in a paper entitled "The Sydney Games: Aboriginal Representations and Symbolisms of an Athlete." Another student put together a complex historiographical overview of the course readings in conjunction with her Olympic journal to explore the question: "Is Cathy Freeman a 'Black' Athlete?" Expanding W. E. B. Du Bois's famous concept of "double consciousness," another probed the conflicts of race and gender via Freeman, Rudolph, and the African running legend Tegla Loroupe in a paper entitled "Overcoming 'Triple' Consciousness to Become One Great Runner." Indeed, after students watched women dominate much of the competition, gender identity became a popular subject. One student wrote a biography of the indomitable Marion Jones, while another won the campus Inez Milholland Boissevain Writing Prize in Women's Studies for her paper, "Passing the Torch: The Significance of the Torch Relay in Celebrating Women in the Olympics."

In their research, students continually challenged themselves to use the historical content of the course in conjunction with the Olympic spectacle in front of them to rethink expansive historical concerns. They granted authority to their own observations, connecting moments in the past with those being created. Students defined their own "texts," whether by exploring such newspapers as the *Zimbabwe Independent* and the *Bahrain Tribune* or by contacting people not usually associated with a history class. Thus they redefined sources of knowledge and expertise to include a range of academic and nonacademic people, including themselves.

Best of all, they collaborated to make the course succeed, and its impact continues. One student has used her "Australian experience" as the basis for her senior thesis project, which explores Jesse Owens and Cathy Freeman to compare the societal meaning of segregation with that of assimilation. Another, after completing papers on representations of black athletes in film and on the assimilation policies of the "stolen generation," will embark on a thesis project about the diplomatic politics of the Olympics. Her inspiration has been her virtual association with Wayne Wilson of the Amateur Athletic Foundation of Los Angeles, whom she "met" during the Sydney Games. This same student conveyed the impact the course had on her when she told me that she still read the *Sydney Morning Herald* online almost every day. "I just can't seem to leave Sydney," she said, perhaps not realizing that she had never actually left Plattsburgh.

Teaching this course also had a profound impact on me. The relationship I established with these students was the strongest in my teaching experience. It broadened my ideas on how students can best capitalize on the multitude of primary and secondary sources available to them, forcing me to innovate on the more traditional pedagogical methods of lectures, note taking, and discussions. It also demonstrated that Plattsburgh's Honors Program allows for unusual flexibility and creativity, engendering a student community strong enough to survive for several weeks without a professor. The next step, then, is to stretch such opportunities to students in the general curriculum, perhaps through the learning communities that have been successful on so many campuses. While doing so would necessitate administrative support and the shattering of rigid registrar schedules, I hope in the future to introduce other courses "outside the box" to a variety of students on a variety of levels, as the rewards are many.

Notes

1. Michelle Dusserre-Farrell, online posting, Sept. 22, 2000, Honors Seminar 129A discussion forum <http://faculty.plattsburgh.edu/amy.bass/disc6_frm.htm> (Jan. 23, 2002); Bob Costas, online posting, Sept. 20, 2000, ibid. (Feb. 16, 2001).

2. Evan Silverman, online posting, Oct. 1, 2000, ibid. (Feb. 16, 2001).

Charles Bright

"It Was As If We Were Never There": Recovering Detroit's Past for History and Theater

This project began in a conversation about Sophocles' tragedy *Philoctetes* and the ancient Greek practice of combining the telling of history with the rituals of theater. It was designed to address two problems I had encountered in teaching a course on the history of Detroit.

First, although the city celebrated its three hundredth anniversary this year with the Detroit 300 festival, it is in most respects a twentieth-century boomtown. Much of its early history has been erased by the power and speed of its dynamic expansion in the first half of the century—and its equally dramatic contraction in the second half. The dominant historical discourse is one of rise and fall, spiked by an immense nostalgia for the city that once (briefly) was.[1] The recent past is often deployed as a cautionary tale about what goes wrong with urban spaces when racism, white flight, and industrial evacuation undercut a city's viability.[2] Such a historical construction places Detroit in a past that is now lost and irretrievable and leaves current residents, especially the African American descendants of those who came to the city during the Great Migration, dangling at the end of history with little hope and no agency. There is a strange disconnect between the history of the city and the people who live in it.

Second, although Detroit is only forty minutes' drive from the Ann Arbor campus of the University of Michigan (UM), a wide chasm separates the average undergraduate from the people of the city. This is not only a racial and class divide, but a gap of purposes in which the large research university tends to treat Detroit as a resource or laboratory, extracting data in the production of knowledge while returning little to the city. Recently, spurred on by the commitment of Provost Nancy Cantor to make the university a "public good," the graduate and professional schools have tried to overcome this legacy and the distrust that goes with it.[3] But little of the new orientation has reached undergraduates. Indeed, my own rather traditional way of teaching Detroit history seemed to reinforce distance: my students did history projects in the city, interviewing residents, poking around archives, looking *into* and *at* the city like spectators, and producing essays, term projects, and research papers that I read, graded, and filed away, lifting here and there a fact or a citation for my own use. But I was open to new possibilities when, in a conversation with my colleague at the Residential College

Journal of American History 88 (2002): 1440–46.

Kate Mendeloff (who had extensive background in community-based theater), the idea arose to use oral histories as the basis for creating stage pieces. We then received strong institutional and funding support from Professor David Scobey, whose Arts of Citizenship program is mandated to build cultural links between the academy and the community.

As initially conceived, the project had three aims: first, to develop a course that took undergraduates out of the classroom to engage residents of the city directly through the collection of life histories; second, to combine interview work with theater improvisations that could be re-presented to our informants as performance pieces that they could react to; and third, to do this work in collaboration with Detroiters, using the resources and skills of the university in ways that would prove relevant to residents and would yield usable cultural products that could be left behind—"owned"—by our partners in the city.

How we did this depended on whom we found to work with. We had to figure out which of the possible partners had compatible objectives and fungible calendars. University participants came to the table concerned with contact hours, weeks in the semester, term projects and assignments, not to mention final products and gradable results. People in the community were on a very different clock, with aims that were both more immediate and longer-running than a university semester. Luckily, in our exploratory discussions, we struck up a relationship with Rick Sperling, artistic director of the Mosaic Youth Theater of Detroit, a remarkably talented troupe of some seventy-five high school students recruited by audition from all over the city. The group produced an original play every year. Sperling was looking for material that would contribute to the Detroit 300 celebration in 2001, and since his is a theater of young people, we thought we might build a play around interviews with Detroit residents about growing up in the city—across racial and ethnic groups, in different communities, and over several decades. For us, the scheme promised to place college students in multiple roles—as learners/researchers, collaborators, and mentors—while helping develop a product that would remain with, and be of use to, our Detroit partners.

In our initial plan, Mendeloff and I were to run a semester-long course in which high school and college students, working in teams, would conduct interviews with Detroiters of various ages about what it was like to grow up in the city. We would then take the material gathered to Mosaic rehearsals for improvisational work that would produce both scenes for the play and problems for my students to investigate further. Over the course of a semester, the students conducted some thirty interviews and did theater and playwriting exercises with the material. The work stretched our organizational capacities and proved very demanding of the students' time, especially that of our high school partners, making stable interview teams impossible to sustain. As the work proceeded, moreover, the Mosaic students became particularly fascinated by the interviews with African Americans who had grown up during the 1940s in Black Bottom, the neighborhood on the near east side where black migrants from the South had been effectively confined. It was on these stories that our work began to focus.

Hastings Street, the main commercial strip running north-south through Black Bottom, was once the center of east European Jewish settlement, but in the interwar years it became a bustling "mixed use" center of African American business, sociability, night life, and underworld activity. All the big bands, jazz artists, and blues singers of the day performed in its bars and juke joints; the street had one of the highest concentrations of black-owned businesses in the country; and the nearby flats and tenements formed a classic "ethnic community" with people of different class and degree living side by side in housing stock that was increasingly crowded and run-down.[4] The war boom of the 1940s brought the twin trajectory of dynamism and decay to a climax, and in the 1950s, the city administration attacked what it called "urban blight" by bulldozing Black Bottom to lay Interstate 75 right down Hastings Street, obliterating even its memory.[5] "It was," said one of our informants, "as if we were never there."

Or so it seemed. Not one of the youngsters in the Mosaic company—95 percent of them African American—had ever heard of Hastings Street. Their school libraries held nothing about it; their history texts were silent. We sent them to ask their grandparents, elderly relatives, and neighbors about Hastings Street, and they came back brimming with stories. Everyone over fifty had something to tell them, and it quickly became clear that we had tapped a gold mine of material rich in theatrical potential but also deeply meaningful to our Detroit partners. Given their growing excitement, we provided tape recorders, questions, and training in interview techniques, then relied on the Mosaic kids to do the interviewing. From then on, the coming-of-age theme blended into a project of recovery, in which high school students discovered broad aspects of their city's past previously invisible to them, and their elders found in the curiosity of the kids reasons to remember and ways, through stories, of instructing and exhorting a younger generation. The stories captured the many deep contradictions of the historic black community: the pride of survival; the nostalgia for neighbors who watched and took care; a familiarity with card games, prostitution, and the numbers; and the lack of contact with a larger white world, coupled with a sustained recognition that this had been an enforced community, created by segregation. As this intergenerational dialogue took shape, the role of the UM participants changed: with the second semester, we brought graduate students into the project and turned over to UM undergraduates the responsibilities for researching, framing, and contextualizing the stories that our community partners discovered. Eventually they created a lobby exhibit of text and photographs to travel with the Mosaic play and provide the audience with a historical context.

The project took an especially important turn when one of our informants mentioned an after-school social group at Black Bottom's Miller High School called the Y-Gees (for Youth Guidance). One of our graduate researchers discovered that this was one of several programs the city created after the race riot of 1943 to keep high school kids occupied and off the streets, that it had been sponsored by the legendary Loving brothers, one of them the first black academic teacher in the Detroit school system, and that it had sustained a small theater company and singing ensemble in the two short years it lasted. High schoolers asked their informants about the Y-Gees and, to our surprise, brought back reports from several who had been members of the club. We brought these original Y-Gees to a meeting with Mosaic. After small-group interviews, the whole company

Mosaic Theater actors tell stories about growing up dancing in the Detroit neighborhood of Black Bottom. *Photograph by david smith Photography. Courtesy Mosaic Theater.*

reconvened, and one by one, the students retold stories they had heard; the elders listened, elaborated, corrected, and added details, showing the youngsters a dance step or a cheerleading routine. Curiosity mixed with recollection to elicit a shared history, and Sperling began to see a story line and the shape of a play: a Y-Gees meeting in 1944 in which the members try to invent a play about their lives. The Mosaic kids would impersonate youngsters of another era and tell "their" stories, using what they had learned from their elders. There would be music, dance, and laughter, but also a war and a race riot to capture. What stories should they include? How would these be enacted? What did each capture or miss about "their" lives in Black Bottom? This would be the play—about a play—and the very process of exploration and creation that the students had been through in developing the dramatic material would become what in theater is called the through-line of the play.

The project was now in the possession of our community collaborators. UM faculty and students continued to help with the interviews, participate in the improvisations, follow up on questions of fact that arose, and offer comment and feedback, but the play belonged to Mosaic. Early in 2001, Sperling assembled the scenes in progress and wrote a script. From then on, the company was working from the text, altering, modifying, refining it, but also now framed by it. Several draft performances before an audience of informants gave elders further opportunity to talk back to the kids—correcting facts, recalling more details, debating the location of a store or the slang used for everyday things—and by their enthusiasm telling these young people that what they were doing was important for the whole community. "I never knew so many people cared so much about Detroit," said one Mosaic student. "This has been the most important thing that ever happened to me," announced an elder Y-Gee. With each session, the play got sharper and more accurate, but it also became a collaboration in which a whole community was involved in the business of shaping a history of itself. The university people were now witnesses on the sidelines. It was one of the happiest moments of my life as a teacher.

In the end, the collaboration with Mosaic and the imperatives of producing a play subordinated my history syllabus to the agendas of our Detroit partners. Yet what they wanted to do demanded historical material, and this took my students beneath the surface of events. It opened questions about social history and the

Actors impersonate the white mobs during the 1943 Detroit race riot. At the end of the scene, they all took off their masks and moved them, wavelike, as the young woman in the front told how a white mob swept down the street in a wave that nobody stopped.
Photograph by david smith Photography. Courtesy Mosaic Theater.

work of memory in a context that gave their historical inquiries immediate relevance. My students learned history with a purpose; the processes of locating a site, tracing a name, and reviving a slang expression or a way of dressing were not esoteric problems for the classroom, but essential details to make the collaboration work. In the recovery of Hastings Street, our partners found a vehicle for achieving other, more immediate aims having to do with community building and intergenerational communication. The real imperatives of our joint project only became apparent in the doing of the work. Together, we discovered common ground in the history we were making. The past became a terrain of exchanges across racial, class, and generational lines.

When Mosaic premiered the play *2001 Hastings Street* to sell-out crowds at Detroit's Music Hall in May 2001, it was more than a good evening's entertainment. The audience "talked back" all through the performance—murmuring assent, remembering and reliving long-forgotten moments across the aisles and in the lobby, and in their applause affirming these young actors as the carriers of their memories and the heirs of their experience. For performers and audience alike, this history, enacted and public, helped to validate the present and to evoke a future. It served a public good. No classroom performance, however eloquent or compelling, could have taught undergraduate students of history so well this deeper lesson about why we study and teach history.[6]

Notes

1. See, for example, Ze'ev Chafets, *Devil's Night and Other True Tales of Detroit* (New York, 1990); and Jerry Herron, *AfterCulture: Detroit and the Humiliation of History* (Detroit, 1993).

2. The best is Thomas J. Sugrue, *The Origins of the Urban Crisis: Race and Inequality in Postwar Detroit* (Princeton, N.J., 1996).

3. Nancy Cantor, "Reinvention: Why Now? Why Us?," paper delivered at the symposium on the Boyer Commission Report, State University of New York, Stony Brook, April 2000, quoted in the "Report of the President's Commission on the Undergraduate Experience," University of Michigan, October 2001 (in the possession of Charles Bright).

4. See Richard W. Thomas, *Life for Us Is What We Make It: Building Black Community in Detroit, 1915–1945* (Bloomington, Ind., 1992).

5. See June Manning Thomas, *Redevelopment and Race: Planning a Finer City in Postwar Detroit* (Baltimore, 1997).

6. The interview tapes are now in the possession of the Arts of Citizenship Program, University of Michigan (and will eventually make their way to the Michigan Historical Collections, Bentley Library, University of Michigan). I have a copy of the script in my possession. Every time it is performed, there are changes, updates, and alterations of one kind or another; it is a work in continual process.

A. Glenn Crothers

"Bringing History to Life": Oral History, Community Research, and Multiple Levels of Learning

In the past three decades, as college pedagogy has come to emphasize the benefits of cooperative classroom environments and experiential learning and as more
historians study their subject from the bottom up, focusing their research on traditionally ignored or disempowered groups, history teaching has increasingly
moved away from the top-down lecture format toward new methods of presenting
history. The benefits of new methodologies are widely recognized. Cooperative
classrooms and experiential learning enable students to engage more fully with
historical materials, to enjoy multiple perspectives on historical evidence, and, it
is hoped, to gain a better understanding of the past and the process of writing history. In contrast, a parallel innovation in college teaching—community-based
research, or service learning—has few advocates in the field of history. Service or
community-based learning engages students in meeting local needs in order to
link the classroom and the community and thereby to create more civic-minded
individuals and a more engaged academic scholarship.[1] That historians should
have generally ignored this method is ironic; after all, many historians claim that
their teaching aims to help produce individuals who are highly engaged in civic
and political life. This report, based on my experience running the Floyd County
Oral History Project at Indiana University Southeast (IUS), demonstrates how
service learning benefits pedagogy. Community-based projects heighten student
awareness of the local impact of broader historical events. Equally important,
service learning increases the opportunities for cooperative and experiential
learning inside *and outside* the classroom. Finally, service-learning projects can
bring the community together, connecting college students and senior citizens
to foster both the preservation of local history and a sense of the responsibilities
of citizenship.

First, a little background. I initiated the Floyd County Oral History Project
in fall 1998, primarily as a way to engage students enrolled in survey-level history courses—"The World in the Twentieth Century" and "U.S. History since
1865"—in the study of history. IUS is a four-year comprehensive college with an
essentially open admissions policy enrolling approximately six thousand students
on its campus in New Albany, Indiana, on the Ohio River. I wanted students to

Journal of American History 88 (2002): 1446–51.

understand how the broad historical events described and discussed in textbooks and in class had profoundly shaped the local community and the lives of its inhabitants. I hoped that by talking to local people and reflecting upon those conversations in short papers, class discussion, and presentations, students would come to recognize the impact of historical events—the human consequences of depression, war, and ideological conflict in their own communities. History would become immediate, tangible, and relevant.

The idea of having students talk to members of the community or (quite often) older members of their families is not new. Many college professors have used this technique effectively. Unfortunately, such projects are seldom employed at the survey level and rarely do they go beyond a conversation and a paper.[2] In contrast, I wanted to involve students in my survey-level courses in making and doing history, to show them how historians use primary and secondary historical sources to try to understand and interpret the past. This meant giving students the opportunity to understand how historians move from evidence to interpretation and involving them in creating a permanent historical resource for the community. In the academic year 1999–2000, students completed some ninety interviews with World War II and Korean War veterans that were edited, bound, and placed in the IUS library and the local county library. The next year students completed sixty interviews with community members who had lived through the Great Depression. The resulting transcripts, generally of high quality, provide an important historical and genealogical resource for southern Indiana. Equally notable, this community research project has blossomed into an invaluable pedagogical tool that enables multiple levels of learning to take place both within the classroom and outside it.

Most students in survey-level classes have no familiarity with the methodology of oral history. The first task, then, is to provide for them a mini-workshop that includes an overview of oral history, instructions about conducting an interview, and an introduction to the subject areas that will be covered in the interview. In general, the guidelines laid out for the students in this class follow those established by the Southern Oral History Program at the University of North Carolina.

A supplementary instructor (SI), a more advanced history major who has completed the class and transcribed her/his own interview, assists students and provides a second level of learning. In their tutoring sessions SIs focus on the oral history project, providing advice and historical context. The SIs are enthusiastic participants, convincing students of the value of the interview and offering hesitant students a different (and positive) perspective on oral history. And the learning is reciprocal. At this second level, the SIs gain experience training others in oral history techniques and in historical subjects.

A third level of learning takes place within the two-member student teams established as interviewing partnerships. In the early class discussions of the project I emphasize the need for proper preparation for the interview, including both adequate research on the subject and the formulation of well-phrased questions. Here partnership between students can pay great dividends. When the partnership works, students effectively mentor one another, sharing research information, collaboratively deciding what questions to ask and how to ask them, and supporting one another through the interview. The most effective partnerships—those involving true collaboration—have resulted in the best interviews. The questions are more probing and more knowledgeable, and the interviews themselves go more smoothly, benefiting from the presence of two prepared students. The partnership also makes transcription a less arduous task.

And the collaboration does not end when the transcription is completed. Although each student must write a separate short reflective essay, the partners make a joint fifteen-minute presentation to the class that, like the paper, requires them to link the interview with the broader historical themes of the class. Students choose an aspect of the interview they believe is important and use a variety of forms of presentation—traditional short lectures, PowerPoint presentations, and, often, collaborative presentations with the interviewee.

The cooperation of narrators points to a critical fourth arena of learning: the interaction between students and local people who have experienced significant historical events firsthand. The interviews enable students to place individual experience within a historical context, to make connections between their own community and regional, national, and international events. Equally important, students become active participants in the creation of a primary document—a historical text—about some aspect of their local community. They not only learn about the history of the community but also become actively involved in preserving that history.

In the process students develop a keen appreciation of the importance of studying history and of the ways their own community was shaped by historical events they might hitherto have considered distant and insignificant. Southern Indiana and Kentucky, students learn, were dramatically impacted by the New Deal programs of Franklin D. Roosevelt, particularly during the 1937 Ohio River flood, though they also learn that local farm families often resorted to strategies of self-sufficiency to survive the worst effects of depression. Interviewees described the enormous changes the military buildup of World War II had on the region, ending the depression and enabling many women who had never worked outside the home to enter local ammunition and boat factories and to develop a new sense of independence. After interviewing World War II and Korean War veterans, students no longer view Pearl Harbor, Normandy, Iwo Jima, Hiroshima, and Inchon as distant locations on a map but as places where young Americans like themselves fought and died in miserable conditions and often without recognition. Students learn that though the veterans invariably remembered their service with pride, most had no desire to repeat the experience. Veterans left permanently disabled, both physically and psychologically, and those who were prisoners of war reinforce the lesson that war, even a "good war," should be entered only with trepidation.

In short, the interviews make a profound impression on students. Many report that their work brought "color & emotion" to the "material we learned in class," that "for the first time I was able to feel and understand some of the emotions and effects of war." Another student put it succinctly: the oral history project helped in "bringing history to life." Students also interact directly with some of the community's most undervalued members, senior citizens, who share the richness of their lives and experiences. As one student noted, "I think the older people [involved in the project] were made to feel important. They had a story to tell and I think college students taking the time to investigate their experience made them feel like someone cared about their sacrifice." Or as another wrote, "I think it would do us all a little good to listen to the stories of our elders." In so doing, students develop an enhanced sense of civic responsibility and involvement, motivating them to want "to learn more" and become citizens with an active interest in the history, culture, and governance of their community.

A fifth level of learning takes place among student assistants, advanced history majors trained in oral history, who work for the project. These students perform a function different from that of the supplementary instructors. They edit and prepare for binding the completed interview transcripts, publicize and speak at public forums, locate prospective interviewees, and maintain and update the project's Web page. I work closely with these students, and the oral history project has become a training program for promising history students interested in local and public history. Most of the student assistants and SIs plan to continue on to graduate school; thus the project strengthens the IUS history program.[3]

In the final level of learning, the community learns more about itself. On the most straightforward level, edited and bound transcripts are easily accessible in the New Albany–Floyd County Public Library where they provide a permanent historical and genealogical resource that captures the voices of the community's elderly residents. Additional bound copies in the IUS library will provide an educational resource to students long after those who had firsthand knowledge of the impact of the depression and World War II on southern Indiana have passed away.

But the project also succeeds in bringing the community together. We depend on ongoing community support, including a mutually enriching partnership with the local historical society. In addition, in collaboration with community groups (and more recently at their invitation), the student assistants and I have organized and spoken at a series of public forums and meetings. These events are a critical part of the project's work, serving multiple functions: educating local people about the project and the community's history; recruiting prospective narrators; and giving both interviewees and students an opportunity to speak in their own voices about the project and their community's history. Indeed, since the project's inception, thirty public events have taken place; the largest, on November 10, 1999, attracted over three hundred community members, grade school and university students, and faculty to IUS. At such events I briefly describe the project, but students and narrators dominate the bulk of the time. The students speak about their experience with the project, and the narrators get another opportunity to tell their stories.

The public meetings have generated strong enthusiasm within the community for the project. Community members seem genuinely pleased with the project's efforts to preserve the region's history and with the interest in the past it has generated among students. As one attendee at a public meeting noted, the oral history project is important because "so much of our history, culture, and traditions will be lost otherwise. Big plus—the project obviously filled your students with interest and enthusiasm plus a new understanding and appreciation for the previous generations."

Can this type of project be duplicated elsewhere? I think so. An institution can benefit tremendously from a community-oriented project. It links the university and the community in partnership while providing new learning opportunities for students, and it increases community and student awareness of the importance of the study of history. The project demonstrates how good things happen when historians broaden their mandate, seeing the university as an integral part of the community in which it functions and using the resources of the institution to benefit not only its students but also the host community. The learning involved in such community-oriented projects is manifold and takes place at multiple levels: incoming freshmen gain a better understanding of the links between classroom and community and an enhanced sense of civic involvement; more advanced students gain concrete experience as teachers and public historians; interested local people learn about both oral history practice and their own community's history; and the historian learns what it means to practice a truly engaged scholarship.[4]

Notes

1. Barbara Jacoby et al., *Service-Learning in Higher Education: Concepts and Practices* (San Francisco, 1996). For the classic statement of the need for an academic scholarship that is engaged with the community, see Ernest L. Boyer, "The Scholarship of Engagement," *Journal of Public Service and Outreach* 1 (Spring 1996): 11–20. See also Carol W. Kinsley and Kate McPherson, *Enriching the Curriculum through Service Learning* (Alexandria, Va., 1995); and David D. Cooper, ed., *Trying the Ties That Bind: Essays on Service-Learning and the Moral Life of Faculty* (Kalamazoo, Mich., 2000). On integrating community-oriented research into the discipline of history, see Ira Harkavy and Bill M. Donovan, eds., *Connecting Past and Present: Concepts and Models for Service-Learning in History* (Washington, D.C., 2000).

2. See, for example, Patrick Hagopian, "Voices from Vietnam: Veterans' Oral Histories in the Classroom," *Journal of American History* 87 (Sept. 2000): 593–601; Pattie Dillon, "Teaching the Past through Oral History," *Journal of American History* 87 (Sept. 2000): 602–5; Donald A. Ritchie, *Doing Oral History* (New York, 1994), 177–83; Marjorie McClellan, "Case Studies in Oral History and Community Learning," *Oral History Review* 25 (Summer/Fall 1998): 8–112; John Forrest and Elisabeth Jackson, "Get Real: Empowering the Student through Oral History," *Oral History Review* 18 (Spring 1990): 29–44; Jean M. Humez and Laurie Crumpacker, "Oral History in Teaching Women's Studies," *Oral History Review* 7 (1979): 53–69; Michael H. Ebner, "Students as Oral Historians," *History*

Teacher 9 (Feb. 1976): 196–201; Robert D. Ilisevich, "Oral History in Undergraduate Research," *History Teacher* 6 (Nov. 1972): 47–50; James Hoopes, *Oral History: An Introduction for Students* (Chapel Hill, N.C., 1979); Van Hastings Garner, *Oral History: A New Experience in Learning* (Dayton, Ohio, 1975); and Charles T. Morrisey, "Oral History as a Classroom Tool," *Social Educator* 32 (Oct. 1968): 546–49.

    3. Student assistants receive small stipends for their work. To pay for these, the project has obtained generous support from the Indiana Campus Compact, the Indiana Humanities Council, and the Kentucky African-American Heritage Commission. Such outside funds have been essential to the project's operation, but its long-term success requires annual institutional support, a commitment still under negotiation with Indiana University Southeast.

    4. After the departure of Professor Crothers from Indiana University Southeast, the project described in this article was discontinued. Transcripts and interviews have been retained in the IUS library.

Cecilia Aros Hunter and Leslie Gene Hunter

La Castaña Project: A History Field Laboratory Experience

Our project, La Castaña, demonstrates the possibilities for teaching outside the box that emerge when an archivist and a history professor join forces to introduce survey-level students to historical research and the excitement of original and primary sources. Our team—Cecilia Aros Hunter, an archivist, and Leslie Gene Hunter, a historian—structured a laboratory experience in which students became discoverers and detectives, joining us in searching trunks, attics, garages, and other family storage areas for documents that will illuminate the history and culture of the peoples of the deep south Texas region in which our university is located.

Our collaboration takes place at Texas A&M University-Kingsville, about ninety miles from the Mexican border and about fifteen miles inland from the Gulf coast, between Brownsville and Corpus Christi, Texas. The university is the oldest in the area, and for seventy-five years it has served a bilingual and multicultural student body that tends to be from small towns and agricultural communities. The students have spent their lives on large ranches and small farms. Although the area is inhabited primarily by people of Mexican descent who speak Spanish, other ethnic communities exist where English is not the primary language; thus the area is both bilingual and multicultural. Recognizing this unique heritage, we named our venture La Castaña, Spanish for "the trunk." Our project has both a pedagogical objective and a specific content goal—helping preserve local history. The two come together when our students realize that history is not something remote, dealing only with people in distant places and ancient times. Rather, we seek to make history immediate and relevant by showing students the drama of the lives of men and women in their local area. By promoting a concept of the archives as a laboratory, we bring students to an understanding of how history is determined, researched, written, and preserved. Students realize that they are making history and are the results of history.

At first we asked our students to focus on locating information about the Mexican and Mexican American communities. We maintained that despite the

Journal of American History 88 (2002): 1456–61.

growing interest in Hispanics, who were quickly becoming the largest minority group in the United States, not enough documents have been collected to report the history of the group accurately, and especially the history of Mexican immigrants into Texas. Although there is a strong community of Tejanos (people of Mexican descent who were in Texas before 1848, when they became Americans as part of the spoils of war), an even larger group of newer immigrants jealously guard their documents. They fear that those documents may be their only link with the past or that their history will not be highly regarded and cared for by archives that have traditionally been Anglo establishments. In time we came to appreciate that other communities had immigrated into the area in the early twentieth century after the discovery of artesian water and the development of irrigation made farming as important to the economy as ranching had been.

We thus expanded our project to ask students to find documents reflecting any ethnic cultural experience, rural or urban, in south Texas. We believed that the youth and enthusiasm of our students could inspire their relatives to seek the needed documents and perhaps to donate them to an archive or to allow us to copy them, thus creating collections that would enrich not only local history but also the larger historical narrative. We do not ask students to seek public documents in courthouses or other governmental agencies, nor do we stress oral history. Our project asks students to locate documents in private possession before they fade, are destroyed or damaged, or disappear. We are careful to explain the difficulty of preserving paper in a hostile environment. South Texas is located near the water and is thus hot and humid, the home of many insects, rodents, and pests who enjoy destroying old paper.

We frame our student laboratory exercise as an alternative to a traditional term paper or book review. In preparation for the assignment, the archivist visits the class to explain the types of materials that are generally collected and the methods by which they are preserved and stored. Students learn that archivists catalog and categorize the information needed by historians, and they discover how historians, following the protocols of archival search strategies, depend upon archives for materials that allow them to find, analyze, interpret, and write about historical facts.

The project requires students to:

1. Locate information about a cultural or historical resource in their home areas or the area of the school.
2. Prepare a survey cover sheet, composed by the historian and archivist, that is included with the assignment. The survey sheet (a copy appears at the end of this essay) includes the name of the potential donor, an address, a map to help locate the donor if his or her residence is rural, and an inventory of the materials located. We ask students to introduce the idea of donating the documents to the South Texas Archives and Special Collections at Texas A&M University–Kingsville, and thus the survey form asks if the owners of documents might be interested in donating them or allowing them to be copied for preservation and research.

3. Write a five-to-seven-page paper evaluating the documents and explaining the significance they might have to future researchers. The student analyzes what the documents may show scholars and the general public about the local Anglo, black, Hispanic, or other cultural community, culture, and way of life. The student then suggests why the items should be included in the collection at the archives.

We do not ask students to "collect" the documents they use, but only to locate them. We emphasize that students should not take physical possession of any documents; they should not remove them from their owners, even to photocopy or to bring them to class. Removing documents, we explain, might hinder the establishment of provenance, the critical archival procedure for determining the creator of a document and the custodians of the document up to the point of archival deposit. They learn that archives establish the authenticity of documents through such procedures, and that a historian relies on the archivist to establish validity.

We remind our students that history is not just about the rich and famous, or infamous. It is also about the everyday happenings of everyday people and the occurrences that explain the contributions of Anglo, African American, Mexican American, and other communities in their local area. In seeking materials, students are urged to think historically about the types of information that will help scholars describe that area. We particularly ask them to seek documents in the following categories:

1. Personal papers and family documents, including correspondence, diaries, and notes.
2. Business documents, including records, bills, tax receipts, banking information, records from ranching and farming activities, and related materials.
3. Newspapers, especially locally created foreign-language newspapers that keep alive the written literary heritage of the culture.
4. Political activity documents, including speeches, records of organizations, flyers, and other pertinent documents. Of special interest would be records of the activities of local ethnic and racial community organizations.
5. Church and religious items and documents, including the records of auxiliary church organizations.
6. Items related to law enforcement.
7. Military documents and items related to military service.
8. Written works that record oral literature, folklore, songs (*corridos*), and traditional medicine.
9. Works of art, including paintings, sculpture, and ceramics.
10. Documents relating to athletics and recreational pursuits.
11. Photographs of activities, dwellings, events, and community leaders.
12. Documents and other items related to educational activities, including certificates, diplomas, grade cards, reports, significant assignments, and items showing the levels of education of the community or reflecting the work of teachers.

13. Immigration documents and items about the immigrant experience.
14. Climatic information that might indicate changes in history due to such events as the huge hurricanes that have destroyed the area or droughts that have devastated the agricultural communities.
15. Documentation of professional activities, especially concerning law, medicine, dentistry, pharmacy, and other professions.

Our students have made remarkable finds since we began our project in 1993. One located eighteen love letters written in Spanish in the local community during the 1930s. At that time south Texas took in many immigrants fleeing the turmoil resulting from the Mexican Revolution of 1910, some of whom were young men still actively involved in revolutionary groups. The authors were an activist young man and the young woman that he was eager to marry. The letters reveal the traditional culture in which they lived: Although the young woman was eager to marry her suitor, she met resistance from her family, which adamantly opposed the marriage for two reasons. Family members were upset by the man's sympathy with the policies and ideas of the Mexican Revolution. They were even more opposed to the marriage because he was not a Roman Catholic. Because she could not gain her parents' approval, the young lady did not feel she could marry the young man. He sent the customary intermediary to try to persuade the parents, but the marriage seemed almost impossible. The woman was hesitantly willing to leave her parents, siblings, and the other members of her extended family. Ultimately, approval was given and the couple married, but the family disowned the young woman. This rich correspondence vividly illustrates the persistence of the area's traditional culture, which bound even these lovers to its standards and mores. Through the letters, this student explored how a major event, the Mexican Revolution of 1910, affected an ordinary person in a seemingly very distant era. The student was profoundly moved because her forebears wrote the love letters.

Another student found hidden away a bound volume of the local high school's student newspaper, including issues published one week before and the month after the bombing of Pearl Harbor in 1941. Following the U.S. entry into World War II, the school newspaper reported the chagrin of students whose fathers, brothers, and friends were being sent to fight in a distant land. The newspaper reported how students prepared to do their part for the war effort. Students were involved in a great historical event. In reporting local reaction, the school newspaper is an illuminating primary source.

When one student asked if her family had anything she could use for the project, her mother looked at her with confusion. When she fully explained the purpose of the project, her mother gave her a pile of photographs and other family items. The student later reported with wonder "the multitude of things that can really be learned from South Texas in such a small chunk of history." She found framed photographs of great-grandparents, showing their activities, their style of dress, and the changes in the appearance of their surroundings. Yet another student found over two hundred letters long forgotten in an old cedar chest given to her grandmother when she graduated from high school. The letters, from her grandfather to her grandmother, began in 1938 and continued through World War II. Tied with old silk ribbons, they had not been touched for over fifty years. The student learned about affection, fear, turmoil, and the uncertainty with which they faced the war. She had not previously even known about her family's involvement in World War II.

Another student thrilled to the "great treasure" discovered in her family's trunk—her great-grandmother's journals, begun in 1918 when she was only eight years old. Written in Spanish, they described the hardships the family had to endure because of the Mexican Revolution, which led the family to move to south Texas.

The documentation for most of the projects does not come to the archives immediately, nor do the possessors generally allow them to be copied, but they are located and appreciated by the students, who learn about their own proud and rich history. Some of the documents arrive at the archives years later when the student who did the original paper inherits them.

On one level, this project results in the use of higher-order thinking skills, including analysis, synthesis, and evaluation; it requires students to examine documents and to determine if they are historically significant by considering the circumstances surrounding their production and by drawing on an understanding of the era. On another level, students who handle documents from the past come to relate to history as "real." They come away with a better understanding of their own history and the history of the area in which they live.

Admittedly, this project posed some challenges for students who did not hail from the local area and thus were too far from their homes easily to ask grandparents or other older relatives for the information they sought. We urged these students to talk to people in senior citizens' establishments, both live-in facilities and those that simply serve the elderly. Social services administrators, ministers, priests, and social workers also helped direct us to elderly people who might have treasure troves of documents. Thus, we believe that our project, La Castaña, can be undertaken in any community, preserving history, connecting students to history, and facilitating the collaboration of archivists and historians.

Appendix: Survey Sheet

La Castaña

A Survey of Historical and Cultural Resources of South Texas

1. Name of potential donor _____

2. Address _____

   City/State/ZIP _____

   Phone _____

   If the address is in a rural area, please include a map showing how to get there.

3. Inventory of items. Include dates; amounts/numbers; conditions. (Attach additional sheets if needed.)

4. If items cannot be donated, can they be copied and the copies stored by the South Texas Archives? If so, what restrictions would be placed on them?

5. What restrictions would be placed on any of the items if they are donated?

6. Is the owner of the documents/items willing to donate them to the South Texas Archives?

   Yes   No

   If yes, when? _____

7. Student's name _____

   Address _____

   City/State/ZIP _____

   Phone _____

Catherine Badura Oglesby

Re-Visioning Women's History through Service Learning

Teaching women's history in southwest Georgia, I commonly hear statements such as "I didn't even know they *had* a history," and "So, do you also teach men's history?" So I have embraced the risk of "teaching outside the box," chancing that it is a risk worth taking. My academic institution, Valdosta State University, fifteen miles north of the Georgia-Florida state line, has a student body of just under nine thousand; 75 percent are white, 21 percent African American, and 4 percent "other." The school serves primarily a forty-one-county area of south Georgia, an area known for diverse pecan types but not for much cultural diversity. A small Asian and Hispanic population barely challenges an ingrained perception that people, issues, and history are largely black and white. Many students see any course prefaced by "women" as either too radical (so they react), or not "real" history (so they do not have to take it seriously). My courses in women's history include rigorous reading and writing assignments that exceed the local norm and disabuse them of the latter attitude. Service work often disarms the former and opens students to learning some of the lessons of history.

For the past four years students in two of my U.S. women's history courses — a course on women activists and a survey from 1869 to the present — have had the option of working fifteen to twenty hours in one of several community agencies that serve, and are directed by, women. Students who choose the service option conclude by writing a paper relating the service to course objectives, the readings, and other topics covered in lectures and class discussions. The alternative to service work is a lengthy, more traditional research paper. Not surprisingly, most students choose service work.

In my approach, service does not replace reading and writing about the historical subject, and I am not suggesting that service is equally valuable in all courses, for all fields, or for all students. Nonetheless, where I have used it (after all, women's history was born "outside the box"), I have found it particularly effective at collapsing the cultural barriers that create "us" and "them" thinking. The service projects are carefully designed to push students to think critically about the ways time, place, and circumstance have intersected to shape women.

Journal of American History 88 (2002): 1431–35.

By linking praxis and theory through experience, service can be especially effective in the discipline of history.

Moreover, the service component I create differs fundamentally from the community service students carry out as members of sororities or fraternities. Students who have had both experiences quickly surmise the difference and often mention it in class or in writing. Among other substantive differences, service required for course work generally leads to direct contact with the dispossessed. Students report that sororities generally screen them from direct interaction. The goal of including service as course work is to educate and transform the student and, by inference, society; the goal in other settings is most frequently charity.

Service projects require a number of set conditions to succeed, in particular, good working relationships between academic faculty and the directors and staff of the chosen agencies. Although my first commitment is to students' learning experience, the projects have to be mutually beneficial to student and agency and, on the larger scale, to the university and the community. Such goals have never been exclusive of each other, but they are not always easy to negotiate. The most common difficulty is balancing the overworked schedules of everyone involved: students (most of whom have jobs in addition to school), agency staff, directors, and faculty. Volunteer coordinators within the agencies help, but not all agencies have coordinators.

Experience has led me to channel most of my students into two agencies: the Haven, a shelter for victims of domestic violence, and New Horizons, a homeless shelter for women and children. The directors of those agencies have helped design the projects for students to satisfy research criteria for course requirements as well as to meet the agencies' needs. For example, one year students working for the Haven surveyed the local newspaper over the past decade to collect articles on cases of domestic violence. Other students researched the different ways social institutions—the criminal justice system, schools, churches, etc.—work together to secure justice for victims of domestic violence. The Haven used the information to help write a sizable grant proposal for public education, which, according to the director, was successful largely due to research contributed by students. Students combing the newspapers learned a great deal about local attitudes toward domestic violence from the location of the articles in the newspaper (back pages) and from the language used to report the incidents. They learned that the social class and race of the victims shaped reporting of the cases and saw how women are doubly victimized when local institutions fail to work together.

The historicizing of such lessons occurs both explicitly and implicitly. First and foremost, course readings are historically focused. Beginning each course with excerpts from familiar historical documents and returning to them frequently as reference points also keeps the class historically situated. Students ponder the time-sensitive meanings of concepts referred to in the Declaration of Independence, the Constitution, and the very familiar Pledge of Allegiance: ideas such as "self-evident truths," "unalienable rights," "general welfare," and "liberty and justice for all." We discuss what those concepts probably meant to the authors, but also how they have been interpreted and appropriated locally and globally ever since. After thinking about what the concepts mean to them personally and what they have meant collectively to any number of peoples, students then wrestle with how they might be interpreted by particular people with whom they work in the shelters—people most of the students had, until then, only vaguely known existed.

When the semester topic for my course on women activists is the historical roots of poverty among women (the specific focus varies each term), students read about the history of social welfare policy and the evolution of attitudes toward poverty since the colonial era. Work at the local homeless shelter makes such reading more meaningful. Students explore how attitudes toward the poor have both changed and remained the same. Also, working with women and children at the shelter helps them think more critically about "welfare reform," stereotypes of welfare recipients, and arguments about welfare's alleged failure.

Several students, black middle-class women and men especially, confronted deep-seated misgivings they had about welfare recipients. Some of the women not only had spent a good deal of energy distancing themselves from the image of the stereotypical "welfare queen," but also had bought into this image and been a part of the chorus of disapproval. After reading about how the female archetypes Jezebel, Mammy, and Sapphire have been used over time to identify, characterize, and oppress black women, and after working at shelters where chronically poor women, black and white, as well as formerly mainstream middle-class women share residence, students' attitudes change dramatically. Historic context provides a missing link. With their new perspective, students reevaluate the degree of personal responsibility for the plight of each individual woman, generally acknowledging that personal history fades in relative importance compared to more comprehensive social and economic forces. In their papers students recall discussions of independence in the introductory part of the course to note now that the dispossessed women with whom they work may be seeking a measure of that coveted independence to take care of themselves and their children—not trying to find clever ways to cheat the system. Students change the focus of their concern from questioning the motive and character of the women struggling in the shelter to thinking about how attitudes and beliefs that undermine women's economic and psychological independence are built into the social structure.

In the survey course, making connections often occurs more implicitly. The readings help students understand how and why women especially are victimized by domestic violence and homelessness. Whether they work at New Horizons or at the Haven, students gain an awareness of how gender has always shaped public attitude and public policy by restricting public awareness. When students work at the Haven, they discuss the difference between the ways women handle a domestic crisis today and the ways they—victim and supporter—might have handled it a hundred years ago. After examining cases of domestic violence in different eras of the past, students compare community attitudes then and now and generally marvel at similarities between eras centuries apart. When they first begin working at the Haven, students discover the pervasiveness of domestic violence in the local community (always a shocking discovery), and then they discuss why it remains such an issue nationally. From readings they learn the historical relationship between the feminist movement and public awareness of domestic violence. After working in the shelter with women and children victims, many female and male students formerly suspicious of anything they perceived as a "feminist agenda" begin to sympathize with some of the primary concerns of feminism. Because service facilitates this sort of change in perspective, it deserves consideration as an alternative to more traditional methods of teaching and learning history.

Although I have used service successfully in my classes, I still have my doubts. It takes time and energy to make the initial community contacts and to sustain those relationships. Colleagues are often skeptical, even when they wish to be supportive. But most important, I know that service work does not serve every student's needs, and distinguishing between those whose historical awareness will be awakened best by service and those who would benefit more from the traditional research paper sometimes eludes me. Students who might fall through the cracks can be found at both ends of the learning curve. Unmotivated students threaten to strain relationships with the agencies and can reflect poorly on the university. Although scheduling is a problem for all students, it becomes a blanket excuse for the unmotivated students. Very often they are either unwilling or unable to work out a schedule with the agency at a time when they can interact with residents. Members of this small minority wind up folding clothes or shelving food and then complain because they do not "get the point." (But then, some conscientious students who do nothing more than fold clothes and shelve food make remarkable connections between their readings and their apparently inane experience.)

But my primary concern is the exceptional student. Some students already have ample experience working in the community; others have sufficient critical thinking skills and abundant empathy for "others" across culture and time. For the former, lessons of service and awareness of the value of diversity are a way of life; for the latter, an appreciation for historical lessons and the value of understanding change over time is already well developed. In the few cases in which students are already active in the community, or in which I judge that the student will benefit more from a traditional research paper, I strongly encourage the latter.

Here, I think of Ann, an especially gifted and highly motivated history major who wanted to do both the service and the traditional research paper. Initially (against my caution), she worked out such a plan but then had to decide between the assignments. During the semester, she reluctantly gave up work at the Haven to devote her time to a paper on the implications of the historiographical debate on the Supreme Court case *Muller v. Oregon* (1908).[1] At the end of the course, she turned in one of the most impassioned and cogently argued research papers I (or some of my colleagues) had ever read. Granted, for this student, a service assignment very likely would have resulted in its own eloquent insights. But she and I might have missed the opportunity this research paper provided—for her an experience that motivated her toward graduate school, and for me the best student paper I have read to date.

That Ann wrote on *Muller v. Oregon* only makes my dilemma more poignant. This historic case and the story surrounding it reveal the nuance, paradox, complexity, and contradictions found in history. Moreover, the case also teaches as well as any single subject why leaving gender out of the analysis eliminates more than merely half the picture. But in roughly ten years of teaching *Muller* expressly to drive home all those salient points, I have never been convinced that even one student completely "got it"—until Ann. By comparison, more students have learned something of this lesson in a visceral way through service. Such a practice cannot be an abuse of the discipline of history if it is our aim to reach more than a handful of students in our careers. When keeping that aim in focus, I struggle less with concerns that tend to divide the mind over whether or not to venture "outside the box" when teaching women's history.

Note

1. *Muller v. Oregon*, 208 U.S. 412 (1908).

Alyssa Picard and Joseph J. Gonzalez

On the Road and out of the Box: Teaching the Civil Rights Movement from a Chrysler Minivan

Each trip had its "moments." In March 2000, we heard Mamie Till describe why she had demanded an open casket for her son Emmett, lynched in 1955: "So that everyone could see what they did to my boy." In 2001, Julian Bond read his student poetry, and John Lewis described how he and Bond resurrected their friendship after both ran for the same congressional seat in 1986. In the Mississippi Delta, the lawyer Jaribu Hill explained why she defends the rights of the poor, rejecting a lucrative private practice: "What do I have to worry about? Some of my clients don't have indoor plumbing, or even front doors."

Each trip had its "moments"—but such moments do not come cheap. In order to appreciate them, we had to implement two experiential learning courses on the civil rights movement, connect with an activist community, and balance academic and experiential learning while writing our dissertations. The effort was worth it. Our first trip, during spring break 2000, was a success, and the second, during spring break 2001, was even better. This year, we will be on the road again, eating fast food, evading speeding tickets, and searching for moments of clarity.

Joseph J. Gonzalez

Why I "Wasted" My Spring Breaks Teaching

> "Our spring break is almost over . . . and we wasted it learning."
> — Jeb Singer, spring break 2000

I "wasted" two spring breaks teaching, and I could not be more satisfied. I had to do it. Years into my doctoral studies, I had taught several writing courses at the University of Michigan. I enjoyed teaching and my students but felt frustrated. Though charming and competent, my students seemed passive, more like guests than participants, learning only enough to write their essays. Their learning—and my teaching—stopped at the classroom door.

Fortunately, I found the Lloyd Hall Scholars Program (LHSP) in 1999. LHSP is a residential learning community at the University of Michigan. Know-

Journal of American History 88 (2002): 1461–67.

ing that its director, Professor David Potter, encourages innovative teaching, I proposed to lead a historical tour of the civil rights movement. The request surprised us both. My knowledge of the civil rights movement rested on a few books hurriedly read for preliminary exams. I knew no one in the movement and had never taught an experiential course, though Douglas Brinkley's *The Majic Bus* provided an inspiring example. But I knew that my students needed to connect their experience with the process of historical change. The civil rights movement, many of its leaders still active and its sites still preserved, seemed ideal for this purpose. In addition, the movement presented a story of heroic struggle and ambiguous results, the legacy of which my students confront every day.[1]

David agreed, and I began planning a one-credit trip for spring break, aided by my wife, Teresa Buckwalter, a graduate student in landscape architecture and teacher in LHSP, and Alyssa Picard, a fellow doctoral candidate in history and teacher in LHSP whose experiments in democratic pedagogy had inspired me. Wanting to emphasize experience, I assigned no reading and adopted a "run and gun" method of lecturing during the trip: "Here's where we are, and here's what happened." Hoping to encourage participation, I asked the students to decide our itinerary and some of our policies.

On February 26, 2000, we left Ann Arbor with nine students. We visited Atlanta, Birmingham, Montgomery, Selma, and Memphis. The trip's high point came at its end, as Mamie Till spoke in front of the Civil Rights Memorial in Montgomery. Then we sang "We Shall Overcome" arm-in-arm with Coretta Scott King and Rep. John Lewis, former chair of the Student Nonviolent Coordinating Committee, who was leading his own civil rights tour that day.[2]

Our students returned tired but energized. Having seen the movement, they wanted to make the movement part of their lives. Four of them formed an organization to promote understanding between Jews and African Americans on campus, while others joined established activist groups. Just as gratifying, our students referred to the class as "our trip." Having assumed a voice in the class, they were participants, not guests.

But we made some mistakes. On the trip, we found the "run and gun" method no substitute for reading. During the trip, I also did too much administration and too little teaching. Finally, we had not seen enough people. The power of Mamie Till's story and the eloquence of John Lewis's testimony inspired me to find more people who were there. After some discussion, we decided to require the members of the next trip to take a semester-long course on the history of the movement, which I would teach. I also resolved to hire an administrative assistant and find more contacts within the civil rights community.

On February 25, 2001, we left Ann Arbor with twenty-one students; Alyssa, on a dissertation fellowship, could not join us. Nonetheless, the trip was better. Having already studied the movement in the classroom, the students understood better the people and places they saw. We met more participants, some famous, such as Julian Bond and Taylor Branch, and some not so famous, such as those who marched in Selma's "bloody Sunday" in 1965 or walked during Montgomery's 1955 bus boycott. We also met present-day activists, including lawyers

Members of the 2000 trip meet Coretta Scott King at the Dexter Avenue King Memorial Baptist Church in Montgomery, Alabama. *Photograph by Michael Simon.*

from both the Southern Poverty Law Center and the Mississippi Workers' Center for Human Rights.

Our second group arrived home as energized as our first. Two students worked for Jaribu Hill the following summer, while others moved into campus activism and internships. For my part, I was no longer the frustrated teacher. After two years of trial and error, I saw students who connected history with their own lives; their learning, and my teaching, only began in the classroom. Perhaps most important, I saw a cohort devoted to living the values of the movement. Students, I now know, are neither naturally passive nor inherently unreceptive to learning; they do, however, need to define their educations and understand historical change inside and outside the classroom. Such an approach may make for better students, but I am not sure. I only know that the civil rights trips made my students better citizens—and me a better teacher.

Alyssa Picard

Democracy Rising: What Our Students Taught Us

The greatest lesson of both the civil rights movement and our civil rights trip is that what young people do (and, therefore, what teachers do with them) *really matters*. Among the Montgomery bus boycotters, the marchers in Selma, and the freedom riders were college students, high school students, and young teachers and parents who risked their lives because they did not want their children to grow up under Jim Crow. The past happened because its makers, some of whom were just our students' age, sought to affect the future: as history teachers and conscientious historians, we are obligated to bring our knowledge of, and respect for, this fact to bear on our relationships with our students. Even when they are quiescent today, they have the potential to be powerful beyond their—and our—wildest imaginations. For me, as for many political and pedagogical progressives, helping students realize that power is one of the central purposes of teaching itself.

The trip was part of my larger experiment with democratic pedagogy, spurred by my visceral identification with John Dewey's claim that education for democracy demands active participation by students and by my reading of Ira Shor's *When Students Have Power*. Shor writes that teachers' sharing of power with students in the classroom creates "the desire and imagination of change while also creating the experience and skills for it."[3] We hoped that our travels with our students would help them to realize, through study and through experience, that social and political change are not only desirable but possible and that young people can, and have, made change happen. In Shor's and Dewey's views, such a lesson can only be taught when students share responsibility for, and authority over, their educational environments. Learning does not get any more participatory than these travel classes: for a time we resided, quite literally, where the rubber of pedagogy hits the road of social change.

Members of the 2001 trip on the front porch of the Martin Luther King Parsonage in Montgomery, Alabama. King lived there during his time in Montgomery, from 1954 to 1960. *Photograph by Brett Mountain.*

But in that first year we assumed too much of students' ability to prepare themselves intellectually independent of any guidance from us. Some of our students, particularly the ones who self-identified as political progressives, did advance reading, and I saw several dog-eared copies of the Martin Luther King reader *A Testament of Hope* circulating around the vans in which we were traveling.[4] Yet only the most motivated students had the level of knowledge we would have liked. So when we found ourselves standing across from, say, the Sixteenth Street Baptist Church in Birmingham, Alabama, where four young women were killed and twenty others injured in the Ku Klux Klan's 1963 bombing, one of us would have to launch into an explanation of what had happened there, trying—and sometimes failing—to convey both factual knowledge and the emotional responses we felt to the place.

Moreover, these sites are living places, not "anachronistic spaces."[5] Worshipers still attend services in the Sixteenth Street Church and at King's Ebenezer Baptist Church in Atlanta—and people still drive across the Edmund Pettus Bridge in Selma, where in 1965 marchers demonstrating for voting rights were attacked by Alabama state troopers wielding clubs and tear gas, every day.[6] We did not want the people who lived in the places we visited to feel that we were treating their hometowns like living history museums—especially because our students were mostly white northerners, with all the historical baggage that entails. But in locations designed for commemoration, we felt more comfortable reflecting on local history: on the fly, we downloaded a copy of King's "I've Been to the Mountaintop" speech, which he delivered for the last time to Memphis sanitation workers the night before he was assassinated, and read it, round-robin fashion, in the parking lot of the Lorraine Motel, where he was killed (and where the National Civil Rights Memorial Museum now stands). The moment underlined the tragedy of King's assassination, the power of his literary and oratorical gift, and the complexity of commemoration all in one fell swoop.[7]

I was glad when Joe nestled the trip into a semester-long course, and I am looking forward to teaching the class myself in 2002 as a co-requisite for the spring break trip. My version of the class will explore how the writing of history relates to the making of it: students will spend a lot of time learning how to read and evaluate primary source documents, will meet and ask questions of the historians who have documented the movement, and will consider the ways in which civil rights commemorations (monuments, museums, and other cultural productions) construct conflicting narratives of the origins, course, and fate of the movement. I will also focus on the centrality of religion to the civil rights movement. During the 2000 trip, we had some memorable exchanges about faith, one of which took place when a student who professed to admire King and wanted to follow in his footsteps dismissed the contemporary religious faith of one of her born-again classmates as "Bible crap." Then, on our last night in Montgomery, the commemoration of the Selma-Montgomery march coincided with the Southern Cultural Independence Heritage Festival being held by several thousand Confederate-flag-toting Rebels on the lawn of the Alabama state house. At our motel, one of the students reported having seen a man carrying an armful of small Confederate flags on sticks and a set of white satin robes into the room next to his. Some students immediately started strategizing about soaping the man's truck windows, letting the air out of his tires so he could not make it to the rally, and other acts of vandalism they could commit to let him know that his politics were unacceptable to them. It was clear to me that the students had not realized the centrality of Christianity to King's program or of nonviolence and love to his religious teaching.

Conclusion: What the Teachers Learned

Our methods and our pedagogy worked well for our course, but they might be used to study many other geographic, social, and political movements in their geographic contexts—the Great Migration, the Trail of Tears, the twentieth-century labor movement.[8] One of the strengths of travel courses is that they preclude the construction of triumphal narratives of days gone by: in every location, and in every application, contemporary travel will reflect the ambiguous legacy of the past. But, perhaps more important, every travel class is indelibly marked with the imprint of the students who take it. We feel privileged to have lived and traveled with some very bright, committed, and reflective young people, and we recommend the experience highly to those who feel, as we do, that the past and the future are profitably brought into contact in the present.

Notes

1. Douglas Brinkley, *The Majic Bus: An American Odyssey* (New York, 1993).

2. For more on John Lewis, see John Lewis, *Walking with the Wind: A Memoir of the Movement* (New York, 1998).

3. Ira Shor, *When Students Have Power: Negotiating Authority in a Critical Pedagogy* (Chicago, 1996), 176.

4. Martin Luther King Jr., *A Testament of Hope: The Essential Writings and Speeches of Martin Luther King Jr.*, ed. James Melvin Washington (San Francisco, 1991).

5. Anne McClintock, *Imperial Leather: Race, Gender, and Sexuality in the Colonial Contest* (New York, 1995), 30.

6. Our students were fortunate enough to have participated in the thirty-fifth anniversary reenactment of the march during the 2000 trip. When the reenactors reached the crest of the bridge that year, they encountered lines of Alabama state troopers saluting them.

7. In Memphis, we confronted the continuing controversy surrounding the building of the National Civil Rights Memorial Museum, which epitomizes the ways in which the urge to commemorate past successes can foster complacency about ongoing problems: in spring 2000, Jacqueline Smith, a homeless black woman, stood outside the museum protesting Memphis's shortage of low-income housing. She handed out literature arguing that King would have wanted the motel converted into a place in which she and others left behind in the much-vaunted economic growth of the 1990s could have lived affordably—and she was right.

8. At Kenyon College, Peter Rutkoff and Will Scott run a two-semester Great Migration travel course; see <www.northbysouth.org/1999/flyaway/flyaway.htm>.

David A. Reichard

"Forgotten Voices and Different Memories": How Students at California State University, Monterey Bay, Became Their Own Historians

> Working on the Fort Ord Project just reinforced my attitude that we need to dig a little deeper and listen to those stories not quite heard.
> —Student evaluation, 2001

During the spring 2001 semester, twenty-seven students in "Out of Many—U.S. Histories" (HCOM 253), a lower-division course at California State University, Monterey Bay (CSUMB), researched, designed, and installed a public history exhibition titled "Forgotten Voices and Different Memories: Fort Ord from Native America to the Twentieth Century and Beyond."[1] Because CSUMB, with about twenty-seven hundred undergraduates, many of whom are commuters, was created in 1994 after the closing of the military base, this topic held particular interest for members of the class. "Ever since I have been here on Fort Ord," one student explained, "I have had many questions about the history. The fact that I was going to school on a military base was enough to pique my curiosity."[2]

"Out of Many—U.S. Histories" fulfills two University Learning Requirements (ULRs) in CSUMB's general education program. One of those ULRs, U.S. Histories, asks students to develop skills that will enable them to become their own historians. In past semesters students had completed independent research papers, collected oral histories, or written historically informed autobiographies in order to attain this outcome. During the spring 2001 semester, I wanted to explore whether public history could make the experience of "becoming your own historian" a more active and collaborative one. What happened confirmed my hope that students would deepen their appreciation of historical practices, enhance their interest in historical content, and become more engaged in their learning experience.[3] We reached back to uncover histories of indigenous people who lived (and still live) around the Monterey Bay area, learned more about the Spanish colonial and Mexican histories of Monterey, examined the origins of the U.S. Army's presence in the area, and speculated about the future. As a result, our own backyard became larger, and our understanding of what it means to interpret the past more complex. One student summed up the process many of us experienced: "We became historians digging up the untold stories of Fort Ord from the indigenous times to the present day. . . . I had never thought

Journal of American History 88 (2002): 1467–71.

much past the fact that I was living on an old army base. I never thought of the indigenous tribes that lived here even before the army bought this land. This really makes me think that there is such rich history engraved everywhere."

Course HCOM 253 encountered numerous challenges. We identified a topic by exploring a variety of ideas in seemingly chaotic brainstorming sessions. We painfully reached consensus on most, if not all, issues. We divided ourselves into working groups to make completion of the project possible in one semester. We had many difficult class discussions that highlighted differences in communication style, historical interpretation, and political positions. Research groups spent hours researching in libraries and on the Internet and interviewing former soldiers and other members of the community. We took digital images of the campus and parts of former Fort Ord. We shopped for materials, designed and constructed kiosks to display our research, wrote text, and tried to keep organized! We completed all of this work on a very tight budget.[4]

One outcome of the course was especially notable to students: discovering the politics of historical interpretation. Some students did so by learning how to evaluate source material. Because HCOM 253 maintains a multicultural focus as a whole, students expected sources for our project to provide multiple perspectives as well. When they discovered that this was not always the case, they frequently expressed regret, surprise, and sometimes anger. As a result, many students began to think more carefully about how historians choose and use source material. For example, one student noticed how difficult it was to uncover "different memories" of Fort Ord, other than those provided in official printed U.S. Army sources. Another student reported, "Doing research, I found a lot of sources that showed the military in one and only one light—a good one. I had to decide for myself if these were true portrayals of what the military experience was really like or if they were watered down to make them look good. This was something that I struggled with throughout the course of researching for this project."

Some students wondered why some histories were more visible than others in our community. As one student expressed it, "Working on this class project was actually depressing for me. I wanted to find libraries of stories of the Ohlone people, and detailed accounts of their lives. But I didn't find them, perhaps because I didn't know where to look. By all rights, they should be as well known as John Steinbeck's life, or the history of Cannery Row. They were the first humans in the Monterey area; their stories count just as much as the white man's." Such recognition had many repercussions. One student suggested that having to question the meaning of history itself was the "greatest challenge faced in the class." "I began to question [what] I had just assumed was the 'whole truth' just because I read it in some history book," the student explained. "It seems naïve now, but I really never questioned whether or not someone else might tell a different story. I figured history was history; how could it be different for any two people? But how wrong I found I was! There are so many untold stories out there, many of which I think teach us much more about human nature, people, and the world around us."

Interpreting historical sources through critical lenses led some students to become creative researchers. "How do we honor and do justice to a variety of groups from a particular period," pondered one student, "when many of those who recorded the histories that we are looking at often ignored the perceptions and experiences of many different people?" From this question, however, the student found inspiration. "One of the main challenges of the project was sifting through the standard materials for tidbits of information that tell a different story." Other students collected stories themselves as a means to overcome the limitations of printed sources. As one student explained, "Being able to research and surface the forgotten voices and different memories of Fort Ord was very important . . . [as they] are just as valuable as those written in history books." What made them most valuable to the student was that "this information was told directly by the people who lived the experiences." After having difficulty finding information about soldiers' experiences, one student concluded "that the only way I [was] going to find out about the soldiers [was] to interview people who were here and [who knew] what it was like to be on Fort Ord during its 'heyday.' This is where I found all the information I needed."

Because the class constructed a public exhibition of our research, we became even more conscious of our own political positions in representing the histories of Fort Ord. For many students, being able to tell "forgotten stories" gave them enormous satisfaction, even pride, in making a contribution to the local community. Noted one student, "We gave [the soldiers] the opportunity to speak, better late than never." Students from the local community were especially conscious of the impact of the project. "I believe that everyone had a piece of themselves displayed in this project. I feel that there was a large piece of myself [in the exhibition] . . . I gave a little back to the men and women who once lived on the land that is now our college campus." Other students drew linkages between the historical research and contemporary political issues, as the representation of the history of the Esselen nation in our exhibit illustrates. "The indigenous struggle for basic rights and recognition continues in the year 2001, and many of the stories I heard [in researching] sound very reminiscent of the issues that Native Americans have been dealing with for the past several hundred years," concluded one student. "This particular portion of the project is helping me to make connections between historical and contemporary issues, and helping me to de-compartmentalize my thinking in terms of historical times, i.e., the indigenous period isn't over!!"

Students also discovered the politics of historical interpretation in efforts to reconcile the content of the research with the design of the public exhibition. Having to collaborate with twenty-seven other people required resolving real differences of interpretation. After we had decided on the project topic, themes, and the time periods we would focus on, we spent one long class discussing the merits of using a timeline, which some students saw as a perfect format to display the research. Other students disagreed, arguing that using a timeline would reinforce the idea that we were presenting one linear history. After much discussion, we decided that multiple-sided kiosks would better reflect the nonlinear and multicultural approach we were pursuing in our research. Rather than present one history displayed as a single narrative line along the wall, we reasoned, kiosks would allow visitors to consider that what became Fort Ord had multiple and complex histories. As one student concluded, "We decided that the presentation and design of the project should reflect the importance of the information. The design needed to have depth, have color, have shapes, layers . . . it needed to reflect the history we were portraying."

At the end of the semester, we installed the final product in the University Center on campus. We arranged three four-sided kiosks around the space, using two walls in the corner for additional displays. Each kiosk highlighted select themes we had identified from our research—"Environment," "Faces," and "Stories & Memories." The theme of "Environment" explored the intersections of humans with other living beings and how those intersections had shaped the landscape. "Faces" gave visitors a glimpse of the people from different cultural backgrounds who had inhabited this land. "Stories & Memories" highlighted written and oral histories of life at what became Fort Ord. We examined each theme over four main periods of time—"Indigenous Histories," "Spanish Colonial and Mexican Periods," "Fort Ord—Heyday," and "Fort Ord—The Future." "Indigenous Histories" explored the histories of Native Americans who lived and continue to live in the region. The "Spanish Colonial and Mexican Period" examined the period between Spanish colonization along the Monterey Bay through Monterey's brief role as the Mexican capital of California. "Fort Ord—Heyday" included text and images about life at Fort Ord and in the surrounding communities during its heyday as an active military installation. Finally, "Fort Ord—The Future" explored what was planned for the former Fort Ord in the years ahead. Thus, each thematic panel gave the visitor perspectives on that theme over four different periods of time. On one wall, we displayed images and text describing "Fort Ord—The Soldiers' Experience," drawn mostly from official U.S. Army sources. On an opposing wall, we displayed examples of underground newspapers created by soldiers on Fort Ord during the war in Vietnam. Headlines such as "Ft. Ord Organizes!," "GI Shot in Escape Attempt," and "Bring the Troops Home Now!" provided a contrast with the official materials on the opposite wall.

As I observed the students meandering through the exhibit after we had completed set-up, I could tell they were proud of what they had accomplished. Most students agreed that the project had allowed them to "become their own historians." Learning that interpreting history is political, collaboration is difficult, and such a project is possible were invaluable lessons for all of us. Moreover, student enthusiasm for what they created was apparent. "The entire process was tedious, fun, exciting, time-consuming, educational, and definitely a learning experience all rolled into one project," noted one student, "along the way I wondered if we would ever get it done. However, the final result was gorgeous! When I came into the University Center to view the whole project during our reception, I was amazed at what we, as a class, and what I, myself, had accomplished. What a wonderful way to share with our school and the community what we learned about the different stories about this piece of land called Fort Ord." As another student concluded in a reflection paper, "I am thankful for the opportunity to have taken this class and to have gone through this learning process with the group. My interest in group work, as well as social history, has been rekindled, and I plan to spend a part of the rest of my life learning from these kind of experiences." Now that's an outcome!

Notes

1. This article is based on a course I offered while I was a lecturer at California State University, Monterey Bay. I would like to recognize the students of HCOM 253 for their untiring efforts on this project. The Institute for Human Communication provided essential funding for the exhibit. An action research grant from the Center for Teaching, Learning, and Assessment at CSUMB and the CSU chancellor's office supported research for this article. An interdisciplinary teaching cooperative of CSUMB faculty that met during the spring 2001 semester nourished the experience—many thanks!

2. Student self-assessment, spring 2001 (in David A. Reichard's possession). With students' permission, I use examples from student reflection papers and other documentation that students produced during the semester. On the conversion from military base to university campus, see California Postsecondary Education Commission, *Creating a Campus for the Twenty-First Century: The California State University and Fort Ord* (Sacramento, 1993).

3. For the text of the U.S. Histories ULR, see <http://CSUMB.edu/academic/ulr/ulr/ushistories.html> (Dec. 7, 2001).

4. Working groups included an administrative group (to find a venue, create a budget, advertise the event, assist in managing the project), two research groups (Indigenous, Spanish, and Mexican periods group and a Fort Ord group), and a design group (to devise how we would present the project to the public, provide technical assistance to the research groups, scan images for presentation, and construct the final product). Collaboration and consensus building were key elements of what made this project ultimately work.

Kathryn Kish Sklar

Teaching Students to Become Producers of New Historical Knowledge on the Web

Historians do a relatively poor job of explaining their work process to others. Perhaps this and the ahistorical bent of our culture explain why my undergraduate students—even history majors—know astonishingly little about historical methods. Too many students think the study of the past consists of reading secondary works and reporting on them. At most they might evaluate a few primary sources. Yet the exceptions to this rule—students who write honors theses—show that undergraduates are capable of more serious work. We can coax them out of the box to become producers of new historical knowledge.

In 1997, in an undergraduate seminar for history majors at the State University of New York, Binghamton, I began a project that rewarded students' efforts with publication of their term projects on the course Web site. Binghamton, one of four university centers in the SUNY (State University of New York) system, attracts a very diverse and highly motivated population of students, primarily from New York City. Partly because we have a strong graduate program in U.S. women's history, we also offer an array of undergraduate courses in U.S. women's history. Focusing on "women and social movements in the U.S.," this seminar had no prerequisites and included nonmajors as well as majors. Students in this and subsequent seminars came to see how their course projects could open exciting new windows onto American history for high school and college students. It is a lot of work—for them and for me—but by becoming historical practitioners themselves my seminar students have gained a much more complete understanding of how historians work. In the process they have also acquired useful skills that help them evaluate information, interpret evidence, and construct arguments.

Do not let the technology scare you; college teachers do not need to be Web wonks to do this. I was not yet on e-mail when I began using Web-based technology in that seminar in January 1997. My conversion to the new order occurred during the first week of class, when I attended a funding panel at the Library of Congress. Meeting with librarians, professors, and teachers of kindergarten through twelfth grade classes, I found myself in the company of colleagues who were creating the vanguard of history Web technology—Ed Ayers of

Journal of American History (2002): 1471–76.

the University of Virginia, Roy Rosenzweig of George Mason University, and John McClymer of Assumption College. I noticed that U.S. women's history was dramatically underrepresented among the submitted proposals and realized that this absence symbolized a growing gender digital divide in U.S. history on the Web. There I also learned from high school teachers that what they needed most from the Web were sites where information was focused in such a way as to permit students to learn something significant in an hour. Browsing the Web might be a way of life for many students, but learning meaningful history is rarely achieved by simple and undirected Web browsing. This made me wonder how the need for pedagogically effective resources in U.S. history could be met by women's history materials, a strategy that would simultaneously address the needs of U.S. history teachers and the gender digital divide.

Returning to my senior seminar, where I had organized a number of likely research topics for students based on microfilm sources, I offered students the alternative of creating document-based projects for the World Wide Web (www). Every student chose the new alternative. The shift from using microfilm for research papers to using microfilm for document-based editorial projects for the Web was easier than I could ever have imagined. Web technology is a perfect match for teaching about history because it permits us to democratize the availability and analysis of documents. The technology boosts our capacities as teachers by giving our students a front-row view of the documentary record of historical change. Moreover, it allows us to teach students how professional historians work with such records. This happy conjuncture of new technology with the possibilities of the history classroom has enormous potential for improving the way we teach history. But to develop that potential we need to design effective models for the classroom use of the new technology.

The model I developed in the spring of 1997 and continue to employ has three features. First, it treats students as the producers of new historical knowledge by requiring them to produce a project containing new historical knowledge. Second, it prescribes a very specific form that the projects must follow, a form that facilitates Web-based learning by offering historical knowledge in units that can be explored in an hour's time. Third, it helps students place their projects on the course Web site, where others can learn from their work.

The course is divided into three parts that reflect these three components. Gradually the course propels students "outside the box." First, each student selects a topic, explores related secondary literature, frames a new question, and locates primary sources that will address the question. Second, the student selects around twenty documents that address the question, writes headnotes for each document, and writes a short interpretive introduction for the whole project. Third, the student transcribes the documents and mounts them with interpretive comments on the course Web site.

Students' final projects are therefore pedagogic units that pose central interpretive questions and provide about twenty primary documents that address each question. Each project also includes footnotes to the introductory materials, annotations of the primary documents, a bibliography, and a list of related Web links.

"Arresting the Girl Strikers for Picketing." *Reprinted from the* International Socialist Review, *Jan. 1910. Part of an editorial project by Deirdre Doherty, State University of New York at Binghamton, May 1998.*

To guide students through this demanding course I have relied on the able assistance of Dr. Melissa Doak, a recent Binghamton Ph.D. in U.S. women's history, who has developed an effective course Web site, <http://bingweb.binghamton.edu/~hist465>. To produce new historical knowledge students learn about a wide array of methodological issues, most of which we discuss on the course Web site under "project guides." There we offer guidance on such matters as:

- learning the distinction between primary and secondary sources;
- compiling a bibliography of secondary sources and developing a perspective on historiography;
- learning what constitutes authoritative information (especially on the www);
- locating and selecting documents for inclusion in the project;
- considering editorial practices to be employed in the transcription process;
- writing headnotes;
- citing documents and secondary sources properly; and
- writing an interpretive introduction for the documents as a whole.

The course Web site also offers html (hypertext markup language) tutorials written by Dr. Doak.

Our course meets once a week for three hours. Classroom discussions focus on the week's assignment: how to frame a historiographically derived question; how to locate documents capable of addressing one's question; how to evaluate and interpret documents; how to create a story from a group of documents; how to search for appropriate images to illustrate one's project; etc. Throughout the course we schedule frequent individual tutorials to discuss students' progress and problems. Early in the course students acquire peer review partners with whom they discuss their work each week.

At the end of the semester, we invite university administrators, librarians, and history faculty to attend the final meeting of the class where students give oral reports on their work and display the products of their labors with large-screen projection facilities. This event rewards the extra effort that most students have put into their course projects. It also reinforces their identity as producers of historical knowledge.

I help with the first stage of the course by preparing page-long descriptions of possible topics, with suggested questions, secondary bibliography, and micro-film sources. Some students prefer to work more independently at this stage, but typically students use these descriptions to launch their projects. My reward for

Jennifer Burns (left) and Gretchen Becht (right), in a senior seminar taught in the collaborative classroom, Fall 1999, compare notes on their project on women's rights conventions of the 1850s. *Photograph by Kitty Sklar.*

this preparatory work is that students become engaged in their projects early enough to complete them within fifteen weeks. I also assume all responsibility for permissions, an extremely time-consuming and arcane task that they could not possibly add to their already-full plates, although I describe that work so they understand that permissions do have to be obtained.

In addition to posting their projects on the course Web site, students aspire to have their work included in the *Women and Social Movements in the United States, 1820–1940,* Web site that my Binghamton colleague Professor Thomas Dublin and I co-direct with the assistance of Melissa Doak, <www.womanhist .binghamton.edu>. That site is visited by about ten thousand visitors a month from sixty different countries. Before student work is placed on that site we revise it in ways that render it fully authoritative and professional. Yet the final products clearly reflect students' work, and we credit them as the original editors.

Although the larger Web site builds on student work, it is not an integral part of this flexible classroom model. This model can be replicated wherever students have access to primary sources that can be used to address historical questions. Variations on the model might include group projects in which students share the responsibility of completing a single project. My students have worked almost exclusively with microfilm sources, but the course could also use archival or even printed materials. The course could be adapted to serve as a year-long framework for honors theses. Teachers without supportive computer technology assistance might rely on my course Web site.

Addressing substantive interpretive questions in the selection and editing of historical documents is a challenging task for students to master in a single semester, as is the acquisition of technical skills, but most of my students have risen to the occasion and done quite remarkable work in the short space of three and a half months. The key to their success is that they become energized by the goal of putting their project on the Web as a learning resource for other students of U.S. history. Inspired by this goal, they have been willing to learn the nitty-gritty features of historical scholarship that otherwise might discourage all but the most dedicated. Students who entered the class with little or no understanding of historical methodology or technical Web expertise leave the class with a command of both. They let themselves "out of the box" to become part of the process by which history is written. And they have fun in the process.

AFTERWORD

Five years after the original publication of this article, the course described here is still an exciting venture in Web-based history teaching, but the *Women and Social Movements* Web site began to publish document projects by historian colleagues rather than students in 2003, the year after this article appeared. When colleagues approached Thomas Dublin and me with ideas about document projects based on their research, we gladly traded the challenge of rendering student

work authoritative for the opportunity to publish document projects that embraced the latest scholarship in U.S. women's history. In 2004 we became an
online quarterly journal and began to co-publish with Alexander Street Press of
Alexandria, Virginia, an alliance that has made the site available through library
subscription and permitted us to expand it enormously. The site is now much
more widely accessed than it was when this article was published. As of September 2007, it offered 78 document projects, 2,300 documents, 860 images, and
31,000 pages of additional primary sources, with new material added quarterly.
Readers whose libraries do not yet subscribe to the site can see many of its features on our editorial page at http://womhist.alexanderstreet.com.

JOHN WERTHEIMER

The Collaborative Research Seminar

At the first meeting of my legal history seminar at Davidson College, I tell my ten students that our goal for the semester is simple: to produce a collaborative research paper that is so well conceived, so thoroughly researched, and so finely written that it gets published. Publication, of course, will not always be possible, though I will thank you not to mention this to my students. But whether or not my seminar accomplishes its stated goal of publication, I am confident that it will always achieve its *unstated* goal: to teach students—and remind me—how to research, write, and love history.[1]

Davidson College is a "highly selective" liberal arts school in North Carolina. It has been a good home to my collaborative research seminar. All of the school's 1,650 students are full-time; almost all live on campus. History is a popular major here, and law a popular career choice. Attracting good, hardworking students to my legal history seminar has not been difficult.

I originally conceived the collaborative research project as a mere training exercise to prepare students for what I thought would be the seminar's capstone: individual research papers. Walking—and talking—through a single research project in the term's first half, I thought, would prepare students to write papers of their own thereafter. Teach the flock to fly together, then watch them disperse and soar.

But a funny thing happened on the way to the individual term paper: the flock became so fond of their collaborative project—and each other—that they refused to separate. They pleaded with me to drop the individual assignment so that they might continue collaborating. I feigned reluctance but was inwardly delighted. I had already noticed that collaboration had ignited a passion for history usually restricted to honors students and departmental groupies. What is more, I too had unexpectedly fallen for our topic (a 1931 arson case involving a group of young, white, female inmates who torched their state-run "training school" to escape its horrors) and did not fancy saying goodbye to it just yet. I agreed to stick with the group project and have never looked back.

I have now taught my seminar four times. Each year my students and I explore a different episode from North Carolina's legal history. In addition to the arson case described above, we have studied a 1914 challenge to a Winston, North Carolina, city ordinance mandating racial residential segregation; the Reconstruction-era prosecution of a black man and a white woman for "fornication," even though the couple was legally married; and a depression-era community's

Journal of American History 88 (2002): 1476–81.

female-led efforts to shut down Greenwich Village, a bawdy roadhouse that had opened in its midst.[2] I am already looking forward to next year.

In what follows, I will discuss organizational detail, wherein lies the devil of the collaborative research seminar or of any effort to teach outside the box. To start, I offer three general suggestions. First, trust your students. Motivate, coordinate, but do not dominate their efforts. Second, be flexible. No matter how well-crafted your syllabus is (and craft it as well as you can), be prepared to make midstream modifications. Third, be as committed to the group project as you expect your students to be. They will make the course a top priority only if they see you doing so.

GETTING STARTED

On the first day of class, following the usual pleasantries and a stirring pep talk, I move directly to topic selection. Because this is a make-or-break point, it sparks immediate student engagement. There are multiple ways of selecting topics. Once I handpicked a topic and fed it to my students on day one. That tactic had several advantages: I knew that the topic was good, I was able to prepare relevant assigned readings in advance, and my class hit the ground sprinting.

I now believe, however, that it is pedagogically preferable for students to generate their own topics—even if it means slower starts and, possibly (though not necessarily), weaker papers. The topic proposal is now my students' first research-and-writing assignment. Since my course deals with legal history, each student proposes a law case that could serve as the centerpiece of our collaborative paper. I limit the dates within which the cases must fall, mandate that the cases come from North Carolina to facilitate off-campus research, and provide an evaluative checklist to help students identify cases that would make good topics.[3]

Each student then explores our library's law books, nominates a case, and writes a short paper explaining the nomination. As with all written assignments in the seminar, students submit their topic proposals electronically, and I post them online for the entire class to see. Students read each other's proposals and come to the next session prepared for deliberation and topic selection. Once a consensus emerges, I celebrate the selection, congratulate all on their good proposals, and paraphrase Thomas Jefferson's first inaugural address on the need to forgive past differences and join together for a common purpose. The semester is short. We have much to do. Let's get to it.

THE RESEARCH

Research begins when each student submits a list of promising secondary sources. I compile them into a master bibliography, which I post online.[4] Students select and read works from the list, jotting down notes on three-by-five index cards. When done, they prepare one-page write-ups, summarizing the works' main points and evaluating their usefulness to the group project. The write-ups go online, so that students can use them when preparing the term's first major writing assignment, the historiographical essay. That assignment asks each student to do two things: analyze the current state of historical understanding of the group topic and describe the original historiographical contributions that the group paper might make. It is a challenging but important assignment.

Although secondary sources are essential, it is the primary source research—especially the off-campus variety—that provides the seminar's magic. After topic selection, I use class discussion to generate a list of research questions. Although many answers will be available right on campus, others will require travel. I work the phones, the Web, and reference librarians to learn about promising holdings in the area. I then send student researchers out with clear travel orders. ("Go snoop around and see what's there," incidentally, is an acceptable travel order.) Student researchers should take good notes, photocopy relevant material, keep their eyes open for unanticipated leads, and prepare thorough research write-ups. Believe it or not, students love the research trips. Anonymous course evaluations describe them as: "very helpful and lots of fun," "extremely helpful," "good, fun experience," "a great learning experience," "very productive," "very beneficial," "hugely helpful—learned how to do research and learned a lot about history," and "central to my learning in the course; I loved them."

Here are four keys to primary-research success:

1. Make off-campus research a requirement, not an option. Students will travel more happily knowing that there are no slackers back on campus, laughing.
2. Tell students that you are well aware that archival research is a hit-or-miss proposition. You will not hold it against them if, despite their best efforts, they return empty-handed.
3. Solicit money from your chair or dean to reimburse student expenses. Even a small amount will have large symbolic value.
4. Insist that students carpool. In transit my students have, as one put it, "bonded." In the archives they have divided unpleasant tasks, celebrated finds with high fives, and learned tremendously from each other. "I remember when we went on our first research trip," wrote Stan, a senior history major, in a peer review of his classmate Mike. "We didn't find much that day besides a good Italian restaurant. Still, I remember being impressed with Mike's resourcefulness. Having researched for four years, I figured there was nothing else I could learn. Mike proved me wrong. As we worked together, we were able to teach one another some of the tricks of the trade. It was a pleasure to get to know him and work with him." Magic.

THE WRITING

The writing for the group paper will be different from any writing students have previously done. It will be collaborative, not individual. It will be made from scratch, not slice-and-bake. And it will be a long-term commitment, not a one-night stand. I begin the process by having each student prepare a tentative outline. In seminar, we consolidate student ideas on the chalkboard. Besides providing for clean narrative flow and clear argumentation, the master outline should divide the material into roughly equal segments whose number matches the seminar's enrollment. Students then decide who will write which section of the paper. Some matches will be obvious. Only Robin, the lone student to explore the Heriot Clarkson papers, wants the Clarkson section. Only Ed, a genealogy buff (honest), volunteers to write about the Spake family's background. Other choices will be less clear. You should be part traffic cop, part auctioneer, and part shepherd. When every slot is filled, have your students distribute all research photocopies and three-by-five cards among themselves according to subject matter.

Allow a couple of weeks for the preparation of a first draft. Prior to the deadline, ask seminar members to bring tentative section outlines to class. Talking through these, in order, will remind students of how their individual parts relate to the whole.

Once students have written and electronically submitted their first drafts, compile and distribute copies of the whole paper. If you like bloated, disjointed, aimless prose, you will love the first draft. If not, you will find it dreadful. Do not despair. Think of it as a teaching opportunity, for so it is. Have each student edit and comment on the draft. In seminar, discuss what needs to be done, section by section. This will be time-consuming but valuable. The second draft will surpass the first; the third will be better still.

To enliven and sharpen the repeated rewriting, seek the comments and guest appearance of an outside reader. I have been blessed with four wonderful outside readers: Nancy Hewitt, Martha Hodes, Steve Kantrowitz, and Brian Luskey. For weeks in advance I invoked their pending visits as a spur to hard work. Our visitors invariably reassured us that there was hope, after all. They also suggested productive ways of rethinking our material, leading us back to old sources with new questions.

After your group paper attains some polish, consider a public presentation. The discipline required to reduce a fifty-page paper to a forty-five-minute presentation is of immeasurable value. Prepare students to present their sections in turn. Prior to the show, have *at least* one full run-through in which students time each other's presentations and you take notes like a theater director. While some of your remarks will involve delivery ("Melvin, lose the gum"), the important ones will involve content. If your pen runs out of ink, feel free to borrow the following remarks, since they will apply: "We need better transitions." "We need to identify the *essential* points of each section and communicate them more clearly." "We need to explain what we are going to say, say it, and then say what we have said." Although such remarks are putatively aimed at the presentation, their ultimate target is the final draft.

Students blossom at the public presentation. They invite friends, professors, and parents. They prepare overhead projections. They dress up and comb their hair. Unaccountably, no matter how crummy the rough drafts and dress re-hearsals, the public presentations are always wonderful. My favorite part might be the question-and-answer session at the end, when students stand shoulder to shoulder and field questions as one.

There remains only the paper's final revision. Students should strive to re-create the clarity achieved at the public presentation. They should also attach brief remarks that begin with the phrase, "If I had unlimited time to research and rework this section, I would improve it in the following ways: . . . " With the sub-mission of final drafts—and an end-of-term party—the collaborative research seminar concludes.

GRADING

Assigning individual grades in a collaborative research seminar is not as difficult as it might seem. Indeed, since students submit written work just about every week, grading options abound. The major writing assignments—historiographi-cal essays and rough draft sections—can be graded, as can less formal assign-ments such as research reports and rough-draft critiques. Assigned readings can be quizzed. A take-home final can be added. Professors who like distributing fre-quent letter grades may easily (and perhaps profitably) do so.

It is also possible, however, to go through an entire semester without assign-ing a single formal grade. I did so last spring and saw no decline in student effort. Students received, in one's words, "critique after critique" of written work during the term, but no letter grades. Every week I wrote notes in my grade book regard-ing each student's performance, both in class and on outside work. By semester's end—especially after reading my students' candid performance reviews of them-selves and each other—I had no difficulty calculating final grades that seemed no more arbitrary than usual. Students did not complain. (Only one student last spring took me up on my offer to hold personal "evaluation conferences" upon request.) One student remarked that the unorthodox system "allowed for greater intensity of research and less stress." Whatever grading scheme you adopt, leave plenty of wiggle room to reward intangible contributions and hold free riders accountable. If the project goes well, grading will be but a pleasant afterthought.

One of my quietest seminar students was Ryan. He listened attentively to group discussions but spoke only when interrogated. After our public presenta-tion Ryan's year, I chatted with him and one of his friends. "I'm glad I finally saw what this group paper is all about," the friend remarked. "Ryan won't stop talking about it!" Several factors explain the collaborative research seminar's rare capac-ity to engage students such as Ryan. Most students enjoy the unusual format, which takes them well outside of conventional academic boxes. Most like the course's hands-on features. ("We learned how to do history, rather than [just] read it—that made this a great class," one course evaluation stated.) Many appre-ciate the "extraordinary amount of responsibility and input" demanded of each class member. And all agree, "It was really cool to work as a group." You too will enjoy working with a group, especially when you see how much your students teach and learn from each other. "Alison helped me a whole lot individually," wrote an appreciative Beth in an end-of-term peer review, "especially with my forum [public presentation] draft—she sat with me for a couple of hours reworking and clarifying it—HUGE help!" Andy's glowing peer evaluations included praise for "help[ing] me with concepts, with the case, with footnotes, with random computer tricks. . . . He took time out to work with me whenever I asked him to."

Last spring Carrie visited my office to discuss her section of the group paper. Seeing that I was with another student, she waited in the hall. Minutes later, after recognizing that the other student was David, another member of our seminar, she came in to join our conversation. "I didn't realize that it was family," she explained. Even if my course never succeeds in publishing another article, comments like Carrie's will make it worth teaching, again and again.

Notes

1. I submitted three of my seminar's four papers for publication consideration. The first paper, written by the 1997 seminar, was published; see Brian Luskey et al., "'Escape of the Match-Strikers': Disorderly North Carolina Women, the Legal System, and the Samarcand Arson Case of 1931," *North Carolina Historical Review* 75 (Oct. 1998): 435–60. The second paper was part of a collection of essays currently under consideration at an academic press; the third paper was accepted conditionally by a state historical journal. Publication was possible thanks to the generosity of Davidson College and the George Lawrence Abernethy Endowment.

2. *State v. Darnell*, 166 N.C. 300 (1914); *State v. Ross*, 76 N.C. 242 (1877); *Carpenter v. Boyles*, 213 N.C. 432 (1938).

3. According to my evaluative checklist, a promising case is one that raises interesting legal issues, touches on interesting historical issues, suggests compelling human stories, and appears amenable to research.

4. I asked each student to submit fifteen titles, including at least three books, three history articles, and three law review articles.

James P. Whittenburg

Using Historical Landscape to Stimulate Historical Imagination: A Memoir of Climbing outside the Box

When I began teaching early American history at the College of William and Mary a quarter century ago, the new social history was running at flood tide. It shaped my personal vision of the past and dominated my syllabi.[1] But if the content of the courses was new, the approach I took with students remained traditional: read, write, and (via some infamous quantitative class projects) count. The publication of Rhys Isaac's *The Transformation of Virginia, 1740–1790*, in 1982 convinced me that it would be possible to use surviving and re-created elements of the early American landscape in teaching, if only I could get students out of the classroom and into the field.[2] I immediately discovered that it was easier to contemplate teaching with historic sites than to do it. Colonial Williamsburg was almost at my doorstep, but merely marching up and down the Duke of Gloucester Street would require more time than the traditional class period allowed.

My initial solution was volunteerism. One of my first doctoral students at William and Mary, Carter Hudgins, now a history professor at Mary Washington College but then an archaeologist, introduced me to other archaeologists at the Virginia Research Center for Archaeology (VRCA). When the Virginia Institute of Marine Science decided to build Waterman's Hall in 1983–1984, the VRCA needed willing hands to excavate the site of Gloucestertown, a seventeenth-century village on the York River.[3] I recruited college students for that work. Many other salvage excavations followed, and for the next half dozen years archaeology would be my standard means to introduce students to material culture and to get them onto historic sites. Eventually, changes at the VRCA and in my own life dictated that I put archaeology aside. Trowel-less, I began to experiment with courses in which visits to historic places were the principal activity. When my department needed an additional freshman seminar for the fall of 1997, I volunteered, with the proviso that we schedule "The Colonial and Revolutionary Tidewater" on Saturdays.

Abandoning the standard format for a class period by taking the plunge into Saturday meetings put me outside a very important academic box. Field trips were no longer optional extras or even required out-of-class assignments. They had become the class. What follows are descriptions and reflections from the first four

Journal of American History 88 (2002): 1481–88.

Students work on a Virginia Research Center for Archaeology (VRCA) salvage archaeology site in the 1980s. *Photograph by James P. Whittenburg.*

editions of my seminar. While I have treated them together, no two semesters have been quite the same in the sites visited, readings, guest speakers, and assignments.

My course addresses topics in the history of Virginia from the founding of Jamestown to the Revolution. I require substantial reading prior to each week's field trip and depend greatly upon discussion. All freshman seminars in history at William and Mary carry a writing requirement. In my class students do most of their writing in the form of electronic journals. They design Web pages where they describe and reflect upon what they have read, seen, heard, and said each week. No computing skill or experience is necessary. In a few labs and many one-on-one sessions, I am able to teach them what they need to know. I find that Web pages are particularly useful for such work. The students can share their thoughts immediately; they can revise instantly; and perhaps no other medium so encourages the interplay of text and images.

We spend very little time in our classroom, which functions mostly as a staging area where I attempt to preface the topic at hand. I often do that with a film clip. Some are from documentaries such as the splendid 1997 video based on Laurel Thatcher Ulrich's *A Midwife's Tale*. The sequence in which Martha Ballard's family awakens to their daily routine makes a fine introduction to our visit to the "tenant house," a small wooden structure that Colonial Williamsburg uses to depict the lives of working-class people. As often as not, however, I use scenes from commercial movies that may not have a historical theme but that compel the viewer's attention. As physical evidence of the Great Awakening is very hard to come by, I use the exquisite barn-raising scenes from the 1985 film *Witness*, about a modern-day Philadelphia detective's sojourn among the Amish of Lancaster

County, Pennsylvania, as a preface for a discussion of Rhys Isaac's 1974 essay, "Evangelical Revolt." I do not suggest that films about the Maine frontier or twentieth-century murder mysteries accurately depict colonial Virginia. My intent is to get my students to think about the past and especially about its relationship to the present.[4]

Half an hour after beginning class, we are on the road. We sometimes see two related sites in a day, comparing, for example, the slave quarter at Carter's Grove plantation with the 1780s yeoman's farm at the Yorktown Victory Center. While most of the students have a very good time on most of the trips, we are not tourists. I select sites that reaffirm, challenge, or extend ideas the students first encounter in readings and discussions. Perhaps an illustration from my own scholarly development may help to make the point. In the late 1970s, interdisciplinary reinterpretation of the early Chesapeake Bay region was standard fare at Institute of Early American History and Culture colloquia. At one meeting, Cary Carson, Norman F. Barka, and William M. Kelso presented an early form of their pathbreaking 1981 *Winterthur Portfolio* article, "Impermanent Architecture in the Southern American Colonies."[5] The authors offered a description of a seventeenth-century landscape dominated by earthfast structures that was remarkably accessible to historians with scant material-culture experience. It has since become a classic of the genre. Yet I did not truly comprehend the work—did not understand how neatly it dovetailed with the demography-driven new social history of the day—until I had myself walked among the traces of a seventeenth-century structure at a VRCA excavation. To build a house, colonists had simply set posts into holes dug into the earth at intervals of a few feet in the outline of a rectangle, attached horizontal members to form a boxlike frame, and covered that with clapboards. Nothing remained above ground, but by pulling back the topsoil, the archaeologists had revealed a striking pattern of small dark stains left by rotted posts in the sterile clay. These "posthole" buildings were the dominant architectural form of the era. They matched in material crudity the harshness of a society in which life expectancy for men and women who managed to reach adulthood was only about another twenty years. I believe my students derive similar insights from the material remains of the colonial past I show them.

Watching the Byrd family mansion, Westover, appear by degrees as one walks up the bank from the James River drives home the true purpose of conspicuous consumption among elite colonial families in ways that texts cannot. Westover is a dramatic presentation of wealth and power that William Byrd II carefully positioned where it would impress other rich and powerful people traveling in relative ease by water. The social contest, my students discover, was mainly between gentry families. The yeomen, the poor, and the enslaved rarely caught a glimpse of the great house. Even so, reading beforehand about elite life-styles and eighteenth-century notions of deference is essential to drawing out the meaning of the house. To prepare for our visit to Westover last fall, students read all of Daniel Blake Smith's *Inside the Great House* and a sizable swath of *The Transformation of Virginia*.[6] As my association with archaeologists has convinced me that the best conversations are those we enjoy over a pleasant meal, my classes typically hold extended lunchtime discussions of the readings for the week and especially of how they intersect with what we find on site. At Westover last year, we picnicked a quarter mile upriver from the main house, where the first parish church once stood. There was something poignant about discussing Evelyn Byrd only a few yards from her tomb. Later, we examined the detailed inscription on the tomb of her father, William Byrd II, as a text for what the Byrds themselves thought it meant to be gentry.

Using material culture as we used the inscription on the Byrd tomb is a staple of my course, but the messages are seldom in written form. Bacon's Castle is a prime example. Built by the merchant-planter Arthur Allen south of the James River in Surry County about 1665, this cruciform brick house served for three centuries as a residence before the Association for the Preservation of Virginia Antiquities (APVA) acquired and restored it in the 1970s. The APVA returned the second floor to its seventeenth-century configuration. The first floor now represents the eighteenth century and retains the panel wall Elizabeth Allen added to convert the two-room arrangement of the seventeenth century into a Georgian central passage flanked by two large rooms, a transformation that is evident from original beams that no longer intersect in the center of a first-floor ceiling. My students can read cultural change in this evolution of interior space. In the seventeenth century, the main entrance of even elite houses opened directly into the most important room. Reflecting the rising importance of privacy in the next century, the development of passages and foyers allowed the masters of great houses to regulate entry into their homes better and to control how deeply visitors might penetrate. Walking around the outside of Bacon's Castle, my students can see the "architectural ghosts" of many other alterations in the form of bricked-up windows and doors, reminders of a scramble over many generations to stay current with architectural styles.[7]

Students ponder the pattern of graves at Bruton Parish Church, Williamsburg, Virginia.
Photograph by James P. Whittenburg.

Inside a house museum such as Bacon's Castle, students have only limited opportunity to explore on their own. Docents conduct us through such buildings as a group, and especially at heavily visited places, the interpretation is often generic. This is not my favorite format for site visits, but tourists mob Monticello for good reasons, and being quickly ushered into, through, and out of such a remarkable house is (perhaps) an acceptable trade-off to not seeing it at all. I compensate by seeking out sections of the site—Mulberry Row, in the case of Monticello—where the pace is left to the visitor. Here I have an opportunity to bend the class back to my original objectives—and most historic places can serve many objectives. As always, pre-reading provides the context for what we see.

I am exceedingly fortunate to have friends, colleagues, and former students (often the same people) who have special knowledge of places or topics and who are very willing to match guest appearances to the themes of my class. Julie Richter's discussions of slavery in Williamsburg and Camille Wells's explanations of Jefferson's life-style at Monticello, to cite two outstanding examples, have added great depth to my fieldtrips. Assigning articles by both people conveys additional authority to their presentations.[8] The students learn from my introductions that Richter and Wells earned their doctorates at William and Mary. I noticed early on that involving alumni contributed to a certain esprit among the undergraduates, and while I had not anticipated the phenomenon, I certainly capitalize on it. My freshmen spend the last Saturday morning before Thanksgiving break exploring the Bruton Parish graveyard in the company of Professor Turk McCleskey and a group of his Virginia Military Institute cadets. McCleskey, who earned his Ph.D. at William and Mary, directs a multilayered exercise in which students discover the patterns of marked graves, deduce from them the presence and placement of an earlier church, theorize about disappeared wooden markers, and draw conclusions about colonial society. But it is not always necessary that guests hold advanced degrees or that they conduct complex activities. Insight and attitude are the keys. While a high school student, my daughter Elizabeth worked as a costumed interpreter at Jamestown Settlement, a state-run museum complex on the mainland near Jamestown Island. Her specialty was interpretation of full-size replicas of the three ships that Captain Christopher Newport used to transport the first colonists to Jamestown in 1607. She and Kyia Dunalak, a recent William and Mary alumna who also worked on the ships, joined one of my freshmen seminars for lunch. The result was an excellent peer-to-peer discussion in a very relaxed setting of shipboard life in the seventeenth century.

Places such as Jamestown Settlement lend themselves to browsing, which I often formalize with specific assignments. A session entitled "Williamsburg Considered as a Shopping Mall" sends students into the businesses along the Duke of Gloucester Street to engage in comparison shopping, combined with role playing. At least one student will draw the role of Eliza Ambler, a Yorktown teenager during the Revolutionary War. A 1997 essay by Catherine Kerrison, another Ph.D. alumna, establishes Ambler's identity.[9] The assignment calls for the student to consider Williamsburg as a sort of eighteenth-century strip mall but also to attempt to see the goods, services, and people of the town/mall as Ambler might have seen them.

Assuming the role of Eliza Ambler requires historical imagination, and the Duke of Gloucester Street is so rich in visual cues that the most difficult part of that assignment may be to simply cover all the possibilities for shopping. But elaborate settings are not essential. A few years after completing her dissertation at William and Mary, Ann Smart Martin, now at the University of Wisconsin-Madison, dazzled my students with a lecture on eighteenth-century ceramic styles built in part around her collection of richly patterned paper plates. I suspect that one group of freshmen will always remember visiting Shadwell, the boyhood home of Thomas Jefferson, in the company of Susan Kern, one of my graduate students who had recently been an archaeologist at nearby Monticello. Well off the beaten path, Shadwell is nothing more than a pasture now. Standing before the pile of brush that is the only indication of the long-vanished house, Kern told them that they were perhaps twenty feet from the room in which Jefferson was born. "Of course," she added, radiating enthusiasm and command of her subject, "we don't know which twenty feet." I doubt it mattered. In the gathering dusk of that late fall afternoon, the site of Shadwell evoked the spirit of the eighteenth century as beautifully as any standing structure.[10]

Landscapes such as the field containing the buried remains of Shadwell, remnants and reconstructions of the physical past, and tableaux depicting people of the past are like works of art: some are in sharp relief, some slightly out of focus. We see photographs and impressionist paintings in different ways, and it is not always easy to classify precisely what they mean to us. Yet they do help us understand both the past and the present, which artists often blend together. So, too, the evocative quality of historic places melds past and present. Jamestown Island, in particular, is a jumble of competing and conflicting reminders of the past and of how Americans have felt about it. Rather different National Park Service (NPS) and APVA approaches to the past overlie evidence from archaeological excavations that began with the construction of a seawall in 1903 and continue now in the celebrated work of William Kelso and the APVA/Rediscovery team. Merely to reach the ongoing excavation of James Fort from the NPS visitor center, one must first pass a giant obelisk from the 1907 Jamestown Exposition, then the 1906 chapel the Colonial Dames of America built over the footprint of the seventeenth-century church just inside the APVA property line. Beyond the church, an earthen Confederate fort sacred to modern devotees of the Civil War sits atop one leg of the triangular stockade that Kelso and company hope to excavate. In the middle of the Confederate fort a twentieth-century shrine celebrates the first Anglican minister at Jamestown.[11] The relationship between past and present tends to be like that: seamless but messy. Dealing with the ambiguities pushes my freshmen to develop their historical imaginations. I can provide them no greater service.

Notes

1. There is now a large literature on the Chesapeake region that one could include in the new social history. In the late 1970s much of it consisted of conference papers and dissertations. For classic treatments, mostly featuring the demographic model, of the sev-

enteenth century, see Thad W. Tate and David L. Ammerman, eds., *The Chesapeake in the Seventeenth Century: Essays on Anglo-American Society* (Chapel Hill, N.C., 1979), esp. Thad W. Tate, "The Seventeenth-Century Chesapeake and Its Modern Historians," 3–50. For a remarkable synthesis ten years further along, see Jack P. Greene, *Pursuits of Happiness: The Social Development of Early Modern British Colonies and the Formation of American Culture* (Chapel Hill, N.C., 1988), chap. 4. For updates and commentary on older work that continued to be important, see Karen Ordahl Kupperman, "The Founding Years of Virginia—and the United States," *Virginia Magazine of History and Biography* 104 (Winter 1996): 102–12; and James P. Whittenburg, "Primal Forces: Three Interlocking Themes in the Recent Literature of Eighteenth-Century Virginia," ibid., 113–20.

2. Rhys Isaac, *The Transformation of Virginia, 1740–1790* (Chapel Hill, N.C., 1982). Much to the delight of my students, Professor Isaac came along on some of our field trips when he was Harrison Professor at the College of William and Mary in 1998–1999.

3. Wilford Kale, "Forgotten Gloucestertown: Site of Tarleton's Surrender, the Old Port Is Archaeological Treasure Trove," *Colonial Williamsburg* 11 (Summer 1989): 21–25.

4. Laurel Thatcher Ulrich, *A Midwife's Tale: The Life of Martha Ballard, Based on Her Diary, 1785–1812* (New York, 1990); *A Midwife's Tale*, dir. Richard P. Rogers, prod. Laurie Kahn Levitt (Blueberry Hill Productions, 1997) (videocassette, 88 mins.); *Witness*, dir. Peter Weir, prod. Edward S. Feldman and David Mombyk (Paramount, 1985) (videocassette, 1 hr., 52 min.); Rhys Isaac, "Evangelical Revolt: The Nature of the Baptists' Challenge to the Traditional Order in Virginia, 1765 to 1775," *William and Mary Quarterly* 31 (July 1974): 345–68.

5. Cary Carson, Norman F. Barka, William M. Kelso, Garry Wheeler Stone, and Dell Upton, "Impermanent Architecture in the Southern American Colonies," *Winterthur Portfolio* 16 (Summer/Autumn 1981): 135–96.

6. Daniel Blake Smith, *Inside the Great House: Planter Family Life in Eighteenth-Century Chesapeake Society* (Ithaca, N.Y., 1980); Isaac, *Transformation of Virginia*, i–135.

7. Stephenson B. Andrews, *Bacon's Castle* (Richmond, Va., 1984).

8. Julie Richter, "Slavery in John Blair's Public and Personal Lives in 1751," *Colonial Williamsburg Interpreter* 20 (Fall 1999): 1–8; Julie Richter, "'The Speaker's Men and Women: Randolph Slaves in Williamsburg," ibid. 47–51; Camille Wells, "The Planter's Prospect: Houses, Outbuildings, and Rural Landscapes in Eighteenth-Century Virginia," *Winterthur Portfolio* 27 (Spring 1993): 1–31.

9. Catherine Kerrison, "By the Book: Eliza Ambler Brent Carrington and Conduct Literature in Late Eighteenth-Century Virginia," *Virginia Magazine of History and Biography* 105 (Winter 1997): 27–52.

10. Ann Smart Martin, "The Role of Pewter as Missing Artifact: Attitudes towards Tablewares in Late Eighteenth-Century Virginia," *Historical Archaeology* 23, no. 2 (1989): 1–27; Ann Smart Martin, "'Fashionable Sugar Dishes, Latest Fashion Ware': The Creamware Revolution in the Eighteenth-Century Chesapeake," in *Historical Archaeology of the Chesapeake*, ed. Paul A. Shackel and Barbara J. Little (Washington, D.C., 1994), 169–87; James P. Whittenburg, notes on a class visit to Shadwell, Nov. 13, 1999 (in James P. Whittenburg's possession).

11. National Park Service, "Jamestown National Historic Site," *Colonial National Historical Park*, <www.nps.gov/jame/index.htm> (Nov. 29, 2001); Association for the Preservation of Virginia Antiquities, "Old Town," *Jamestown Rediscovery*, <www.apva.org/tour/tour.html> (Nov. 29, 2001).

Michael Zuckerman

A Modest Proposal: Less (Authority) Is More (Learning)

It is easy to denounce the lecture format. It is not so easy to dismantle it or to give it up.

Lecturing to hundreds of very smart young people is a heady experience. I talk, they duly note what I say. I stand in the spotlight, they sit in the shadows. I dazzle, they defer to my brilliance. It is gratifying. I like adulation as much as the next guy.

But the lecture does not do nearly as much for my students as it does for me. It keeps them from an active, participatory engagement in their own education. And by my lights it does not do anything desirable for society, either. It confirms my students in their understanding of themselves as consumers and of their society as founded upon the star system.

I have always been aware that I have more than enough control of my classes. I have always experimented with ways of sharing that control with my students. I am under no illusion that I can abdicate authority. If nothing else, I still assign the grades at the end of the semester. But I have become more and more convinced that I can give some of my control away and still have enough left and that I can give my students a lot more voice in their own education when I do.

About a dozen years ago, I instituted my first major change. In all my alleged lecture courses at the University of Pennsylvania—courses with enrollments of a dozen, or twenty-five, or forty students—I began dividing the class into groups of three or four or five, making each of those groups responsible for the conduct of an entire class session. I arrange the syllabus so that we discuss a set of readings every week. The group conducts the discussion on Tuesday, and I respond to the group's presentation on Thursday. I try to tie things together or take things apart. I add to or subtract from what the group said and what the class said.

I emphasize to the students that they are welcome to present the texts as inventively and vivifyingly as they can. Still, they always astound me. When I began, I thought they might stage debates or role-plays. Over the years, they have concocted multimedia extravaganzas, composed and performed original music, created their own videos, taken the class on location, staged sound-and-light

Journal of American History 88 (2002): 1488–93.

shows, conducted polls, performed costume dramas, had the class fingerpainting, mounted parodies, prepared food, invited confessions, and much else.

The exuberance and daring that my students display is just a part of the pleasure and the power of the group presentations. There is more.

In my classes, students see their fellow students create interpretive matrices richer and denser than their professor does. They come to respect one another's intelligence in the formal setting of the classroom as they already do in the informal settings of college life. And there is more.

Pretty consistently, students prepare more conscientiously for class—and participate more thoughtfully in it—when the groups teach than when I do. They know that the group counts upon them to be responsive, whereas they assume that I will manage even if they are not. They know too that one day they will be part of the group and depend on the others. And there is more.

Several times a semester, students complain wistfully that the class they conducted was anticlimactic. Such students do not lament that the class went badly. They lament that it went so swiftly and that there was so much still to say. In an hour and a half, it was over. These are students in groups that truly caught fire. They grew accustomed to long hours of intense disputation with one another as they prepared their presentation. Only after it was done did they realize how much more they had learned in preparing than in performing, and from one another in the wee hours of the morning than from me the following Thursday. And there is more.

The authority that a group holds for that hour and a half on Tuesday lasts at least a semester, if not longer. I know because I read my students' final papers. Routinely, those papers embrace, or play with, conceptions that the student presentations set forth and that I thought I had refuted. In a democracy, I think it may matter that several of them said it while only I said nay. In a meritocracy, I think it may matter that they often said it in a more dramatic and vibrant way than I said nay. And in the forum for free thought that I fantasize I create, it may be that the mere fact of multivocality fosters freer thought. Think of Solomon Asch's experiments on conformity.[1] If all of the experimenter's accomplices say that a shorter line matches the standard one, a large percentage of the true subjects of the experiment do too. But if just one of the accomplices chooses the true match, virtually every single true subject does too. It is possible that, sometimes, I truly think the shorter line the true match. It is possible that my teaching groups enable my students to say that, however ingeniously I argued otherwise, the shorter line is shorter. When authority is pluralized, the range of permissible truth on student papers is extended too.

But all of this is just a start. It gets students into the classroom as teachers. It does not get the class out of the classroom itself. Community service does that.

About a half-dozen years ago, I instituted my second major change. I began sending the students in my course in American national character into the schools of West Philadelphia. We still meet for an hour and a half every Tuesday and Thursday. But now they spend an hour or two—or three or four—working in the community each week as well.[2]

The specific arrangements change every year. The informing purpose remains constant. I get the students out of the cocoon of the university and out of my control.

On Tuesdays as well as Thursdays, I set the agenda. I choose the readings; I decide the framework that the readings elaborate; I have a heavy hand—on Thursdays—in the subjects we discuss and the turns our discussion takes.

In the city schools, I determine none of this and influence almost none. The students go according to their own schedule, not mine or our common one. They generally work with different teachers, and they almost always work with different students.

I do not even set my students their initial assignments for the community work. I confess that I have tried to do it and that I still think it would be grand if they were all engaged in a common endeavor. Every year, my Penn-based collaborator, the schoolteachers, and I come up with something: school-to-work, or the mayoral campaign, or the new journalism charter. And every year, most of my students opt out. They find other assignments they prefer to the ones we have devised, sometimes even at other schools than the one in which we are working.

More than that, my students inevitably come at their diverse community assignments with diverse attitudes. Some of them do as their teachers tell them to. Others do as their ingenuity invites. They have organized an elementary school co-ed soccer team so successful that it inspired the creation of an entire league. They have instigated a school newspaper so successful that it became a community newspaper. They have created a "girl talk" program so successful that it spread to other high schools. They have formed jazz clubs, taught neighborhood history classes, and started an after-school gardening program that now sells its harvests to local restaurants.

Whether they innovate or just help out, they confront their own problems and venture their own solutions. We do devote a part of class each week to talking about the challenges they face, but I do not lead, and generally do not even intervene in, those discussions.

A student "teaching assistant" presides over them. Each year, I ask a student who took the class the year before to coordinate community service. She and I speak often, both before and during the course, but I assure her that she is to treat the community service component as a course within the course and that that course is hers, not mine. My assistants have initiated routines of journal keeping, journal sharing, and weekly e-mail postings for the students. It is, I think, a measure of their triumph that, in their e-mailings as in our class discussions, students soon stop speaking to the assistant and speak directly to one another.

The real point of the community service work, beyond the service itself, is to *authorize* the students. For the final paper for the course, I ask them to synthesize the reading that we do on contemporary West Philadelphia and their own experience of the neighborhood. I ask that they treat the two sources of information and ideas as coordinate and that they recognize the primacy of their own expertise in their fieldwork.

Students from University City High School sell their produce at the Powelton Farmers' Market at Drew Elementary School in West Philadelphia. UCHS senior Charles Martin finds that Bright Lights chard can sell for $3 a bag. *Photograph by Danny Gerber.*

And they do. Again and again in their papers, they ponder the implications of their experience for the books that they have read. Sometimes they argue that, in the slice of life they have observed, things are not as bad as some of our authors allege. Sometimes they argue that things are even worse. And sometimes they get past that polarity and argue more ingeniously. But always they are empowered to argue with what they have read. They do not depend passively or reactively on Jonathan Kozol or Elijah Anderson, John Wideman or Carl Nightingale.[3] They have had an immersion of their own in a life that had, before, been alien to their experience. They have needs of their own to make sense of that experience.

Of course, I do eventually get to set some of my own views before them. I do get those four Thursdays over the last third of the course. But by the time I begin, they have been in their schools for a couple of months. I try not to preach at them when we get to that concluding segment on contemporary America. But even if I fail, they have had the better part of the course to figure out where they stand before I even begin speaking to their immediate experiences.

Some months ago, David Brooks caused a stir with a piece in the *Atlantic Monthly* on "The Organization Child." Like William Whyte half a century before, Brooks hung out with his subjects—in this case, students at Princeton University—and observed them sharply. He found a lot to like in those young people, or at least a lot to admire. But he also found that, to them, the world they live in seems fundamentally just. If you work hard, behave pleasantly . . . you will

Students from the University of Pennsylvania cultivate eggplants with students in the Urban Nutrition Initiative Summer Camp at Drew Elementary School in West Philadelphia. *Photograph by Danny Gerber.*

be rewarded with a wonderful ascent in the social hierarchy. . . . There is a fundamental order to the universe, and it works. If you play by its rules and defer to its requirements, you will lead a pretty fantastic life.[4]

My University of Pennsylvania students come from the same elite families in the same elite suburbs that Brooks's Princetonians do. They went to the same elite high schools, and they will go to the same elite law schools and ultimately join the same elite firms.

But very few of my students come out of History 443 believing that the world is "fundamentally just." Scarcely a one deludes himself about his "wonderful ascent in the social hierarchy." More than a few come out tormented by the *disparity* between their prospect of "a pretty fantastic life" and the bleak outlook of the students at West Philadelphia High School. Nearly all come soberingly to see that they are where they are by an accident of birth. If they read Brooks, nearly all would reach the disturbing realization that he is wrong on one crucial thing. They are not ascending the social hierarchy. They will—if they are good enough and lucky enough—do no more than maintain their parents' position. But for the grace of their privileged birth, they would not be at Penn. Had they been born black and poor, they too would have gone to West Philly and not much further.

I do not teach my students any of that. They learn it by themselves, for themselves.

Notes

1. Solomon Asch, *Studies of Independence and Conformity* (Washington, D.C., 1956).

2. Michael Zuckerman, "The Turnerian Frontier: A New Approach to the Study of the American Character," in *Connecting Past and Present: Concepts and Models for Service-Learning in History*, ed. Ira Harkavy and Bill M. Donovan (Washington, D.C., 2000), 183–202.

3. Jonathan Kozol, *Savage Inequalities: Children in America's Schools* (New York, 1991); Elijah Anderson, *Code of the Street: Decency, Violence, and the Moral Life of the Inner City* (New York, 1999); John Wideman, *Philadelphia Fire* (New York, 1990); Carl Nightingale, *On the Edge: A History of Poor Black Children and Their American Dreams* (New York, 1993). For some specification of the sorts of things my students write, see Zuckerman, "Turnerian Frontier."

4. David Brooks, "The Organization Child," *Atlantic Monthly* 287 (April 2001): 40–54, esp. 50. William H. Whyte, *The Organization Man* (New York, 1956).

PART FOUR

THE SCHOLARSHIP OF TEACHING AND LEARNING . . . AND TESTING

Excellence in college teaching has traditionally been regarded as an art, not a science. Yet in recent years an influential set of critics—including prominent government officials—has demanded that colleges and universities prove that they deliver "value added" benefits commensurate with the money they charge. These critics argue that institutions of higher education, like other schools, should be held accountable for the "learning outcomes" of their students. Meanwhile, from a very different direction, champions of the liberal arts have questioned whether what passes today for quality instruction at many colleges and universities is really effective in teaching students how to think critically, rather than how to regurgitate information on standardized tests of the sort advocated by the "value added" set. Inspired by Ernest L. Boyer's *Scholarship Reconsidered*, this second set of critics has called on the academy to study more carefully what really succeeds in promoting critical thinking at the college level.[1] Proponents of this approach call their enterprise "the scholarship of teaching and learning."

How, then, should we assess success in the history classroom? When we first approached this subject, we had reservations: Would we be moving into the domain of education departments and teacher certification programs that addressed such issues as the relative merits of various classroom technologies, the effective construction of multiple-choice tests, and the mysteries of the grading rubric, all to serve us better in our quest for efficient "content delivery"? Would we be presented with mind-crushing correlations between student assessment scores and proportions of lecture/discussion observed for various courses at distinct levels of the curriculum? Would we see lesson plans for successful classes presented like recipes in a "best practices" cookbook? To our relief our skepticism proved misplaced. The work presented in Part Four is analytically sophisticated, well grounded in empirical research, and provocative. It demands that we engage questions not just about the merits of particular pedagogies, but about our central purposes as academics who both study and teach the American past.

Above all, the scholars whose work appears in Part Four taught us that exploring teaching and learning in history requires that we consider our goals before we turn to evaluating our methods. What are we trying to teach? What do we want students to know after they have completed a history course, and for how long do we expect them to retain that knowledge?

Contributors to this part recognized and registered the familiar concern with the lack of historical knowledge today's students manifest, but rather than simply trying to fill empty vessels with incontestable, abstracted, and correct facts, they sought to help students develop an appreciation for history as the practice of interpretation and narration, based in the systematic analysis of evidence. In this way, they argued, students learn both content and what to do with it. In other words, these practitioners illuminated strategies for teaching historical thinking, not a long list of names and dates or even a short list of "the lessons of history." These case studies are rich with discussions of the components that constitute our disciplinary mode of analysis: posing historical questions; evaluating contested interpretations; interrogating and contextualizing sources; using evidence to create a narrative; revising established narratives in light of new findings. The best historians use these skills unselfconsciously. They are part of our cast of mind. But how do we teach these skills to our students so that they will think like historians, not just memorize the thoughts of their teachers? The scholarship of teaching and learning not only encourages us to bring our skills as researchers into our work as teachers; it also asks us to articulate the core substance and significance of our distinctive expertise as historians. Perhaps, as T. S. Eliot has said, "the end of all our exploring will be to arrive where we started and know the place for the first time."[2] Teaching history may yet be reconnected with doing history.

The section that follows has three components. It begins with Lendol Calder's article on how he radically restructured the American history survey in light of the scholarship of teaching and learning. Calder, who teaches history at Augustana College in Rock Island, Illinois, was a 1999 Fellow in the Pew Scholars Program at the Carnegie Academy for the Scholarship of Teaching and Learning (CASTL). The second article is a collaborative essay by five historians who worked together on the Visible Knowledge Project (VKP) from 2000 through 2005: Michael Coventry (Georgetown University), Peter Felten (Elon University), David Jaffee (City College of New York and the Graduate Center, City University of New York), Cecilia O'Leary (California State University, Monterey Bay), and Tracey Weis (Millersville University). Directed by Randy Bass of Georgetown University and co-directed by Bret Eynon of LaGuardia Community College, the VKP sought "to improve the quality of college and university teaching through a focus on both student learning and faculty development in technology-enhanced environments."[3] As the participating historians explained, questions of teaching and learning quickly became central to their thinking about how to engage their students in using visuals and new media to develop a sophisticated approach to history. Bringing new forms of evidence and analysis into their history classrooms helped them not only to promote the cognitive processes they sought to foster in novice learners but also to understand better the methods we use as historians in our research and writing for others in the profession.

The last article in Part Four is by Sam Wineburg, professor at Stanford University, co-director of the National Center for History Education, and prizewinning author of *Historical Thinking and Other Unnatural Acts: Charting the Future of Teaching the Past.*[4] Wineburg surveyed the results of standardized American history tests over the past century and found student performance remarkably consistent. The reason, he explained, has less to do with how history is taught or what students really know than with how historical knowledge is measured. He described in wonderfully accessible detail how standardized tests are constructed and why we should not expect to see improvement in test scores anytime soon. Despite doubts that standardized tests would disappear, he sketched an alternative approach to history education and assessment that would liberate students and teachers from the inexorable demands of the bell curve.

Notes

1. Ernest L. Boyer, *Scholarship Reconsidered: Priorities of the Professoriate* (Princeton, N.J., 1990).

2. T. S. Eliot, "Little Gidding," in T. S. Eliot, *The Complete Poems and Plays, 1909–1950* (New York, 1962), 145.

3. On the Visible Knowledge Project, see http://crossroads.georgetown.edu/vkp/.

4. Sam Wineburg, *Historical Thinking and Other Unnatural Acts: Charting the Future of Teaching the Past* (Philadelphia: Temple University Press, 2001).

Lendol Calder

Uncoverage: Toward a Signature Pedagogy for the History Survey

History professors say the darnedest things. Like the one who summed up his teaching philosophy declaring, "If I said it, that means they learned it!" Or the colleague who scoffed at "trendy" educational reforms because, as she put it, "You can't teach students how to think until you've taught them what to think." Then there was the time an eminent historian rose to speak after my presentation on how *not* to teach the history survey. "I may be doing it wrong," conceded this gifted, award-winning teacher, "but I am doing it in the proper and customary way."[1]

The professor's droll remark points to where we stand today in the teaching of history surveys, perhaps especially the U.S. history survey. Generations of undergraduates can testify that introductory surveys are taught in a "proper and customary way." "First you listen to a lecture, then you read a textbook, then you take a test," is how a student described her survey to me, adding, significantly, "It wasn't different, really, from my other introductory courses." Here historians flirt with calamity.

When the only history course most people ever take from a professionally trained historian tempts students to believe there is little difference between history and sociology or history and biology except for the facts to be learned, it is not surprising that teachers occasionally sense they might be "doing it wrong."[2]

The feeling is as old as it is accurate. For as long as there have been survey courses, some teachers have suspected that the vacant expressions on students' faces (so famously portrayed in the "Anyone? . . . Anyone?" history-class scene in the movie *Ferris Bueller's Day Off*) are not so much indications of the students' shortcomings as predictable products of the survey itself, whose basic design requires professors and textbooks to pass on essential information about a historical period. This emphasis on "coverage" accounts for the course's trademark routines—earnest lectures, stolid textbooks, decontextualized assessments, flagrant and routine violations of Auerbach's law (as in Arnold "Red" Auerbach, the distinguished learning theorist and coach of National Basketball Association [NBA] legends, who summarized his teaching philosophy by declaring, "It's not what you say; it's what they hear").[3] Some teachers have always suspected that to make the survey "a serious house . . . proper to grow wise in," to borrow imagery from

Journal of American History 92 (2006): 1358–70.

Philip Larkin, it would not be enough to juice up the lectures and write better textbooks. Nor would it be enough to tinker with content by assigning a few novels, or rearranging the chronology, or reorganizing lectures around a set of new themes. For at least a century, some have asserted that nothing less will do than a complete redesign of the survey, from its basic assumptions up.[4]

So when I claim that the typical, coverage-oriented survey is a wrongheaded way to introduce students to the goodness and power of history, I am not saying anything outrageous or new. But pedagogical inertia happens. While everything else touching the survey has changed—think back to the days of the presidential synthesis, when classroom technology meant pull-down maps and chalkboards, when tweedy professors lectured to what back then were called "freshmen"—the old routines of coverage remain firmly in place. Thus the problem that bedeviled our teachers and their teachers before them continues to vex us today: What is to be done with the history survey?

I hope it is not useless to argue yet again for significant changes in the way we teach these most important of history courses. True, obstacles that defeated earlier calls for reform have not gone away. Professional reward structures continue to discourage careful inquiry into the problems of teaching. Institutional constraints still make large classes obligatory, while old folk beliefs about learning continue to be impervious to cognitive science. Neither do current political trends favor reform, unless one believes that narrow testing regimes and a return to "traditional" American history should define the horizon of what is possible.

But other developments are more encouraging. Everywhere, the mystique of coverage is abating. Teachers no longer believe they can cover everything of importance, and more feel the awkwardness of teaching about social differences in the past while disregarding what this knowledge might mean for the construction of authority and teacher-student interactions in present-day classrooms. Meanwhile, a wired student generation sends up its own drumbeat for change, tap-tapping their laptops, MP3 players, and PDAs in battles against classroom tedium.

Checking e-mail in class is rude and immature, but it is also a predictable response to a worn-out pedagogy that no longer has a place in the history survey. Now that cognitive scientists have developed a basic consensus on the principles of learning, and now that historians are playing a significant role in efforts to field-test and expand this research through a scholarship of teaching and learning, it is a good moment to remind ourselves what the introductory survey could be (and what it already is for some teachers) if we replaced generic pedagogies of coverage with teaching and learning marked by the distinctive signature of history.

This essay will describe such a course, a U.S. history survey I have been teaching and studying since becoming a Carnegie scholar in 1999.[5] But my course is not unique. Other courses laid out along similar lines are being developed by teachers at many different types of institutions.[6] So much experimentation is going on, in fact, that one wonders whether historians might not be close to establishing a new "signature pedagogy" for the introductory history course.

What is a signature pedagogy? And what would it look like in a history survey? Consider the distinctive method used for teaching and learning in a typical law school. In the case-dialogue method, a law professor calls on a student to summarize a case. If the summary of essential facts is incoherent or factually wrong, public embarrassment follows. If the answer is lucid, the student is not yet let off the hook; now the professor grills the student to determine the limits of what he or she knows, often by changing the facts of the case into hypothetical scenarios—"hypos"—for which students are asked to rule on the new facts and explain their reasoning. It is a demanding classroom routine that is part Socratic dialogue, part Spanish Inquisition. The goal is to teach beginning students to think like lawyers, which means less a perfect recall of little-known cases than a habitual fidelity to established law. So when a student inevitably complains, "I know that's what the law says, but it hardly seems fair," the professor seizes the opportunity to correct the student's untutored inclination to view legal questions as a problem of justice or fairness, reminding the class that they are training to become lawyers, not ethicists or politicians. Some professors do this more gently than others, and every professor contributes a personal style to her or his course. But the basic pedagogy for teaching law students is everywhere the same.

And so it goes across the professions, observes Lee S. Shulman, president of the Carnegie Foundation for the Advancement of Teaching, who for the last ten years has been directing studies on preparation for the professions. Medical schools train physicians through the bedside ritual of clinical rounds; engineering faculty put students together in collaborative-design studios; theological seminaries mingle study with prayer and community service. It is a hallmark of professional education that each discipline has developed characteristic forms of teaching and learning that, like the name of a person written in his own hand, are done in the same way from teacher to teacher and institution to institution. These signature pedagogies, as Shulman refers to them, disclose important information about the personality of a disciplinary field—its values, knowledge, and manner of thinking—almost, perhaps, its total world view. Shulman's team of scholars finds that signature pedagogies are more common in fields like law and medicine than in the liberal arts, perhaps because teachers in the professions must answer to practitioners for what students know. "Knowing" in the professions means more than filling in the blanks with correct answers—it refers to what a person can *do*. For reasons Shulman and scholars at the Carnegie Foundation are continuing to study, signature pedagogies make a difference in shaping future performance and passing on the values and hopes of the members of disciplinary fields.[7]

A signature pedagogy, then, is what beginning students in the professions have but history beginners typically do not: ways of being taught that require them to do, think, and value what practitioners in the field are doing, thinking, and valuing. Which is exactly the way it should be, some will stoutly maintain. Professional schools are graduate schools. How could instructional methods intended for graduate students possibly work for novices who lack even basic information about the past? Facts must come first, a lot of history teachers will say. Only after a groundwork of factual knowledge has been laid can students go on to more advanced interpretive work. In this commonsense view of the matter, history can lay claim to a signature pedagogy of its own—the research seminar—but this method is reserved for upper-level students and those pursuing advanced degrees.

The "facts first" view is based on half-truths that deserve to be taken seriously. Historical facts are important, and instruction should be fitted to the level of the students. But defenders of traditional survey methods who want students to know certain things—what Reconstruction was, or why slavery happened, or who fought whom in World War II—risk the negation of their objectives by a very large error. Many of the assumptions historians make about learning have been shown by cognitive scientists to be quite wrong, including what Sam Wineburg calls the "attic theory" of cognition. As it happens, people do not collect facts the way homeowners collect furniture, storing pieces in the attic for use at a later time. Teachers may like to think they are "furnishing the mind," but since the late 1950s, investigations of human mental functioning have shown that this metaphor falls apart when taken too literally. Facts are not like furniture at all; they are more like dry ice, disappearing at room temperature. Cognitive science has much to teach history teachers about memory, about the relation between facts and thinking, and about the nature of historical thinking itself.[8] Or we could listen to our own. When Charles G. Sellers heard University of California, Berkeley, alumni reflecting on the value of their history courses, he resolved to abandon his "facts first" survey. In an address to the 1969 meeting of the American Historical Association, Sellers explained why:

> The notion that students must first be given facts and then at some distant time in the future will "think" about them is both a cover-up and a perversion of pedagogy. . . . One does not collect facts he does not need, hang on to them, and then stumble across the propitious moment to use them. One is first perplexed by a problem and then makes use of facts to achieve a solution.[9]

Cognitive scientists have shown Sellers to be right.

The problem with defenders of traditional surveys, then, is not that they care about facts too much but that they do not care about facts enough to inquire into the nature of how people learn them. Built on wobbly, lay theories of human cognition, coverage-oriented surveys must share in the blame for Americans' deplorable ignorance of history.[10]

The late Roland Marchand wondered: Why are historians so incurious about learning?[11] For historians who are also teachers, not being curious about learning is an uncharacteristic failure of the scholarly imagination—and perhaps the moral imagination too, as when professors write off students who learn little from lectures or have not excelled in school, in short, the ones who are not like themselves. The distance historians traditionally have kept from research on learning is obvious in the way historians talk about teaching, as was apparent several years ago in a round table discussion of the U.S. history survey published in this journal. The participants, prominent scholars and gifted teachers all, talked cogently and perceptively about aspects of their teaching but not a single reference was made to serious studies of cognition, learning, historical thinking, or course design.[12] The problem with this kind of autodidactic conversation is that although able professors will develop a certain wisdom of practice, a knowledge based on hunches, personal experience, and limited scholarly reading will also lead them to make what expert authorities regard as appalling blunders and howlers. Preoccupied with what to teach while ignoring the equally important matter of *how* to teach it, historians have been aptly described by David Pace as "amateurs in the operating room."[13]

But change is coming. The scholarship of teaching and learning is bringing home to historians valuable knowledge about learning in our own language and journals.

Research-based studies of exceptional history teachers show that whereas no two accomplished teachers teach in exactly the same way, effective history teaching is oriented toward what Grant Wiggins and Jay McTighe call "uncoverage."[14] In traditional surveys "to cover" a subject means "to travel over" or "to go the length of" a period. But coverage has other meanings too; it can mean "to conceal," "to cover up," or "to throw a blanket over" something. Covering up history as historians know it is one thing that traditional surveys do very well—hiding what it really means to be good at history.[15] But it does not have to be this way. Survey instructors should aim to uncover history. We should be designing classroom environments that expose the very things hidden away by traditional survey instruction: the linchpin ideas of historical inquiry that are not obvious or easily comprehended; the inquiries, arguments, assumptions, and points of view that make knowledge what it is for practitioners of our discipline; the cognitive contours of history as an epistemological domain.

The theory and research justifying uncoverage approaches are already in place. What we still need are professionwide conversations about how to translate theory into good practice. To fire up that debate, I offer here an example of what uncoverage looks like in practice.

What follows is a description of a survey course I teach called "U.S. History: World War II to the Present."[16] The ten-week course is taught to thirty-five students but would be adaptable to larger classes with minor adjustments and the help of teaching assistants. It is not my claim that the course in all its details constitutes a signature pedagogy for the history survey. It is on the deeper structures of the course—the goals, student performances, and course routines—that history's signature is inscribed.

"U.S. History: World War II to the Present" does not actually begin with World War II. Rather, my survey begins with a prologue or overture in which students consider the nature of historical study itself. Taking place over four class meetings, the prologue is designed around questions and exercises meant to uncover important aspects of the historical enterprise: What is history? Why study it? What problems trouble historical knowledge? What stories, tropes, and patterns do people typically see in the past?

Committing time to problems normally reserved for historiography courses seems justified by Sam Wineburg's observation that "the problem with students is not that they don't know enough about history. The problem is that they don't know what history is in the first place."[17] Students come to college thinking that history is what one finds in a textbook: a stable, authoritative body of knowledge that, when remembered, somehow makes the world a better place. The prologue features exercises designed to expose the inadequacies of such a view. For example, when students write brief "histories" of a civil disturbance in the Spike Lee movie *Do the Right Thing*, they are surprised to learn just how different people's interpretations of an event can be, even when everyone works from the same evidence.[18] Historical knowledge, the students learn, is fraught with difficulties, which means that the stories and claims made by historians will always be contestable. This is a truth expert historians often assume everyone knows, but in fact they do not—it has to be uncovered. My prologue does not give students a deep understanding of history. But it is enough to expose students' basic misconceptions about the nature of history and prepare them mentally for the hard work that is to come.

After the prologue, the remaining weeks of the course are given to eight problem areas spanning the course's chronological boundaries. Beginning with World War II, we examine "Origins of the Cold War," "Society and Culture in the Fifties," "The Civil Rights Movement," "Kennedy/Johnson Liberalism," "Vietnam," "Sixties Cultural Rebellion," "1980s Culture Wars," and "The End of the Cold War." Each topic is given three class meetings, with each of the three devoted to a different kind of study: the first to visual inquiry, the second to critical inquiry, the third to moral inquiry. I make no attempt to cover the topics thoroughly or to provide a seamless, authoritative narrative or argument. Rather, the problem areas become opportunities for students and teacher to do history themselves, to encounter the past in all its messy, uncertain, and elusive wonder. Can beginning students learn to do history the way professionals do it? Of course not. But my studies have found they can learn to execute a basic set of moves crucial to the development of historical mindedness. I want students to learn six such moves, or cognitive habits: questioning, connecting, sourcing, making inferences, considering alternate perspectives, and recognizing limits to one's knowledge, all in the service of understanding American history since 1945.[19] Here is how it works.

Historical thinking, like other forms of disciplinary thinking, begins with clear-eyed wonder before the world. But questioning is an extraordinarily difficult skill for most students, probably because for their whole lives teachers and textbooks have posed the questions for them ("Write an essay on the following question . . ."). Feeding students a steady diet of other people's questions is a sure-fire prescription for mental dyspepsia. So the first move students need to learn is that of asking good historical questions. To this end the first meeting in every unit is designed to intensify students' desire to inquire.

I find that films are good for this purpose. A well-chosen film orients students to basic information about a subject and motivates them to take an empathic leap into the past. Films make good launch pads for thought as they provide interpretations students can push against with their own questions ("Was World War II really a 'good war' like Frank Capra said?"). Most of the films screened in my course are documentaries, with an occasional historical Hollywood drama or period propaganda film on the schedule. On film day my objective is to teach students how to learn from film, how to view moving images with an awareness of the manipulations involved. Visual literacy is essential to both liberal education and the study of the recent past, for which the moving image is an important source of information. But in addition to literacy and student motivation, my ultimate objective on the first day of each unit is to create an environment so rich in information and so charged with interesting problems that students who are inert in the face of lectures and textbooks will be stirred to ask a few historical questions. After the film awakens their capacity for wonder, I then send students out to do what historically minded people do: follow a question that takes them beyond what they already know.

Following the meeting given to visual inquiry, students prepare for the second meeting in the unit—we call it "history workshop"—by examining primary documents pertaining to the week's subject (I use document readers for this purpose). Students write three- to five-page essays on questions of their choosing using the evidence they have examined. When the history workshop convenes, this essay is everyone's ticket to class—no one is allowed entry without it. This requirement has a marvelous effect on the quality of class discussions. It ensures that everyone not only has read the documents but also has read them closely enough to construct a historical argument, thus making each student the class expert on at least one facet of the subject. At the beginning of class, students submit notecards with the questions that prompted their essays. While I collate the cards into piles of similar questions, students pass their papers around and read what others have written. When I am done sorting the questions, the papers are handed back, and the history workshop begins.

This meeting has two objectives. My first goal is to facilitate discussion of the questions students have brought. The second goal is to introduce each week a new intellectual move characteristic of the way historians think. I work toward these goals in the manner of a coach—but not like a tennis coach standing on one side of the net opposite a group of students on the other, volleying back and forth. Rather, on workshop day I work like a soccer coach, throwing questions into play from my position on the sideline and then watching as students kick the questions around, advancing toward tentative conclusions as they learn to play the fun yet serious game of academic discourse. As the discussion proceeds, I look for opportunities to call time-out, stopping intellectual play to conduct short clinics on elements of analytic reading, persuasive argument, or historical thinking. For example, on the very first workshop day I almost always have to coach students to respond to each other's contributions with a version of what I call the "But" move and Gerald Graff calls "Arguespeak": "She said X, but I say Y."[20] Later I coach them to ask the useful little question: "What is the evidence or reason for believing what you just said?" Until intellectual moves like these are uncovered, students rarely talk about history the way historians do with each other. That is because they have been schooled to think that being good at history means being ready to supply a correct answer. It takes some doing to get them to believe that a good question is worth a dozen hasty opinions.

As it happens, questioning is the first of six cognitive moves I introduce one at a time in the history workshop days following the prologue. Until all have been explained, practiced, and practiced some more, the papers students bring to the workshops are really quite *terrible*. And why shouldn't they be? No one has ever made plain to them how one makes sense of historical texts. With so much to do in the workshop meetings, it never happens that we cover all the questions students bring to class. This, too, is an important lesson about historical investigation. Students come to understand what a difficult, untidy business it is to create historical knowledge—what is covered up behind the neat, handsome pages of a history textbook. Writing their own histories, students come to understand what history is not: a definitive story, facts strung together, a clear-cut and painlessly acquired knowledge of the past.

Writing their own histories primes students to read what professional historians have written. So for the third meeting in a unit, students read selections from two histories of the United States: Howard Zinn's *A People's History of the United States* and Paul Johnson's *A History of the American People.*[21] These "untextbooks" support the goal of uncoverage in several ways. Their status as best sellers means students will be learning to think discerningly about the kind of popular history they are most likely to encounter in future years as adults. Students appreciate that the texts are inexpensive, while I appreciate that Zinn and Johnson between them will cover most of the topics a historically literate person should be familiar with for our period. Thus if the 1954 Central Intelligence Agency (CIA) military coup in Guatemala does not happen to come up in class, students still will have read two accounts of it in Zinn and Johnson (two accounts—that is critically important). Even though these histories are completely lacking in charts, sidebars, pictures, and Web support, students actually read these histories and even hold onto them after the course is over, rarely selling them back to the campus bookstore. Why? Because it is not dry coverage that drives the two histories but compelling moral visions expressed in provocative arguments. When students read Zinn's and Johnson's strikingly different interpretations of American history, their attention is drawn by the thrill of a quarrel, then captured and held by the gravity of each author's *telos*. They must now confront, inescapably, an essential feature of historical mindedness—that history is "an argument without end." A textbook can say this, of course. But it cannot repeal Auerbach's law.

Our third class day, then, is for inquiry and reflection on the meaning of past events. Class begins with a quiz on the main points of the assigned readings. To students who have been taught to read textbooks for information, it is a revelation to discover that historians are not just storytellers but case makers too. Initially, they struggle to recognize the main claim of a reading. But by the end of the term, the recurring quizzes have made most students adept at recognizing historical arguments. With the quiz out of the way, I lead the class in examining the contrasting interpretations of the two historians, comparing what they say with conclusions we have reached in our previous workshop. The histories by Zinn and Johnson become prompts for inquiring into the moral significance of historical events: what the past means for our ethics and self-knowledge and how knowledge of the past shapes our general understanding of the world (and vice versa).

In this third meeting I exercise greater control than in the second, sometimes lecturing for minutes at a time on the interpretive questions I want to consider that day. But by the third meeting students can be so primed with questions and historical arguments of their own that sometimes it is impossible to talk uninterrupted for long. When students see their own arguments from the history workshop showing up in the works of professional historians, their self-confidence grows. At the same time, students are more likely to read authorities with a critical eye because the historical arguments they wrote from primary documents have given them an understanding of the choices confronting Zinn and Johnson when they created their histories—choices to ask certain questions but not others, to emphasize certain themes while ignoring other topics, to reason from anecdotes or quantitative data.

At the end of the course, students complete a final assignment that calls for them to pull together everything they have learned. With Zinn and Johnson in mind, they write a memo to Sen. Robert C. Byrd arguing for one of the books as the best history to adopt for a program of adult education. It is an impossible assignment. Both books are arguably good histories, or bad ones. But impossible tasks call for the utmost one is capable of. That is the point of this summative assignment: to see what students have learned to do after ten weeks of training. What kinds of questions are they capable of asking? Can they recognize connections between disparate sources of information? How do they read texts: as neutral sources of information or as human-stained palimpsests of authorial limitation and intention requiring careful deciphering and positioning in a social context? How well do they marshal evidence to support claims about U.S. history? Do they consider arguments and perspectives different from their own? What is the quality of their critical self knowledge— are they humble about what they claim to know? These are the six cognitive moves the course is designed to support. My survey uncovers history only imperfectly, but the thinking I see in even the worst of these papers convinces me students are learning more now than in the lecture and textbook surveys I offered years ago.

Teachers often fear to break from coverage-oriented pedagogies because they worry that with less content being covered, students will know less about the past.[22] This fear is not groundless, but it is usually exaggerated. The largest studies completed to date of teaching and learning in the sciences show that stepping away from lectures and textbooks, far from condemning students to knowing fewer facts about a subject, appears to lead to better understanding of foundational knowledge.[23] We lack comparable studies of understanding and remembering for students in history courses. But in my department, when several of my colleagues and I converted our survey courses from coverage to uncoverage, we noted that the pass/fail rate of students taking a licensing examination for certifications as history teachers remained unchanged. Apparently, our uncoverage orientation is not cheating students of the ability to do well on traditional multiple-choice history tests.

But the kinds of learning promoted in uncoverage courses are not measurable with bubble tests. To find out if my students become more adept at the six cognitive habits taught in my survey, I designed a simple assessment procedure employing think-aloud protocols to compare what students were able to do with historical documents before and after taking my course. Think alouds are a widely used research tool developed by cognitive psychologists to study how people solve problems. In my think alouds, participants were trained to give voice to any and all thoughts as they attempted to make sense of seven to ten short historical documents on the battle of the Little Big Horn (before the course) and the Haymarket bombing (after the course). Their verbalized thoughts were recorded and transcribed for later analysis to determine patterns of cognition used to make sense of the documents. In fields such as reading comprehension, mathematics, chemistry, and history, think alouds have proved very useful for identifying what constitutes "expert knowledge" as distinguished from the thinking processes of beginners in the field. But in my pair of studies, I used think alouds to measure changes in thinking patterns over time for selected individuals enrolled in my survey.

Of course, I could have studied the cognitive development of students by comparing papers written early and late in the course, and I did. But as finished products, papers conceal as much as they reveal. The advantage of think alouds over graded student work is that they allow one to observe the process of thinking in a raw, unvarnished state. Think alouds reveal not only what a student thinks but also how she came to think it. Think alouds expose the stumblings, the hesitations, the blind alleys, the good ideas entertained and abandoned, the inner workings of a mind trying to make sense of the past. Listening to my students think out loud as they tried to make sense of documents is the single most eye-opening experience I have had in my years as a teacher.

What my studies revealed is that even in a short, ten-week course students on average make modest to occasionally dramatic gains in all six aspects of historical thinking taught in the course. The ability to formulate historical questions led all other areas of improvement (though ironically, and somewhat disturbingly, evidence from post-course surveys indicates that students consistently rate questioning as the *least* valuable skill to be learned in the course). Another finding from my investigations may reassure those who worry that students will react negatively to departures from the comfortable routines of old-school surveys: while students in my survey complain that uncoverage increases their work load, they overwhelmingly prefer uncoverage to more traditional course designs, and they report that their regard for history and desire to study it increases over the length of the course. For more about student learning in my survey and how I went about studying it, please visit the course Web site at www.indiana.edu/~jah/textbooks/2006/calder.

To return now to my theme of a signature pedagogy: Why does my course (or any course) make a difference for students? Some say what matters most is that teachers have a thorough knowledge of their subject. Others say enthusiasm is the truly indispensable thing, while still others say it is the ability to project an ethic of care. All of these qualities matter. But when students reflect on their experiences with my course they point most often to design features shared by all signature pedagogies, elements Lee Shulman suggests may explain why these ways of teaching are so effective for learning.[24]

First, signature pedagogies unfold from big questions that students are likely to find meaningful, questions that are useful for uncovering how expert practitioners in a discipline think and act. In the case of my survey, instead of asking, What does the textbook say? or What does the professor say?, my course begins with an important question students are already asking—What is the story of American history?—and goes from there. Who are Americans? What have we accomplished? How do we judge what we have done? Are things getting better or worse, or are metanarratives even possible to believe in the first place? I have learned from one of my prologue assignments ("Write a two-page history of the United States, without looking up any facts.") what Peter Seixas and others have pointed out: students who have been making sense of their society and national identity since before preschool have been greatly influenced by heritage tales and mythhistory, which is why the history survey must start there.[25] My course takes what students already know and tests it against a different way of knowing the past, the way professionally trained historians construct knowledge. So the second big question of the course is: How do historians know what they claim to know? And the third question follows from the second: Why would one want to think the way historians think? Every element of the course directly addresses one or more of these big questions.

A second characteristic of signature pedagogies is that the intellectual project envisioned by their big questions is advanced through a standard pattern of instructional routines. Routines are essential for learning. Routines provide students with a necessary scaffolding of instructional and social support as they struggle to learn the "unnatural act" of historical thinking. Teachers often say that "critical" or "historical" thinking is a goal of their course. But without effective routines, the goal is unreachable for all but a few students. Professors who ask students to read primary documents know that the exercise can often be a frustrating experience. In fact, good intentions may lead to unintended consequences, as when students become so frustrated with multiple sources of text that they disengage from the course, or worse, form serious misconceptions about historical analysis, believing that primary documents have more inherent veracity than other documents or that one person's perspective is as good as another.[26] In my early attempts to have students work with primary documents, my efforts misfired because I did not realize how much scaffolding it takes for students to learn the unfamiliar, even off-putting habits of mind historians can take for granted. I thought it would be enough if students watched me model historical thinking in class, but this assumption proved to be terribly wrong. Students need models, but it is routines that form habits. This is why I limit the number of cognitive moves uncovered in my course to six and give students repeated opportunities to practice them in their weekly workshop essays. Recurring assignments that require students to make sense of primary documents are crucial for learning the signature of history.

My survey supports student learning with two levels of routines. On the day-to-day level there is what I refer to as "batting practice"—repeated exercises like the main-point quizzes and the primary-document essays that teach specific skills. At the larger level of the overall course design are the routines of "visual inquiry" for questioning, "critical inquiry" for constructing historical knowledge, and "moral inquiry" for reflective application. The pattern of three integrated course meetings is very popular with students. It satisfies their need for stable expectations while appealing to different learning styles. Indeed, there is evidence to suggest that hybrid pedagogies like mine, combining student-centered, active-learning approaches (the history workshop meeting) with teacher-centered approaches (the first and third days of each unit) are more effective at producing deep understanding than either approach alone.[27]

Finally, as with other signature pedagogies, my course requires regular, public student performances. "Your students are so busy," observed a colleague visiting my class on a workshop day. What he saw was students working collaboratively, like students in an engineering-design studio, examining each other's papers for examples of the cognitive move introduced at the previous workshop and making suggestions for how to improve each other's work. On other days my class looks more like law school, as I cold-call on students to source a document or to respond to claims made by Zinn or Johnson. At times we even do something a little like clinical rounds, as when students huddle around a document and I ask the group for an opinion on what problems of interpretation confront us in this source. Following Shulman, it seems to me that active performances like these are important for at least two reasons. To begin with, they push students into moments of uncertainty comparable to the ambiguous situations they will face outside class, when historical judgment may be all that separates the discerning from the deceived. Additionally, putting students on the spot creates "atmospheres of risk-taking and foreboding, as well as occasions for exhilaration and excitement." In other words, it gets students engaged. "To be honest," a student wrote on her evaluation, "I was kind of scared shitless because I wasn't sure I could meet the demand of changing my thinking like you were asking." The performance element in signature pedagogies, Shulman is tempted to conclude, produces the pain that is necessary for gains in intellectual formation.[28] Of course, what teachers will want to aim for is the sweet spot between paralyzing students with fear and lulling them to sleep. Bruce Kochis of the University of Washington, Bothell, first showed me what this spot looks like when I was a young assistant professor full of illusions of competence about my teaching. Kochis summed up the crucial matter of student performances with questions I still ask myself on the way to class: Am I a professor? Then what will I say today? But if I am a teacher, what will they *do* today?

No course is ever finished or fully realizes the intentions of its designer. Twelve years ago, I took a deep breath, checked to see that no one was looking, and yanked my survey free from the "proper and customary way." Students freaked. Their teacher floundered. But eventually my intentions were rescued by the scholarship of teaching and learning. The work done by teachers and scholars in that field has made it possible to ground the design of my survey in knowledge more solid than handed-down folk wisdom or my own intuitions.

By presenting my survey as an example of uncoverage, I am not proposing that my course be the signature pedagogy every survey teacher should adopt. Is it really possible (or desirable) for history professors to adopt a distinctive pedagogy for the survey on the order of the case-dialogue method in law or clinical rounds in medicine? The question deserves consideration. Perhaps we will decide to call the analysis of historical texts history's signature pedagogy and leave it at that. I hope that we will be more ambitious. Let us at least talk more publicly and more deliberately about what we are doing in our courses.[29] Those who stay isolated in their classrooms will continue to say and believe the darnedest things. Exploring together the potential of uncoverage, a community of scholarly teachers may find ways to impress the signature of history on the history survey.[30]

Notes

1. He later told me he was quoting George Bernard Shaw.

2. On the "disciplinary homogenization" caused by introductory courses, see Sam Wineburg, *Historical Thinking and Other Unnatural Acts: Charting the Future of Teaching the Past* (Philadelphia, 2001), 79–80. Evidence for a "proper and customary way" to teach surveys can be seen in a recent study of eight hundred U.S. history survey course syllabi posted on the World Wide Web. See Daniel J. Cohen, "By the Book: Assessing the Place of Textbooks in U.S. Survey Courses," *Journal of American History* 91 (March 2005): 1405–15. For a report on the "remarkable stability and uniformity in the design and structure of the U.S. and European history introductory courses" based on a 2003 nationwide survey, see Robert Townsend, "College Board Examines Survey Course," *OAH Newsletter* 33 (Aug. 2005): 1. On the roles, functions, and consequences of textbooks in introductory courses in other disciplines, see Paul W. Richardson, "Reading and Writing from Textbooks in Higher Education: A Case Study from Economics," *Studies in Higher Education* 29 (Aug. 2004): 505–21.

3. *Ferris Bueller's Day Off*, dir. John Hughes (Paramount, 1986); "Red Auerbach: True Stories and NBA Legends," Morning Edition, National Public Radio, Nov. 2, 2004.

4. For old debates over the introductory course among historians at Stanford University, see Larry Cuban, *How Scholars Trumped Teachers: Change without Reform in University Curriculum, Teaching, and Research, 1890–1990* (New York, 1999). For recent programmatic calls to amend the survey, see David Trask, "Rethinking the Survey Course," *OAH Newsletter* 30 (May 2002): 3–6; and Peter Stearns, *Meaning over Memory: Recasting the Teaching of Culture and History* (Chapel Hill, N.C., 1993), 172–205. For recent efforts to improve history instruction, see Allan E. Yarema, "A Decade of Debate: Improving Content and Interest in History Education," *History Teacher* 35 (May 2002): 389–98.

5. The Carnegie Scholars Program brings together outstanding faculty from a variety of disciplines and institutions committed to investigating and documenting significant issues in the teaching and learning of their fields. For information about individual scholar projects, go to the Carnegie Scholars list at <www.carnegiefoundation.org/CASTL/highered/scholarlist.htm> (Nov. 22, 2005).

6. Recent examples of innovation in history surveys can be found in Peter N. Stearns, "Getting Specific about Training in Historical Analysis: A Case Study in World History," in *Knowing, Teaching, and Learning History: National and International Perspectives*, ed. Peter N. Stearns, Peter Seixas, and Sam Wineburg (New York, 2000), 419–36; Stuart D. Sears, "Reinventing the Survey: Pedagogical Strategies for Engagement," *AHA*

Perspectives 43 (Feb. 2005): 21; Julie Roy Jeffrey, "The Survey, Again," *OAH Magazine of History* 17 (April 2003): 52–54; and Russell Olwell, "Building Higher-Order Historical Thinking Skills in a College Survey Class," *Teaching History* 27 (Spring 2002): 22–32.

7. Lee S. Shulman, "Signature Pedagogies in the Professions," *Dædalus* 134 (Summer 2005): 52–59; Lee S. Shulman, "Pedagogies of Uncertainty," *Liberal Learning* 91 (Spring 2005): 18–25.

8. For summaries of cognition as it relates to learning, see John D. Bransford, Ann L. Brown, and Rodney R. Cocking, eds., *How People Learn: Brain, Mind, Experience, and School* (Washington, D.C., 1999), 8–16, 30, 147–51, 225–26; and Cameron Fincher, "Learning Theory and Research," in *Teaching and Learning in the College Classroom*, ed. Kenneth A. Feldman and Michael B. Paulsen (Needham Heights, Mass., 1998), 57–80. Sam Wineburg referred to the "attic theory" of cognition in conversation with me in 2000.

9. Charles G. Sellers here paraphrased words by another scholar, S. Samuel Shermis. See Charles G. Sellers, "Is History on the Way out of the Schools and Do Historians Care?" *Social Education* 33 (May 1969): 511.

10. Sam Wineburg, "Crazy for History," *Journal of American History* 90 (March 2004): 1413–14. For a summary of studies demonstrating that students remember very little from lecture-based, coverage-oriented courses, see L. Dee Fink, *Creating Significant Learning Experiences: An Integrated Approach to Designing College Courses* (San Francisco, 2003), 2–4.

11. Roland Marchand, "Further Comment on Daniel D. Trifan's 'Active Learning: A Critical Examination,'" *AHA Perspectives* 35 (March 1997): 29.

12. Gary Kornblith and Carol Lasser, eds., "Teaching the American History Survey at the Opening of the Twenty-First Century: A Round Table Discussion," *Journal of American History* 87 (March 2001): 1409–41.

13. David Pace, "The Amateur in the Operating Room: History and the Scholarship of Teaching and Learning," *American Historical Review* 109 (Oct. 2004): 1171–92.

14. Grant Wiggins and Jay McTighe, *Understanding by Design* (Alexandria, Va., 1998), 98–114. For a summary of research on effective history teachers, see Richard J. Paxton and Sam Wineburg, "Expertise and the Teaching of History," in *Routledge International Companion to Education*, ed. Bob Moon, Sally Brown, and Miriam Ben-Peretz (New York, 2000), 855–64.

15. Sam Wineburg, "Teaching the Mind Good Habits," *Chronicle of Higher Education*, April 11, 2003, p. B20; Wineburg, *Historical Thinking and Other Unnatural Acts*, 12–17; Robert B. Bain, "Into the Breach: Using Research and Theory to Shape History Instruction," in *Knowing, Teaching, and Learning History*, ed. Stearns, Seixas, and Wineburg, 334–36. On what it means to be "good" at history, the landmark text is Wineburg, *Historical Thinking and Other Unnatural Acts*, 3–27, 63–112.

16. For more about the course, including all activities and assignments, answers to frequently asked questions, and evidence I have collected to study how well the course meets its goals, readers are directed to the course Web site at www.indiana.edu/~jah/textbooks/2006/calder. I invite critique and welcome others to help themselves to anything they please, as I have done with other teachers' ideas—there is no plagiarism among pedagogues.

17. Sam Wineburg, "Probing the Depths of Students' Historical Knowledge," *AHA Perspectives* 30 (March 1992): 1.

18. Bain, "Into the Breach," 336–37; *Do the Right Thing*, dir. Spike Lee (40 Acres and a Mule Filmworks, 1989).

19. For definitions of historical thinking, see Wineburg, *Historical Thinking and Other Unnatural Acts*, 3–27, 63–112; and Kathryn T. Spoehr and Luther W. Spoehr, "Learning to Think Historically," *Educational Psychologist* 29 (Spring 1994): 71–77.

20. Gerald Graff, *Clueless in Academe: How Schooling Obscures the Life of the Mind* (New Haven, Conn., 2003), 22–25, 156–72.

21. Howard Zinn, *A People's History of the United States* (New York, 1980); Paul Johnson, *A History of the American People* (New York, 1998).

22. Daniel D. Trifan, "Active Learning: A Critical Examination," *AHA Perspectives* 35 (March 1997): 23; Sean Wilentz, "The Past Is Not a Process," *New York Times*, April 20, 1996, p. E15.

23. Thus far, comparative studies have mostly targeted the sciences. Two important studies are R. R. Hake, "Interactive-Engagement vs. Traditional Methods: A Six Thousand Student Survey of Mechanics Test Data for Introductory Physics Courses," *American Journal of Physics* 66 (Jan. 1998): 64–74; and S. E. Lewis and J. E. Lewis, "Departing from Lectures: An Evaluation of a Peer-Led Guided Inquiry Alternative," *Journal of Chemical Education* 82, no. 1 (2005): 135–39. A thoughtful summary of research on active learning can be found in M. Prince, "Does Active Learning Work? A Review of the Research," *Journal of Engineering Education* 93 (July 2004): 223–31.

24. Shulman, "Signature Pedagogies in the Professions," 56–58.

25. Peter Seixas, "The Purpose of Teaching Canadian History," *Canadian Social Studies* 36 (Winter 2002) <www.quasar.ualberta.ca/css/Css_36_2/index36_2htm#Articles> (Nov. 22, 2005); David Lowenthal, *Possessed by the Past: The Heritage Crusade and the Spoils of History* (New York, 1996).

26. Bain, "Into the Breach," 334–36; Susan A. Stahl, Cynthia R. Hynd, Bruce K. Britton, and Mary M. McNish, "What Happens When Students Read Multiple Source Documents in History?" <http://curry.edschool.virginia.edu/go/clic/nrrc/hist_r45.html> (Nov. 22, 2005). See also results from a three-year Spencer/MacArthur Foundation–supported study of professional development for California history teachers and how it affected student learning: Kathleen Medina et al., "How Do Students Understand the Discipline of History as an Outcome of Teachers' Professional Development?" (2000). For copies of this report contact Kathleen Medina at kmmedina@ucla.edu.

27. S. Nadkarni, "Instructional Methods and Mental Models of Students: An Empirical Investigation," *Academy of Management Learning and Education* 2, no. 4 (2003): 335–51.

28. Shulman, "Signature Pedagogies in the Professions," 57.

29. For other models for public description and reflection on one's survey, see Patrick Allitt, *I'm the Teacher, You're the Student: A Semester in the University Classroom* (Philadelphia, 2005); Peter J. Frederick, "Four Reflections on Teaching and Learning History," *AHA Perspectives* 39 (Oct. 2001); Tom Holt, *Thinking Historically: Narrative, Imagination, and Understanding* (New York, 1995).

30. Lendol Calder wishes to thank Gary Kornblith, Kathy Knight Calder, and the Faculty Research Group of Augustana College for their generous help as he was finishing this article. Many of the ideas in this essay were first formulated in working sessions with fellow historians and Carnegie Scholars David Pace, T. Mills Kelly, William Cutler, Orville Vernon Burton, Bob Bain, and N. Gerald Shenk. He would also like to thank Tim Hall, Noralee Frankel, and Sam Wineburg for their assistance with his Carnegie project, and for their many fine criticisms, the historians and other faculty who attended workshops he conducted on survey pedagogy at Rice University, University of Illinois, University of Virginia, University of Kansas, Arizona State University, Trinity College, Lewis University, Salisbury State University, and the University of Wisconsin system schools.

Michael Coventry, Peter Felten, David Jaffee, Cecilia O'Leary, and Tracey Weis, with Susannah McGowan

Ways of Seeing: Evidence and Learning in the History Classroom

INTRODUCTION

In a recent essay, David Pace decried the "chasm" between current practices in research and those in teaching in our profession. For more than a century, historians have worked together to build a research enterprise "infused with a commitment to rigor and collective responsibility." Yet the discipline's approach to teaching could hardly differ more. Because we generally teach in isolation, behind doors that keep our students in and our colleagues out, a significant gap exists, in both orientation and practice, between our research and our teaching. We tend to frame problems in our research as exciting opportunities, and we often seek out colleagues to discuss our work. When it comes to teaching, however, we see problems as disreputable, something to be hidden, rather than as invitations to further the knowledge of a community of practitioners through discussion and scholarship.[1]

Over the past decade, an increasing number of academics, including many historians, have explored the scholarship of teaching and learning (SoTL) as one way to bridge the chasm by giving the same careful, methodical attention to problems in teaching as to problems in research. As in other forms of scholarship, knowledge claims in SoTL must be embedded in a body of knowledge, open to peer review, and accessible for exchange with and use by disciplinary colleagues. In SoTL for history, then, professional historians consider the questions about student learning that matter to them and apply standards of historical scholarship to tackle those questions. Their lines of inquiry often begin with questions about classroom practice—"How can I help students understand and use primary documents better?"—but return to issues fundamental to teaching and learning historical knowledge. The fundamental questions are varied, but historians engaged in SoTL have concentrated on two broad lines of inquiry: "What do students bring to the history classroom that may have a major impact

Journal of American History 92 (2006): 1371–1402.

on their learning?" and "What mental operations and procedures must [students] master in order to think historically?"[2]

Those initial questions motivated the five authors of the case studies that follow. We are historians at institutions ranging from open-admission public colleges to highly selective private universities and were participants in the Visible Knowledge Project (VKP), a grant-supported project funded by the Atlantic Philanthropies that involved over seventy humanities faculty members on twenty-one campuses across the United States.[3] Over the five years of the project (August 2000 to October 2005), VKP participants sought to make visible and to open for inquiry problems in teaching and student learning across the fields of history, American Studies, and ethnic studies, among others. In these case studies we report research into student learning that responds to three developments. First, the scholarship of teaching and learning, or the *pedagogical turn* in the profession, engages historians in investigations of how students learn to think historically, treating student work as evidence to be evaluated using discipline-specific research methods.

Second, the *pictorial turn* in culture studies prompts historians to reconsider the significance of images in the construction of historical understanding. Despite the ubiquity of images in online archives, in classrooms, and in the broader culture, many history students and scholars struggle to devise reading strategies or protocols that are as rigorous and rewarding as those used to interrogate textual sources. Finally, the *digital turn* in the profession encourages scholars and students to experiment with the use of digital media to develop new forms of historical discourse, through the creation of Web- and multimedia-based articles, archives, and narratives.

THE PEDAGOGICAL TURN

At the beginning of the Visible Knowledge Project, our research explored intersections between new digital environments and our classroom practice. Over the course of our investigations, technology became secondary to questions about student learning and historical thinking. We gradually shifted from asking what new media could do for us as teachers to exploring how students learn historical-thinking skills and content knowledge in our classes. Student work became our crucial source of evidence as we probed to see when and how students made incremental steps (or, more rarely, large leaps) toward historical understanding. Our emphasis was on the processes by which students become more expert in their thinking, so rather than concentrating on the final products of a course (such as exams or research papers) we collected evidence throughout the term, focusing on what the scholar of historical cognition Sam Wineburg has called "the moments of confusion before an interpretation emerges, while indecision and doubt reign and coherence remains elusive." We then approached that evidence as we would sources in our scholarly research—systematically performing close and contextualized readings to develop a narrative response to our original research question.[4]

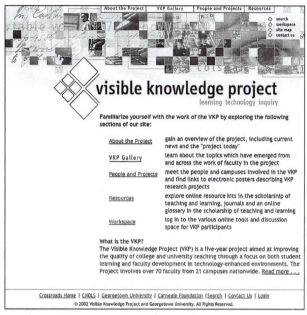

The Visible Knowledge Project (VKP) Web site provides links to syllabi, sample assignments, and multimedia projects from the authors' classes as well as those of colleagues from across fields related to American history and culture. See <http://crossroads.georgetown.edu/vkp/> (Jan. 22, 2006). *Courtesy Visible Knowledge Project, Center for New Designs in Learning & Scholarship, Georgetown University.*

As in traditional historical scholarship, our individual work became part of a larger scholarly discourse about fundamental questions—in this case, about how students learn history in our classrooms, how the use of visual sources shapes and disrupts historical narratives, and how new media can provide innovative opportunities for the expression of historical understanding. Because we based our inquiries on evidence rather than intuition, we could examine our separate projects together to understand crucial issues better. We have attempted to go beyond the anecdotal, beyond the teacher-centered narrative, to analyze evidence rigorously and to engage theoretical aspects of the related scholarship. We apply to all of these strategies what the SoTL theorist Mariolina Rizzi Salvatori has called "unprecedented attentiveness to students' work." For us, this significant move has converted our classrooms into places where, as Salvatori envisions, evidence of student learning becomes "a litmus test for the theories that inform a teacher's approach."[5] Three core factors characterized our effort to undertake research in the scholarship of teaching and learning:

1. *Questions*: a sustained inquiry guided by questions about how students develop historical understanding

2. *Methods*: the use of discipline-based research methods to analyze evidence of student learning
3. *Scholarship*: the connection of individual research projects and findings to a larger body of related scholarship on teaching and learning

This approach has allowed us to begin the process that David Pace has described as "replac[ing] an understanding of teaching based on folk traditions and unfounded personal impressions with one rooted in a rigorous and collective examination of what fosters student learning."[6]

THE PICTORIAL TURN

While an emerging body of scholarship addresses the development of historical-thinking skills using textual sources, little has been published on how the pictorial turn might simultaneously complicate the study of history and offer new opportunities for faculty to teach students to think historically. If, as the historian Robert B. Bain has suggested, "the problem for history teachers begins with trying to understand what defines meaning making in history," then the growing emphasis on understanding history through visual images as artifacts and sources suggests that our inquiries into how students come to understand historical-thinking skills should not be restricted to written texts. Our decision to make images central in our classrooms reflects a convergence of factors. Many cultural theorists argue that we are in the midst of a major transformation. In 1994 W. J. T. Mitchell, a theorist of images, asserted that this change marked the end of the centuries-long text-based linguistic turn in Western society. But historians have been slower than their colleagues in other disciplines to accept the pictorial turn. "If historians have heard of it," the historian of education Sol Cohen noted in 2003, "they have ignored it." Historians traditionally have preferred textual over visual sources, and traditional historians continue to argue for the primacy of written texts. Yet, increasingly some historians have begun to rely on images as essential sources for scholarship, and recent investigations of photographs and portraits, advertisements and buildings, have illuminated significant aspects of the past.[7]

Technological changes have made it easier to use images and other primary sources to teach history, but abundance and availability do not guarantee historical understanding. In the past decade, visual archives have burst onto the World Wide Web in ever-increasing numbers, making it simple to paste images onto class Web sites and into PowerPoint presentations. Textbook publishers offer teachers and students a dazzling array of sources, graphics, and other visual materials. While visuals have become commonplace in history classrooms and texts, rarely do images move to center stage to become the focus of interpretation or the source of new insights. Pedagogically, visual materials are too often used only as presentational props.[8] A slick slide shown in class or an appealing Flash movie posted on a course Web site might transmit information effectively, but such uses fail to capture the interactive possibilities of images and new media, used together, in promoting students' historical understanding.

Students might enjoy, even demand, visual stimulation, but students do not necessarily enter a college classroom able to give visual sources the disciplinary reading that furthers their historical thinking. As Wineburg has argued, historians read primary documents in a distinct way, applying a "sourcing heuristic"—that is, a set of questions about a document, its author's intentions, and its reliability—to use texts to build arguments about the past. Students, in contrast, read sources in a less sophisticated way, as sources of information, or "content knowledge." But because many historians have been so skeptical of images, we have few conventions for reading images as historical sources. Louis Masur maintains that pedagogy is perhaps the most challenging aspect of the emerging image-based scholarship: "Letting one's students interrogate, speculate, and often hyperventilate is an alarming business, especially when at the [end of class] you cannot tell them definitely how to read a picture or precisely how an image shaped history." The point of our classes is not to entertain our students, but to help them learn to think historically—to develop their facility for making historical meaning from the images, texts, and objects in the world around them.[9] Responding to the pictorial turn will require historians to help our students become sophisticated readers—and perhaps even authors—of image-based historical narratives.

THE DIGITAL TURN

Teaching students to craft engaging and effective historical interpretations, a perennial challenge, becomes even more problematic in the digital classroom where faculty ask students to design multimedia- and Web-based projects that demonstrate their ability to think historically. In comparison to more traditional assignments such as term papers, multimedia compositions allow students to use various forms of evidence (text, images, audio clips, and music) to experiment with new forms of critical analysis and narrative. Individual and collaborative multimedia authoring in the classroom—involving multiple skills and points of view and frequently connecting a public audience to student work—resembles, on a much more modest scale, the efforts of historians to develop new forms of scholarship tailored to the digital medium.[10] Can the digital turn do what William G. Thomas III and Edward L. Ayers, pioneers in digital authoring, envision—can it make visible or reconfigure "deeper connections among documentation, evidence, and analysis than a single plane of fixed text can offer"?[11] What opportunities and obstacles do electronic environments offer novice and expert historians interested in rethinking historical narratives? How might the scholarship of teaching and learning help us better understand how the digital turn affects the development of historical thinking in our students?

Bridging the Chasm: Case Studies from the Visible Knowledge Project

In the sections that follow, each of us outlines how her or his own scholarship of teaching and learning research has explored the intersection of visual evidence, multimedia authoring, and historical understanding. Working with our students in new-media environments, we are generating evidence of how historical thinking with visual arguments *develops* in our students. Our analysis of that evidence leads us to posit five interrelated themes, each foregrounded in one of our essays:

1. In "Thinking Visually as Historians: Incorporating Visual Methods," David Jaffee discusses how pushing our students to see visual evidence contextually can help us teach historical reasoning better.
2. In "Confronting Prior Visual Knowledge, Beliefs, and Habits: 'Seeing' beyond the Surface," Peter Felten illustrates how engaging students through a seemingly familiar and self-evident visual culture can also direct them to confront both their deeply held beliefs in particular historical narratives and the constructed nature of any source.
3. In "What's the Problem? Connecting Scholarship, Interpretation, and Evidence in Telling Stories about Race and Slavery," Tracey Weis explores how watching students connect evidence and scholarship as they construct historical arguments reveals ways to use new media to enrich student understanding of historical investigation and argumentation.
4. In "Moving beyond 'the Essay': Evaluating Historical Analysis and Argument in Multimedia Presentations," Michael Coventry proposes that combining argument and evidence in multimedia historical narratives drives faculty and students to rethink the limits of writing as a way of representing historical knowledge.
5. In "Connecting to the Public: Using New Media to Engage Students in the Iterative Process of History," Cecilia O'Leary documents how students become citizen historians by creating digital histories that not only connect them personally to the history they study but also give them the tools to make history public.

Our collaboration has helped us see that the very openness and uncertainty at the heart of the task of interpreting visual materials provide an opportunity to introduce students to the complexity of the past. That complexity often stands in direct opposition to prior knowledge and beliefs about history. Our research also leads us to propose that the confrontation with complexity and the sense of power gained in creating a visual argument replicate for students some of what practitioners experience as we create historical narratives in both traditional and nontraditional media. Making the process of student learning visible offers possibilities both for our students to learn to think historically and for us to develop a rigorous and open approach to our pedagogy, bridging the chasm between research and classroom practice in our profession.

David Jaffee

Thinking Visually as Historians: Incorporating Visual Methods

When students encounter images, they often offer incomplete readings, demonstrating difficulty integrating their insightful visual readings with contextual historical understanding. When asked to "look" and "react" to images, they frame responses that open and close with immediate reactions. All too often, visual materials promote relatively simplistic emotional interpretations because the student viewers offer freestanding responses based solely on the image before them, unencumbered by the context or additional documentation historians use to make meaning with such powerful visual documents. Studying the way my students looked at visual materials, I realized that word and image needed to be reunited if students were to learn to think visually as historians. I came to this conclusion by taking the pedagogical turn: watching my students look, paying attention to the intermediate steps they took on their way to understanding historical problems and mastering the use of sources. Analyzing their work in the light of the scholarship of teaching and learning has helped me develop a strategy that pushes students to see historical context, connection, and complexity as they develop interpretative strategies for visual sources.

For several years, I have collected evidence of student learning as a result of doing the online viewing assignments in my urban culture course, Power, Race, and Culture in the U.S. City, taught at the City College of New York. From the start, students were eager to look at the images as well as the historical and literary texts I posted for them. But the exercise of putting them together, of moving back and forth as a historian might do, proved elusive for many. When they moved onto the terrain of images, many students offered suggestive readings of the individual images before them, and they even referred to other visual materials, but few could integrate multiple sources into an interpretative narrative.

I saw evidence of this difficulty when I asked my students to look at the 1941 murals at the Health and Human Services Building, created by Seymour Fogel, and to describe and interpret what they saw. Henry wrote:

> The painting "Industrial life" by Seymour Fogel (1941) echoes an Urban industrial society. In the painting, we can view five men at work. The artist is trying to project a sense of economic labor values that all America should follow and be aware of. Labor and Industrial is seen as one, the viewer in 1941 should have seen this painting as a positive step for his country. In the painting different labor is being introduced, from the scientist to the train conductor. The colors of the painting are flat tones and the drawings are simple in form. The art work was being [produced] in the Washington. D.C. Health and Human [Services] building, words to encourage the people to *strive forward!!*

Most students followed Henry, with general comments about the industrial character of the objects, drawn from the murals' titles, for example, and from the

David Jaffee uses Seymour Fogel's *Industrial Life* (1941) in an image-viewing assignment for his course Power, Race, and Culture in the U.S. City at the City College of New York. *Courtesy Smithsonian American Art Museum, Transfer from the General Services Administration.*

figures. They referred to the image's visual qualities or its historical significance but were unable to weave the parts into a larger whole. A few students expressed more complicated understandings of the images as visual constructions. Olivia perceived that portrayal of industrial work in a "romanticized light" as a historical change from earlier representations. Arthur, commenting on another of the murals, pointed out their idealized nature, connecting them to other New Deal and World War II–era art, including the paintings of Norman Rockwell and the photographs of Dorothea Lange, both discussed in earlier classes. He could relate the medium of the mural as well as the significance of Fogel's style of drawing (which he likened to "a way that marble might be sculpted into statues") to the murals' message, their "monumental" representation of the force of family life.[12]

Yet, like most other students, Arthur did not raise relevant questions of patronage and audience or muse about the historical "purpose" of the mural project.[13] Henry did attend to placement, but his visual analysis was slim and unconnected to his thematic framework. Even when Olivia and Arthur offered sophisticated understandings of the images, they did not connect their visual readings to text-based course materials—primary and secondary. Even the best students that first year offered separate, unintegrated readings of texts—visual and literary.

Analyzing their efforts, I realized that students needed more scaffolding so that they could learn to move between historical, literary, and visual materials. Perhaps, I thought, I could create an online miniarchive, selecting sources that could enrich the complexity of their readings while helping them keep the context in sight. I wanted their experience in the miniarchive to model how scholars revisit their assumptions in a recursive process of intertextuality, repeatedly moving back and forth among texts and other sources as they weave them together.

My new assignment asked students to look at two 1837 portraits of Indian leaders: *Wi-jún-jon, Pigeon's Egg Head (The Light) Going To and Returning From Washington* by George Catlin and *Keokuk: Chief of the Sacs* by Charles Bird King.[14] Each then wrote "a paragraph or two explaining what you see," a provisional interpretation the student shared with a partner before moving into a miniarchive containing documents selected to help the students situate the two representations: more portraits; speeches by Keokuk; text from Thomas Loraine McKenney's *History of the Indian Tribes of North America*, where the Keokuk portrait appeared; writings by George Catlin about Pigeon's Egg Head; and two extensive Web sites. From this miniarchive, students selected two documents that they thought added context and meaning to their initial reaction to the portraits.

Students encountering George Catlin's 1837–1839 portrait of Pigeon's Egg Head often flatten their readings to fit into what they initially understand as the

At the City College of New York, David Jaffee asks students to use a miniarchive of documents to assist them in interpreting George Catlin's *Wi-jún-jon, Pigeon's Egg Head (The Light) Going To and Returning From Washington* (1837–1839). *Courtesy Smithsonian American Art Museum, Gift of Mrs. Joseph Harrison Jr.*

starkly contrasting choices of accommodation or resistance, sellout or revolt, facing Native American leaders in the early nineteenth century. The visual and textual materials of the miniarchive prodded students to move beyond those dichotomies, developing their historical reasoning and realizing more complex understandings. Using these additional sources to inform her reading of the Catlin portrait, Isadora imaginatively reconstructed the Assiniboines' response to their leader's foolish exchange of his "impressive Indian accoutrements" for foppish attire, including his high-heeled boots, fan, and umbrella, and the liquor bottle in his back pocket, interpreting his actions as compromise in the face of overbearing force. When Isadora turned to the Keokuk portrait, she continued to wrestle with the ambiguity of the image:

> When looking at this painting of Keokuk, one feels that there is something different about this majestic Indian chief. The feathers and animals' skins indicate that he is a powerful, typical Indian chief. . . . But what makes this Indian chief sort of ambiguous? Why does he convey both Indian pride and strength and the acceptance of whites' values?

Additional sources, McKenney's *History of the Indian Tribes of North America* and information on the interpretative stance of the painter Charles Bird King, helped her contextualize the portrait:

> In fact, Keokuk refused to collaborate with another Sac chief (Black Hawk) to fight against the whites, who were going to take their lands. He accepted to exile [sic] with his followers and was therefore much respected by the American government. He succeeded in constantly convincing his people not to join the war because he knew—according to Thomas McKenney, who was commissioner of Indian affairs between 1824 and 1830—that they would be defeated. He is generally depicted as a strong, determined and very tactic [sic] person. And [King] clearly depicts this sort of dichotomy that characterizes Keokuk: he was both a typical Indian chief who, with calm and realism, governed and protected his people and a good negotiator who knew how to deal with the whites. That is why he still appears as a majestic, respected chief on the painting, unless the painter, as it was often said about him and his passion for the Indians, idealized the character and improved the reality of the time.

Moving beyond conventional accounts that frame Native American choices as either accommodation or resistance, Isadora had begun to tell a far more complex and messy historical story of a leader who had to wend his way through competing native factions and a welter of governmental officials, local and national, as well as deal with the divergent demands of settlers and reformers. She also understood that the sources—both texts and visuals—were not unmediated; the Native American voice—and body—comes down to us through Anglo hands and transcriptions. Yet, looking at the portraits by Catlin and King, she had seen some of the layers of complexities that allowed their subjects to represent themselves through pose and costume rather than merely to be represented by the painter. Like John Singleton Copley's wealthy merchant subjects, Catlin's Pigeon's Egg Head and King's Keokuk collaborated in constructing their likenesses. Isadora demonstrated how students can learn to read portraits in their historical context, appreciating complexity.[15]

Like most students, Isadora had plunged into the miniarchive to select specific texts directly relating to the portraits. Her classmate Judy used the miniarchive differently. She chose sources seemingly distant from the original portraits: an appeal by the Cherokee chief John Ross protesting Indian removal in the 1830s and the exoticized depiction of vanquished Indian leaders on the cover of an early twentieth-century popular periodical. These she deployed to explore the broader topic of the perils of assimilation. Here, she modeled the practice of an expert or professional historian who enters an archive with a series of questions or a tentative hypothesis in search of evidence, pulling apparently unconnected texts into a relationship and then constructing a plausible story.

By yoking portraits and prose together, this exercise moved beyond the mere addition of images as illustrations, instead helping students think visually as historians. In creating the miniarchive, I wanted to push students away from freestanding looking and toward historically contextualized seeing of the visual evidence. Watching Isadora and other students move from examining a single image to comparing two images and then to contextualizing particular portraits within a miniarchive of word and image, I learned how students gain an understanding of the complex strategies that Indian leaders devised in the early nineteenth century. Students discovered for themselves the coexistence of choice and constraint. They came to appreciate how the power and pressure of the new American state limited Pigeon's Egg Head and Keokuk but how the two leaders nonetheless deployed imaginative strategies to navigate the new political world that they faced.

Like their subjects, historians too face constraints—the use of evidence, modes of documentary analysis, the need to connect the local event to larger themes or topics—that close off possibilities and hem in interpretations. But we also have choices—about what we teach and how we teach. I have used the scholarship of teaching and learning to develop new strategies for integrating visual materials with other sources to help students comprehend context, to develop their understanding in a way not possible using textual sources alone. My intention is to build scaffolding that helps students to see beyond the simple, to formulate provisional questions for inquiry, to encounter new sources, and then to revise their earlier assertions. In this way, I hope to help students learn the process of historical reasoning.

Peter Felten

Confronting Prior Visual Knowledge, Beliefs, and Habits: "Seeing" beyond the Surface

Students enter our classrooms with knowledge, beliefs, and ways of thinking about both past events and the study of history. Although many of our students were born in the late 1980s, prior schooling and popular culture have helped them construct well-defined "cultural memories" of the assassination of John F. Kennedy, the Vietnam War, and even more ancient history. Indeed, we all bring into the classroom knowledge, beliefs, and habits of thought that shape how we make sense of class material. Older students and faculty who have lived through a historical period being studied cannot rely on personal recollections for an objective version of the past. My scholarship of teaching and learning research explores how visual sources can be used to reveal and disrupt such historical and cognitive assumptions, helping students take necessary steps toward more complex understandings of the past.[16]

The first time I taught a senior seminar on the United States in the 1960s at Vanderbilt University, I came to understand just how powerful cultural memories could be. Most of my fifteen seniors, nearly all history majors, entered the course with a shared and deeply ingrained vision of the decade. The typical student story, which I attributed to the film *Forrest Gump*, went something like this: The 1960s began with a unified nation (except for some backward white southerners) making bold progress in all endeavors, but the Vietnam War and assassinations tore the country apart, leaving chaos and fragmentation at the end of the decade.[17] That story emerged repeatedly during the semester as many students struggled to reconcile our course work with their prior understandings—and when conflicts emerged, *Forrest Gump*'s simple narrative often trumped more complex views of the decade. Many white students, for example, regularly shifted the rise of black power to the end of the decade, implicitly assuming that only the assassination of Martin Luther King Jr. could have produced such militancy. Throughout the semester, I seemed to repeat: "It's more complicated than you think."

The next time I taught the course, I began the semester with an exercise designed to confront student beliefs about the decade. Before we even discussed the syllabus, I gave the students ten primary sources from the 1960s, including excerpts from Richard M. Nixon's 1969 inaugural address and from King's "I have a dream" speech and photographs from demonstrations for civil rights and arms control. I also played for them a Janis Joplin song and the 1971 "Hilltop" television advertisement for Coke. I then asked pairs of students to put the sources in chronological order and to explain why they placed each source where they did. After thirty minutes, I called the class together to compare notes. None of the pairs had sequenced the sources correctly, but that was not really the point. Instead, as students talked about each source, *they* began to see the holes in the *Forrest Gump* narrative—and then students began saying, "It's more complicated than I thought." Because this experience disrupted knowledge and beliefs about the 1960s that students brought to class, we were able, together, to use the semester to develop new and more complex understandings of the decade. In a little over an hour on the first day of class, the source-sequencing exercise had transformed the course and had taught me how interrogating visual knowledge could disrupt students' constructed narratives and habits of analysis.

This experience confirmed for me what cognitive scientists have found: that people "come to formal education with a range of prior knowledge, skills, beliefs, and concepts that significantly influence . . . their abilities to remember, reason, solve problems, and acquire new knowledge."[18] Our students live in a highly visual world, where images are fundamental in shaping their understandings of history before they ever enter our classrooms. I now realized that I must recognize and confront my students' prior visual knowledge and cultural memories to help them move beyond a *Forrest Gump* version of history.

The source-sequencing exercise began that pedagogical process, but it also demonstrated that my students often struggled to interpret primary sources, particularly visual ones. To give my students practice making historical sense of complex sources, including images, I interspersed a series of short source-reading exercises through the semester. In each, I provided students with a packet of three or four primary sources (typically including photos and excerpts from newspapers, letters, or speeches). I instructed every student to answer the question "What significant things do you know, and don't you know, about each source?" I also asked students to rank the items according to their reliability as historical sources and to explain their rankings.[19]

Although I expected these exercises to reveal a range of student capacity to read sources, over multiple semesters I found a troubling consistency in student response to visual images. A few students could offer fairly sophisticated readings of photographs, asking, "Who took these pictures? What is context of the last photo?" and even probing how and why each picture was taken. But most students, including the most sophisticated readers, fell back on cultural assumptions about photographs when asked to assess their dependability as sources. Colin, one of my most capable students, wrote: "These pictures record a moment that clearly happened. Pictures shot candidly tend to not have inherent prejudices, though it is easy to interpret them as you will. Pictures are basically neutral." Other students echoed this view. Melanie noted that "the Photo Collection is the most trustworthy source—images often speak louder than words." Jane referred to the photos as "snapshots of what actually happened." Marvin summarized the typical student analysis when he wrote, "Photos—the almost most objective evidence there is."

Just as students had brought the *Forrest Gump* narrative into the classroom, they had also brought beliefs that shaped how they made sense of historical sources. "The myth of photographic truth" overruled what my students had learned in history classes (including mine) about the constructed nature of any source.[20] At the same time, many students spent far less time evaluating visual sources than textual ones, resulting in facile readings that typically ignored aspects of analysis they routinely applied to texts. In one class exercise, for instance, Jill began her close reading of two textual sources with comments on the author and audience. But she failed to consider such issues when examining two photographs; instead, she performed a quick reading of the people depicted in the photographs, concluding, "You know the man pictured [Bobby Seale] must be at least slightly liberal by his hairstyle." Jill, it seemed, read the photographic sources as she might read a pictorial spread in a magazine, rather than transferring the analytical techniques for reading primary texts that she had developed in history classes.

Yet the same source-reading exercises that raised troubling questions about students' understanding of photographs as constructed sources demonstrated that they could perform sophisticated analysis of documentary film footage. Student readings of video-based sources often paid particular attention to the ways moving images are edited and produced. Angela, who struggled with photo analysis, performed expertly with one video excerpt.

> Don't know context—setting of events also unclear. Don't know who filmed or what was purpose of film. Don't get to hear from anyone being filmed . . . so don't know their intentions. Don't know how film has been edited—what it doesn't show—only a few minutes excerpted from several days. Can get more of an idea of state of mind of protestors by watching body language than through other sources which rely on description—give good feel.

Other students identified similar issues. Lilly noted that "[I] don't know the persons or organizations responsible for the film and any biases they may have." Mark wondered, "Who directed it? What were the judging criteria for what clips made the video? Is there other footage which might have contradicted the video's overall theme?" Colin asked similar questions about the video production ("Who shot it? Who compiled it?"), but he took his analysis one step further: "Does [the video] have legitimate claim to the omniscient tone with which it narrates events?"

In marked contrast with readings of photographs, then, students consistently noticed the constructed nature of the documentary film source, asking how both the video images themselves and the video editing shaped the source. Maria highlighted what appeared to be the central distinction for most students: "Video [is] similar in content to photos but editing . . . can put a spin on images." Marvin echoed this view: "The clip is an edited representation of those events and *even though the footage may be authentic*, the editing [is] not."[21] For Marvin and many of his peers, the constructed nature of the video robbed the images it contained of the inherent objectivity of stand-alone photographs. The editing process corrupted the fundamental "photographic truth" of video.

By understanding the rich but problematic visual knowledge, beliefs, and habits that students bring to the history classroom, we can develop new and more effective strategies to help students learn historical content and reasoning. In my class, I have tried both to work with students' visual liabilities, using images to confront the popular but flawed history they bring into the classroom, and to build on their visual assets, helping students transfer techniques for reading moving images to the analysis of still ones. Thus, the scholarship of teaching and learning offers us an opportunity to attend systematically to the prior visual understandings and the habits of looking that students bring to our classrooms. In my own work, I will continue to collect and analyze evidence of how students read and reason from visual sources and use such evidence to help them develop more critical and contextualized visions of history.

Tracey Weis

What's the Problem? Connecting Scholarship, Interpretation, and Evidence in Telling Stories about Race and Slavery

For years students seemed to come to my African American history course with the *Gone with the Wind* interpretation of slavery that collapses four centuries of history on four continents into the plantation production of cotton in the Deep South in the late antebellum period. I want them to comprehend how slavery "worked" in different places and times and to understand the role of slavery in the making of America.[22] I knew I could use the traditional lecture format to tell them about the complexity of the peculiar institution. Even so, I wondered if they could show me how they navigated between their prior knowledge and beliefs about slavery and the new forms of evidence and scholarship they would encounter in my course. The scholarship of teaching and learning has helped me address two persistently pressing pedagogical concerns: (1) how to get students to see beyond their visions of slavery as monolithic; and (2) how to make the process of historical interpretation and narrative construction more visible for myself and for novice historians such as my students. It has guided me in developing multimedia exercises for students that combine text, image, and narration in ways that make visible to them the complexity of historical research and the knowledge it produces.

My interest in having students broaden and complicate their narratives of slavery led me to devise "Telling Stories about Slavery at America's Historic Sites," a three-week unit that culminates in student PowerPoint slide shows based on their assessments of how the Web sites of Monticello, Mount Vernon, Colonial Williamsburg, and the National Park Service interpret slavery and race. Small groups of students work together to combine their readings of the Web sites with other relevant visual and text sources; they then produce a research report consisting of fifteen to twenty PowerPoint slides accompanied by a narrative—a script—for class presentation. Functioning as visual paragraphs, the slides show the relationships between the evidence students select from the Web sites, the historiography they locate in the America: History and Life database, and the arguments about slavery they develop as they maneuver back and forth among the sources. The deliberate juxtaposition of historical incidents, types of evidence, and scholarly analyses helps them grasp the complexity of slavery and its interpretation. Contrasting four colonial-era historic sites would, I hoped, allow students to see how they had privileged antebellum cotton plantations as the singular sites of slavery.[23]

I first introduced the unit in fall 2001. In reviewing the initial round of presentations, I realized I did not know how to assess the messy complexity of what students were learning about slavery as they researched, produced, and presented their multimedia narratives. Yet, within six months, collaborative work with colleagues in the Visible Knowledge Project who shared my interest in multimedia student authoring resulted in the development of a common framework for evaluating multimedia projects.[24] With a better understanding of how to evaluate narrative organization, thoughtfulness in the use of images, and the process of multimedia authoring, I was ready to try again.

The following fall I tried to map student presentations frame by frame so that I could see how students were assembling primary and secondary texts, images, scripts, and audio narration into narratives. A close reading of their work helped me recognize that students had begun to grasp the need to create a contextualized narrative that acknowledged both the existence of many stories about slavery and, to quote the historian Ira Berlin, the complicated and protracted ways "Americans have situated their own history in terms of the struggle between freedom and slavery—and freedom's triumph."[25] Nonetheless, their capacities for incorporating visual evidence into their historical explanations were uneven and at best generally at the novice stage. Below, I discuss what I learned from one presentation that analyzed the Web site of Colonial Williamsburg.

The substance of the student presentation began with a slide that contained three elements: an image of shackles, a photograph of a contemporary historical interpreter at Colonial Williamsburg, and a reference to a required course reading by the historian James Oliver Horton. But the script that the student had created as narration referred to neither of the images; instead, it summarized Horton's argument that "historic places give concrete meaning to our history and our lives as no spoken or written word alone can do," a claim that served as a compass for my students as we tacked back and forth between the familiar and the unfamiliar, the local and the national, in our efforts to situate and to scrutinize slavery. Surprisingly, the presentation did not include or interrogate the caption of the photograph from the Web site: "Old Paris, played by Robert C. Watson, awes with tales that teach." While an expert historian might have chosen to juxtapose the harshness of the shackles and the benign image of a grandfatherly storyteller to raise questions about the contradiction between the brutality of punishment and the benevolence of paternalism, the novice historian seemed unable to exploit the interpretative potential of the juxtaposition.[26]

Similarly, the student author of the next slide used a photograph of the reconstructed slave quarters at Carter's Grove plantation, run by Colonial Williamsburg, to illustrate her evaluation of the organization's Web site. Although she had probably read "Representing Slavery: A Roundtable Discussion" in the issue of the online journal *Common-Place* that included the photograph, her script did not refer to it directly. The accompanying narration—"the Williamsburg site gives us the impression of a quaint, small, harmless slave community without all the cruelties that were experienced"—only obliquely pointed back to the discussion, in an article in the roundtable, of the daily challenge African American interpreters face in trying to "strike a balance between being truthful and being tasteful." Yet the student's assessment did acknowledge the contradictions between Colonial Williamsburg's visual representation of master-slave relations and the scholarship on the subject. Labeling her argument, "The Good, the Bad,

A student in Tracey Weis's class at Millersville University used a 1993 image of Robert Watson Jr. as Old Paris, a first-person interpreter at Colonial Williamsburg, in order to analyze contemporary reenactments of slavery. *Courtesy Colonial Williamsburg Foundation.*

and Pretty Ugly," she identified as positive the site's insertion of information about the working lives of slaves.[27] This inclusion of African American presence was undercut, however, by the Web site's misrepresentation and omission, termed the "Bad" and the "Pretty Ugly" by the student critic. The student pointed out how the Web site "completely glossed over" the brutality of slavery and "the mistreatment of human life that occurred there." These contradictions prompted other members of the class to ask whether the images and text on the Colonial Williamsburg Web site reflected the content and tone of the living-history presentations.

In the next two slides, a new author explicitly juxtaposed scholarship and visual evidence to advance critical interpretations. Tellingly, she titled her two companion slides "Slavery through the Eyes of Whites" and "Slavery through the Eyes of Slaves." In the former, she set Jean-Baptiste Le Paon's 1783 portrait of General Lafayette accompanied by his orderly James Armistead against a rather lengthy caption: "Slavery, in the eyes of whites, was glossed over. Not everyone agreed with slavery, but the ones who did made slavery out to be a pleasant experience. White people would make comments such as 'they were fed and sheltered, what more did they want?'"[28]

Her skepticism of the benevolent paternalism that the portrait announced was evident. But, I wondered, had she brought that wariness, informed by her own experiences as a young African American woman, into the classroom at the

Through the Eyes of Whites

Slavery, in the eyes of whites, was glossed over. Not everyone agreed with slavery, but the ones who did made slavery out to be a pleasant experience. White people would make comments such as "they were fed and sheltered, what more did they want?"

For students in Tracey Weis's class at Millersville University, the task of contextualizing Jean-Baptiste Le Paon's *Lafayette at Yorktown* (1783) illustrated the challenges of interpreting images of slavery. The man next to Lafayette is believed to be his orderly, James Armistead. *Courtesy Lafayette College Art Collection, Easton, Pa. Gift of Mrs. John Hubbard.*

beginning of the semester? Or had she refined her understanding based on her consideration of the experience of the first-person interpreter at Colonial Williamsburg?[29] In any event, her conclusion that the visual evidence misrepresented James Armistead included an awareness of authorial intent: "This picture portrays the idea of noble savage. Whites who did not want to believe that slavery was wrong called African Americans noble servants rather than slaves. This picture gives a false image of how slaves dressed. When looking at this picture one might believe that African Americans were treated equal to whites when in reality that was not the case."

In the next slide, this same student author offered a bulleted summary of some of the harsh aspects of slavery in visual juxtaposition to *The Old Plantation*, an undated and unsigned (perhaps late eighteenth-century) picture found in Columbia, South Carolina, that depicts playful slave leisure:

- Taken from their home only to be forced to do laborious work for white men
- Treated as if they had no soul
- Torn apart from their families[30]

The student's narration for this slide included quotations from several scholars speaking to the difficulty of African American survival in the face of the brutality of slavery. After featuring an analysis of slavery in the antebellum period, she turned next to the words of a freedman extracted from a secondary source on Reconstruction: "We haven't got our rights yet, but I expect we're go'n to have 'em soon. . . . We're men now, but when our masters had us we was only change in their pockets." She then invoked Frederick Douglass to conclude her analysis: "A man's troubles are always half disposed of when he finds endurance the only alternative. I found myself here; not getting away; and naught remained for me but to make the best of it." Once more she used scholarship and textual sources to challenge visual evidence that portrayed master-slave relations as benevolent. Yet, although her slides were conceptually rich and interpretatively sharp, the student seemed untroubled that they were analytic collages comprising visual and textual "traces" from different historical eras and places.[31]

Taken together, these excerpts from the Colonial Williamsburg presentation illustrate both the increasing complexity of students' understandings of slavery and the persisting unevenness of their analyses. Looking back on the evidence I collected, I can identify three distinct moments when students' understandings faltered and suggest what I learned about intervening in those episodes:

First, students unaccustomed to critically evaluating visual historical evidence tended to employ a cut-and-paste approach to images. They either extracted an image as a free-standing item devoid of context or pulled an image and its accompanying scholarly commentary as a unified and coherent item. This, I learned, reflected their inexperience in working with primary sources of any kind. I needed to help them develop their understanding of how—and why—expert historians attend to context and authorial intent.[32] Then these young scholars could apply their newfound skepticism about veracity and motive to subsequent analyses of all primary sources.

Second, neither my students nor I had begun the class with an understanding of how contemporary culture shaped the knowledge of slavery that they brought with them. My presumption that they shared the *Gone with the Wind* interpretation worked against making their prior knowledge and beliefs about slavery visible. Nor had I considered the images of slavery they carried with them from such films as *Amistad* or from illustrations in high school textbooks. Moreover, references to "White America" and "White people" in the slides had alerted me to the necessity of making students' prior knowledge and beliefs about *race* more explicit in the classroom so that we could all see how these interrupted our analytic efforts to "compare and contrast differing sets of ideas, values, personalities, behaviors, and institutions" in the past. Recognizing that images evoked both cognitive and affective responses from students led to the realization that exploring students' prior beliefs meant encouraging them to articulate desires, fantasies, and fears as well as rational reactions—a daunting challenge indeed, but one I found necessary if our learning were to proceed.[33]

Third, students displayed particular historical-thinking skills when they undertook particular tasks in their analyses of slavery, but they seemed unable to bring their multiple competencies together. As a result, their efforts to move beyond novice interpretative strategies were haphazard rather than systematic and often generated collages rather than narratives. Yet, by bringing together the content of historical interpretations on the one hand and the organization and form of the analysis on the other, they had taken important steps toward understanding the complexity of historical representation. When they constructed their individual slides, they understood the tension between showing (demonstrating) and telling (narrating). Peer-review discussions of the presentations pushed this learning even further, as students asked each other to justify their selections of images and texts: *Why* did you select this image? What *point* were you trying to make? How does *that image* relate to *this excerpt* from a primary document? The students were demonstrating how the technique of juxtaposition enhanced their understanding of how historical narratives are constructed. By gaining competencies in composing the individual "visual paragraph" for each slide, students were preparing to take the next step in narrative construction: creating more coherent and more comprehensive explanations of causation and consequence.

Inspired by the scholarship of teaching and learning to contemplate students' work more closely and more carefully, I am challenged to refine my strategies for helping students develop the skills and dispositions of historical inquiry. The multimedia format of the historic site reviews made the problems and possibilities of historical argumentation and narrative visible even as the collaborative review of the multimedia interpretations put the *process* of historical interpretation on display. Evaluating students' efforts to incorporate visual evidence into their analyses, however, is making me rethink the limits of writing as a way of representing historical knowledge. Like David Jaffee and Peter Felten, I recognize that many students need more practice in *reading* visual sources with skill before they can effectively use them to present compelling and coherent historical interpretations. Nonetheless, like Michael Coventry and Cecilia O'Leary, I am excited by the new forms of historical argumentation emerging in multimedia narratives. I am optimistic that working together, as scholars and educators, we can continue to build our knowledge of teaching and learning in ways that will advance both the pedagogical and professional practice of history.

Michael Coventry

Moving beyond "the Essay": Evaluating Historical Analysis and Argument in Multimedia Presentations

What might it look like if our media-savvy students expressed their historical analysis through new media? What can we learn about how historical knowledge is created by watching students make and present their work in new-media forms? Because at times written description has seemed inadequate to communicate the richness of the visual and aural record of popular culture, my students and I experiment with creating short multimedia narratives as a way of exploring those questions. In these projects, students intermingle images, music, and voice narration to form a multimedia, multidimensional critique. Becoming interpreters and explainers of the cultural past and present, they analyze their objects of study and create multimedia projects in order to tell interpretative stories, to show the viewer examples and evidence to support their interpretations, and to connect their stories to larger themes in culture and history studies. In this essay I use tools from the scholarship of teaching and learning to describe my students' learning and some of its constituent features through an examination of student multimedia experiments.[34]

As the only historian teaching in an interdisciplinary media, technology, and culture studies M.A. program, I introduce my discipline and its habits of thought to students. My students come from a variety of backgrounds, possessing bachelor's degrees in journalism, film studies, political science, or business, to name just a few possibilities. Their degree program exposes them to a broad range of issues raised by networked technologies and new media. Most come into my courses with intricate frameworks for understanding media, and they eagerly embrace opportunities to think about how to interpret and analyze in formats that move beyond writing.

Using evidence of various sorts—digitized film or video footage, images, photographs, music—my students build multimedia analysis by the juxtaposition of this historical evidence with their own analytic voices presented in recorded narration or titles. In written narratives, historians present textual evidence through quotations, numeric evidence through tables, and visual evidence through reproductions of photographs, maps, or cartoons. We surround this evidence with interpretation, placing quotations among our statements or directing our reader's eye to images or tables reproduced above or beside our analysis. But too often—and this is most apparent in the case of video or music—we are forced to represent visual evidence and pinpoint our analysis to specific parts of it through written description. Multimedia allows audiences to see or hear moving pictures or songs; it allows authors to show multiple examples quickly with narration over them or to guide viewers over specific parts of an image and show analysis directly beside or over a specific point.[35] When projects are successful, they engage in the sort of insightful, carefully considered argument we expect from written work, but the means of expression can be very different. Multimedia allows my students to *show* their subjects as they analyze them. Such work thus illustrates both the possibilities—and some of the limits—of multimedia authoring for academic work.

Looking closely at my students' projects reveals that multimedia work in history depends on the relationship of two key techniques: (1) the compression of argument and (2) the use of simplistic cultural memories for complicated ends. The multichanneled, multilayered nature of multimedia authoring allows—indeed relies on—compression of argument, conveying a great deal of information quickly and by a variety of means. Compression intentionally invokes simplistic cultural memories to make its argument. It occurs in all forms of communication, including writing, but multimedia authoring brings compression to the fore: the viewer must recognize an era or associate a sound with a particular cultural milieu. The best multimedia authoring projects will then explain, clarify, or challenge the cultural memory in question.

Two student multimedia projects showed me how the two interrelated techniques are central to the presentation of historical analysis in new-media narrative forms. Alyson Hurt's digital story revealed the historical construction of simplistic cultural memories, while deploying compression to show that the very cultural knowledge she invokes as evidence is historically contingent. Malgorzata Rymsza-Pawlowska used a period style of filmmaking to evoke, through compression, an entire era. She then mixed evidence and argument to read her subject outward, into a larger historical argument. Alyson Hurt's digital story explored a contemporary television program starring actor Ben Sander in drag as Brini Maxwell, a "domestic goddess" who guides viewers to perfect home life through exemplary cooking, cleaning, and decorating. Hurt's story used multimedia capabilities to establish a historical context for her subject. Hurt illustrated the continuity of domestic goddess ideals in American culture with a montage of 1950s and 1960s photos and TV footage of Donna Reed—an actress famous for her popular television portrayal of a perfect housewife—and similar TV and magazine images of the 1990s celebrity domestic expert Martha Stewart. Hurt then introduced Maxwell, a cross-dressing television personality whose use of the domestic diva tradition helps show the historical construction of gender, particularly the performance of housewife and domestic goddess. Working in new media, Hurt could accentuate the ways Maxwell self-consciously performs and destabilizes the domestic diva tradition. Maxwell's clothing and sets exist in a no-man's-land between contemporary style and the aesthetic of the late 1950s–early 1960s, when Reed's show was popular. This is intentional: according to Hurt, "Maxwell cites Reed as one of her biggest inspirations."[36] The connection to Martha Stewart is effected through Maxwell's blonde wig and statuesque height. While both connections could be conveyed in writing (as I have just done), multimedia allowed Hurt to demonstrate her point more vividly. Viewers could *see* in chronological order the domestic icons from whom Maxwell creates her satirical performance. In this sense, multimedia provided the cultural evidence alongside Hurt's analytic voice.

Just as she simultaneously showed Maxwell performing a particular femininity and documented its construction, Hurt used the show's intentionally simplistic cultural memory of the history of femininity to demonstrate that memory's instability. As she wrote in her reflective essay, the show "both celebrates and satirizes these 'old-school' values. Brini's sensibility seems intentionally anachronistic, provoking dissonance between Brini and the perceived sensibilities of 'modern' women and further underscoring the fact that Brini is a constructed persona."[37] Throughout the project, Hurt relied on this dissonance between the viewer's sensibilities, the mythical womanhood Maxwell portrayed, and Maxwell's outrageous and self-referential performance in order to make a critique. Hurt assumed that the viewer would recognize the satire in Maxwell's performance. In this sense, Hurt was working with key features of new-media argument: the multimedia author relies on the viewer's store of cultural knowledge and uses images, music, or other keys to evoke that knowledge and to show complex juxtapositions of meaning. Yet compression works only if viewers possess the cultural knowledge needed to give a story the intellectual and emotional effects the author intends. Compression functions paradoxically as a limitation and strength of multimedia: when Hurt "reveals" her subject's "true" gender, we are forced to question all the assumptions we have brought to bear in viewing the entire piece.

In her multimedia project, Rymsza-Pawlowska used the style of a silent newsreel to evoke the 1920s. She interwove still images, clips from period movies, and full screens of text (intertitles) to present her analysis of smoking as a symbol of women's modernity and relative freedom in 1920s popular culture. Her choice of genre allowed her to present evidence and analysis together. "The film clips and advertising stills speak for themselves," she reflected, "and with the help of the intertitles, indicate a strong case" for historical change. She chose the "gushing style" of the newsreel as a way of "conveying the excitement of the modernity that was very much a feature of the decade."[38] Through the creative use of the newsreel format, Rymsza-Pawlowska both evoked the era and made her argument seem to come from within that very era.

Like Hurt, Rymsza-Pawlowska opened her piece with a rapid montage of images: a headline about woman suffrage, a headline about shortening skirts, and a clip of women typing in an office, signaling some of the "large-scale socioeconomic and political transformations that would profoundly affect the lives of

Michael Coventry's student Malgorzata Rymsza-Pawlowska evokes the 1920s by mixing her own intertitles with historical film clips and accompanying them with period music. She connects women, smoking, and female performances of modernity and independence. "Lighting Up at the Dawn of Modernity," digital story, Communication, Culture, and Technology Program, Georgetown University, Dec. 2004. Clip segments: above from *Possessed*, dir. Clarence Brown (Warner Brothers, 1931); and below from *Three on a Match*, dir. Mervyn Le Roy (Warner Brothers, 1932). *Courtesy Malgorzata Rymsza-Pawlowska.*

American women" in the early twentieth century.[39] Thus she set the stage for her overall argument: the connections between smoking in popular culture as a symbol of women's independence and the real changes in women's lives in the 1900s–1920s. Again like Hurt, Rymsza-Pawlowska used compression in her opening montage to establish context. But while Hurt sought to establish a lineage showing the ways gender is a historical construct, Rymsza-Pawlowska evoked and established multiple historical factors using artifacts from a single period. She then placed her subject—smoking—in this context as a symbol and expression of white middle-class women's "new freedoms" in the decade.

Also like Hurt, Rymsza-Pawlowska relied on and attempted to undermine our prior cultural knowledge of the era. After evoking the context of social change, Rymsza-Pawlowska showed how smoking signaled the flapper's freedom while symbolizing more significant developments. She used images of a variety of women engaged in relatively new public leisure activities (with and without men) while smoking to help us understand the broader reach of this symbol beyond the flapper stereotype.[40] But unlike Hurt, who, reading inward or deeply, focused on one subject in detail over time, Rymsza-Pawlowska read one subject (modern woman/flapper/female smoker) outward through advertisements, still images, and movie clips. She connected her subject to a variety of discourses to show that subject's ubiquity and the force of its meaning across 1920s culture.

Both Hurt and Rymsza-Pawlowska relied on compression of argument, and both evoked cultural memories and stereotypes to produce their historical analyses. Yet, to most historians, those very moves might at first glance seem to flatten intellectual complexity. How do we know that accounts are critiquing, not replicating, the simplistic cultural memories they invoke when they undertake compression? How can we tell when stereotypical images reproduce old interpretations or when they instead open interpretative possibilities? To answer those questions, historians can turn to the scholarship of teaching and learning for methods that help us watch carefully as students make choices about bringing together video clips, images, narration, and music to build their arguments. Due to the very compression of the form, we might at first glance miss the deep complexity of the arguments. It is easy for those of us trained to argue using words to focus solely on the narration of a digital story, without paying attention to the ways the words work with, over, and against the visual narrative constructed by the student. We need to learn to read new-media forms so that we can recognize the intended argument within them. In addition to strengthening our own knowledge of multimedia communication, another way to ascertain complexity is to ask students to reflect on their own intentions, whether in written proposals for projects, post-project reflective papers, or video- or audiotaped reflections. Like a successful research paper, a successful multimedia narrative project in history is based on solid research and analysis and is the product of multiple drafts and revisions. Asking students to share draft scripts with the professor, to turn in bibliographies, or to write reflections— all are ways of increasing our understanding of student intentions, sophistication of argument, and (relative) success in their projects. The standards of argument are the same, but the possibilities for making them are decidedly different.

Cecilia O'Leary

Connecting to the Public: Using New Media to Engage Students in the Iterative Process of History

As a cultural historian in an interdisciplinary department—New Humanities for Social Justice—at California State University, Monterey Bay, I continually grapple with what to emphasize in the one required history course for majors. At the Visible Knowledge Project Summer Institute in 2000, colleagues encouraged me to foreground the digital turn in history by linking new media with my longtime goal of inspiring students to become citizen historians.

Citizen historians understand their right both to learn and to make history: they assume responsibility for contributing to the ongoing project of uncovering the diversity of our past and expressing that historical knowledge in a public forum. In *Multicultural History in the New Media Classroom*, I combine traditional approaches to reading and writing with an assignment that requires students to present their research projects in new-media forms. Students are

This collage is the logo for Cecilia O'Leary's course *Multicultural History in the New Media Classroom* at California State University, Monterey Bay. O'Leary's student Yael Maayani designed the collage in 2000, using the artist Rini Templeton's drawings. Templeton created the drawings between 1974 and 1986 for public use by activists in Mexico and the United States. *Courtesy Betita Martinez.*

involved in authentic tasks—that is, the kind of work undertaken by historians, including complex inquiry and analytical thinking—and accept accountability for the "public dimension of academic knowledge."[41]

Self-consciously applying the scholarship of teaching and learning to evaluate my course and its outcomes, I have been able to document how digital history assignments helped my students develop two key historical-thinking skills. First, my students developed the ability to place themselves in history; this is an especially significant achievement since many of them are working-class and first-generation college students from migrant families who work in the fields surrounding my university. Although such students are too often seen only as hampered by deficits associated with inadequate preparation, my students in fact bring critical assets to the classroom—family and community experiences that help them write narratives of social change and move those stories from the margins into the mainstream of history.[42] Second, my students discovered the iterative nature of historical knowledge—that is, the need for historians to revise their findings in light of the knowledge they discover in the process of research and presentation. In their own efforts to stitch together the patchwork of evidence they have collected, they learned how to refocus, rewrite, and rethink the stories they tell.[43]

Making digital histories presents students with daunting technical challenges. But these new-media narratives also foster student learning in large part because of the real stakes in presenting history to a wider audience. As deadlines approach, students try to fill holes in their research and to comprehend whether new information strengthens their original interpretation or raises new directions. The very act of going back over the evidence they have collected involves them in the pattern of recursive iterations that "separates good historians from not very good historians."[44]

The particular historical period or pedagogical approach I take varies each year as I incorporate lessons garnered from evidence of student learning from the previous semester. Recently, in spring 2005, I decided to create my own course reader so that students could have models of how both academic and nonacademic writers combine personal approaches with the telling of history. Each section contained articles that took students on an intellectual journey from "Theory: Framing Identities and Histories" to "Practice: Storytelling and History-making" and finally to "Visions: What Are You Going to Do to Make History?" Articles included excerpts from Raymond Barrio's *The Plum, Plum Pickers*, Roxanne Dunbar-Ortiz's "Invasion of the Americas and the Making of the Mestizocoyote Nation," and Paul Takagi's "Growing Up as a Japanese Boy in Sacramento County."[45]

Learning the different ways historians portray the past is an important part of the scaffolding— instructional support—students need to author their own history. They choose their own research topics, often from their lived experiences or out of a commitment to social justice or a desire to learn about struggles for equality ignored or minimized by their high school history textbooks. They are required to write an abbreviated research prospectus that describes the topic, takes a metacognitive look at initial assumptions, details research questions, and lists sources. They explore the campus library, online archives, and resources in surrounding communities. I encourage them to look at a range of possibilities for primary materials: published and unpublished sources such as newspapers and diaries; visual records found in photo albums and films; everyday artifacts including family cookbooks and clothing; evidence from the built environment seen at local cemeteries and in memorials; and aural sources encompassing oral histories as well as music.

I involve my students in a cognitive apprenticeship by making visible and explicit to them my own thinking about the construction of historical narratives. I explain how I decide which sources to use, question evidence, and analyze findings.[46] I work with students to unwrap the art of storytelling and the discipline of critical thinking while my education technology assistant demystifies how to create computer-generated short films. As they might in drafting an outline of a paper, but working with multiple layers of evidence, students juxtapose images, text, special effects, and sound in what video makers call a storyboard. Students also write a reflection on the reasoning behind their choices. As these storyboards change during the course of the semester, I collect evidence of how students are learning the iterative nature of historical knowledge as they undertake successive edits of their digital narratives, visually rearranging the elements on their storyboards.

What follows are three short examples of how students grow into their roles as citizen historians, learning to place themselves in history, and to present their narratives to a wider public, including fellow students, their families, and communities.

"Look what I have found!" declared one of my students, the daughter of farmhands who work in the fields surrounding California State University, Monterey Bay. Proudly, Marisa produced a picture of her grandfather marching with César Chávez, her little sister in his arms. After many hours of researching the United Farm Workers (UFW) movement at the local library, she had found the photograph buried in the newspaper archive. With this discovery, Marisa now felt confident that she could document her family's connection to making history. The subsequent revision in her research focus, from abstract to personal, informed her choice to create a bilingual, bicultural film, using both Spanish and English audio narration, Latino and Anglo visual representations, and music from both cultures. Her film presented the photo of her grandfather surrounded by the red and black colors of the United Farm Workers while other clips featured compelling images drawn from magazines, newspapers, and family photo albums. Marisa had succeeded in weaving her family's personal experiences into a broader social history—one that made sense to her and to her community.

Another project, "A Place to Remember," told the history of a nine-year battle in San Francisco to keep the International Hotel (I-Hotel), home to Filipino seniors, from being torn down. It opened with a full-screen image of an empty lot filled with weeds and remnants of a concrete foundation while Megan, the film's narrator, asked, "What does an address mean? Whose lives and what histories lay behind the numbers?" The film later cuts to images of thousands of protesters juxtaposed to scenes of Filipino elders being dragged out of the I-Hotel by deputy

In 1970, when California vegetable growers refused to recognize the United Farm Workers (UFW) union, the workers went on strike, and their leader, César Chávez, called for a nationwide boycott of lettuce and in consequence was jailed. Cecilia O'Leary's student Marisa Jimenez searched the local history room of the Steinbeck Library in Salinas, California, and found a December 1970 clipping of her grandfather Antonio Margarito supporting the boycott. She included it in a media presentation for O'Leary's course *Multicultural History in the New Media Classroom*. Slide from "The Life of Antonio Margarito: The Bracero Program," California State University, Monterey Bay, fall semester, 2002. *Courtesy Marisa Jimenez.*

sheriffs. The audience hears Megan's voice reading an excerpt from an interview: "It filled my heart with anger, I hated how the city let something like this happen. If they were white it probably wouldn't have happened." Taken by surprise, the audience learns that those are the words of her father, Rey Mojica, "one of the thousands of protesters there that morning." Part Filipina, the student producer had embarked on her research because she had wanted to find out more about her heritage. In her research Megan found out that her own father had been one of the protesters. That discovery enabled her to revise her understanding of her connection to the struggle and to place herself and her family within it. At the close of the semester, she planned to give copies of her film to the International Hotel Senior Housing Organization and to share it with her parents, hoping her project "touches my father as much as it has touched me."

In a third project, Nicole chose to focus her digital history on an aspect of Italian culture in San Jose. Enthusiastic about the film she had created, she showed it to her large extended family. Everyone crowded around the television, taking great pride in seeing how Nicole's grandfather, a high school dropout, became a leading figure in bringing Italian accordion music to California's Bay Area. Images from scrapbooks, newspapers, wedding invitations, and community programs moved across the screen. At the end Nicole had included a clip of accordion music, but to her surprise, instead of applause, a heated debate erupted. The family demanded to know why she had used "Sicilian" rather than "Italian" music to conclude her film. Until that moment, Nicole had not realized the two were significantly different. Her family's enthusiasm for making sure the evidence she used was right made the reciprocal nature of constructing historical knowledge possible and visible in her very own living room. Their heated response spurred her to want to revise her digital history and get it right—although our class had already ended.

Going public can involve risks, as in Nicole's case. But the public presentation of the digital history increases students' excitement about the relevance of the past as they see themselves as citizen historians imparting knowledge to others. After close readings of student evidence culled from over three semesters of collecting digital histories, student reflections, and videoed exit interviews, I am confident that my students leave my classes with the ability to contextualize themselves in history. They are aware of the reciprocal nature of constructing historical knowledge and the iterative process in which new evidence constantly reshapes ideas and interpretations. They can, in the words of one student, not only "dialogue with books and communicate with primary sources from the past" but also integrate words, sounds, and visuals in the public representation and narration of history.[47]

A Conclusion

"Insofar as knowledge about teaching is anecdotally conveyed, it cannot be systematically traced . . . neither can it be systematically built on, since it cannot be accurately retrieved," Mariolina Rizzi Salvatori has argued. In short, an anecdotal approach to teaching "does not conform to most commonly accepted criteria of traditional scholarship."[48] In order to build our knowledge of teaching and learning in our own field, we realized that we had to engage the growing literature about the scholarship of teaching and learning being developed by historians with zeal and with a collective rather than an individual gaze.

Our intense collaboration has brought us together in electronic networks, conferences, and VKP writing residencies, where we have shared and critiqued each other's ideas and drafts. We have wrestled with questions of what constitutes historical understanding and how to present history in the classroom. We have together explored the openness and uncertainty of interpreting visual materials—recognizing in our work the complexity of the past and the challenge to our prior knowledge—an exploration that we now think essential for our students as they strive to acquire historical understanding. Our evidence has enabled us to see that process better.

What does it mean to think historically? That question has been central to us. As numerous recent critics have argued, history has traditionally been reluctant to engage in reflection on its own practice.[49] But we believe that these theoretical and philosophical problems are empirical issues for exploration in our own classrooms. Through careful attention to how students learn, we have come to fresh insight into our own practice as both researchers and teachers of history. Watching novice historians develop historical skills forces us—the expert practitioners—to uncover and articulate those skills and practices that we have internalized over time.

Our VKP work in the scholarship of teaching and learning has made us conscious that engagement is the first step in historical inquiry; that historians read both visual and traditional texts with attention to context and heuristic sourcing; that juxtapositional complexity enhances and deepens our understanding of history. We are learning from and with our students to be self-conscious about the intricate choices we make when constructing historical narratives, and the compression we use when we invoke visual or textual representations involves intricate choices. We study our students as they reenact our iterative processes of research and revision; and we struggle with them to make meaning with and for a larger public.

Whether as readers or researchers, our observations of students making meaning with visual and written sources now inform our own scholarly practice. Curriculum specialists often deliberate over how to ensure the transferability of skills from one class to another as a student moves through a curriculum. Analogously, we ask whether our scholarship of teaching and learning after the pictorial and digital turns transfers not only to the next class we teach but also to our more traditional scholarship as historians of particular countries, eras, and topics. These case studies push us to move beyond our opening question: Why do we use visual approaches in our teaching? to ask the disciplinary question: *Why are we not* using visual evidence and visual modes in the presentation of our own practice and research? How can visual evidence inform, or provide alternative perspectives to, our traditional research practices? What kinds of historical narratives can we visualize, construct, and present within our field and to a larger public?

We conclude that the pedagogical-visual-digital turn offers an alternative perspective for historical understanding and historical presentation. As we explore how historical meaning is constructed from new, relatively unfamiliar types of sources and presented to a public increasingly accustomed to visual communication, we grow in understanding of our own often-unexamined disciplinary practices. The scholarship of teaching and learning offers a new way for historians to see their discipline—to think, write, and communicate about history, in the classroom and beyond.[50]

Notes

1. David Pace, "The Amateur in the Operating Room: History and the Scholarship of Teaching," *American Historical Review* 109 (Oct. 2004): 1171. On viewing teaching problems

as positive and worthy of research, see Randy Bass, "The Scholarship of Teaching: What's the Problem?" *inventio* 1 (Feb. 1999), <www.doiiit.gmu.edu/Archives/feb98/randybass.htm> (Sept. 20, 2005).

2. The questions are from Pace, "Amateur in the Operating Room," 1176. On early work that takes the evidence-based approach advocated here, see Lendol Calder, William W. Cutler III, and T. Mills Kelly, "History Lessons: Historians and the Scholarship of Teaching and Learning," in *Disciplinary Styles in the Scholarship of Teaching and Learning: Exploring Common Ground*, ed. Mary Taylor Huber and Sherwyn Morreale (Washington, D.C., 2002), 46, 52–54. We adapt this definition of scholarship from Lee Shulman and the Carnegie Foundation for the Advancement of Teaching, who expand the work of Ernest L. Boyer. See Lee Shulman, "Course Anatomy: The Dissection and Analysis of Knowledge through Teaching," in *The Course Portfolio: How Faculty Can Examine Their Teaching to Advance Practice and Improve Student Learning*, ed. Pat Hutchings (Washington, D.C., 1988), 5, and Ernest L. Boyer, *Scholarship Reconsidered: Priorities of the Professoriate* (Princeton, N.J., 1990).

3. On the Visible Knowledge Project (VKP), see http://crossroads.georgetown.edu/vkp/ (Sept. 25, 2005). In July 2003 the Atlantic Philanthropies ended its program of grant making in higher education to focus on areas such as population growth and human rights. See the Atlantic Philanthropies, <www.atlanticphilanthropies.org/areas_of_support/earlier_programs.asp> (Dec. 13, 2005).

4. Sam Wineburg, *Historical Thinking and Other Unnatural Acts: Charting the Future of Teaching the Past* (Philadelphia, 2001), 91. Entries for "history teaching" indexed in *America: History and Life* increased from 253 (1985–1989), to 260 (1990–1994), to 357 (1995–1999), and to 428 (2000–2005). Important book-length investigations include Paul Gagnon, ed., *Historical Literacy: The Case for History in American Education* (New York, 1989); Peter N. Stearns, *Meaning over Memory: Recasting the Teaching of Culture and History* (Chapel Hill, N.C., 1993); Robert Blackley, ed. *History Anew: Innovations in the Teaching of History Today* (Long Beach, Calif., 1993); Gary B. Nash, Charlotte Crabtree, and Ross E. Dunn, *History on Trial: Culture Wars and the Teaching of the Past* (New York, 1997); Peter N. Stearns, Peter Seixas, and Sam Wineburg, eds., *Knowing, Teaching, and Learning History* (New York, 2000); Wineburg, *Historical Thinking and Other Unnatural Acts*; Jonathan Zimmerman, *Whose America? Culture Wars in the Public Schools* (Cambridge, Mass., 2002); Linda Symcox, *Whose History? The Struggle for National Standards in American Classrooms* (New York, 2002); and Thomas Bender et al., *The Education of Historians for the Twenty-first Century* (Urbana, Ill., 2004).

5. Mariolina Rizzi Salvatori, "The Scholarship of Teaching: Beyond the Anecdotal," *Pedagogy* 2 (Fall 2002): 298.

6. Pace, "Amateur in the Operating Room," 1189.

7. Robert B. Bain, "Into the Breach: Using Research and Theory to Shape History Instruction," in *Knowing, Teaching, and Learning History*, ed. Stearns, Seixas, and Wineburg, 332; W. J. T. Mitchell, *Picture Theory: Essays on Verbal and Visual Representation* (Chicago, 1994), 11; Sol Cohen, "An Innocent Eye: The Pictorial Turn, Film Studies, and History," *History of Education Quarterly* 43 (Summer 2003): 251. For a survey of approaches to images, see Peter Burke, *Eyewitnessing: The Uses of Images as Historical Evidence* (Ithaca, N.Y., 2001). For examples of the recent shift toward visual evidence, see George H. Roeder Jr., "Filling in the Picture: Visual Culture," *Reviews in American History* 26 (March 1998): 275–93; Joshua Brown, *Beyond the Lines: Pictorial Reporting, Everyday Life, and the Crises of Gilded Age America* (Berkeley, Calif., 2002); and Peter H. Wood, *Weathering the Storm: Inside Winslow Homer's Gulf Stream* (Athens, Ga., 2004).

8. Louis Masur, "'Pictures Have Now Become a Necessity': The Use of Images in American History Textbooks," *Journal of American History* 84 (March 1998): 1409; David Jaffee, "'Scholars will soon be instructed through the eye': E-Supplements and the Teaching of U.S. History," *Journal of American History* 89 (March 2003): 1463–82. For speculations on moving images to the center of historical accounts, see Katherine Martinez, "Imaging the Past: Historians, Visual Images, and the Contested Definition of History," *Visual Resources* 11, no. 1 (1995): 27.

9. On students and images, see James H. Madison, "Teaching with Images," *OAH Magazine of History* 18 (Jan. 2004): 65. For a detailed approach to understanding the textual reading practices of historians, see Wineburg, *Historical Thinking and Other Unnatural Acts*, 89–112. On the need for conventions for reading images, see Robert M. Levine, *Insights into American History: Photographs as Documents* (Upper Saddle River, N.J., 2004), ix. Wineburg's model was adapted by the Center for History and New Media, the American Social History Project, and the Visible Knowledge Project in the production of the Making Sense of Evidence Web site. See Center for History and New Media, Making Sense of Evidence <http://historymatters.gmu.edu/browse/makesense/> (Sept. 20, 2005). For another project that works with college, university, and high school teachers of history and the use of images in the classroom, see American Social History Project, Learning to Look: Visual Evidence and the U.S. Past in the New Media Classroom <http://web.gc.cuny.edu/ashp/LTLNMC> (Sept. 20, 2005). See also Masur, "'Pictures Have Now Become a Necessity,'" 1423.

10. On the complexities of multimedia authoring in humanities classrooms, see Visible Knowledge Project, Multimedia Authoring Gallery <http://crossroads.georgetown.edu/vkp/themes/poster_showcase_writing.htm> (Sept. 20, 2005). See also Randy Bass and Bret Eynon, eds., *The Difference That Inquiry Makes* (forthcoming), and Randy Bass and Bret Eynon, "Teaching Culture, Learning Culture, and New Media Technologies: An Introduction and Framework," *Works and Days* 16, nos. 1–2 (1998): 11–96. For examples of new digital scholarship in history, see Robert Darnton, "An Early Information Society: News and the Media in Eighteenth-Century Paris," *American Historical Review* 105 (Feb. 2000): 1–35; Roy Rosenzweig et al., "Forum on Hypertext Scholarship: AQ as WebZine—Responses to AQ's Experimental Online Issue," *American Quarterly* 51 (June 1999): 237–83; and the contents of the special issue "Hypertext Scholarship in American Studies," ed. Roy Rosenzweig, *American Quarterly* 51 (June 1999) <http://chnm.gmu.edu/aq> (Sept. 20, 2005). See also the introduction to an online article on slavery: William G. Thomas III and Edward L. Ayers, "The Difference That Slavery Made: A Close Analysis of Two American Communities," *American Historical Review* 108 (Dec. 2003): 1299–1307; and the article: William G. Thomas III and Edward L. Ayers, "The Difference That Slavery Made: A Close Analysis of Two American Communities," *American Historical Review* 108 (Dec. 2003) <www.vcdh.virginia.edu/AHR> (Sept. 20, 2005).

11. Thomas and Ayers, "Presentation," in "The Difference That Slavery Made," <www.vcdh.virginia.edu/AHR> (Sept. 22, 2005).

12. Olivia: "'The Industrial life' picture seems to view industrial work in a romanticized light, which contrasts with the way it originally used to be represented. Early in the century, industrial life was seen as unsanitary, dangerous, menial work, fit for only the poor. This picture, however, uses vivid, warm colors, clean cut and clear drawn lines. I think after WWII (this picture was created in 1941) there seemed to be more of a romanticized view of technology and industry and all that can be accomplished. The picture shows types of work being done that are necessary to an industrial society. There's the scientist, the architect, the worker, and I guess the engineer. "The second picture 'Security

of the Family' is supposed to represent family life and roles during the 40s. The woman (the mother) is seen holding a child—obviously meaning that women were expected to be mothers and child rearers. The Father is seen as being more 'intellectual,' sitting down at the table, seeming to have an important air about him. The girl is drawing, to represent that girls are seen as being artistic. The young boy is playing tennis. It shows that girls are supposed to 'act like girls,' being calm and 'cultured.' Boys seem to have more liberties in their manner of behavior." Arthur: "Seymour Fogel's painting, 'Security of the Family,' reminds me of Norman Rockwell's paintings, 'The Four Freedoms.' The Rockwell image from that group that comes to mind most immediately is the one where the child is being tucked into bed with the father looking on holding a newspaper containing terrifying headlines." Both Rockwell and Fogel are presenting idealized images of American society, but they're different. Fogel is not seeking to portray the warmth and intimacy of the kind that Rockwell seeks to portray. Fogel's figures, drawn in the way that marble might be sculpted into statues, present Family Life as a monumental, larger than life force. "The sky overhead may be gray and over cast, but the mother—staring out into the undefined future much as the mother in Lange's 'Migrant Mother'—is, like the other members of the family, stolid, sturdy, unwavering in their march forward into the unknown."

13. See Barbara Melosh, *Engendering Culture: Manhood and Womanhood in New Deal Public Art and Theater* (Washington, D.C., 1991).

14. "Exercise Two," *History 31516: Power, Race, and Culture in the U.S. City*, Fall 2003, City College of New York, <www.ccny.cuny.edu/humanities/jaffee/nyc/exer2.html> (Dec. 1, 2005).

15. See Brian W. Dippie, *George Catlin and His Indian Gallery* (Washington, D.C., 2002); Thomas Loraine McKenney, *History of the Indian Tribes of North America*, with Biographical Sketches and Anecdotes of the Principal Chiefs Embellished with One Hundred and Twenty Portraits from the Indian Gallery in the Department of War (3 vols., Philadelphia, 1838–1844); Richard White, *The Middle Ground: Indians, Empires, and Republics in the Great Lakes Region, 1650–1815* (New York, 1991); Carrie Rebora, *John Singleton Copley in America* (New York, 1995).

16. Peter Seixas, "Preservice Teachers Assess Students' Prior Historical Understanding," *Social Studies* 85 (Jan.–Feb. 1994): 91–95; Wineburg, *Historical Thinking and Other Unnatural Acts*, 232–55; Sam Wineburg, Susan Mosborg, and Dan Porat, "What Can Forrest Gump Tell Us about Students' Historical Understanding?" *Social Education* 65 (Jan.–Feb. 2001): 55. See also Marita Sturken, *Tangled Memories: The Vietnam War, the AIDS Epidemic, and the Politics of Remembering* (Berkeley, Calif., 1997).

17. *Forrest Gump*, dir. Robert Zemeckis (Paramount, 1994).

18. John D. Bransford, Ann L. Brown, and Rodney R. Cocking, eds., *How People Learn: Brain, Mind, Experience, and School* (Washington, D.C., 2001), 10.

19. I adapted the ranking question from Wineburg, *Historical Thinking and Other Unnatural Acts*, 75; and Roy Rosenzweig and David Thelen, *The Presence of the Past: Popular Uses of History in American Life* (New York, 1998), 91. For a detailed explanation of both the source-sequencing exercise and its results, see Peter Felten, "'Photos—The Almost Most Objective Evidence There Is': Reading Words and Images of the 1960s," *Reader* 52 (Spring 2005): 77–94.

20. Marita Sturken and Lisa Cartwright, *Practices of Looking: An Introduction to Visual Culture* (New York, 2001), 17.

21. This aligns with Roy Rosenzweig and David Thelen's findings that films and television are widely considered to be untrustworthy sources of historical knowledge. See Rosenzweig and Thelen, *Presence of the Past*, 91, 97–101. It seems, however, that some

people may internalize a historical narrative presented on film or TV (such as *Forrest Gump*) even though they tell researchers and teachers that such video sources are of dubious historical value. Emphasis added.

22. Russell Olwell, "New Views of Slavery: Using Recent Historical Work to Promote Critical Thinking about the 'Peculiar Institution,'" *History Teacher* 34, no. 4 (2001): 459–69.

23. "Syllabus," History 272: African American History, Fall 2002, Millersville University <http://muweb.millersville.edu/~ugrr/272> (Sept. 20, 2005). For more on this assignment, see <http://muweb.millersville.edu/ugrr/272/tsoutline.pdf> (Sept. 20, 2005). In addition, each team had to investigate the Web site of a historic site that challenged or contradicted the presentation of master-slave relations at the first site. The paired sites were: (1) Monticello <www.monticello.org> (Sept. 20, 2005) and Kingsley Plantation <www.cr.nps.gov/goldcres/sites/kingsley.htm> (Sept. 20, 2005); (2) Mount Vernon <www.mountvernon.org> (Sept. 20, 2005) and Seacoast New Hampshire Black History <http://seacoastnh.com/blackhistory/ona.html> (Sept. 20, 2005) (featuring the story of Ona Judge Staines, who escaped the Executive Mansion in Philadelphia in 1796 and made her way to Portsmouth, New Hampshire); (3) Colonial Williamsburg <www.colonialwilliamsburg.com> (Sept. 20, 2005) and Common-Place <www.common-place.org> (Sept. 20, 2005); and (4) selected sites administered by the National Park Service <www.cr.nps.gov/aahistory> (Sept. 20, 2005).

24. We drew on several resources to develop our rubric for assessing multimedia narratives. For the elements that make a "good story," see the Cookbook from the Center for Digital Storytelling <www.storycenter.org/memvoice/pages/cookbook.html> (Sept. 20, 2005). For the components of effective historical narratives, see the National History Standards <www.sscnet.ucla.edu/nchs/standards> (Sept. 20, 2005). For guidance in using images in a historical interpretation, see Martinez, in "Imaging the Past," 21–45. For rubrics of narrative construction, see "Digital Storytelling: Some Selected Online Resources," *VKP Community Newsletter* (Sept. 2002) <http://crossroads.georgetown.edu/bkp/newsletter/0902/resources.html> (Sept. 20, 2005).

25. For a sample assessment grid, see <http://muweb.millersville.edu/~ugrr/VKP/triad/vkp.html> (Sept. 20, 2005). Ira Berlin, *Generations of Captivity: A History of African-American Slaves* (Cambridge, Mass., 2003), 10.

26. James Oliver Horton, "On-Site Learning: The Power of Historic Places," *CRM Online* 23, no. 8 (2000) (access by subscription only). See also James O. Horton, "Presenting Slavery: The Perils of Telling America's Racial Story," *Public Historian* 21 (Fall 1999): 19–38. The photograph of the historical interpreter appeared on the Colonial Williamsburg Web site. See Colonial Williamsburg: African-American Experience <www.history.org/Almanack/life/Af_Amer/aalife.cfm> (Sept. 20, 2005). For another perspective on "tales that teach," see Lawrence W. Levine, *Black Culture and Black Consciousness: Afro-American Folk Thought from Slavery to Freedom* (New York, 1977).

27. Karen E. Sutton, "Confronting Slavery Face-to-Face: A Twenty-first-Century Interpreter's Perspective on Eighteenth-Century Slavery," *Common-Place* 1 (July 2001) <www.common-place.org/vol-01/no-04/slavery/sutton.shtml> (Sept. 20, 2005). Christopher D. Geist, "African-American History at Colonial Williamsburg," *CRM Online* 20, no. 2 (1997) (access by subscription only); Jeffrey J. Crow, "Interpreting Slavery in the Classroom and at Historic Sites," *AHA Perspectives* 36 (March 1998).

28. The painting appears as an illustration in Alex Bontemps, "Seeing Slavery: How Paintings Make Words Look Different," *Common-Place* 1 (July 2001) <www.common-place.org/vol-01/no-04/slavery/bontemps.shtml> (Sept. 20, 2005).

29. Interpretations that informed this student's reading of the master-slave relationship in colonial-era Williamsburg included Shane White, "Introduction: Representing Slavery; A Roundtable Discussion," ibid.; Sutton, "Confronting Slavery Face-to-Face"; and Bontemps, "Seeing Slavery." On variations in historical understanding among students of various national, ethnic, and racial backgrounds, see Keith Barton, "Research on Students' Historical Thinking and Learning," *AHA Perspectives* 42 (Oct. 2004): 21.

30. This unsigned painting (c. 1777–1794), held by the Abby Aldrich Rockefeller Folk Art Center in Williamsburg, Virginia, appeared in Bontemps, "Seeing Slavery." The paper on which it was painted shows a paper maker's watermark from 1777–1794. Historians speculate it shows a scene from the late eighteenth or early nineteenth century on a plantation between Charleston and Orangeburg, South Carolina.

31. Frederick Douglass, *My Bondage and My Freedom* (New York, 1855), chap. 4; Burke, *Eyewitnessing*, 13–16.

32. Additionally, as the National Standards for History urge, students must develop competencies to interrogate "a variety of visual sources such as historical photographs, political cartoons, paintings, and architecture in order to clarify, illustrate, or elaborate upon the information presented" in written narratives. National Center for History in the Schools, *National Standards for History* (Sept. 20, 2005).

33. *Amistad*, dir. Steven Spielberg (DreamWorks, 1997). Standard 3B Historical Analysis and Interpretation, National Standards for History <http://nchs.ucla.edu/standards/thinking5-12_toc.html> (Sept. 20, 2005).

34. For other explorations of digital storytelling, see Tracey M. Weis et al., "Digital Storytelling in Culture and History Classrooms," in *Engines of Inquiry: Approaches to Teaching, Learning, and Technology in American Culture Studies*, ed. Michael Coventry (1998; Washington, D.C., 2003), 397–413; Viet Than Nguyen, "How Do We Tell Stories?," ibid., 363–96; and Joe Lambert, *Digital Storytelling: Capturing Lives, Creating Community* (Berkeley, Calif., 2002). From the literature on new media, see Mark Stephen Meadows, *Pause and Effect: The Art of Interactive Narrative* (Indianapolis, 2003); Gunnar Liestol, Andrew Morrison, and Terje Rassmussen, eds., *Digital Media Revisited: Theoretical and Conceptual Innovations in Digital Domains* (Cambridge, Mass., 2003); Lev Manovich, *The Language of New Media* (Cambridge, Mass., 2001); and Mary E. Hocks and Michelle R. Kendrick, eds., *Eloquent Images: Word and Image in the Age of New Media* (Cambridge, Mass., 2003). On describing features of student learning, see Pat Hutchings, "Approaching the Scholarship of Teaching and Learning," in *Opening Lines: Approaches to the Scholarship of Teaching and Learning*, ed. Pat Hutchings (Menlo Park, Calif., 2000), 4.

35. On juxtaposition, see Nancy Barta-Smith and Danette DiMarco, "Same Difference: Evolving Conclusions about Textuality and New Media," in *Eloquent Images*, ed. Hocks and Kendrick, 159–78; and Jennifer Wiley, "Cognitive and Educational Implications of Visually Rich Media: Images and Imagination," ibid., 201–15. On visual arguments, see Gunther Kress and Theo van Leeuwen, *Reading Images: The Grammar of Visual Design* (New York, 1996); N. Katherine Hayles, *Writing Machines* (Cambridge, Mass., 2002); and Edward R. Tufte, *Visual Explanations: Images and Quantities, Evidence and Narrative* (Cheshire, Conn., 1997).

36. Alyson Hurt, "How to Be a Domestic Goddess," digital story, *Communication, Culture, and Technology Program*, Georgetown University, May 2004; Alyson Hurt, "How to Be a Domestic Goddess," reflective paper, *Communication, Culture, and Technology Program*, Georgetown University, May 11, 2004, 1 (in Michael Coventry's possession).

37. Hurt, "How to Be a Domestic Goddess," reflective paper, 6. The theory of gender performance also influenced Hurt's reading. See, for example, Judith Butler, *Gender Trouble: Feminism and the Subversion of Identity* (New York, 1990).

38. Malgorzata Rymsza-Pawlowska, "'Lighting Up at the Dawn of Modernity,'" digital story, *Communication, Culture, and Technology Program*, Georgetown University, Dec. 2004; Malgorzata Rymsza-Pawlowska, "'Lighting Up at the Dawn of Modernity': The 1920s Woman and Smoking as a Performance of Social Change," reflective paper, *Communication, Culture, and Technology Program*, Georgetown University, Dec. 16, 2004 (in Coventry's possession).

39. Rymsza-Pawlowska, "'Lighting Up at the Dawn of Modernity,'" digital story; Rymsza-Pawlowska, "'Lighting Up at the Dawn of Modernity,'" reflective paper, 2.

40. Rymsza-Pawlowska, "'Lighting Up at the Dawn of Modernity,'" reflective paper, 5.

41. On the relationship between new-media pedagogy and elements of quality learning, see Randy Bass, "Engines of Inquiry: Teaching, Technology, and Learner-Centered Approaches to Culture and History," in *Engines of Inquiry*, ed. Coventry, 3–26.

42. What students bring into the history classroom is a crucial area for future research on student learning. See Pace, "Amateur in the Operating Room." On assets-based approaches to multicultural learning, see the special issue "Pedagogies for Social Change," ed. Susan Roberta Katz and Cecilia Elizabeth O'Leary, *Social Justice* 29 (Winter 2002): 1–197.

43. In approaching documents, students enact processes similar to those of historians. See Wineburg, *Historical Thinking and Other Unnatural Acts.*

44. T. Mills Kelly, "For Better or Worse? The Marriage of the Web and the Classroom," *Journal of Association for History and Computing* 3 (Aug. 2000) <mcel.pacificu .edu/JAHC/JAHCIII2/ARTICLES/kelly/kelly.html> (Sept. 25, 2005).

45. Raymond Barrio, *The Plum, Plum Pickers* (Binghamton, N.Y., 1971), 84–94; Roxanne Dunbar-Ortiz, "Invasion of the Americas and the Making of the Mestizocoyote Nation: Heritage of the Invasion," *Social Justice* 20 (Spring–Summer 1993): 52–55; Paul Takagi, "Growing Up as a Japanese Boy in Sacramento County," *Social Justice* 26 (Summer 1999): 135–49.

46. On teaching strategies, see Bain, "Into the Breach," 334–35.

47. Matthew Fox, "Student Reflection," Spring 2005, California State University, Monterey Bay (in Cecilia O'Leary's possession).

48. Salvatori, "Scholarship of Teaching," 369–94.

49. See Dominick LaCapra, *History in Transit: Experience, Identity, Critical Theory* (Ithaca, N.Y., 2004); John H. Zammito, "Reading 'Experience': The Debate in Intellectual History among Scott, Toews, and LaCapra," in *Reclaiming Identity: Realist Theory and the Predicament of Postmodernism*, ed. Paula M. L. Moya and Michael R. Hames-Garcia (Berkeley, Calif., 2000); Joan W. Scott, "Experience," in *Feminists Theorize the Political*, ed. Judith Butler and Joan W. Scott (New York, 1992), 22–40; and John E. Toews, "Intellectual History after the Linguistic Turn: The Autonomy of Meaning and the Irreducibility of Experience," *American Historical Review* 92 (Oct. 1987): 879–907. See also Peter Novick, *That Noble Dream: The "Objectivity Question" and the American Historical Profession* (New York, 1988).

50. The authors wish to thank the editors of the *JAH*, and especially Gary Kornblith and Carol Lasser, "Textbooks and Teaching" section editors, for their invaluable help. David Pace was instrumental throughout, facilitating discussion at our writing residency and reading drafts. Roy Rosenzweig kindly read and offered detailed comments on an

early draft. Susannah McGowan, assistant director for curriculum design at the Center for New Designs in Learning and Scholarship at Georgetown University, assisted in the writing of this essay by participating in conversations about its shape, compiling early versions of the pieces, and commenting on drafts. We acknowledge with gratitude her important contribution to our thinking. The authors thank Randy Bass and Bret Eynon and all of their colleagues from the Visible Knowledge Project (VKP) for providing a nurturing space for the exploration of these ideas. We each express thanks to our students for permitting us to quote and paraphrase their work. Our title echoes that of John Berger's influential book, *Ways of Seeing* (1972).

SAM WINEBURG

Crazy for History

In 1917, the year the United States went to war, history erupted onto the pages of the American Psychological Association's *Journal of Educational Psychology*. J. Carleton Bell, the journal's managing editor and a professor at the Brooklyn Training School for Teachers, began his tenure with an editorial entitled "The Historic Sense." (A companion editorial examined the relation of psychology to military problems.) Bell claimed that the study of history provided an opportunity for thinking and reflection, qualities lacking in many classrooms.[1]

Bell invited his readers to ponder two questions: "What is the historic sense?" and "How can it be developed?" Such questions, he asserted, did not concern only the history teacher; they were ones "in which the educational psychologist is interested, and which it is incumbent upon him to attempt to answer." To readers who wondered where to locate the elusive "historic sense," Bell offered clues. Presented with a set of primary documents, one student produces a coherent account while another assembles "a hodgepodge of miscellaneous facts." Similarly, some college freshmen "show great skill in the orderly arrangement of their historical data" while others "take all statements with equal emphasis . . . and become hopelessly confused in the multiplicity of details." Did such findings reflect "native differences in historic ability" or were they the "effects of specific courses of training"? Such questions opened "a fascinating field for investigation" for the educational psychologist.[2]

Bell's questions still nag us today. What is the essence of historical understanding? How can historical interpretation and analysis be taught? What is the role of instruction in improving students' ability to think? In light of his foresight, it is instructive to examine how Bell carried out his research agenda. In a companion article to his editorial, Bell and his colleague David F. McCollum presented a study that began by laying out five aspects of the historic sense:

1. "The ability to understand present events in light of the past."
2. The ability to sift through the documentary record—newspaper articles, hearsay, partisan attacks, contemporary accounts—and construct "from this confused tangle a straightforward and probable account" of what happened.
3. The ability to appreciate a historical narrative.

Journal of American History 90 (2004): 1401–14.

4. "Reflective and discriminating replies to 'thought questions' on a given historical situation."
5. The ability to answer factual questions about historical personalities and events.[3]

The authors conceded that the fifth aspect was "the narrowest, and in the estimation of some writers, the least important type of historical ability." Yet, they acknowledged, it was the "most readily tested." In a fateful move, Bell and McCollum elected the path of least resistance: of their five possibilities only one—the ability to answer factual questions—was chosen for study. While perhaps the first instance, this was not the last in which ease of measurement—not priority of subject matter understanding—determined the shape and contour of a research program.[4]

Bell and McCollum created the first large-scale test of factual knowledge in United States history and administered it to fifteen hundred Texas students in 1915–1916. They compiled a list of names (for example, Thomas Jefferson, John Burgoyne, Alexander Hamilton, Cyrus H. McCormick), dates (1492, 1776, 1861), and events (the Sherman Antitrust Act, the Fugitive Slave Act, the Dred Scott decision) that history teachers said every student should know. They administered their test at the upper elementary level (fifth through seventh grades), in high schools (in five Texas districts: Houston, Huntsville, Brenham, San Marcos, and Austin), and in colleges (at the University of Texas, Austin, and at two teacher-training institutions, South-West Texas State Normal School and Sam Houston Normal Institute).

Across the board, results disappointed. Students recognized 1492 but not 1776; they identified Thomas Jefferson but often confused him with Jefferson Davis; they uprooted the Articles of Confederation from the eighteenth century and plunked them down in the Confederacy; and they stared quizzically at 1846, the beginning of the U.S.-Mexico war, unaware of its place in Texas history. Nearly all students recognized Sam Houston as the father of the Texas republic but had him marching triumphantly into Mexico City, not vanquishing Antonio Lopez de Santa Anna at San Jacinto.

The overall score at the elementary level was a dismal 16 percent. In high school, after a year of history instruction, students scored a shabby 33 percent, and in college, after a third exposure to history, scores barely approached the halfway mark (49 percent). The authors concluded that studying history in school led only to "a small, irregular increase in the scores with increasing academic age." Anticipating jeremiads by secretaries of education and op-ed columnists a half century later, Bell and McCollum indicted the educational system and its charges: "Surely a grade of 33 in 100 on the simplest and most obvious facts of American history is not a record in which any high school can take great pride."[5]

By the next world war, hand-wringing about students' historical benightedness had moved from the back pages of the *Journal of Educational Psychology* to the front pages of the *New York Times*. "Ignorance of U.S. History Shown by College Freshmen," trumpeted the headline on April 4, 1943, a day when the main story reported that George Patton's troops had overrun those of Erwin Rommel at

Al-Guettar. Providing support for the earlier claim made by the historian Allan Nevins that "young people are all too ignorant of American history," the survey showed that a scant 6 percent of the seven thousand college freshmen tested could identify the thirteen original colonies, while only 15 percent could place William McKinley as president during the Spanish-American War. Less than a quarter could name two contributions made by either Abraham Lincoln or Thomas Jefferson. Often, students were simply confused. Abraham Lincoln "emaciated the slaves" and, as first president, was father of the Constitution. One graduate of an eastern high school, responding to a question about the system of checks and balances, claimed that Congress "has the right to veto bills that the President wishes to be passed." According to students, the United States expanded territorially by purchasing Alaska from the Dutch, the Philippines from Great Britain, Louisiana from Sweden, and Hawaii from Norway. A *Times* editorial excoriated those "appallingly ignorant" youth.[6]

The *Times*'s breast-beating resumed in time for the bicentennial celebration, when the newspaper commissioned a second test, with Bernard Bailyn of Harvard University leading the charge. With the aid of the Educational Testing Service (ETS), the *Times* surveyed nearly two thousand freshmen on 194 college campuses. On May 2, 1976, the results rained down on the bicentennial parade: "*Times* Test Shows Knowledge of American History Limited." Of the 42 multiple-choice questions on the test, students averaged an embarrassing 21 correct—a failing score of 50 percent. The low point for Bailyn was that more students believed that the Puritans guaranteed religious freedom (36 percent) than understood religious toleration as the result of rival denominations seeking to cancel out each others' advantage (34 percent). This "absolutely shocking" response rendered the voluble Bailyn speechless: "I don't know how to explain it."[7]

Results from the 1987, 1994, and 2001 administrations of the National Assessment of Educational Progress (NAEP, known informally as the "Nation's Report Card") have shown little deviation from earlier trends.[8] In the wake of the 2001 test came the same stale headlines ("Kids Get 'Abysmal' Grade in History: High School Seniors Don't Know Basics," *USA Today*); the same refrains of cultural decline ("a nation of historical nitwits," wagged the *Greensboro* [North Carolina] *News and Record*); the same holier-than-thou indictments of today's youth ("dumb as rocks," hissed the *Weekly Standard*); and the same boy-who-cried-wolf predictions of impending doom ("when the United States is at war and under terrorist threat," young people's lack of knowledge is particularly dangerous).[9] Scores on the 2001 test, after a decade of the "standards movement," were virtually identical to their predecessors. Six in ten seniors "lack even a basic knowledge of American history," wrote the *Washington Post*, results that NAEP officials castigated as "awful," "unacceptable," and "abysmal." "The questions that stumped so many students," lamented Secretary of Education Rod Paige, "involve the most fundamental concepts of our democracy, our growth as a nation, and our role in the world." As for the efficacy of standards in the states that adopted them, the test yielded no differences between students of teachers who reported adhering to standards and those who did not. Remarked a befuddled Paige, "I don't have any explanation for that at all."[10]

To many commentators, what is at stake goes beyond whether today's teens can distinguish whether eastern bankers or western ranchers supported the gold standard.[11] Pointing to the latest NAEP results, the Albert Shanker Institute, sponsored by the American Federation of Teachers, claimed in a blue-ribbon report, "Education for Democracy," that "something has gone awry. . . . We *now* have convincing evidence that our students are woefully ignorant of who we are as Americans," indifferent to "the common good," and "disconnected from American history."[12]

One wonders what evidence this committee "now" possesses that has not been gathering moss since 1917 when Bell and McCollum hand tallied fifteen hundred student surveys. Explanations of today's low scores disintegrate when applied to results from 1917-history's apex as a subject in the school curriculum.[13] No one can accuse the Texas teachers of 1917 of teaching process over content or serving up a tepid social studies curriculum to bored students—the National Council for the Social Studies (founded in 1921) did not even exist. Instead of being poorly trained and laboring under harsh conditions with scant public support, the Texas pedagogues were among the most educated members of their communities and commanded wide respect. ("The high schools of Houston and Austin have the reputation of being very well administered and of having an exceptionally high grade of teachers," wrote Bell and McCollum—it is hard to imagine that sentence being written about today's schools.)[14]

Historical memory shows an especial plasticity when it turns to assessing young people's character and capability. The same Diane Ravitch, educational historian and member of the NAEP governing board, who in May 2002 expressed alarm that students "know so little about their nation's history" and possess "so little capacity to reflect on its meaning" did a one-eighty eleven months later when rallying Congress for funds in history education:

> Although it is customary for people of a certain age to complain about the inadequacies of the younger generation, such complaints ring hollow today. . . . What we have learned in these past few weeks is that this younger generation, as represented on the battlefields of Iraq, may well be our finest generation.[15]

The phrase "our finest generation" of course echoes the journalist Tom Brokaw's characterization of the men and women who fought in World War II as the "greatest generation." Those were the college students who in 1943 abandoned the safety of the quadrangle for the hazards of the beachhead. Yet only in our contemporary mirror do they look "great." Back then, grown-ups dismissed them as knuckleheads, even questioning their ability to fight. Writing in the *New York Times Magazine* in May 1942, a fretful Allan Nevins wondered whether a historically illiterate fighting force might be a national liability. "We cannot understand what we are fighting for unless we know how our principles developed." If "knowing our principles" means scoring well on objective tests, we might want to update that thesis.[16]

A sober look at a century of history testing provides no evidence for the "gradual disintegration of cultural memory" or a "*growing* historical ignorance." The only thing growing seems to be our amnesia of past ignorance. If anything, test results across the last century point to a peculiar American neurosis: each generation's obsession with testing its young only to discover—and rediscover— their "shameful" ignorance. The consistency of results across time casts doubt on a presumed golden age of fact retention. Appeals to it are more the stuff of national lore and wistful nostalgia for a time that never was than a claim that can be anchored in the documentary record.[17]

ASSESSING THE ASSESSORS

The statistician Dale Whittington has shown that when results from the early part of the twentieth century are put side by side with those of recent tests, today's high school students do about as well as their parents, grandparents, and great-grandparents. That is remarkable when we compare today's near-universal enrollments with the elitist composition of the high school in the teens and early twenties. Young people's knowledge hovers with amazing consistency around the 40–50 percent mark—despite radical changes in the demographics of test takers across the century.[18]

The world has turned upside down in the last one hundred years, but students' ignorance of history has marched stolidly in place. Given changes in the knowledge historians deem most important, coupled with changes in who sits for the tests, why have scores remained flat?

Complex questions often require complex answers, but not here. Kids look dumb on history tests because the system conspires to make them look dumb. The system is rigged.

As practiced by the big testing companies, modern psychometrics guarantees that test results will conform to a symmetrical bell curve. Since the thirties, the main tool used to create these perfectly shaped bells has been the multiple-choice test, composed of many items, each with its own stem and set of alternatives. One alternative is the correct (or "keyed") answer; the others (in testers' argot, "distracters") are false. In the early days of large-scale testing, the unabashed goal of the multiple-choice item was to rank students, rather than to determine if they had attained a particular level of knowledge. A good item created "spread" among students by maximizing their differences. A bad item, conversely, created little spread; nearly everyone got it right (or wrong). The best way to ensure that most students would land under the curve's bell was to include a few questions that only the best students got right, a few questions that most got right, and a majority of questions that between 40 and 60 percent got right. In such examinations (known as "norm-referenced" tests because individual scores are compared against nationally representative samples, or "norms"), items are extensively field-tested to see if they behave properly. The testers' language is revealing: A good item is of medium difficulty and has a high "discrimination index"; students with higher scores will tend to get it right, and students with lower scores will tend to get it wrong. Items that deviate from this profile are dropped. In other words, only the questions that array students in a neatly shaped bell curve make it to the final version of the test.[19]

When large-scale testing was introduced into American classrooms in the 1930s, it ran counter to teachers' notions of what constituted average, below average, and exemplary performance. Most teachers believed that a failing score should be below 75 percent, and that an average score should be about 85 percent, a grade of B. Testing companies knew there would be a culture clash, so they prepared materials to allay teachers' concerns. In 1936 the Cooperative Test Service of the American Council on Education, ETS's forerunner, explained the new scoring system to teachers:

> Many teachers feel that each and every question should measure something, which all or at least a majority of well taught students should know or be able to do. When applied to tests of the type represented by the Cooperative series, these notions are serious misconceptions. . . . Ideally, the test should be adjusted in difficulty [so] that the least able students will score near zero, the average student will make about half the possible score, and the best students will just fall short of a perfect score. . . . The immediate purpose of these tests is to show, for each individual, how he compares in understanding and ability to use what he has learned with other individuals.[20]

The normal curve's legacy accompanies us today in the tests near and dear to the hearts of American high school students: the SAT (Scholastic Assessment Test). No matter how intelligent a given cohort of young people may be, no matter what miracles the standards movement may perform, no matter how much we close the "achievement gap" between students of different races and classes, it is impossible for the majority of students to score 1600. If that happened, the normal curve would not be normal, and Lake Wobegon, where "all of the children are above average," would not be fictional.[21] It is impossible to have a basketball league in which every team wins most of its games. Similarly with the normal curve: there can be no winners without losers.

In spite of the odds against their scoring well, students at an SAT summer camp in Milton, Massachusetts, spend at least five hours a day studying and taking practice tests. *Courtesy National Center for Public Policy and Higher Education.*

If all students get an item correct, they do not necessarily know the material; the item's distracters may be lousy. Therefore, when we examine the names and events included among the distracters in the 2001 NAEP examination—for example, the mutiny of British forces under General Howe, the Wobblies, the Morrill Land Grant Act, and the relation between the coinage of silver and an economic downturn—we must remember that those facts do not appear because of their inherent worth or because they were taught in the high school curriculum or even because a blue-ribbon commission declared that every American high school student should know them. Rather, General Howe, the Wobblies, the Morrill Land Grant Act, and countless other bits of information appear on the test because they "work" mathematically; they snare their targets in sufficient numbers to boost the item's "discrimination index." It is modern psychometrics in the driver's seat, not sound historical judgment.[22]

What would happen if the smart went down with the dumb, or, to put it more delicately, if students who knew the most history were stumped by items answered correctly by the less able? Again, the technology of testing makes sure that does not happen. Large-scale tests rely on a mathematical technique known as the biserial correlation in which each test item is linked mathematically to students' total scores and individual items that do not conform to the overall test pattern are eliminated from the final version.[23] Imagine an item about the *Crisis* magazine, which W. E. B. Du Bois edited, that is answered correctly at higher rates by black students than by whites, while overall white students outscore blacks on the test by thirty points. The resulting correlation for the Du Bois item would be zero or negative, and its chances of survival would be slim—irrespective of whether historians thought the information was essential to test.[24] Technically, such examinations as the history NAEP are "standards-based" (hypothetically, every student should be able to "reach standard") rather than fit to a predetermined curve. But the practices of item analysis, discrimination, biserial or item-test correlations, and spread are so ingrained in psychometric culture that for all intents and purposes, results from all large-scale objective tests fit the traditional bell curve.[25] Indeed, this was confirmed by Steven Koffler, an administrator with the NAEP program that designed the 1987 history test, who reported that traditional item analysis and biserial correlations were used to create that supposedly standards-based test.[26]

What does all of this mean, practically? First, in addition to handicapping students who possess different historical knowledge from those in the mainstream, it means that no national test can allow students to show themselves historically literate. If ETS statisticians determined during pilot testing that most students could identify George Washington, "The Star-Spangled Banner," Rosa Parks, the dropping of the bomb on Hiroshima, slavery as a main cause of the Civil War, the purpose of Auschwitz, Babe Ruth, Harriet Tubman, the civil rights movement, the "I Have a Dream" speech, all those items would be eliminated from the test, for such questions fail to discriminate among students. So, when the next national assessment rolls around in 2010, do not hold your breath for the headline announcing, "U.S. schoolchildren score well on the 100 most basic facts of American history." The architecture of modern psychometrics ensures that will never happen—no matter how good a job we do in the classroom.[27]

ASSESSING THE FUTURE

Whether or not students have known history in the past begs our present concerns. Shouldn't we be worried when two-thirds of seventeen-year-olds cannot date the Civil War or half cannot identify the Soviet Union as our ally in World War II? No one concerned with young people's development should remain passive in the face of such results. Any thinking person would insist that such knowledge is critical to informed citizenship. In this sense, E. D. Hirsch, an educational critic and proponent of "cultural literacy," is right when he claims that without a framework for understanding—the ability to identify key figures, major events, and chronological sequences—the world becomes unintelligible and reading a newspaper well-nigh impossible. So why is it that many young people emerge from high school lacking this core knowledge?[28]

One narrative popular on both sides of the political aisle (as well as among historians who should know better) is that the social studies lobby and its agents warp young minds in ways reminiscent of a North Korean reeducation camp, wasting their time on mind-numbing "critical thinking" skills devoid of content. The problem with this armchair analysis is that, although we might find some support for it in the education school curriculum, the empirical data on what goes on in classrooms paint a different picture. Summarizing results from the 1987 national assessment, Diane Ravitch and Chester E. Finn concluded that in the typical social studies classroom, students

> listen to the teacher explain the day's lesson, use the textbook, and take tests. Occasionally they watch a movie. Sometimes they memorize information or read stories about events and people. They seldom work with other students, use original documents, write term papers, or discuss the significance of what they are studying.[29]

Similar conclusions emerged from a study of history and social studies instruction in Indiana in the early 1960s, as well as from John I. Goodlad's *A Place Called School*, the most extensive observational study of schooling in the twentieth century, involving twenty ethnographers in 1,350 classrooms observing 17,163 students. The high schools visited by Goodlad's team in 1977 all offered courses in American history and government. Yet, while teachers in those courses overwhelmingly claimed that their goals fit snugly with "inquiry methods" and "hands-on learning," their tests told a different story, requiring little more than the recall of names and dates and memorized information. The topics of the history curriculum are of "great human interest," wrote Goodlad, but "something strange seems to have happened to them on their way to the classroom." History becomes removed from its "intrinsically human character, reduced to the dates and places readers will recall memorizing for tests."[30] Even at the height of the "new social studies" in the late 1960s and early 1970s, those who ventured into classrooms saw something different from the image conveyed by then-fashionable teachers' magazines. In the history classrooms Charles Silberman visited in the late 1960s, the great bulk of students' time was "devoted to detail, most of it trivial, much of it factually incorrect, and almost all of it unrelated to any concept, structure, cognitive strategy, or indeed anything other than the lesson plan." In a 1994 national survey of about fifteen hundred Americans conducted by Indiana University's Center for Survey Research (under the direction of Roy Rosenzweig and David Thelen), adults were asked to "pick one word or phrase to describe your experience with history classes in elementary or high school." "Boring" was the single most frequent description. Instruction lacked verve not because of projects, oral histories, simulations, or any of the other "progressive" ideas drubbed in print by E. D. Hirsch and others, but because of what the historian of pedagogy Larry Cuban has called "persistent instruction"—a single teacher standing in front of a group of 25–40 students, talking. A sixty-four-year-old Floridian described it this way: "The teacher would call out a certain date and then we would have to stand at attention and say what the date was. I hated it."[31]

Textbooks dominate instruction in today's high school history classes. These thousand-plus-page behemoths are written to satisfy innumerable interest groups, packing in so much detail that all but the most ardent become daunted.[32] Many social studies teachers are forced to rely on the books because they lack adequate subject matter knowledge. Drawing on data from the National Center for Educational Statistics, Ravitch has shown that among those who teach history at the middle and secondary levels, only 18.5 percent possess a major (or minor!) in the discipline. Thus over 80 percent of today's history teachers did not study it in depth in college. While states have tripped over each other to beef up content standards for students, they have left untouched the minimalist requirements for those who teach history. The places that train teachers, colleges of education, are held hostage by accreditation agencies such as the National Council for Accreditation of Teacher Education (NCATE), which promote every cause, but not the stance that teachers should possess deep knowledge of their subject matter. Although federal efforts such as the Teaching American History program help individual teachers (and provide a boondoggle to many in the profession, including this author), at a policy level they are a colossal waste of money. One does not repair a rickety house by commissioning a paint job—one brings in a backhoe and starts digging up the foundation. Helping veteran teachers develop new subject matter knowledge for two weeks in the summer is a worthy cause, but not one likely to have any lasting impact. Change will occur only by intervening at the policy level to ensure that those who teach history know it themselves. Until that happens, we should expect no miracles.[33]

What should we do while we are waiting for the revolution? First, we should admit that we cannot have our cake and eat it too. We cannot insist that every student know when World War II began and who our allies were while giving tests that ask about the battles of Saratoga and Oriskany. Today's standards documents, written to satisfy special interest groups and out-of-touch antiquarians, are a farce.

When the majority of kids leaving school cannot date the Civil War and are confused about whether the Korean War predated or followed World War II, how far do we want to go in insisting that seventeen-year-olds know about the battle at Fort Wagner, Younghill Kang's *East Goes West*, Carrie Chapman Catt, Ludwig von Mises, and *West Virginia State Board of Education v. Barnette* (Massachusetts State History Standards); John Hartranft (Pennsylvania State History Standards); Henry Bessemer, Dwight Moody, Hiram Johnson, the Palmer raids, the 442nd Regiment Combat Team, Federalist Number 78, and *Adarand Constructors, Inc. v. Peña* (California History–Social Science Standards, grades 11 and 12); the policy of Bartolomé de Las Casas toward Indians in South America, Charles Bulfinch, Patience Wright, Charles Willson Peale, and the economic effects of the Townshend Acts (NAEP standards)? As William Cronon remarked after examining another pie-in-the-sky scheme, the ill-fated National History Standards, he would have been ecstatic if his University of Wisconsin graduate students had known half of this stuff. Or, in words that today's teenagers might use, let's get real.[34]

NONE OF THE ABOVE

The dilemmas we face today in assessing young people's knowledge differ little from those confronted by J. Carleton Bell and David F. McCollum in 1917. Few historians would argue that large-scale objective tests capture the range of meanings we attribute to the "historic sense." We use these tests and will do so in the future, not because they are historically sound or because they predict future engagement with historical study, but because they can be read by machines that produce easy-to-read graphs and bar charts. The tests comfort us with the illusion of systematicity—not to mention that scoring them costs a lot less than the alternatives.

Psychologists define a crazy person as someone who keeps doing the same thing but expects a different result. As long as textbooks dominate instruction, as long as the ETS dictates the history American children should know, as long as states continue to play a "mine-is-bigger-than-yours" standards game for students while hiding from view content-free teacher standards, as long as historians roll over and play dead in front of number-wielding psychometricians, we can have all the blue-ribbon commissions in the world but the results will be the same. Technology may have changed since 1917, but the capacity of the human mind to retain information has not. Students could master and retain the piles of information contained in 1917 or 1943 textbooks no better than they can retain what fills today's gargantuan tomes. Light rail excursions through mounds of factual information may be entertaining, but such dizzying tours leave few traces in memory. The mind demands pattern and form, and both are built up slowly and require repeated passes, with each pass going deeper and probing further.[35] If we want young people to know more history, we need to draw on a concept from medicine: triage. As the University of Tennessee's Wilfred McClay explains,

Memory is most powerful when it is purposeful and *selective* . . . it requires that we possess stories and narratives that link facts in ways that are both meaningful and truthful, and provide a . . . way of knowing what facts are worth attending to. . . . We remember those things that fit a template of meaning, and point to a larger whole. We fail to retain the details that, like wandering orphans, have no connection to anything of abiding concern. . . . The design of our courses and curricula must be an exercise in *triage*, in making hard choices about what gets thrown out of the story, so that the essentials can survive. . . . We need to be willing to identify those things that every American student needs to know and insist upon them . . . while paring away vigorously at the rest.[36]

Mechanical testing tempts us with the false promise of efficiency, a lure that whispers that there is an easier, less costly, more scientific way. But the truth is that the blackening of circles prepares us only to blacken more circles in the future. The sooner we realize this, the sooner we will be redeemed from our craziness.[37]

Notes

1. J. Carleton Bell, "The Historic Sense," *Journal of Educational Psychology* 8 (May 1917): 317–18.

2. Ibid.

3. J. Carleton Bell and David F. McCollum, "A Study of the Attainments of Pupils in United States History," *Journal of Educational Psychology* 8 (May 1917): 257–74, esp. 257–58.

4. Ibid., 258.

5. Ibid., 268–69. Five years later the Bell and McCollum survey was replicated, though on a much smaller scale. See D. H. Eikenberry, "Permanence of High School Learning," *Journal of Educational Psychology* 14 (Nov. 1923): 463–81. See also Garry C. Meyers, "Delayed Recall in History," *Journal of Educational Psychology* 8 (May 1917): 275–83.

6. *New York Times*, April 4, 1943, p. 1; Allan Nevins, "American History for Americans," *New York Times Magazine*, May 3, 1942, pp. 6, 28. The *Times* survey followed an earlier exposé on the scarcity of required courses in American history at the college level. See *New York Times*, June 21, 1942, p. 1. For the editorial, see *New York Times*, April 4, 1943, p. 32. On how the general media reported this survey, see Richard J. Paxton, "Don't Know Much about History—Never Did," *Phi Delta Kappan* 85 (Dec. 2003): 264–73.

7. *New York Times*, May 2, 1976, pp. 1, 65.

8. Diane Ravitch and Chester E. Finn, *What Do Our Seventeen-Year-Olds Know? A Report on the First National Assessment of History and Literature* (New York, 1987); Educational Testing Service, National Center for Education Statistics, *NAEP 1994 U.S. History Report Card: Findings from the National Assessment of Educational Progress* (Washington, D.C., 1996) <http://nces.ed.gov/pubsearch/pubsinfo.asp?pubid=96085> (Nov. 24, 2003). Compare Edgar B. Wesley, *American History in Schools and Colleges* (New York, 1944). At the height of Cold War anxieties, *McCall's* commissioned a survey of college graduates' knowledge of the Soviet Union. Over a quarter could not name Moscow as the capital, and nearly 80 percent were unable to name a single Russian author. Harrison E. Salisbury, "What Americans Don't Know about Russia," *McCall's Magazine* 84 (June 1957): 40–41.

9. *USA Today*, May 10–12, 2002, p. 1; *Greensboro* [North Carolina] *News and Record*, May 13, 2002, p. A8; Lee Bockhorn, "History in Crisis," *Weekly Standard*, May 13, 2002, available at LexisNexis Academic. Diane Ravitch quoted in the *Palm Beach* [Florida] *Post*, May 10, 2002, p. 13a.

10. Michael A. Fletcher, "Students' History Knowledge Lacking, Test Finds," *Washington Post*, May 9, 2002 <www.washingtonpost.com/ac2/wp-dyn/A60096-2002May9 ?language=printer/> (Dec. 4, 2003). For the quotations from National Assessment of Educational Progress (NAEP) officials, see *USA Today*, May 10–12, 2002, p. 1. Rod Paige quoted in David Darlington, "U.S. Department of Education Releases Results of Latest U.S. History Test," *Perspectives Online*, Summer 2002 <www.theaha.org/perspectives/ issues/2002/Summer/naep.cfm> (Nov. 24, 2003). In the 2001 administration of NAEP, scores on the fourth grade test rose four points from 1994, and on the eighth grade test three points (from 259 to 262 out of 500 total). Twelfth graders' scores remained stagnant. The NAEP examination in history is not solely multiple-choice but includes some "constructed-response" (short answer) questions. Sample questions are available at <http:// nces.ed.gov/nationsreportcard/ITMRLS/pickone.asp> (Dec. 4, 2003).

11. Students did surprisingly well on the gold standard item, with 56 percent answering it correctly. See items for the 2001 history NAEP at the user-friendly Web site of the National Center for Educational Statistics <http://nces.ed.gov/nationsreportcard/> (Dec. 4, 2003).

12. Albert Shanker Institute, "Education for Democracy" (2003) <www.ashankerinst .org/Downloads/EfD%20final.pdf> (Nov. 13, 2003), pp. 6, 7. Emphasis added.

13. History achieved a stronger position in the curriculum in the first two decades of the twentieth century than at any other time in American history. "By 1900," a historian of education wrote, "history . . . received more time and attention in both elementary and secondary schools than all the other social studies combined." History dominated from about 1890 to 1920, although its apex was probably about 1915. Edgar B. Wesley, "History in the School Curriculum," *Mississippi Valley Historical Review* 29 (March 1943): 567.

14. On the school curriculum in this period, see Hazel W. Hertzberg, "History and Progressivism: A Century of Reform Proposals," in *Historical Literacy: The Case for History in American Education*, ed. Paul Gagnon and the Bradley Commission on History in Schools (New York, 1989), 69–102. Bell and McCollum, "Study of the Attainments of Pupils in United States History," 268.

15. The date for the first statement is May 9, 2002; see Associated Press Online, "HS Seniors Do Poorly on History Test," available at LexisNexis Academic. The second is from Diane Ravitch, "Capitol Hill Hearing Testimony," April 10, 2003, LexisNexis Academic (Sept. 6, 2003).

16. Nevins, "American History for Americans," 6.

17. E. D. Hirsch cited in Chester E. Finn and Diane Ravitch, "Survey Results: U.S. Seventeen-Year-Olds Know Shockingly Little about History and Literature," *American School Board Journal* 174 (Oct. 1987): 32; Rod Paige quoted in "Students and U.S. Secretary of Education Present a Solution for U.S. Historical Illiteracy," June 8, 2002, Ascribe Newswire, available at LexisNexis Academic. For the adjective "shameful," see Ravitch and Finn, *What Do Our Seventeen-Year-Olds Know?* 201. On the early volleys of what came to be known as the "history wars," see Arthur Zilversmit, "Another Report Card, Another 'F,'" *Reviews in American History* 16 (June 1988): 314–20; and Sam Wineburg, *Historical Thinking and Other Unnatural Acts: Charting the Future of Teaching the Past* (Philadelphia, 2001), esp. 3–27. For manifestations of this neurosis in other national contexts, see Jack Granatstein, *Who Killed Canadian History?* (Toronto, 1998); and Yoram Bronowski, "A People without History," *Haaretz* (Tel Aviv), Jan. 1, 2000.

18. Similar test results mean, not that what students know today is identical to what they knew in the past, but "that each group performed about the same on the particular set of test questions designed for them to take. This observation is buttressed by the comparison of the distributions of item difficulty. The shape and location of these distributions for tests covering a span of 42 years are strikingly similar." Dale Whittington, "What Have Seventeen-Year-Olds Known in the Past?" *American Educational Research Journal* 28 (Winter 1991): 759–80.

19. The origins of multiple-choice testing go back to the first mass-administered examination in American history, the Army Alpha and Beta, during World War I. See Daniel J. Kevles, "Testing the Army's Intelligence: Psychologists and the Military in World War I," *Journal of American History* 55 (Dec. 1968): 565–81; Franz Samelson, "World War I Intelligence Testing and the Development of Psychology," *Journal of the History of the Behavioral Sciences* 13 (July 1977): 274–82; and John Rury, "Race, Region, and Education: An Analysis of Black and White Scores on the 1917 Army Alpha Test," *Journal of Negro Education* 57 (Winter 1988): 51–65. For critical and nontechnical overviews of modern testing, see Stephen Jay Gould, *The Mismeasure of Man* (New York, 1981); Banesh Hoffmann, *The Tyranny of Testing* (New York, 1962); Leon J. Kamin, *The Science and Politics of IQ* (Potomac, Va., 1974); and Paul L. Houts, ed., *The Myth of Measurability* (New York, 1977). An evenhanded assessment from a major figure in modern psychometrics is Lee J. Cronbach, "Five Decades of Public Controversy over Mental Testing," *American Psychologist* 30 (Jan. 1975): 1–14.

20. Cooperative Test Service of the American Council on Education, *The Cooperative Achievement Tests: A Handbook Describing Their Purpose, Content, and Interpretation* (New York, 1936), 6.

21. For Garrison Keillor's famous phrase, see "Registered Trademarks and Service Marks" <www.prairiehome.org/content/trademarks.shtml> (Dec. 4, 2003).

22. Even professional historians do poorly when staring down items outside their research specializations. When historians trained at Berkeley, Harvard, and Stanford universities answered questions from a leading high school textbook, they scored a mere 35 percent—in some cases lower than a comparison group of high school students taking Advanced Placement U.S. history courses. See Samuel S. Wineburg, "Historical Problem Solving: A Study of the Cognitive Processes Used in the Evaluation of Documentary and Pictorial Evidence," *Journal of Educational Psychology* 83, no. 1 (1991): 73–87.

23. For non-multiple-choice items, the functional equivalent is the item-test correlation. Biserial or item-test correlations range from –1.00 to +1.00, with –1.00 being a score for a completely ineffective test item and +1.00 one for a perfect item. A +1.00 correlation would be achieved if all students in the highest scoring group got a particular item correct and all students in the lower scoring group got it incorrect (conversely, for a perfect negative correlation). Most multiple-choice items on large-scale tests have biserial correlations that range from +.25 to +.50.

24. For recent updates on bias in large-scale achievement testing, see Roy O. Freedle, "Correcting the SAT's Ethnic and Social-Class Bias: A Method for Reestimating SAT Scores," *Harvard Educational Review* 73 (Spring 2003): 1–43. For nontechnical overviews of Freedle's argument, see Jeffrey R. Young, "Researchers Charge Racial Bias on the SAT," *Chronicle of Higher Education*, Oct. 10, 2003, p. A34; and Jay Matthews, "The Bias Question," *Atlantic Monthly* 292 (Nov. 2003): 130–40.

25. Perfect normal curves are extremely rare in nature and typically result from experiments in probability, such as tossing a thousand quarters in the air over and over, each time plotting the number of heads; as the number of tosses approaches infinity, the curve

becomes more and more symmetrical. Only by fixing the results beforehand can something as diffuse as historical ability fall into such even and well-shaped patterns. The best critique of the normal curve is by a physicist; see Philip Morrison, "The Bell Shaped Pitfall," in *Myth of Measurability*, ed. Houts, 82–89. See also Irving M. Klotz, "Of Bell Curves, Gout, and Genius," *Phi Delta Kappan* 77 (Dec. 1995): 279–80.

26. Whittington, "What Have Seventeen-Year-Olds Known in the Past?" 778. The use of biserials (and their equivalents, now employed with Item Response Theory methods) is predicated on the unidimensionality of the "construct" being tested. That is, "historical knowledge" is considered a single entity, not a woolly construct composed of different factors and influences in the spirit of J. Carleton Bell's 1917 formulation. Typical of psychometric reasoning is the following statement: "Items that correlate less than .15 with the total test score should probably be restructured. One's best guess is that such items do not measure the same skill or ability as does the test on the whole. . . . Generally, a test is better (i.e., more reliable) the more homogeneous the items." Jerard Kehoe, "Basic Item Analysis for Multiple-Choice Tests," *Practical Assessment, Research, and Evaluation* 4 (1995) <http://pareonline.net/getvn.asp?v=4&n=10/> (Jan. 13, 2004).

27. As the Cooperative Test Service explained to teachers in 1936, "The purpose of the test is to discover differences between individuals, and this must also be the purpose of each item in the test. Items that *all* students can answer will obviously not help to discover such differences and therefore the test should contain very few such items." Cooperative Test Service, *Cooperative Achievement Tests*, 6.

28. The first question is from the 1987 exam, the second from 2001. E. D. Hirsch, *Cultural Literacy: What Every American Needs to Know* (Boston, 1987).

29. Sean Wilentz, "The Past Is Not a Process," *New York Times*, April 20, 1996, p. E15. Wilentz predicted that the "historical illiteracy of today's student will only worsen in the generation to come," without referring to similar baleful predictions from 1917, 1943, 1976, or 1987. Ibid. Ravitch and Finn, *What Do Our Seventeen-Year-Olds Know?* 194.

30. Maurice G. Baxter, Robert H. Ferrell, and John E. Wiltz, *The Teaching of American History in High Schools* (Bloomington, Ind., 1964); John I. Goodlad, *A Place Called School* (New York, 1984), esp. 212. See also James Howard and Thomas Mendenhall, *Making History Come Alive* (Washington, D.C., 1982); and Karen B. Wiley and Jeanne Race, *The Status of Pre-College Science, Mathematics, and Social Science Education: 1955–1975*, vol. III: *Social Science Education* (Boulder, Colo., 1977).

31. Charles Silberman, *Crisis in the Classroom: The Remaking of American Education* (New York, 1970), 172; Larry Cuban, "Persistent Instruction: The High School Classroom, 1900–1980," *Phi Delta Kappan* 64 (Oct. 1982): 113–18; Larry Cuban, *How Teachers Taught: Constancy and Change in American Classrooms, 1890–1980* (New York, 1993); Roy Rosenzweig, "How Americans Use and Think about the Past: Implications from a National Survey for the Teaching of History," in *Knowing, Teaching, and Learning History: National and International Perspectives*, ed. Peter N. Stearns, Peter Seixas, and Sam Wineburg (New York, 2000), 275. The full survey is reported in Roy Rosenzweig and David Thelen, *The Presence of the Past: Popular Uses of History in American Life* (New York, 1998).

32. Textbook wars are often portrayed as political battles between Left and Right, but they also manifest internecine struggles within the Left. See the account of the Oakland, California, textbook adoption process in Todd Gitlin, *The Twilight of Common Dreams: Why America Is Wracked by Culture Wars* (New York, 1995). On textbooks, see Harriet Tyson Bernstein, *A Conspiracy of Good Intentions: America's Textbook Fiasco* (Washington, D.C., 1988); Frances FitzGerald, *America Revised* (New York, 1979); Gary B. Nash,

Charlotte Crabtree, and Ross E. Dunn, *History on Trial: Culture Wars and the Teaching of the Past* (New York, 1997); Diane Ravitch, *The Language Police* (New York, 2003); and Jonathan Zimmerman, *Whose America? Culture Wars in the Public Schools* (Cambridge, Mass., 2002). On the readability of textbooks (or lack thereof), see Isabel L. Beck, Margaret G. McKeown, and E. W. Gromoll, "Learning from Social Studies Texts," *Cognition and Instruction* 6, no. 2 (1989): 99–158; and Richard J. Paxton, "A Deafening Silence: History Textbooks and the Students Who Read Them," *Review of Educational Research* 69 (Fall 1999): 315–39.

33. Diane Ravitch, "The Educational Backgrounds of History Teachers," in *Knowing, Teaching, and Learning History*, ed. Stearns, Seixas, and Wineburg, 143–55. Compare today's efforts at improving history instruction with the last federal infusion of millions into the history and social studies curriculum. An extensive evaluation of the 1960s curriculum projects found that by the mid-1970s, the effects of the "new social studies" had largely vanished from public schools. See Wiley and Race, *Status of Pre-College Science, Mathematics, and Social Science Education*, III; and Peter Dow, *Schoolhouse Politics: Lessons from the Sputnik Era* (Cambridge, Mass., 1991). On historians' involvement with the new social studies, see the statement by its leader, a Carnegie Mellon University historian: Edwin Fenton, *The New Social Studies* (New York, 1967). The jewel of the crown of these efforts was the Amherst History Project, whose curriculum materials remain in print. Richard H. Brown, the force behind the project, provided an early analysis of problems with its conceptualization and a requiem for it. See Richard H. Brown, "History as Discovery: An Interim Report on the Amherst Project," in *Teaching the New Social Studies in Secondary Schools: An Inductive Approach*, ed. Edwin Fenton (Boston, 1966), 443–51; and Richard H. Brown, "Learning How to Learn: The Amherst Project and History Education in the Schools," *Social Studies* 87 (Nov.–Dec. 1996): 267–73.

34. See "Massachusetts Curricular Frameworks" <www.doe.mass.edu/frameworks/current.html> (Dec. 4, 2003); "Pa. History Is Put to the Test," *Philadelphia Inquirer*, June 4, 2003, available at LexisNexis Academic; "History–Social Science Framework for California Public Schools, Kindergarten through Grade Twelve" <www.cde.ca.gov/cdepress/hist-social-sci-frame.pdf> (Dec. 4, 2003); and "U.S. History Framework for the 1994 and 2001 National Assessment of Educational Progress" <www.nagb.org/pubs/hframework2001.pdf> (Dec. 4, 2003). William Cronon, "History Forum: Teaching American History," *American Scholar* 67 (Winter 1998): 91.

35. On contemporary learning theory, see a consensus report: U.S. National Research Council, *How People Learn: Brain, Mind, Experience, and School* (Washington, D.C., 1999), available online at <http://books.nap.edu/books/0309065577/html/index.html> (Dec. 17, 2003). The volume echoes statements first enunciated in Jerome Bruner, *The Process of Education* (Cambridge, Mass., 1960).

36. Albert Shanker Institute, "Education for Democracy," 16.

37. Sam Wineburg wishes to acknowledge Gary Kornblith for his counsel and patience during the preparation of this article and Shoshana Wineburg and Simone Schweber for their keen editorial acumen. Cathy Taylor provided essential technical advice and saved me from error. I thank them all.

PART FIVE

TEACHING RE-CENTERED SURVEYS IN THE TWENTY-FIRST CENTURY

As we approached the end of our term as editors of T&T, we returned to thinking about how to teach American history survey courses, intentionally plural here, for this time we began not with the emphasis on *Unum* but on *E Pluribus*. What happens when we make a group other than straight, white, Euro-Americans the primary focus of a survey? What is the result when we move the distinctive histories of African Americans, Latinos/as, Native Americans, Asian Americans, and lesbian/gay people from margin to center? How does such teaching change our perspective on the relationship of previously underrepresented groups to our national narratives?

We asked five scholars to reflect on their experiences teaching those kinds of surveys: Ned Blackhawk (University of Wisconsin), Allison Dorsey (Swarthmore College), Scott Kurashige (University of Michigan), Pablo Mitchell (Oberlin College), and Nancy C. Unger (Santa Clara University). We wanted to know about their goals for their courses and how their courses "work"—periodization, pedagogy, audiences, and assignments. Their "field reports" from this cutting edge of American history teaching are both fascinating and provocative.

The authors underscored the dynamism of the scholarship in their fields, as well as the challenge of synthesizing new research for presentation to undergraduates. They reflected on the choices they make about enrollment targets and about negotiating issues of authenticity and identity in the classroom. They also cited the impact of institutional context on how they teach about the history of race, class, religion, sexual orientation, and ethnicity. Many enlist students in the project of creating new knowledge in their fields, encouraging oral histories and document-driven research projects. All are unafraid to connect past and present.

The authors illuminated the relationship of their courses to other offerings in American history at their institutions, demonstrating how, "by pivoting the center . . . new themes, approaches and questions become visible."[1] From their various perspectives, our contributors demonstrate how their efforts in the class-room have the potential to reshape the terrain of history teaching—and of histor-ical scholarship. They suggest how their surveys might transform "traditional" approaches to teaching American history, changing themes, periodization, and subjects and re-centering our understanding of the meaning of "nation" and of our collective past. They remind us that the study and teaching of American his-tory are forever changing. History professors may always look backward, but they also must move forward. Certainly they can't stand still, or their subjects and their students will pass them by.

Note

1. Patricia Hill Collins, "Gender, Black Feminism, and Black Political Economy," *Annals of the American Academy of Political and Social Science* 568 (March 2000): 543. For another work that uses the concept of "pivoting the center," see Bettina Aptheker, *Tapestries of Life: Women's Work, Women's Consciousness, and the Meaning of Daily Experience* (Amherst, Mass., 1989), esp. 12, 20. For an even earlier use of the notion, see Benjamin Brawley, *Social History of the American Negro, Being a History of the Negro Problem in the United States, Including a History and Study of the Republic of Liberia* (New York, 1921). See also Earl Lewis, "To Turn as on a Pivot: Writing African Americans into a History of Overlapping Diasporas," *American Historical Review* 100 (June 1995): 765–87.

Ned Blackhawk

Recasting the Narrative of America: The Rewards and Challenges of Teaching American Indian History

With eleven federally recognized tribes, Wisconsin remains central to America's Indian past. The western center of the Great Lakes fur-trading empires, the nineteenth-century home to thousands of Algonquian, Siouan, and Iroquoian speakers, and the site of several of the most intense political standoffs in the twentieth century, Wisconsin has always been and remains "Indian country."[1]

I knew such generalities upon appointment to the University of Wisconsin, Madison, Department of History and American Indian Studies Program (AISP) in the fall of 1999. In fact, working in an environment seemingly so well situated for Indian history powerfully attracted me to the position. I had no idea, however, how challenging enacting curricular initiatives amid such historical currents could be. For, while recent studies of American Indian history have forced reconsideration of innumerable aspects of the American experience, translating the achievements of such scholarly profusion into accessible lectures and navigable syllabi remains a constant struggle. Indian history appears increasingly critical to nearly all epochs of the nation's past, while in the classroom reconciling commonplace assumptions about America with the traumatic histories of the continent's indigenous peoples can be an exceedingly turbulent endeavor. What follows are reflections based on my experience teaching the semester-long American Indian history survey course at Madison for the last seven years. My teaching has been uniquely rewarding, but it has sparked both challenges and concerns.

First, as in any recently ascendant field of inquiry, scholarly insights and public consciousness move at different speeds. What may seem to be the most important academic finding may not work so well in the classroom; given its historic marginalization, Indian history is particularly prone to such discrepancies. That American history was taught for so long without attention to the continent's original inhabitants and was written to celebrate certain chapters of the national story over others compounds this field's comparative disadvantages. The endless cacophony of simplistic media representations only deepens the challenge of engaging one of America's most complicated narratives.

Such challenges are in many ways accentuated by several of Madison's general education requirements, particularly an ethnic studies requirement that was

Journal of American History 93 (2007): 1165–70.

introduced in the 1990s. Housed within an amalgam of ethnic studies program units, nearly all of Madison's AISP courses in 1999, including my American Indian history survey, fulfilled that requirement. From the outside, that status might seem beneficial both to the course and to the larger program. Under such initiatives, many of the nation's ethnic studies and American cultures departments have seen large enrollments and, as a result, garnered additional resources, especially teaching assistants and faculty, thus broadening their curricular impact. At Madison, however, faculty and teaching assistant positions have not kept pace with increased demand. The university's nearly thirty thousand undergraduates in twenty-one different schools and colleges demand entrance into a handful of ethnic studies courses, including mine.

As on any campus and as in any ethnic studies field, the currents of multiculturalism flow into the classroom, and with them, varying social and political positions. I initially designed my first lecture course for students who I assumed were somewhat interested in American Indian history. Now I have recast the American Indian history survey both to engage those with interest and to challenge those without. I see America's Indian past as one of underrecognized trauma as well as triumph, the epitome of several of the nation's darkest chapters and, recently, its noblest ideals. Students entering this class now encounter a variety of pedagogical strategies aimed at recasting various commonly held assumptions about America. Indeed, the juxtaposition between one-dimensional portraits of "America" and of its "Indians" begins the course.

It goes without saying that "Indians" remain iconographic Americans. I use the tensions that arise from conjoining two of our nation's most powerful adjectives—American and Indian—as heuristic guides in profitably organizing my survey. Embedded in that conjuncture are lessons and truths that can potentially transcend what either term provides in isolation. I begin the course by telling students that despite recent attempts to shed the racist, limiting, and painful history of the term "Indian," we will use such terminology purposefully, trying to recapture and revise the representational power of one of America's oldest pejoratives. While at times interchanging "Native American" or simply "Natives" with "American Indians," we proceed from the premise that the once historically disparate subjects of U.S. history and American Indian history must be understood together and as mutually interanimated.

With such pedagogical guides, it is tempting to follow many scholarly trends by foregrounding Indian historical actors in many of the most dramatic chapters in the nation's past: the innumerable encounters of the colonial era; the imperial and revolutionary struggles of the late eighteenth century; the early republic and its westward expansion; and the nineteenth-century Indian wars and their traumatic aftermath. While the overwhelming number of monographs in American Indian history generally fall within such periodization, the teaching of that history must also extend beyond such parameters to interrogate normative assumptions about the nation's past and the place of Indian peoples in it. Within and outside the academy, a cascade of challenges and contemporary Indian community concerns confront those entering into the currents of this field, challenges and concerns that make Indian history and teaching it a unique and particularly rewarding opportunity. Among the many possible approaches, I have identified four that offer engaging, structuring principles for my survey course.

First, I attempt to destabilize assumptions about the uniformity of American Indian experience; the tremendous diversity of the continent's indigenous populations may partially explain the nation's historic reluctance to engage the history of the Native Americans. With over 560 contemporary, federally recognized Indian communities in the United States, one cannot fully gauge the regional, cultural, linguistic, religious, intellectual, economic, legal, and political distinctiveness of each of America's indigenous nations. Engaging students in such diversities of experience, however, is possible as well as necessary, especially in academic environments close to contemporary Indian communities and with Indian student populations. As far too many Indian people know too well, simplistic assumptions of a uniform Indian experience pervade popular culture, and challenging students to recognize and reformulate such received knowledge remains essential, particularly because the legacies of conquest have so often been rationalized with, and accompanied by, monolithic and dehumanizing caricatures.

Several strategies can be used to transcend monolithic portraits of Indian life, and historicizing the multiplicity of American Indian experiences through combinations of texts, novels, poems, oral histories, films, life histories, and other media can deepen students' understandings. For example, detailing both the spread of equestrianism onto the Plains and the ubiquitous history of Plains Indian iconography invites students to engage important aspects of Indian history while also recognizing the mythologies embedded in visual constructions. In such context, one can weave together eighteenth-century Plains Indian history, Meriwether Lewis and William Clark's journey up the Missouri River, and Kevin Costner's mythic West, profitably deploying them against each other to convey critical, ongoing aspects of the field.[2] One need not be familiar with Hollywood's representations of Indians or the history of equestrianism to see various connections between them, nor to see which elements of these pasts have been chosen for memorialization and which others have not.

Second, while introducing the diversity of Indian experiences can fragment a survey effort, common themes can unify it, particularly the centrality of Indian peoples to the making of America. Many undergraduates may recoil at this structuring principle, particularly if the instructor makes the end of the American Revolution the halfway point of a single-semester survey, as I do. Given their general unfamiliarity with early American history, many are unprepared for the relentless assault of Indian-imperial relations in sixteenth-, seventeenth-, and eighteenth-century North America. Unaware that England and its Atlantic colonies were not the major centers of colonial America until a century after Spanish exploration, many students bemoan the constellation of competing indigenous and imperial actors set before them. I try to ameliorate these concerns with outlines, lists of exam study questions, and select readings; the "middle ground" forms a lecture, not a required text. Ultimately, however, I find little resolution to that impasse. The first three centuries of colonial intrusion into the Americas form a necessary introduction to indigenous history, particularly when investigating both the influence of native peoples on the continent's development and the devastating impacts of European influence on the Americas.[3]

That third and latter theme, I believe, is one of the hardest to integrate into a survey course, and I have encountered similar difficulties when teaching the first half of the U.S. survey course. That the largest loss of human life in world history followed the arrival of Europeans in the Americas remains so incongruent with prevailing assumptions about America and its history that many are unprepared, reluctant, or simply too overwhelmed to engage this foundational aspect of our nation's past. "Depressing," "politically motivated," and even "anti-American" are not uncommon reactions to my survey course on student evaluations. Some wonder why I place so much emphasis on Spanish contact and the Columbian exchange at all. More often, however, students are intrigued and begin interrogating critical elements from the postcontact era. How responsible were Europeans in the spread of unknown microbes throughout the Americas? What do the varying debates about the size of precontact native populations reveal about the nature of academic scholarship? What other social forces impinged on native communities' capacities to withstand the spread of diseases? Most important, what lessons, legacies, and conclusions can one draw from these devastating generations of contact? Such engagement, I believe, is critical both to understanding the postcontact development of America and also to formulating alternative visions about the nature of our nation's past and the place of Indians within it.[4]

Emphasis on the traumatic impacts of European contact may reify notions of Indian victimization. However, other critical lessons emerge from foregrounding Indian agency amid such disruptions: namely, the resilient, adaptive capacity of Indian groups to respond to colonialism in challenging and often deadly circumstances. Ultimately, such emphasis may reorient the broader meanings associated with both Indian and American history. For example, studying the experience of settler-Indian relations within a hemispheric or even global context recasts critical elements of the national past. A comparative history of the Americas is unimaginable without analyses of indigenous people. Highlighting the exciting transnational turn that increasingly links the experiences of indigenous communities across the hemisphere and the Pacific Rim encourages such internationalization. Similarly, students and scholars alike often forget that the two most recently admitted states to the Union have sizable indigenous populations. Their histories parallel and intersect with those in the continental United States and Canada and others in the Pacific. Conjoining Alaskan and Hawaiian native histories, then, with those in the lower forty-eight states as well as with Canadian First Nations and Pacific Islander experiences can stimulate such interconnections.[5]

Lastly, while such comparative attention can generate greater linkages and awareness, sustained focus on the uniqueness of Indian-white relations in the United States, particularly from a legal and constitutional perspective, must invariably characterize significant portions of any Indian survey. I make the end of the Revolutionary War the halfway point of the survey so that federal Indian policy spans the entire second half. I do so purposefully in a state and on a campus with a sizable Indian population. While many students find the machinations of Indian law and sovereignty confusing, communicating the constitutionally unique standing of Indian communities vis-à-vis other American groups remains central to my course. Despite the enormous gains made in the scholarship of early America, without more sustained examinations of the national histories of particular Indian nations, the field of Indian history may remain slightly behind or out of step with the dramatic achievements currently being made throughout Indian country. Such achievements, as Charles Wilkinson has effectively demonstrated, have come largely from the continued activism of Indian community leaders and from within the nation's legal system. The narrative of Indian history ends neither in the nineteenth century nor in defeat, and contextualizing the recent successes of America's indigenous nations within a historically and constitutionally informed perspective remains among the most pressing challenges for the field. Fortunately, Wilkinson's *Blood Struggle* is now in paperback, and twentieth-century Indian history has become far more established, as have rich interpretations of the origins and particularities of Indian sovereignty.[6]

Toward those ends, I offer exams and teach texts specifically aimed at recasting the narrative of Indian victimization and disappearance and highlight the ways Indian communities endured, adapted, and refashioned the world around them, particularly after reservation confinement. Frederick E. Hoxie's *Parading through History*, for example, skillfully details the many ways Montana's Crow Indians came together in the late nineteenth century and established the capacious religious, political, and social institutions that over time have made them into a modern Indian nation. Continuing where many conclude, Hoxie's study of the reservation era nicely conveys the ties between pre- and post-confinement history. Students marvel at his concluding section on the Crow leader Plenty Coups's grace and dignity during the Armistice Day celebration at Arlington National Cemetery following World War I, when this venerable Crow leader began the ceremonies with a prayer in his native language. Hoxie also includes a revealing photograph of Plenty Coups and the French field marshal Ferdinand Foch, who sought out the Crow leader in Montana during his tour of America. The text and photo nicely communicate each leader's respective *national* standing and highlight the larger themes of adaptation and survival found throughout the book. While students, ultimately, may identify as national leaders those who negotiated the Treaty of Versailles in 1919 more readily than they would identify Plenty Coups as one, I remind them that many state legislatures now host annual addresses delivered by tribal leaders. Each spring, for example, Wisconsin's state legislature—located at the opposite end of State Street from our campus—sponsors a State of the Tribes Address, and the university's Indian faculty, students, staff, and alumni are well represented in the audience.[7]

I also not only insist that students engage John Marshall's interpretation of the Constitution's commerce clause but also that they link such Supreme Court rulings to their own world here in Wisconsin, whose Indian history has recently found powerful synthesis in Patty Loew's *Indian Nations of Wisconsin*. In fact, I know of few other state or regional surveys as successful as Loew's, and I encourage the use, adoption, and continued creation of such regionally specific texts. Loew's work provides vivid overviews of Wisconsin's Indian nations and useful up-to-date political and legal profiles of their current development. Denied voice and recognition in so many narratives of America, contemporary Indian communities demand increased historical focus, particularly in academic institutions that were often created shortly after their dispossession; at Madison, my classes meet on Ho-Chunk Indian homelands. I believe a successful semester requires bringing Indian community members into class, encouraging attendance at local Indian events, and communicating respect for the challenges and sacrifices so many Indians, particularly Indian veterans, have endured.[8]

Not all texts or initiatives work in the classroom. Students often maintain an undercurrent of resentment due to their perceptions of my political intentions. I try to highlight the political diversity found in Indian country and its supporters; Arizona's Republican senator John McCain not only blurbed Wilkinson's book *Blood Struggle* but is also a consistent advocate for Indian rights. However, in a class where, as on the campus as a whole, nine out of ten undergraduates are white, racial politics and representation are unavoidable, particularly given my own identity as a self-identified and enrolled tribal member. Whereas American Indian men constitute approximately 10 percent of the inmate population at the federal correctional institution in Oxford, Wisconsin, sixty miles north of Madison, on campus Indians are less than 0.5 percent of the student population. Although I work closely with Indian undergraduates, native students have never totaled more than 20 percent of students in the course. The educational and pedagogical obstacles to American Indian higher education are well reflected, then, in my class demographics.[9]

While the task of covering over five hundred or five thousand years of indigenous history in North America may seem both potentially daunting and depressing, the resiliency of Indian peoples illustrates an underrecognized form of American achievement, one that can reorient the often linear teleology of America and offer insight into the ongoing transformations of its indigenous communities. Laden with pain, Indian history is also filled with surprising moments of joy, satire, and celebration. Its fiction and forms of cultural production reveal both pathos and humor, perhaps none better than the works of the Spokane and Coeur d'Alene author Sherman Alexie. In the opening story to his recent collection, *Ten Little Indians*, Alexie contemplates the nature of Indian identity, rhetorically asking,

> But who could blame us our madness? . . . We are people exiled by other exiles, by Puritans, Pilgrims, Protestants, and all of those other crazy white people thrown out of a crazier Europe. We who were once indigenous to this land must immigrate into its culture. I was born one mile south and raised one mile north on the Spokane River where the very first Spokane Indian was ever born, and I somehow feel like a nomad.

Such expressions of exile form appropriate entryways into the contested, vibrant, and contemplative landscapes offered by teaching North American Indian history, providing vistas of insight into the evolving patterns of American history. Teachers of Indian history, no longer an anecdotal, cursory, or shadowy component of the national epic, now possess a wealth of materials to guide students into the field, so that we may all someday, perhaps, become nomads no more.[10]

Notes

1. Patty Loew, *Indian Nations of Wisconsin: Histories of Endurance and Renewal* (Madison, Wis., 2001), 12–112.

2. *Dances with Wolves*, dir. Kevin Costner (Tig Productions and Majestic Films, 1990).

3. Richard White, *The Middle Ground: Indians, Empires, and Republics in the Great Lakes Region, 1650–1815* (Cambridge, Eng., 1991). For one of the most successful surveys of Indian-imperial relations before 1800, see Alan Taylor, *American Colonies: The Settling of North America* (New York, 2001).

4. For estimates of the collapse of Native American populations after 1492, see Charles C. Mann, *1491: New Revelations of the Americas before Columbus* (New York, 2005), 92–112; Russell Thornton, *American Indian Holocaust and Survival: A Population History since 1492* (Norman, Okla., 1987), esp. 3–42; and William M. Denevan, ed., *The Native Population of the Americas in 1492* (Madison, Wis., 1992).

5. For select studies engaged with the transnational currents of indigenous history, see Cole Harris, *The Resettlement of British Columbia: Essays on Colonialism and Geographic Change* (Vancouver, 1997); Cole Harris, *Making Native Space: Colonialism, Resistance, and Reserves in British Columbia* (Vancouver, 2002); Paige Raibmon, *Authentic Indians: Episodes of Encounter from the Late-Nineteenth-Century Northwest Coast* (Durham, N.C., 2005); Noenoe K. Silva, *Aloha Betrayed: Native Hawaiian Resistance to American Colonialism* (Durham, N.C., 2004); and Linda Tuhiwai Smith, *Decolonizing Methodologies: Research and Indigenous Peoples* (London, 1999).

6. Charles Wilkinson, *Blood Struggle: The Rise of Modern Indian Nations* (New York, 2005).

7. Frederick E. Hoxie, *Parading through History: The Making of the Crow Nation in America, 1805–1935* (New York, 1995), 344–74.

8. *Worcester v. Georgia*, 31 U.S. 515 (1832); U.S. Const. art. I, par. 8, cl. 1; Loew, *Indian Nations of Wisconsin*, 40–47.

9. The federal correctional institution at Oxford, Wisconsin, hosts an annual powwow and regularly holds community meetings for its Indian inmates. For general information about Oxford, see Federal Bureau of Prisons, "FCI Oxford," <www.bop.gov/locations/institutions/oxf/index.jsp>.

10. Sherman Alexie, *Ten Little Indians* (New York, 2003), 40.

Allison Dorsey

Black History Is American History: Teaching African American History in the Twenty-first Century

> History, despite its wrenching pain, cannot be unlived,
> and if faced with courage, need not be lived again.
> –Maya Angelou, "On the Pulse of Morning," 1993

In the spring of 2003, I received an invitation to the screening of the HBO film *Unchained Memories: Readings from the Slave Narratives* at the Prince Music Theatre in Philadelphia. The film features black actors reading from the text of the 1930s Works Progress Administration–sponsored Federal Writers' Project interviews with former slaves. At the reception following the screening, I overheard the conversation of a group of professional thirty-something African American women, all of whom seemed stunned by the film. Most remarked that they had no previous knowledge of the Works Progress Administration project, and many reported being amazed that "slaves" could have articulated their life experiences so clearly. Reluctant to enter the conversation as a know-it-all historian, I remained silent until one of the women remarked that she would have to figure out how to get to the Library of Congress in Washington, D.C., so she might gain access to the narratives herself, to find "our own history that has been hidden away from us." "Hidden?" I sputtered in response. "No, it is not hidden. And you don't have to go to Washington, D.C. You can go to a library and ask for all or part of George Rawick's many volumes of *The American Slave!*"[1]

My spirited outburst sparked a spontaneous, lengthy "teach-in" session that left me feeling socially inept and intellectually frustrated. How was it, I wondered as I boarded the train home, that in 2003, a group of college-educated, professional black women were so unaware of the tremendous body of work, researched and written by hundreds of scholars, about slavery or African American history and culture in general? Equally perplexing, why did some of the women in question, with computers and knowledge of the World Wide Web, continue to hold the rather dated belief that "our" history was "hidden" and inaccessible? And, just as troubling, if middle-class and rising black women did not know their

Journal of American History 93 (2007): 1171–77.

history, what might that mean for other people of color or whites in the larger society?

I strode into class the next day determined to teach with such intensity and passion as to ensure that no Swarthmore College student would leave school without knowing the history of African-descended people in the United States and that this history is readily accessible and belonged to all Americans. Sadly, I do not have the power to compel any student at Swarthmore to take African American or any other type of history course. Still, I continue to teach the African American history survey in service to the Department of History, to the Black Studies Program, and to my core belief that knowledge of American history is vital for all citizens. For the American story simply cannot be told without discussion and analysis of the experiences of black people whose labor created the nation's wealth, whose enslavement undergirded and undermined the concept of democratic freedom, and whose civil exclusion sparked the political revolutions of the twentieth century.

The year-long survey in African American history (7A, "African American History, 1500–1865" and 7B, "African American History, 1877–Present") that I teach was originally divided to acknowledge the formal end of American slavery and to allow space for my upper-level course: "Black Reconstruction." In current practice that periodization has become a bit of a misnomer. The first semester always ends with a discussion of the Civil War and Reconstruction, and the second semester always begins with a more detailed discussion of Reconstruction. The survey is designed to provide a general knowledge of the social, political, and cultural history of the people who would become African Americans, from the development of the sixteenth-century Atlantic world to the presidency of William Jefferson Clinton. The earliest lectures focus on life among the many peoples of West Africa prior to European contact and, *by necessity*, emphasize the development and evolution of the concept of race, one of the themes of the course. I learned in my earliest years of teaching that American undergraduates, products of what Toni Morrison has identified as "the wholly racialized society that is the United States," need to confront and begin to dismantle their ingrained notions of race as a fixed and static concept in order to make possible any genuine understanding of the past.[2]

The course work for 7A is comprised of readings from a textbook and ten to twelve additional texts, including a few novels and historical monographs. Lectures and discussions move the course through the processes of enslavement, the development of slave culture, the formation of free communities, the rise of abolitionism, and the experience of life in the immediate postemancipation era. The 7B course includes a discussion of the hopes and failures of Reconstruction, an outline of the rise of Jim Crow and early black political protest, and highlights of the Great Migration and the Harlem Renaissance. Analysis of the debates about and within the growing black middle class gives way to discussion of the black experience during both world wars, and then the course inevitably gets bogged down in my detailed discussion of the modern civil rights movement. The survey ends with a discussion of the 1996 Welfare Reform Act, the urban crises, the rise of black conservatives, and the dangers of the "ghetto trance." I place great emphasis on the diversity of the black experience. To disrupt the assumption of a monolithic, universal black experience, I instruct students to pay careful attention to the impact that time, location, and occupation had on the lives of black people in the past. The interplay of gender within the black community, as well as gendered limitations imposed on the black community by white society, runs like a bold stripe through the course. Beginning with a discussion of Edmund Morgan's thesis found in *American Slavery, American Freedom* linking black enslavement and white liberty, I foreground issues of class: class formation, class mobility (or lack thereof), and class solidarity. My own interest in black community studies creeps into my lectures, and students leave the survey with at least an awareness of the titles of the most recent literature in that subfield.[3]

I have spent the bulk of my teaching career at small liberal arts colleges: Oberlin, Hamilton, and currently, Swarthmore. Working at an affluent, predominately white institution, I have no expectations that a majority of my students will be of African descent, neither recent immigrants nor descendants of American slaves. Indeed, students of color are a distinct minority at most such institutions. As a result, the course was not and is not designed to appeal to any particular category of student—save my accurate assumption that most of my students have graduated from an American high school. Most also come from upper- and middle-class backgrounds; such students are well read, write well, and have had some small exposure to American history, though considerably less to African American history. I seek to provide more of an "event history" of African Americans—the who, what, when, where, and why—and less of a historiographical overview in the survey course. I am more interested in students understanding the work of contemporary scholars, such as Leslie Harris's study of blacks in pre–Civil War New York, Charles Payne's dynamic analysis of the civil rights movement, or Steven Hahn's discussion of the black pursuit of freedom and political equality in the era of Reconstruction, than I am in studying the works of Ulrich B. Phillips and company. While discussions of the exclusion of black scholars by the mainstream history profession, the work of the Dunning school and of black ethnographers of the Chicago School, and the of rise of post–World War II "revisionist" scholars bubble to the surface on occasion, I believe it is generally far more important that students in the survey course learn about the lives and struggles of the vast majority of black people in America (in addition to improving their writing and learning how to do research). It is my hope that they will leave the course with, among other things, a clear understanding that slavery flourished well above the Mason-Dixon line, a knowledge of the difference between the Emancipation Proclamation and the Thirteenth Amendment, an understanding of the political and social activism of blacks in the post–Civil War era, and a recognition of why the full name of the 1963 March on Washington for Jobs and Freedom matters.[4]

African Americans are, as stated in the syllabus, the subject matter of the course. Rather than discussed as an "add-on," or as simply part of a special unit on the Civil War or World War II, the black experience is the center of the story.

At the same time that I seek to center the African American experience, I emphasize that this history is quintessentially American history. From before the beginning of the nation, Africans were an integral part of what would become America; their status as enslaved persons cannot diminish their contributions to the creation and success of the nation. Historians have long acknowledged that fact, though it may be new to undergraduates. Writing in *Slavery and Public History*, Ira Berlin notes that, "Simply put, American history cannot be understood without slavery. Slavery shaped America's economy, politics, culture, and fundamental principles. For most of the nation's history, American society was one of slaveholders and slaves."[5] Slavery fostered notions of race for all Americans, notions that mutated over the centuries of that peculiar institution and through the Jim Crow era, ultimately influencing the whole of the nation's life. Later freed, though for most of the nation's existence barred from the rights and status of citizens, black men and women met all the challenges that tested other Americans and left their mark on the nation's intellectual life, culture, and industry. How can the nation fail to recognize black history as American history? The senior scholar John Hope Franklin, speaking in a recent television interview, reflected on the notion of black history as American history.

You can't be a historian of blacks without distorting the relationship between blacks and whites; you can't be a historian of whites without distorting the relationship. They're all here together; they interact all the time. Sometimes it's not favorable or exciting or good, but the interaction is there. And you have to take into consideration all these aspects of American history before you can say that you're really a historian of the United States.[6]

The emphasis on black history as American history often provokes questions about why the African American survey continues to be taught separately from the U.S. history survey. My pragmatic response focuses on time and reading load. If each of the three Americanists currently teaching in my small department offers a course on some portion of American history, with a different emphasis on sexuality or class or period, and each has corresponding lectures and a reading load that averages about two hundred pages a week, combining them into a gigantic American history survey would not do justice to either the themes or texts we are attempting to teach. The students would be overwhelmed and the faculty would be frustrated. I have no concerns that either of my well-trained colleagues, one white female and one white male, could not teach a basic survey in African American history in the same way that I often teach the U.S. history survey. We are distinguished more by our work and subfields than by our sex or race.

Swarthmore students tend to understand my rejection of notions of "authenticity" regarding the phenotype of the person teaching a course. My deep concerns with authenticity have to do with the preparation and skill of any given scholar. Is the scholar well trained? Has he or she studied and become well versed in the literature of the field? Is the research for his or her publications exhaustive and well presented? Does the scholar in question acknowledge and engage with the work of other scholars in the discipline? An affirmative response to those questions makes the historian in question authentic much more than

does his or her race. In my experience, the instructor's race has only been significant when the person in question evidences overtly racist behavior or an uncon-
scionable racial insensitivity. For example, the social scientist who can find only
black examples when discussing criminality or drug abuse, or the scholar whose
racial insecurity manifests in inappropriate humor and storytelling. It is hoped
that such experiences are rare.

 On the few occasions that a student has expressed concerns about authenticity, I have used the moment to teach about the dangers of assuming that all
people of any given race, religion, or creed think or act alike and of believing in
the illusion of perfect racial solidarity. I have also taken some wicked pleasure
in highlighting the dangers of racial stereotype and identity politics. For some
students, my phenotype and working-poor background make me much more
authentic than some of my peers or colleagues. I remind them that my phenotype and life experiences are representative of one type of collective black experience and that there have always been many black experiences, all of them
authentic. I also remind students of the dangers of the flip side of the authenticity question. If they reject out of hand a white scholar doing African American
history because of his or her race, then they must also accept that an African
American scholar would be inauthentic doing the history of the white working
class or, for that matter, analyzing the sonnets of Shakespeare, a conclusion they
all reject as untenable. Lastly, I have been known to highlight the fact that some
of the authors of their assigned texts, scholars they have judged to be excellent
and authentic (especially if they agree with the thesis of the text), are not, in fact,
African American.

 Swarthmore students are famous for their nose-to-the-grindstone, shoulder-
to-the-wheel approach to their education. They are also known for their love of
challenge and debate, a good part of the joy of teaching at this particular institution. I expect students in the survey to engage in classroom discussion of the
assigned text, which is structured into the course for one meeting per week, but
generating student discussion is always a challenge. Some are silent because it is
their nature to be reticent, others because they have not completed the reading.
Some students, often male students, assume that they have the right to the floor
and hold forth until gently encouraged to let others participate. These are normal patterns of discussion. Still, discussions in the African American survey are
somewhat distinct.

 In most years there are only a few students of color, including African American and self-identified "multi" students, in the survey—they are no more likely
to take the course than other students. Nevertheless, I am often troubled by what
I understand to be the self-imposed silence of some of the students of color who
do enroll. That silence is sometimes connected to their failure to recognize that
naïve knowledge of the black past is not the same as historical knowledge; students should not assume that being of African descent gives them more historical
knowledge of the black past than other students have. Yes, black students reared
in black homes, having attended black churches with parents who may have
belonged to black fraternities or sororities, will undoubtedly have some basic

awareness of the black experience in the past and a lived understanding of being black in the twenty-first century. That is not, however, historical knowledge of the black past, which requires research, study, and familiarity with documents, texts, and critical debates, as does the historical knowledge of any other past. Racial identity does not in and of itself produce historical knowledge. Some students of African descent erroneously assume that they "should know this history already" and are therefore likely to be intimidated into silence when they discover that they have as much to learn as everyone else in the class.

Other times, it is clear that this silence, especially in 7B as the class is struggling with the story of African American life in the twentieth century, is connected to something else. After class and, more frequently, during my office hours, students of color have reported tremendous frustration, and sometimes legitimate anger, at arguments expressed by some of their white peers. When asked why they did not speak in class, why they did not challenge a peer on the merits of the case, they respond, "It is just too hard," or "Professor Dorsey, this stuff is just too close, I don't want to shout or lose my cool in front of those white kids." More than one student has shed tears in my office while recounting some deeply personal experience—with racism or with harassment by law enforcement, experiences rooted in the everyday life of urban black America. Faced with what they see as the glib commentary of their white peers, many retreat to silence rather than try to explain their reality. Some white students also retreat to silence and have been known to shed tears in my office—pressed by their own professed sense of "white guilt" or more often because they fear being perceived as a racist.

This classroom dynamic is both baffling and frustrating. I have great empathy for my students of color struggling to come to voice around issues of race and class. I also have some faint understanding of the fear of being charged as a racist. Yet, as I remind my students every year, the college classroom is the safest place in the nation to study, debate, challenge, argue, or even shout. I struggle to remind these thin-skinned youngsters that they will not be forever marked or damaged by disagreeing or even by being charged as a racist. The history classroom is to my mind the very best place for Americans to engage in the process of coming to grips with our complex story of slavery and freedom, racial exclusion and participatory democracy. Here, we root our arguments and defend our positions with evidence; here, we have the tools—words, documents, photos, and songs—to create knowledge of the past and to glean some new understanding of our present. When my classroom feels safe for all, when students recognize that heated disagreement *can* be resolved in dialogue, when I have encouraged all students to push past their comfort zones to achieve intellectual breakthroughs, I deem the survey a success. Some terms are better than others.

The African American survey fits nicely into the core of courses on American history offered at Swarthmore. There is very little sequencing of history courses at Swarthmore, though students who take my colleague's Civil War course may follow it by enrolling in 7B. Similarly, students who take 7A may move on to another colleague's course on American labor history. Ideally, the African American survey would serve as a feeder course for upper level and double credit honors seminars.[7] This is not necessarily the case, and, as a consequence, some students enter the honors seminar on slavery or black communities with no background in African American history. Most students will overcome that lack with extra study and reading. Unfortunately, others will assume that training in this field is unnecessary—resulting in anemic contributions to seminar discussions and lackluster essays.

The study of any history is reading and research intensive, and because many students come to the field with little knowledge of research methods, I have added a research skills component to the survey course. This decision to require more research in primary-source documents is grounded in my hope of teaching a new skill and in my frustration with reading yet another paper on the Tuskegee experiment or *Brown v. Board of Education*.[8] While those papers are usually well written and reference the required five secondary sources, the work represents a sameness, a failure to understand how much other subject matter might be investigated. I have discovered that exposure to primary-source documents helps students develop their own ideas about what topics need study and what questions should be asked.

I also aspire to other revisions of the survey. I have not yet found a satisfying way to incorporate more literature on music and the music industry from the era of Scott Joplin or to address the transformation of the cultural landscape created by the hip-hop revolution. Nor have I found time within the structure of the class to address black theater and art seriously. There is much to add to the syllabus each year: the history of interaction between African Americans and Latinos in the West or Asians in the South, the story of black immigration from the Caribbean and Africa in the nineteenth and twentieth centuries, and issues of sexuality beyond the dynamic of black heterosexual relationships. This challenging predicament is revealing of the vibrancy of the field of African American history.

At the close of the survey, I distribute a "Summer Reading List in African American History." Conceding that I cannot require students to read from the list and test them in the fall, I encourage them to explore some of the themes we have not addressed in the course. Over the years, a number of students have reported that they were "working" through the list. I choose to believe that the survey in African American history has created in some a lifelong interest in the field and, I hope, it has sparked more than one heated, well-informed debate about the American story. Though the spontaneous "teach-in" at the reception for *Unchained Memories* may have been too little and too late for my thirty-something auditors-of-the-moment, I hope, in a way shared by every other educator, that the students who have taken my survey courses are better prepared to recognize the survival and importance of the historical in the present and to understand the myriad sources and the vast number of stories out of which "our" American history is made.[9]

Notes

1. *Unchained Memories: Readings from the Slave Narratives*, dir. Ed Bell (HBO, 2003). George P. Rawick, ed., *The American Slave: A Composite Autobiography* (19 vols., Westport, Conn., 1972); George P. Rawick, ed., *The American Slave: A Composite Auto-*

biography. Supplement, Series 1 (12 vols., Westport, Conn., 1977); George P. Rawick, ed., *The American Slave: A Composite Autobiography*. Supplement, Series 2 (10 vols., Westport, Conn., 1979).

2. Toni Morrison, *Playing in the Dark: Whiteness and the Literary Imagination* (Cambridge, Mass., 1992), xii.

3. Peter Edelman, "The Worst Thing Bill Clinton Has Done," *Atlantic Monthly* 43 (March 1997): 43–58. William Julius Wilson, *When Work Disappears: The World of the New Urban Poor* (New York, 1996). Mary Pattillo-McCoy, *Black Picket Fences: Privilege and Peril among the Black Middle Class* (Chicago, 1999), 119–20. Edmund S. Morgan, *American Slavery, American Freedom: The Ordeal of Colonial Virginia* (New York, 1975).

4. Leslie M. Harris, *In the Shadow of Slavery: African Americans in New York City, 1626–1863* (Chicago, 2003); Charles M. Payne, *I've Got the Light of Freedom: The Organizing Tradition and the Mississippi Freedom Struggle* (Berkeley, Calif., 1995); Steven Hahn, *A Nation under Our Feet: Black Political Struggles in the Rural South, from Slavery to the Great Migration* (Cambridge, Mass., 2003); Ulrich B. Phillips, *American Negro Slavery: A Survey of the Supply, Employment, and Control of Negro Labor as Determined by the Plantation Regime* (New York, 1918).

5. Ira Berlin, "Coming to Terms with Slavery," in *Slavery and Public History: The Tough Stuff of American Memory*, ed. James Oliver Horton and Lois E. Horton (New York, 2006), 2.

6. For Gwen Ifill's interview with John Hope Franklin, see "Civil Rights Activist, Historian Discusses New Autobiography," transcript, June 15, 2006, *Online NewsHour*, <www.pbs.org/newshour/bb/entertainment/jan-june06/franklin_06-15.html>.

7. For information on the Swarthmore College Honors Program, see <www.swarthmore.edu/honors.xml>.

8. *Brown v. Board of Education*, 347 U.S. 483 (1954).

9. Allison Dorsey thanks her former student Rachel Burstein and former colleague Victoria Vernon for their feedback and assistance with this essay. Thanks also to Swarthmore College student Kelsey Baldwin '07 for her research assistance.

Scott Kurashige

Exposing the Price of Ignorance: Teaching Asian American History in Michigan

For the final meeting of my Asian American history survey during the winter 2006 semester at the University of Michigan, we studied the narratives of three immigrants whose journeys to the United States followed harrowing experiences that had shaped the course of world history. The first saw his Philippine childhood shattered by the Japanese occupation during World War II. While aiding the guerrilla resistance, his eldest brother was imprisoned and executed. From humble Chinese peasant origins, the second subject saw the Communist revolution transform his family's status. As a Red Guard militant, he was granted a rare opportunity to attend college. By contrast, the final subject witnessed the extreme deprivation dictatorial Communist rule caused in Cambodia. After she fled to a refugee camp to escape the genocidal regime of the Khmer Rouge, she eventually resettled in Michigan, as the other two had. Asian American historians are blessed with the type of rich source material that pushes forward studies of race, class, gender, war, and migration in transnational context and situates the field at the cutting edge of the discipline of history. Such narratives do more than breathe new life into the foundational concept of America as a nation of immigrants. They demonstrate how the struggle of Asians to establish a home in America offers new modes of rethinking the meaning of national identity.

Those narratives were drawn neither from my primary nor my secondary research. They were instead the product of course-assigned research papers, which in these cases focused on oral histories of the students' parents. Monica Kim, a Department of History Ph.D. student and graduate instructor, was so impressed by the quality and originality of these projects that she and I asked the student authors to share their findings with the class. By recognizing how their class projects place them at the frontiers of scholarly research, students come to appreciate how histories of marginal subjects stretch the boundaries of knowledge production. My goal is for students to see themselves as history makers— possessing the power both to write and to change the course of history.

As I teach at a large research university in the Midwest, the regular schedule for my Asian American history survey includes three hours of lecture per week and one hour of discussion led by a graduate instructor. It generally draws fifty to

Journal of American History 93 (2007): 1178–85.

seventy students. I could not imagine putting the curriculum together without the graduate school training I received at the University of California, Los Angeles, home to the nation's largest Asian American studies department. But living and toiling in the hinterlands of Asian American settlement has led me to alter my approach in several critical ways. I will outline the key historical themes I highlight and the methods I use to engage them. Finally, I will try to convey a sense of how students have responded to the course and some of the ongoing challenges I face.[1]

I want my students to appreciate that history making is a political endeavor; they need to understand the specific politics surrounding the teaching and writing of Asian American history. My syllabus does not start with the ancient empires of Asia or the first Asian sailor to disembark in the Americas. Instead, we open with the creation of Asian American studies as an academic field out of social movements in the late 1960s. I seek to make an important historiographic point here. Increasing attention to the significance of Asians in American history was not the result of internal developments within the discipline. To the contrary, activist-minded scholars and students pushed historians to acknowledge, grudgingly, what a growing number in the discipline now take for granted—a linear master narrative cannot explain the nation's multiethnic history; "orientalist" discourse has been integral to the construction of race; and the expansion of the U.S. empire into Asia is implicated in the fabric of American national identity. San Francisco State University and the University of California, Berkeley, built the first Asian American studies programs because activists there mobilized massive strikes under the banner of the "Third World Liberation Front." In that historical moment it was clear that "Asian American" served not as a generic marker of racial identity but as a signifier of radical politics. Indeed, those adopting the moniker "Asian American" were quick to denounce those "Orientals" past and present whom they viewed as exploiting immigrant workers, whitewashing their ethnic identity, and collaborating with oppressors. Thus, the field of Asian American history has been defined not only by the subjects students and scholars examine but more significantly by the critical and oppositional stance they adopt.

As the construction of Asian American identity has been a political project, one cannot genuinely teach the experience of diverse Asian ethnicities as a collective history without having some investment in it. In a technical sense, the history of people who identified as "Asian American" dates back only four decades. My curriculum thus ties together the histories of peoples who often failed to embrace a shared identity and sometimes found themselves immersed in interethnic conflict. I stress that the panethnic "Asian American" rubric through which we examine both pre- and post-1960s history is built on principles that shaped Asian American studies during its movement-era origins. Without glossing over the historical specificities that distinguish one group from another, I lay out two bases for a common approach to the study of multiple Asian ethnicities and nationalities.

First, I situate Asian American history in a global context that recognizes not only the importance of "push" factors that spurred migration from Asia to the

United States but also the omnipresent relevance of imperialism. We reflect, for instance, on the trans-national significance of U.S. intervention in Indochina. The wars in Vietnam, Cambodia, and Laos galvanized Asian Americans to unite, not only to stop the bloodshed but also to confront the racist "gook" discourse in American militarism. At the same time, those wars forced hundreds of thousands of Southeast Asians to seek refuge in America, where their new experiences with discrimination (because they "looked like the enemy") led them into Asian American organizing circles.

Second, I situate Asian American history in the multiethnic construction of race. In particular, I point out that those who identified as Asian American consciously resisted the assimilationist imperatives in "model minority" ideology. As conservatives deployed images of high-achieving and politically passive Asians to discredit African American protest and rebellion, young Asian American activists turned for inspiration to the black power movement and elder radicals such as Yuri Kochiyama of Harlem and Grace Lee Boggs of Detroit. While we read narratives from this era, I present evidence of black-Asian relations dating back more than a century, such as Frederick Douglass's arguments against the Chinese Exclusion Acts, which foreground the relationship between Asian immigration and Reconstruction.[2]

Although I am a less than perfect practitioner, I am philosophically committed to a problem-posing method rooted in the belief that people's convictions are strongest when they draw their own conclusions. I attempt to let actors on all sides of historical debates and conflicts speak for themselves through primary documents. For instance, members of the Japanese American community still debate today the actions of the Nisei who resisted the draft during World War II. Did their refusal to be drafted out of internment camps damage a community that was already politically vulnerable? Or was their stand a patriotic defense of constitutional rights? We read a statement from the Japanese American Citizens League advocating cooperation with the government alongside a petition from the Fair Play Committee at the Heart Mountain, Wyoming, internment camp justifying civil disobedience. Then I ask the students, "How would you have acted under these circumstances?" In the end, I try to reiterate that we are not evaluating the students' opinions, but the strength of their analysis. While we trace the origins of Asian American identity to the radicalism of the sixties, I do not expect that the students will become activists themselves (though some inevitably do). What I want them all to recognize is that history is alive, and that it is constantly shaping our sense of identity, reality, and possibility. That may be stating the obvious to students majoring in history, but the overwhelming majority of history majors at Michigan never set foot in my course. In fact, most of my students admit that they have generally found the study of history (based largely on textbook-driven high school experiences) to be dry and uninspiring.

Why, then, are they taking my course? Some have developed an interest in ethnic studies as undergraduates, and others are trying to satisfy various requirements. But some vague curiosity motivates the largest group. Three out of four claim Asian ancestry, and those students suspect that they will have a chance to learn something about "their" history. But with very few exceptions, what is common across all students in the course is that Asian American history never received more than a cursory nod throughout their precollege education. That is especially true for those reared in Michigan, where, to my knowledge, I am the only teacher statewide at any level of education hired as an Asian American history specialist. Hence, most of the students (Asian and non-Asian alike) have never done any serious thinking about the course topic.

That deficiency creates the basis for the central problem I pose in this course: What is the price of ignorance? Such a question can be interpreted both individually and socially. It resonates most clearly at the individual level with the Asian American students, many of them raised in predominantly white, midwestern neighborhoods. Often for the first time, those students are able to see how their families' experiences contribute to broader historical patterns, providing a context for their personal struggles with issues of exclusion and assimilation. During the first week of class, I run an exercise in which I ask students to plot the date, place of origin, and occupation of their first known ancestor in America on a giant timeline. Without fail, the resulting portrait is the same every time I do this at Michigan. In the section before 1850 there are the postings of a sprinkling of non-Asian students tracing their ancestry to the *Mayflower*, African slaves, indigenous people, and Irish laborers. Next comes a clump reflecting the "new" immigration of the late nineteenth and early twentieth centuries. Most were pulled by the demand for labor, including Asian immigrants like my great-grandfather who sailed from Japan to Hawaii as a contract laborer in 1889. There is a noticeable gap between 1924 and 1965 marking the palpable impact of racist exclusion laws. Finally, we come to the largest bloc, comprising post-1965 immigrants and refugees from Asia. Probing further, we discover that the majority in that group are professionals in the fields of medicine, science, and engineering, rendering the impact of immigration preference categories abundantly clear (as well as the overrepresentation in "elite" public universities of students from upper middle-class families). As such trends reveal the operation of power, students are drawn to new questions about the social significance of history.[3]

Debates about the price of ignorance at the social level bring into sharper focus the degree to which the production of historical knowledge is a high-stakes endeavor. While Michigan students are used to hearing that they represent the "best and brightest" of their generation, they recognize that even their vigorous pursuit of education has never afforded them the opportunity to study Asian American history. As they begin to realize that historical omissions and distortions are not accidental but deliberate, it is not hard for them to appreciate how and why racist stereotypes and half-truths have so frequently been used to justify colonialism and white supremacy in American history. For example, John Dower has marshaled ample evidence of how the intense and dehumanizing anti-Japanese racism of the Americans (matched by the anti-Americanism of Japanese chauvinists) led to the devolution of the Pacific war into a "war without mercy." The same totalizing racist logic led the U.S. government to conclude that Japanese American civilians were a threat to national security. Because I recognize that most of my students would rebel against Dower's prizewinning—but long—scholarly texts, I try to make that point in one lecture after screening *Bugs Bunny Nips the Nips*, showing an editorial cartoon by Dr. Seuss that cast Japanese Americans as saboteurs, and passing out the December 1941 *Time* article "How to Tell Your [Chinese] Friends from the Japs."[4]

Students also recognize that the marginalization of Asian American perspectives distorts our conception of America's past, present, and future. When asked how many died due to the Korean War, most students estimate between twenty-five thousand and three hundred thousand persons. They are shocked to learn that the actual figure is closer to 4 million. Moreover, few are aware that American soldiers massacred Korean civilians at No Gun Ri, an event that journalists confirmed in 1999 to end a half-century cover-up. As students discover the degree to which a war of that magnitude could be reduced to little more than a footnote in the standard American curriculum, they begin to question how and why our nation has developed collective amnesia. My hope is that history's significance to the present and future is clear. A lack of appreciation for the legacy of the Korean War hampers the public's ability to make sound judgments regarding potential military actions against North Korea.[5]

As public consciousness of Asian American history is geographically uneven, my course takes that reality into account. While Asian American organizing since the 1960s has provided new mechanisms to establish community and overcome discrimination, that process of empowerment bypassed much of the Midwest, where Asians are still frequently viewed as an intrusive alien presence. Over the past three decades, the hardships caused by the failing rust belt economy have intensified anti-Asian sentiments generated in response to the Vietnam War and the trade war with Japan. The award-winning documentaries *Blue Collar & Buddha* and *Who Killed Vincent Chin?* put a spotlight on two notorious hate crimes by respectively examining the bombing of a Laotian temple in Rockford, Illinois, and the death of a Chinese American in Detroit by two white auto workers using a baseball bat. They depict disturbing scenes, ranging from grass-roots bigotry to gross displays of institutionalized racism, forcing students out of their comfort zones. After viewing such films, students often ask, "Why did I never learn about this?" Some exclaim that they have been "lied to," "cheated," and "robbed" of a relevant education. My goal is not simply to agitate them but to challenge them to think creatively about unresolved societal problems.[6]

While it would not be difficult to fill a semester of lectures with stories of anti-Asian racism, Asian American history is driven by events and personalities that resist innocent narratives of victimization. The pioneering historian Yuji Ichioka—who is credited with coining the signifier "Asian American" in 1968—argued stridently that scholars must reclaim the agency denied Asian American historical actors by recovering what he called the "buried past." I attempt to drive that point home on day one by playing my acoustic guitar and singing "We Are the Children" from the landmark 1970s album *A Grain of Sand* by the folk trio Chris Kando Iijima, Joanne Nobuko Miyamoto, and Charlie Chin. Its lyrics begin:

We are the children of the migrant workers
We are the offspring of the concentration camp
Sons and daughters of the railroad builder
Who leave their stamp on Amerika

Taken as a statement of identity and class politics, the song reveals the relationship between Asian American movement activism and the construction of narratives rooted in a progressive conception of social history, moving non-elite actors from the margin to the center of analysis. My course materials draw heavily on research that was part and parcel of that search for the buried past, mostly conducted by researchers outside, or at best on the margins of, the academy. While I employ Sucheng Chan's concise overview as a reference text, the vast bulk of my reading list consists of first-person accounts.[7]

We study the post-1882 era of Chinese exclusion, for example, by reading poems inscribed on the walls of the Angel Island Detention Center in San Francisco Bay. These writings entered the consciousness of historians through the work of a community-based reclamation project spearheaded by Judy Yung, Genny Lim, and Him Mark Lai; translations were published in the book *Island*. Authored by migrants whose entry to the United States was delayed or denied, they convey resignation, resentment, and resilience. I complement those assigned readings with a lecture on the politics of exclusion and a screening of the documentary *Carved in Silence*, featuring oral interviews with Angel Island survivors describing the subversive means they deployed to circumvent racist laws and outwit authorities. Next, I ask students to complete a writing assignment involving both historical analysis and imagination. Drawing on course materials, they reconstruct the life of a Chinese immigrant using one or more detainee poems as clues as to why the subjects left their homeland, why they were drawn to America, and how detainment reshaped their attitudes and goals. By having them write those essays in the first person, I hope to encourage the students, most of whom are immigrants or children of immigrants, to see their personal connection to history. Finally, we push that connection further through online and graduate instructor–led discussions that ask students to consider how our understanding of the past (or lack thereof) informs or should inform contemporary political debates about immigration.[8]

My course ties the study of immigrant pioneers to the collective formation of Asian American communities. It is especially designed to help students from post-1965 immigrant families connect with a past they would not otherwise identify as theirs. (I will never forget the course evaluation of one student who criticized my history course for dwelling too much on the past.) Just as I attempt to make non-Asian students see the impact of Asian American history on their lives, I similarly push post-1965 Asian students to see how historical patterns of racialization, struggles for justice, and transnational politics dating back to the nineteenth century or earlier have shaped their lives. For instance, I emphasize the tremendous legacy created by the small early twentieth-century wave of Asian Indian migration and quickly curtailed by racist exclusionists. As Karen Isaksen Leonard's writings have shown, Punjabi Sikh immigrants fought to democratize

American citizenship and to overthrow British colonialism in India. Sikhs, including leaders such as Bhagat Singh Thind and Dalip Singh Saund, persisted in the face of labor exploitation, political repression, and racist violence, while uniting with other Indians as well as Mexicans to establish permanent communities in America. That legacy, however, is lost on the frighteningly large numbers of Americans who have berated and attacked turban-clad Sikh Americans for "looking like the terrorists." Students were shocked to read that more than five hundred post-9/11 bias incidents have been reported on the Sikh Coalition Web site, yet they simultaneously acknowledged that their own total (prior) ignorance of Sikh American history was symptomatic of a wider problem in America.[9]

Much of my current curriculum is a product of adjustments I have made over the past six years. One of the harsh realities of working at a large public institution is that teaching is always a popularity contest, given that course enrollments influence departmental funding. As a result, I try to be sensitive to the cultural orientation of MTV generation students without giving in to the consumerist ethos that has been branded onto them. For starters, I dropped my overheads two years ago and created the now universally requisite PowerPoint presentations filled with eye-catching photos and graphics. In addition to playing folk songs, I present poems, retell dramatic anecdotes, and occasionally rap. I have also been known to accentuate historical analysis with spot-on impressions of Elvis Presley, President John F. Kennedy, George "Mr. Sulu" Takei on *Star Trek*, and other prominent figures. Now I would be lying if I did not admit that part of my goal is to use humor and entertainment both to keep the students alert and to indulge my alter ego as an open-mic performer in Detroit coffeehouses.

But there is another method to that madness, which may or may not have something to do with Zen simplicity and *wabi-sabi* aesthetics. Any attempt to teach all of the periods, events, and groups that constitute Asian American history in one semester cannot hope to achieve any semblance of complete coverage. What I try to do with each lecture is hammer home a few themes and leave some lasting impressions. That is especially crucial to reiterate to the many science and engineering majors in my course, who would otherwise spend eighty minutes frantically writing down everything they heard while comprehending only a fraction of it. I lead the students through creative exercises like these: We do role-playing to demonstrate how the 1854 California Supreme Court decision *People v. Hall* facilitated racist mob violence. Participants witness a heinous murder, then realize through a mock trial that they as Chinese are barred from testifying against a white defendant. After discussing the exclusionary 1924 Immigration Act and the U.S. Supreme Court's 1922 *Ozawa* decision denying Japanese immigrants the right to naturalized citizenship, I ask the students to write a seventeen-syllable haiku poem.[10]

When it comes to aspects of the course I consider core elements, I am far less willing to compromise. Although many students are known to avoid courses that assign a research paper, I insist on retaining this requirement. In my eyes, the papers are far more crucial than the final exam, which I include primarily to ensure that students complete assigned readings. I particularly encourage students to conduct oral histories so that they see themselves as participants in the ongoing search to reclaim the buried past. As I stated at the outset, those projects often produce the most profound and memorable discoveries for both students and instructors. In addition, though mandating an additional hour of class can also inhibit enrollment, I structure the course with discussion sections to encourage peer interaction and to provide a rare opportunity to train Ph.D. students to teach Asian American history. Lastly, I choose not to have this course satisfy the university-wide "race and ethnicity" requirement, which would boost enrollment but alter the dynamics of the classroom by introducing students who felt "forced" to be there.

In the end, what impact does my course have on students? For some, it may be just another line on a transcript. Nevertheless, I can attest that more than a handful undergo life-changing experiences. I have witnessed first-year students go on to take several of my courses and specialize in Asian/Pacific Islander American studies, science majors switch to humanities or social sciences, and seniors shift career aspirations from medicine or engineering to law, social work, or public policy. More commonly, students maintain their majors and career paths but orient themselves toward Asian American concerns through sponsorship of campus programs, engagement with community activism, or teaching in public schools. What I hope that all take away is a sense of responsibility to pass along the knowledge they have acquired and produced, thereby transforming public discourse in large and small ways. Moving from Los Angeles to Detroit and correspondingly from a place of high to a place of minimal Asian American consciousness, has sharpened my awareness of how critical historical narratives are to giving us our sense of place and status in American society. Asian American history is not likely to be a part of the formal education of the average midwesterner for the near future. But if I have done my job well, the students completing my course will understand that Asian American history is too important to be confined to the classroom.

Notes

1. For my first college teaching experience in 1992 at the University of California, Los Angeles, I had the good fortune to serve as a teaching assistant for Valerie Matsumoto's Asian American history survey. My oral history assignments are largely drawn from her course.

2. For a valuable collection of primary documents, see Philip Sheldon Foner and Daniel Rosenberg, *Racism, Dissent, and Asian Americans from 1850 to the Present: A Documentary History* (Westport, Conn., 1993). My assigned readings on the Southeast Asian refugee experience include the riveting memoir by Andrew X. Pham, *Catfish and Mandala: A Two-Wheeled Voyage through the Landscape and Memory of Vietnam* (New York, 1999). For recollections by activists from the 1960s and 1970s, see Steve Louie and Glenn Omatsu, eds., *Asian Americans: The Movement and the Moment* (Los Angeles, 2001). I also assign excerpts from Grace Lee Boggs, *Living for Change: An Autobiography* (Minneapolis, 1998); and Yuri Kochiyama, *Passing It On: A Memoir*, ed. Marjorie Lee, Akemi Kochiyama-Sardinha, and Audee Kochiyama-Holman (Los Angeles, 2004).

3. I learned this exercise from popular education advocates at Asian Americans United, a community organization in Philadelphia.

4. John Dower, *War without Mercy: Race and Power in the Pacific War* (New York, 1986); *Bugs Bunny Nips the Nips*, dir. Fritz Freleng (Warner Brothers, 1944); "Dr. Seuss Went to War: A Catalog of Political Cartoons by Dr. Seuss," Mandeville Special Collections Library, University of California, San Diego, <http://orpheus.ucsd.edu/speccoll/dspolitic>; "How to Tell Your [Chinese] Friends from the Japs," *Time*, Dec. 22, 1941, p. 33.

5. Charles J. Hanley, Sang-Hun Choe, and Martha Mendoza, *The Bridge at No Gun Ri: A Hidden Nightmare from the Korean War* (New York, 2001).

6. *Blue Collar & Buddha*, dir. Taggart Siegel (Siegel Productions, 1986); *Who Killed Vincent Chin?* dir. Christine Choy and Renee Tajima-Pena (1987).

7. *Encyclopedia of Japanese American History: An A-to-Z Reference from 1868 to the Present*, updated ed., s. v. "Ichioka, Yuji"; Chris Kando Iijima, Joanne Nobuko Miyamoto, and Charlie Chin, *A Grain of Sand: Music for the Struggle by Asians in America* (LP record; Paredon 01020; 1973); Sucheng Chan, *Asian Americans: An Interpretive History* (Boston, 1991). Memoirs I have assigned with success include Mary Paik Lee, *Quiet Odyssey: A Pioneer Korean Woman in America* (Seattle, 1990); and Jeanne Wakatsuki Houston and James D. Houston, *Farewell to Manzanar: A True Story of Japanese American Experience during and after the World War II Internment* (Boston, 1973).

8. Him Mark Lai, Genny Lim, and Judy Yung, eds., *Island: Poetry and History of Chinese Immigrants on Angel Island, 1910–1940* (Seattle, 1991); *Carved in Silence*, dir. Felicia Lowe (1987).

9. I assign excerpts from Karen Isaksen Leonard, *The South Asian Americans* (Westport, Conn., 1997), 39–66; Reports of bias incidents can be found at <www.sikhcoalition.org/ListReports.asp>.

10. An imperfect translation of *wabi-sabi* is "appreciating the beauty in the imperfect way things are." *People v. Hall*, 4 Cal. 399, 404 (1854); *Immigration Act of 1924*, 43 Stat. 153 (1924); *Takao Ozawa v. United States*, 260 U.S. 178 (1922); Chan, *Asian Americans*, 47–48, 55.

Pablo Mitchell

Playing the Pivot: Teaching Latina/o History in Good Times and Bad

I will begin with a confession. As I see it, the first time I taught Latina/o history was a disaster. It was fall 2000, and I was a newly hired assistant professor at Oberlin College. I had just finished my dissertation over the summer and had almost zero teaching experience—I had been a teaching assistant for several courses in graduate school. I also did not like the idea of standing in front of dozens of twenty-year-olds and lecturing them on history-related topics, or on anything else for that matter. I had been fairly content squirreled away in the Pittsburgh hills, and the thought of several rows of skeptical students leaning back in their chairs, arms crossed, as I lectured did not thrill me. It did not help that I had gone to a small liberal arts college and had been precisely that kind of student—capable and engaged, but also skeptical and even a little suspicious of my professors.

At the same time, I was thrilled to be able to teach a course in Latina/o history. My colleagues placed no restrictions on me, no hints to stay away from this topic or nudges to include that event. I thought, and still do, that there are enough similarities between the histories of Chicanas/os and Puerto Ricans and Cuban Americans, not to mention immigrants from the Dominican Republic and Central America and elsewhere in Latin America, to justify treating their diverse experiences in the United States within a single, semester-long course.

As I saw it, I could go in two directions. I could treat the history of each group as a relatively discrete unit—a section on Chicana/o history followed by one on Puerto Ricans, and so on, with transition days between topics to highlight similarities and differences. Alternatively, I could move chronologically from the sixteenth century to the near present, ending more or less with the Mariel boatlift in the 1980s. Along the way, I would shuttle around in space rather than in time, from the Mexican North and the American Southwest to the Spanish Caribbean and Miami and New York, describing what life was like in Cuba and Puerto Rico in 1848 when the Treaty of Guadalupe Hidalgo was signed, how *nuevomexicanas/os* in 1898 reacted to the Spanish American War, or how Puerto Ricans viewed the Peter Pan flights from Cuba in the 1960s.

I chose the latter approach. I chose poorly. Without an adequate textbook, I spent the semester feverishly writing lectures, a man on the run trying to unite

Journal of American History 93 (2007): 1186–91.

disparate histories into coherent narratives. I compared slavery in the nineteenth-century Caribbean with slavery in the Southwest; honor and shame in New Mexico and Puerto Rico; Desi Arnaz and Rita Moreno. Some lectures worked well; others were failures. I limped to the end of the semester and vowed, never again. Since then I have stuck, even clung, to the first option, organizing the course around individual groups. I still do not use a textbook, though I experimented one term with Ilan Stavans and Lalo Alcaraz's *Latino U.S.A.: A Cartoon History* and was fairly happy with the thematic coverage, if not the obviously thin content (it is a cartoon history, right?). I use transition classes at the end of each section to reemphasize broader themes in Latina/o history. Sometimes I even compare slavery systems and talk about honor and shame.[1]

While the format of the class has changed, the goals have pretty much stayed the same. First, of course, I want students to learn something about the history of people of Latin American descent in the United States. I highlight major themes such as work, political activism, migration, and key individuals and events—Alvar Núñez Cabeza de Vaca, José Martí, Dolores Huerta; 1848, 1898, 1980. We watch clips from *Zoot Suit, I Love Lucy, Salt of the Earth, High Noon,* and *West Side Story* and migrate from Los Angeles to San Antonio to Chicago, Miami to New York, the islands to the rust belt to the sun belt. In addition, I incorporate the history of Latinos in Lorain, Ohio, into the class at several points. Oberlin is less than ten miles from Lorain, the home of prominent and longstanding Puerto Rican and Mexican American communities. In fact, Latinos have had a significant presence in Lorain for over seventy-five years. Mexicans and Mexican Americans arrived in the 1920s to work in Lorain's steel mills, and thousands of Puerto Rican workers were recruited to the mills in the late 1940s and made their home in the city. Besides lecturing about the arrival of, first, ethnic Mexicans and then Puerto Ricans to the region, I ask the class to analyze assorted primary sources from the city's past. We examine 1930 manuscript census schedules from Lorain listing Mexicans, Spaniards, Puerto Ricans, and Peruvians living side by side with Eastern European immigrants and native Ohioans on the south side of Lorain. The class also discusses articles from local newspapers from the 1950s and 1960s that describe, for instance, Puerto Rican social events and meetings of Mexican mutual aid organizations.[2]

I also see the class as a place to challenge students with a more complicated view of American race relations than many of them, especially those early in their college careers, have encountered in other courses. Most of the students see American history as filled, for the most part, with white people—with a few Native Americans present at first and a handful of important African Americans. Sexuality is another major theme of the course. It is one of my main research interests and an important intellectual topic for both white and nonwhite students. In fact, I think many students in the course would have serious misgivings about any survey of Latina/o history that did not directly address sexuality and sexual politics. In addition to lectures on topics such as sexual assault in the Southwest and antimiscegenation laws, I include primary sources ranging from newspaper accounts from across the country to poetry and film clips. Students also read essays on rape and Spanish colonialism, abortion rights mobilization by Puerto Rican nationalists, and Cuban gay men during the Mariel boatlift.[3]

Entwined with those more formal goals are other commitments. Precious few self-identified Latinos and Latinas attend Oberlin, and they are a mixed lot. They come from the Southwest and the Northeast, the Caribbean and Latin America, Chicago and small-town Ohio. Some speak Spanish, others do not. Some have one Latino parent, some have two. All, whether they articulate it or not, have an intimate relationship with Latino culture. But many, especially those of mixed heritage or those not fluent in Spanish, feel distant from what they (mis)perceive to be real Latinos. I think often about these Latino students during the semester, but especially in the first few weeks of the term when class schedules are still fluid and the particular features of the class are still emerging: that is, when they still might drop the class. I know that for many of these students a Latina/o history class or a Spanish class are early steps in coming to terms with their mixed ethnicity, and I am very careful not to alienate or discourage them with talk of "true" Latinos or "real" *latinidad*. I talk about my own nonnative Spanish and Anglo father and tell students that cross-cultural mixing is fundamental to Latina/o culture. It's a little hokey, not to mention paternalistic, but I never had a Latina/o history class in college, and it would have meant a lot to me to know that I was one in a long line of *mestizos* and mixed bloods.

From the beginning, I also wanted students to work closely with primary sources. With my recently completed dissertation still fresh in mind, I imagined my students as colleagues, even co-conspirators, in the creation of new knowledge about the history of Latinas/os. At the same time, I was leery of assigning long research papers, perhaps projecting my own undergraduate bumps and bruises onto my students. Instead, I assigned three five-page papers spread out over the semester. The format of those assignments has hardly changed over the past six years. Each paper requires students to compare a primary source, such as a newspaper or magazine article or a census document (they can either dig one up or use the sources handed out in class), with one of the secondary sources in the class. Another constant in the course over the years has been the time and day of the week of the class. While I have toyed with the idea of switching to a fifty-minute, Monday, Wednesday, Friday format, teaching the class in two seventy-five minute chunks on Tuesday and Thursday has been hard to shake. I lecture for about forty or fifty minutes and then turn to small group discussions about primary sources or assigned readings.

One of the biggest problems I have yet to solve is finding a decent textbook. I simply have not found a textbook that both provides a sophisticated overview of Latina/o history and adequately addresses gender and sexuality. That problem aside, I have been generally quite happy with the other reading assignments for the class. Besides the handful of articles, many of them sexuality-related, I include three books in the syllabus, one each on Chicana/o, Puerto Rican, and Cuban American history. I recently added Vicki L. Ruiz's *From Out of the Shadows* to the older standards, María Cristina García's *Havana USA* and Ruth Glasser's *My Music Is My Flag*, and have been quite pleased with all three books, especially when students compare them during discussion sections. The books vary in chronology (from Ruiz's twentieth century scope to the several decades covered by García and Glasser), historical method, and writing style.[4]

Since the Cuban American section comes late in the semester, I always appreciate García's political history and more formal prose. Almost invariably, at least one student, usually a self-described history major, will praise the book as "real history." That is a nice, if a little annoying, opening for discussions of writing history and how some historians choose to write concrete, authoritative prose, while others open possibilities in their writing for dissent and counter-argument, and how we as writers and readers need to recognize the advantages and disadvantages of each approach. Central to that discussion is the fact that García, unlike Ruiz and Glasser, does not explicitly situate herself in her writing. Ruiz elegantly places herself at particular moments within her narrative, and Glasser's introduction makes quite clear her "outsider" status as a non–Puerto Rican studying Puerto Rican musicians. Placed side by side the three books work marvelously in both conveying critical information and stimulating important discussions about history and history writing.

College-wide changes have also had a significant effect on the course. When I arrived in Oberlin in 2000, my position was one of five continuing positions in American history. Besides Latina/o history, the positions were in environmental history, Asian American history, nineteenth-century women's history, and a position spanning the colonial era through Reconstruction. With an American historian in the college's African American studies department, American race relations figure prominently in the history curriculum. That emphasis on race and ethnicity, however, has not come at the expense of chronological coverage. My specialty is the Gilded Age and Progressive Era, and I have taught courses on Gilded Age America and U.S. history since 1877, while colleagues in environmental history and Asian American history have offered courses on recent American history and the 1960s. The lesson here is that even small departments can "pivot" and diversify their curriculum by devoting full-term positions to particular fields (Latina/o history and Native American history, for example) and by hiring with an eye toward chronological coverage.

It is also important to recognize the close ties between fields such as Latina/o history and ethnic studies. A commitment to ethnic studies is critical to the teaching of Latina/o history, at both large and small institutions. Ethnic studies needs several things to be viable at a small college such as Oberlin. First and foremost, the college must have a strong African American studies program. Oberlin fortunately has such a program, with four full-time, permanent positions and several associated faculty. Ethnic studies at a small college also needs at least two permanent full-time positions in at least two other specialties. A strong African American studies program and one professor each in Latina/o and Asian American studies, for instance, are great, but not enough. The pressures placed on faculty of color, especially female faculty of color, can be intense, even in a relatively diverse setting. When there is only one specialist in a given field, demands on that person's time and energy (such as to represent diversity on alumni panels, admissions gatherings, or faculty committees; to advise, formally and informally, students of color; not to mention, to meet the high teaching expectations typical of liberal arts colleges) can easily be overwhelming. Finally, there must also be a critical mass of likeminded scholars, an intellectual community attuned to racial heterogeneity, to support research and writing.

Oberlin, for a moment, had that elusive critical mass in ethnic studies. For a couple of years, I was the only Latina/o studies professor at the college. I was also one of the very few teaching and writing about sexuality. In 2003, two new tenure-track colleagues changed that situation. The newly formed Comparative American Studies Program hired Gina Pérez to teach Latina/o studies and Meredith Raimondo to teach LGBTQ (lesbian/gay/bisexual/transgendered/queer) studies. Increasingly, students entered my classes with a deeper understanding of contemporary race relations and current social theory. Students have far better interdisciplinary training, and I have noticed more sophisticated discussions on, for instance, interlocking hierarchies of race and sex in Latina/o communities in a variety of historical contexts. At the same time, knowing that my colleagues address more recent events allows me to focus the class more tightly on the period before 1960, where I am, to be honest, more comfortable. Perhaps most importantly, along with a handful of other newly arrived faculty with ethnic studies specialties, there is now at Oberlin an interdisciplinary cohort of teachers and scholars committed to rethinking how the country understands race and sex. In such a setting, Latina/o history has become a critical aspect of a much larger, community endeavor.

The time of faculty expansion at the college, however, has for the moment come to an end. Two years ago, trustee demands forced college faculty into making a tough choice: either eliminate seven continuing positions or have seven positions cut for them. One of the first positions considered for elimination was, unfortunately, the Asian American history position, one of two positions in Asian American studies. That history position, which was similar to my position in Latina/o history, had been recently vacated by an assistant professor who went to a prestigious research university. Of the first four positions considered for elimination, only Asian American history was not returned immediately: the position was "tabled," and a final decision about its permanent return was postponed.

The ensuing struggle to reinstate the Asian American history position drew together student activists, who rallied in support of the position, and faculty and administrators, including the president of the college, who argued elegantly and persuasively in favor of a permanent place for Asian American history in the college curriculum. As this essay went to press, the permanent position was reapproved, and, to my delight, a tenure-track search is now in process.

With the return of the Asian American history position, there is a renewed excitement among faculty, including myself, about the shared project of studying and teaching about American race relations at a small college. The return of the position is also a victory for the history department and its commitment to diversifying its curriculum. Like Latina/o history, Asian American history helps draw American history away from traditional topics. Without sacrificing chronological coverage, the history department can once again offer students a curriculum in American history that begins to truly represent the country's racial heterogeneity. It was also reassuring to me personally. My position in Latina/o history is obviously similar to the Asian American history position, and it was, I admit, hard not to view the "tabling" of that position as a not-so-subtle comment on my own courses and scholarship in Latina/o history. The strong support for Asian American history signaled support for many forms of new knowledge at the college, including new knowledge produced by students and teachers of Latina/o history.

The fact remains, however, that Asian American history came very close to disappearing from Oberlin's curriculum. Under different circumstances Latina/o history could have suffered a similar fate. It is a grim reminder that during periods of contraction, institutions large and small can all too easily roll back many of the advances that have allowed the development of fields like Latina/o history. Sad to say, we have pivoted the center, but the center lurks, willing and able to pivot back.[5]

Notes

1. Ilan Stavans and Lalo Alcaraz, *Latino U.S.A.: A Cartoon History* (New York, 2000).

2. *Zoot Suit*, dir. Luis Valdez (Universal, 1982); "Lucy Goes to a Rodeo," prod. Lucille Ball and Jess Oppenheimer, dir. William Asher and James V. Kern (episode of *I Love Lucy*, ex. prod. Desi Arnaz), Desilu (CBS, Nov. 28, 1955); *Salt of the Earth*, dir. Herbert J. Biberman (Independent Productions, 1954); *High Noon*, dir. Fred Zinnemann (Stanley Kramer Productions, 1952); *West Side Story*, dir. Jerome Robbins and Robert Wise (Mirisch, 1961). U.S. Bureau of the Census, *Fifteenth Census of the United States, 1930, Lorain County, Ohio* (Washington, D.C., 1930). The newspaper articles we discuss include *Lorain Morning Journal*, Aug. 4, 1949, p. 21; *Lorain Morning Journal*, Nov. 2, 1949, p. 12; *Lorain Morning Journal*, Nov. 22, 1950, p. 9.

3. Antonia I. Castañeda, "Sexual Violence in the Politics and Policies of Conquest: Amerindian Women and the Spanish Conquest of Alta California," in *Building with Our Hands: New Directions in Chicana Studies*, ed. Adela de la Torre and Beatríz M. Pesquera (Berkeley, Calif., 1993), 15–33; Jennifer A. Nelson, "Abortions under Community Control: Feminism, Nationalism, and the Politics of Reproduction among New York City's Young Lords," *Journal of Women's History* 13, no. 1 (2001): 157–80; Susana Peña, "Visibility and Silence: Cuban American Gay Male Culture in Miami" (Ph.D. diss., University of California, Santa Barbara, 2002).

4. Vicki L. Ruiz, *From Out of the Shadows: Mexican Women in Twentieth-Century America* (New York, 1998); María Cristina García, *Havana USA: Cuban Exiles and Cuban Americans in South Florida, 1959–1994* (Berkeley, Calif., 1997); Ruth Glasser, *My Music Is My Flag: Puerto Rican Musicians and Their New York Communities, 1917–1940* (Berkeley, Calif., 1995).

5. Pablo Mitchell extends his thanks to Gary Kornblith, Carol Lasser, Beth McLaughlin, Kevin Marsh, and the staff at the *Journal of American History* for their thoughtful comments and editorial assistance on this piece.

Nancy C. Unger

Teaching "Straight" Gay and Lesbian History

The importance of offering a lesbian and gay American history course was initially impressed upon me in 1986. A newly minted Ph.D., I was teaching my very first class: a U.S. history survey at San Francisco State University (SFSU). The course required each student to review a book of his or her choice on any topic in U.S. history. One student chose John D'Emilio's *Sexual Politics, Sexual Communities: The Making of a Homosexual Minority in the United States, 1940–1970* from my list of suggested titles and wrote a thoughtful, enthusiastic review.[1] At the bottom of the review was a handwritten note: "Thanks for recommending this book. As a gay man, I didn't know I *had* a history." Didn't know he had a history?! My fellow historians will share my sense of dismay and my determination to remedy this unthinkable state of affairs.

I have always included the history of gay men and lesbians in my various classes, not as a sop to "political correctness" and not because it is an amusing/interesting "add on" to "real" history, but because it is a vital component of a more complete understanding of American political, economic, social, legal, military, and religious history. For example, my courses that focus on the twentieth century include the significant role that the campaign against homosexuals played in McCarthy-era persecutions; in "U.S. Historical Geography" (which examines the role physical geography has played in the development of the United States), we study how and why the coastal cities of New York and San Francisco emerged as major centers of homophile populations; in women's history courses we examine the controversy and contributions lesbians brought to various feminist movements.

Around 1989, a contingent of gay and lesbian SFSU students who appreciated the inclusion of their history in my classes came to my office to formally request that I offer a course on the history of American homosexuality. The curriculum committee approved my proposal, and the course was introduced. To my disappointment, because of a quirk in university policy, I, a lowly lecturer, was not allowed to teach "my" course. It was officially assigned to a tenure-track colleague but in fact taught by an exceptionally qualified graduate student.[2]

In 1994 I came to Santa Clara University (SCU), a Catholic, Jesuit institution in the heart of California's Silicon Valley. Based on my undergraduate education at the more conservative Gonzaga University (also a Jesuit school), I

Journal of American History 93 (2007): 1192–99.

assumed that teaching my own lesbian and gay course was now a complete impossibility. I continued to incorporate gay and lesbian history into much of my research and my courses, however, and was pleasantly surprised to find that my desire to offer a dedicated course on that topic was supported by students, faculty, and administrators. That support included a $4,000 Building Partnerships for Diversity grant in 2001 from the university's Center for Multicultural Learning to fund the development of the course. Ironically, the center did not recognize issues of sexuality in its definition of "multicultural"—the funding was granted to support the course's emphasis on the role of race within homosexual communities.

Despite the widespread support I was receiving, as I developed the course I continued to worry about the reaction of older alumni. Considering Santa Clara University's setting in the traditionally liberal San Francisco Bay area, I felt less trepidation than I would have if I were offering the course on a campus in a conservative stronghold. Nevertheless, based on letters to the editor of the alumni magazine, I knew that while most alumni are delighted about the university's serious commitment to social justice, especially its emphasis on the dignity of all persons, others are still fuming over the "radical" decision to admit women to the university in 1961.

Once the course was officially on the books, the university's Jesuit president sought from the chairs of the English and history departments a response to a letter he had received from a parent whose child was considering applying to SCU. This parent had been appalled to find gay and lesbian subject matter in the course catalog and clearly envisioned my course not as social history but as something along the lines of "Great Gays in American History," which would feature lots of lectures beginning with, "Did you know that [insert famous name here] was gay?" My response to the president spells out the course's actual themes and objectives:

> The author [of the complaint letter] states the belief that "when individual authors or historical figures are identified by their orientation and their contributions 'celebrated,' there is the implication of support for their lifestyle." I would like to reassure this person that no history course at Santa Clara University seeks "celebration" as its goal. The discipline of history seeks to understand the past and, in so doing, develop the crucial skills of critical thinking, particularly the ability to prepare and communicate well supported arguments and interpretations. A course on the Holocaust, for example, would not be offered to celebrate genocide, but to understand why and how such unspeakable acts could be carried out against fellow human beings.
>
>   . . . for the past several decades, the history of a number of groups and movements previously overlooked has been a major emphasis. Courses on labor, racial minorities, women, and gender have proliferated across the nation. More recently environmental history and historical geography have been added to the mix. The combined result of all these new courses is not a series of isolated studies, but a much more complete picture of the many complex issues and interactions that make up American history. History is a tool of understanding rather than celebration. The gay and lesbian course does not seek to defend or denounce homosexuality any more than the women's courses defend or denounce women, or historical geography courses defend or denounce physical geography.

Cross-dressing occurred throughout American history. In this picture postcard (c. 1890–1930), unidentified women dress as men, possibly for a theatrical production. *Courtesy William Lipsky.*

The university's president thanked me for my "thoughtful, thorough" response, and that was the end of any opposition I have encountered at SCU as a result of offering the course.[3] My only other negative encounter came at a local community college when I gave a guest lecture on lesbians in the nineteenth century. Because I was at a public rather than religious institution, I anticipated that I would encounter no resistance. What I had not counted on was the presence of a fundamentalist Christian who quoted Bible verses as I began my lecture. That experience made me appreciate anew my own religious institution's emphasis on social justice.

"Gays/Lesbians in U.S. History," an upper-division course (History 177), was first offered at Santa Clara University in the spring of 2002. I gave it that title for two reasons. First, I did not want there to be any confusion about the course's content. Even with a title such as "Diverse Sexualities in American History," students might still expect a class focused primarily on heterosexual themes. Secondly, although the course touches on queer, transgendered, and bisexual issues (to provide appropriate context, I begin with a brief section on queer theory), I wanted it to be clear that the course had a straight (that is, exclusive) gay and lesbian emphasis.

Having settled on the title, I fretted about it. Roughly half of SCU's students are Catholic, a few are Muslim. Would they sign up for this course? Even if they were interested, would they want the words "gay" and "lesbian" on their college transcripts? SCU is an expensive private school, and, although many students work part time, most are partially or fully funded by their parents. Would parents pay to have "those words" on their children's official record? The course satisfied the college's U.S. core requirement as well as the women's and gender/ethnic studies requirement (a double dipper!), but I was still nervous about attracting sufficient enrollments to justify not just this initial offering but subsequent sections. For the first time in my career, I advertised a class, posting flyers throughout the history and women's and gender studies departments.

The course quickly reached its cap of twenty-five students. An equal number were on the waiting list, a pattern that has been repeated in subsequent offerings (the course is offered every year). In that first offering, as in subsequent years, the students were primarily juniors and seniors, with men and women represented in equal numbers. I do not inquire as to my students' sexualities, but their personal histories are sometimes revealed during discussions. Of the students who make their sexual identification known, the majority identify as straight. Some of them are drawn to the class because of a gay or lesbian parent or sibling, but most enroll because they are interested in the subject matter (and in fulfilling two core requirements). The others who self-identify are gay or lesbian in roughly equal numbers. Only a few identify as bisexual, with only one (so far) identifying as "gender outlaw."

As part of a phenomenon described by Stephanie Fairyington in the *Gay and Lesbian Review* as "The New Post-Straight" (concerning straight academics who teach queer studies), I never explicitly discuss my own sexuality, but I wear makeup, dresses, and a wedding ring. Straight women hardly have a monopoly on those accoutrements, but I expect that most of my students assume, correctly, that I place on the heterosexual side of the Kinsey scale. As such, I am never bothered by issues of "authenticity" in teaching the course. After all, as a scholar trained in the study of the Gilded Age and Progressive Era, I authored a biography of Robert M. La Follette and never once worried that my lack of authenticity (I am not a powerful politician nor am I male or dead) disqualified me from writing that book or from teaching about lots of other dead men once in political power. What is important to me and to my students in all the courses I teach is not whether I am like or unlike the people we study, but whether I have the scholarly expertise to teach the class to the highest standards. The fact that it was a contingent of gay and lesbian students who originally urged me to offer my lesbian and gay history course fostered my belief that my sexual identity does not hinder my credibility with my students. Gay and lesbian students have told me that my being straight adds to their sense of the course's credibility. I urge them to consider, however, what it might mean to them to have someone such as our university's only openly lesbian professor (the renowned LGBTQ [lesbian/gay/bisexual/transgendered/queer] scholar Linda Garber, associate professor of English and director of the Women's and Gender Studies Program) teaching gay and lesbian history as a respected faculty member on our Jesuit campus. They agree that having openly homosexual professors provides important role models, but by no means do they think that professors must be what they teach.[4]

The dynamics for the class are established on the first day. I begin by explaining that the course will focus primarily on the history of American lesbians and gay men, and I suggest that we start by defining our terms. I ask the class what makes a woman a lesbian. A few tentative definitions are proposed, but other students find them too broad or too narrow. Debates quickly ensue, setting the tone for the thoughtful, wide-ranging discussions I strongly encourage. I throw out a few questions to stir the pot. Is it only desire that "counts," or do actions matter as well? What if a woman's heartfelt sexual attraction is to other women, but she never acts on it? If such a woman marries a man, bears children, and never has a sexual relationship with another woman, is she a lesbian? What about a "political lesbian," a woman who desires men sexually, chooses to remain celibate, yet identifies as a lesbian because she believes it impossible for a woman to have a truly egalitarian relationship with a man? What if that same woman does have sexual relations exclusively with women? What about a woman who has satisfying sexual relationships exclusively with men, but who enjoys fantasies about other women?

This complicated and often volatile effort to answer the "simple" question of what makes a woman a lesbian sets the stage for the first reading, an excerpt from Annamarie Jagose's *Queer Theory*. In their end-of-term evaluations, most students list this as the most difficult of all the readings. A few, however, love to grapple with issues of theory, appreciate the opportunity to contextualize the course, and throw themselves into the discussion with gusto. Others save their enthusiasm for discussions of the more fact-based readings on homosexuality in American history. I have continued to assign the books I chose for the course's initial offering: Leila Rupp's brief but delightful overview, *A Desired Past: A Short History of Same-Sex Love in America*; Lillian Faderman's *Odd Girls and Twilight Lovers: A History of Lesbian Life in Twentieth-Century America*; and *Cures: A Gay Man's Odyssey*, the first volume of Martin Duberman's memoirs. To augment those materials I used some of my grant monies to compile a reader consisting of fourteen essays selected as a sampling of some of the best writing and newest thinking in the field. They were also selected to cover the very wide range of subjects noted in the course description. Although modern notions of heterosexuality and homosexuality are relatively new, I want my students to appreciate that same-sex desire has always played an important role in American history. The course reader includes an article on pre-Columbian Native American sex/ gender systems from *Living the Spirit: A Gay American Indian Anthology*, and "Hearing Voices," an essay on same-sex sexual practices in Africa and their impact on relationships among the enslaved in colonial America. A particularly popular reading is Richard Godbeer's "Sodomy in Colonial New England," in which surprisingly tolerant attitudes about same-sex acts reveal much about seventeenth-century colonial law, religion, and community relationships. Because a significant portion of my students are Asian American, the readings from Russell Leong's *Asian American Sexualities: Dimensions of the Gay and Lesbian Experience* also tend to generate a great deal of interest.[5]

What all my students have in common is enthusiasm for the subject matter. No one ever complains, "Gay and lesbian history *again*?" Although all of the signposts are familiar from countless American history classes from kindergarten on (the pre-Columbian period, the Revolutionary War, the Civil War, the Gilded Age and Progressive Era, and so on), the course material is new—a combination

Although modern notions of heterosexuality and homosexuality are relatively new, same-sex desire has always played an important role in American history. A suggestion of same-sex intimacy is depicted in this unidentified artist's rendering of men in the Old West. Faced with a shortage of women, they dance with each other. Plate 150 in Owen C. Coy, *Pictorial History of California* (Berkeley, 1925). Reprinted in William Lipsky, *Images of America: Gay and Lesbian San Francisco* (Charleston, 2006).

students seem to appreciate. The course not only fills in the blanks in the more conventional histories, but it also raises questions vital to the study of history and to critical thinking. We discuss, for example, Charles Clifton's "Rereading Voices from the Past," which suggests that many male slave narratives include coded language indicating that the authors were raped by their male owners.[6] Clifton argues that such coded language deserves the same careful study as the language in female slave narratives, and he suggests that male/male rape is an aspect of the American slave experience that has been overlooked. His article generates much lively discussion about historical sources and the limits of interpretation.

My gay and lesbian history course is one of the most successful I have ever taught. In their anonymous evaluations at the end of the course, my students frequently refer to the class as "one of the best" and even "the best" of their university experience. For many students, it is like finding the missing piece to a puzzle—it rounds out their understanding of history acquired in previous classes even as it inspires them to learn more. Others are profoundly empowered by learning for the first time of a history of gay men and lesbians with whom they share some experience or identity. Although I would like to report that it is my lectures that consistently receive top marks, in truth, what many students cite as particularly valuable are the three documentaries shown in class: *Before Stonewall, After*

Stonewall, and *The Celluloid Closet*. The first two always evoke a sense of wonder and amazement: Old people! Talking about *sex*! The history they have been reading, pondering, and discussing in a fairly intellectual way suddenly comes alive. They feel the despair and pain caused by institutionalized homophobia and are shocked by the depth and breadth of legal discrimination. They see how a marginalized group strategized to acquire civil rights, then responded to a deadly epidemic. In *After Stonewall*, when they witness members of ACT-UP (AIDS Coalition to Unleash Power) disrupting a Mass in New York's St. Patrick's Cathedral, many of my students (and not just the Catholics) literally gasp, they are so struck by the power of that painful, highly controversial confrontation. *The Celluloid Closet* (a documentary on the depictions of homosexuals in popular film) elicits discussion on the power of popular culture in inculcating, challenging, and changing attitudes and perceptions.[7]

The combination of readings, films, and discussions gives my students important historical perspective on current issues, ranging from the controversies over gay marriage and adoption to the military's policy of "don't ask, don't tell." They appreciate the value of history, not just as a collection of stories about the past, but as a vital tool in the efforts to resolve present-day questions and problems.

While I consider the course to be highly successful, I have been less successful in bringing gay and lesbian history into high school classrooms. I have given a series of talks to groups of high school teachers on how to incorporate

As a study of an oppressed people's struggle for civil rights, gay and lesbian political actions offer valuable insight into American history. Here, on Armed Forces Day, May 21, 1966, gay men hold a rally on the steps of the federal building in San Francisco's Civic Center to protest their exclusion from the military. *Courtesy GLBT Historical Society of California, San Francisco, California.*

gender history into their course curricula (emphasizing that it is not an "add on") as a new and exciting way to meet some of the existing state requirements. They are openly leery of discussion in their classrooms of anything to do with homosexuality for fear of generating controversy that will get them into trouble. I suggest that they tackle the issue head on: Before launching into a lesson plan, explain that they are not seeking a discussion of personal views on homosexuality, but rather offering an instructive new way of examining the American past by exploring the history of an overlooked minority. One approach might be to look at how some gay and lesbian individuals and organizations consciously borrowed from the African American civil rights movements of the 1950s and 1960s and the women's rights movements of the 1960s and 1970s. Such a comparative approach invites study of the larger issues and strategies involved in all civil rights struggles, while it also points out the differences in the various groups' challenges and solutions. It can also elicit useful questions about identity, as many Americans were (and are) members of more than one oppressed group. Members of my audiences of teachers nod and take notes, but in their e-mails to me, in which they excitedly report back on their success in working some of my suggestions into their lesson plans, their selections are always from my material on women's, rather than gay and lesbian, history.

I am excited that History 177 is now routinely included in my annual course offerings, but I am also rather daunted by the task of continually updating my course readings. There has been such an explosion of superb research in recent years that I have found it impossible to keep up even with LGBTQ book *reviews*, let alone the actual books, articles, and scholarly papers. One of the great benefits of allowing students to pick their own research paper topics is that they are doing much of my work for me, investigating the most recent and exciting scholarship on a vast array of topics. I look forward to many more years of learning and writing about gay and lesbian people and movements, and to teaching this lively course so integral to the study of history.[8]

Notes

1. John D'Emilio, *Sexual Politics, Sexual Communities: The Making of a Homosexual Minority in the United States, 1940–1970* (Chicago, 1983).

2. The LGBTQ (lesbian/gay/bisexual/transgendered/queer) scholar Linda Heidenreich, today associate professor of women's studies at Washington State University, Pullman, was the graduate student who taught the course.

3. Santa Clara University provost Denise Carmody pasted the complaint by the parent of the prospective student into an e-mail she sent to the chair of the history department, Thomas Turley. I sent a response to the president of the university, Paul Locatelli, S.J. Denise Carmody to Thomas Turley, e-mail, April 18, 2002 (in Nancy Unger's possession); Nancy Unger to Paul Locatelli, S.J., e-mail, April 23, 2002, ibid. Locatelli to Unger, e-mail, April 23, 2002, ibid.

4. Stephanie Fairyington, "The New Post-Straight," *Gay and Lesbian Review* (Nov./Dec. 2004): 33–34. Nancy C. Unger, *Fighting Bob La Follette: The Righteous Reformer* (Chapel Hill, N.C., 2000).

5. Annamarie Jagose, *Queer Theory: An Introduction* (New York, 1996), 1–21. Leila Rupp, *A Desired Past: A Short History of Same-Sex Love in America* (Chicago, 2002); Lillian Faderman, *Odd Girls and Twilight Lovers: A History of Lesbian Life in Twentieth-Century America* (New York, 1992); Martin Duberman, *Cures: A Gay Man's Odyssey* (Boulder, Colo., 2002). Midnight Sun, "Sex/Gender Systems in Native North America," in *Living the Spirit: A Gay American Indian Anthology*, ed. Will Roscoe (New York, 1988), 32–47; Cary Alan Johnson, "Hearing Voices: Unearthing Evidence of Homosexuality in Precolonial Africa," in *The Greatest Taboo: Homosexuality in Black Communities*, ed. Delroy Constantine-Simms (Los Angeles, 2001), 132–48. Richard Godbeer, "Sodomy in Colonial New England," in *Major Problems in the History of American Sexuality: Documents and Essays*, ed. Kathy Lee Peiss (Boston, 2001), 92–106. Russell Leong, ed., *Asian American Sexualities: Dimensions of the Gay and Lesbian Experience* (New York, 1995).

6. Charles Clifton, "Rereading Voices from the Past: Images of Homo-Eroticism in the Slave Narrative," in *Greatest Taboo*, ed. Constantine-Simms, 342–61.

7. *Before Stonewall: The Making of a Gay and Lesbian Community*, dir. John Scagliotti, Greta Schiller, and Robert Rosenberg (Before Stonewall, Inc., 1985); *After Stonewall*, dir. John Scagliotti (First Run Features, 1999); *The Celluloid Closet*, dir. Rob Epstein and Jeffrey Friedman (Sony Pictures, 1995).

8. Mary Whisner made valuable contributions to this essay.